A Book Of

COST ACCOUNTING

B.B.M. Semester - II
(Bachelor of Business Management)

Dr. Suhas Mahajan
B.A., M.Com., Ph.D. (Finance)
Research Guide, Univeristy of Pune and YCMOU,
Nashik.

Dr. Mahesh Kulkarni
M.Com., M. Phil., L.L.B., D.T.L., Ph.D. (Management)
Research Guide, Univeristy of Pune and YCMOU,
Nashik.

N2941

Cost Accounting (BBM : Semester II)   ISBN 978-93-83750-39-9

Third Edition : January 2016
© : Authors

The text of this publication, or any part thereof, should not be reproduced or transmitted in any form or stored in any computer storage system or device for distribution including photocopy, recording, taping or information retrieval system or reproduced on any disc, tape, perforated media or other information storage device etc., without the written permission of Authors with whom the rights are reserved. Breach of this condition is liable for legal action.

Every effort has been made to avoid errors or omissions in this publication. In spite of this, errors may have crept in. Any mistake, error or discrepancy so noted and shall be brought to our notice shall be taken care of in the next edition. It is notified that neither the publisher nor the authors or seller shall be responsible for any damage or loss of action to any one, of any kind, in any manner, therefrom.

Published By :
NIRALI PRAKASHAN
Abhyudaya Pragati, 1312, Shivaji Nagar,
Off J.M. Road, PUNE – 411005
Tel - (020) 25512336/37/39, Fax - (020) 25511379
Email : niralipune@pragationline.com

Printed By :
Repro Knowledgecast Limited,
Thane

☞ DISTRIBUTION CENTRES

PUNE
- **Nirali Prakashan** : 119, Budhwar Peth, Jogeshwari Mandir Lane, Pune 411002, Maharashtra
  Tel : (020) 2445 2044, 66022708, Fax : (020) 2445 1538
  Email : bookorder@pragationline.com, niralilocal@pragationline.com
- **Nirali Prakashan** : S. No. 28/27, Dhyari, Near Pari Company, Pune 411041
  Tel : (020) 24690204 Fax : (020) 24690316
  Email : dhyari@pragationline.com, bookorder@pragationline.com

MUMBAI
- **Nirali Prakashan** : 385, S.V.P. Road, Rasdhara Co-op. Hsg. Society Ltd.,
  Girgaum, Mumbai 400004, Maharashtra
  Tel : (022) 2385 6339 / 2386 9976, Fax : (022) 2386 9976
  Email : niralimumbai@pragationline.com

☞ DISTRIBUTION BRANCHES

JALGAON
- **Nirali Prakashan** : 34, V. V. Golani Market, Navi Peth, Jalgaon 425001,
  Maharashtra, Tel : (0257) 222 0395, Mob : 94234 91860

KOLHAPUR
- **Nirali Prakashan** : New Mahadvar Road, Kedar Plaza, 1st Floor Opp. IDBI Bank
  Kolhapur 416 012, Maharashtra. Mob : 9850046155

NAGPUR
- **Pratibha Book Distributors** : Above Maratha Mandir, Shop No. 3, First Floor,
  Rani Jhanshi Square, Sitabuldi, Nagpur 440012, Maharashtra
  Tel : (0712) 254 7129

DELHI
- **Nirali Prakashan** : 4593/21, Basement, Aggarwal Lane 15, Ansari Road, Daryaganj
  Near Times of India Building, New Delhi 110002
  Mob : 08505972553

BENGALURU
- **Pragati Book House** : House No. 1, Sanjeevappa Lane, Avenue Road Cross,
  Opp. Rice Church, Bengaluru – 560002.
  Tel : (080) 64513344, 64513355,Mob : 9880582331, 9845021552
  Email:bharatsavla@yahoo.com

CHENNAI
- **Pragati Books** : 9/1, Montieth Road, Behind Taas Mahal, Egmore,
  Chennai 600008 Tamil Nadu, Tel : (044) 6518 3535,
  Mob : 94440 01782 / 98450 21552 / 98805 82331,
  Email : bharatsavla@yahoo.com

niralipune@pragationline.com | www.pragationline.com
Also find us on www.facebook.com/niralibooks

Preface ...

There are a number of books on the subject of **'Cost Accounting'** available in the learner's market, but they do not meet the basic requirements of **B.B.M. (Bachelor of Business Management) Semester - II**. This book is written as per the syllabus for B.B.M., Semester - II, students from June, 2013. We do hope that this book will definitely help to meet the growing requirements of students of B.B.M., from the faculty of commerce. This book adopts a modern and novel approach towards the study of Cost Accounting in view with the specific requirements of the readers and practitioners of this subject.

All the topics included in the syllabus are explained in simple, but apt language so that the students coming from different faculties can also understand them very easily. Besides the language, care is also taken to solve the problems at the end of each unit with the help of appropriate illustrations, wherever necessary. This will help the students in understanding the different topics properly. We have taken tabular representation of classified cost statements. Proper emphasis is also given on charts and graphs to simplify the cost accounting theories and practices. This book has been designed to serve as a self sufficient text for B.B.M. Semester - II students. It will definitely add to our satisfaction if this book would be more useful as a reference for practicing accountants, professional managers, dynamic entrepreneurs and enthusiastic teachers of the subject concern. This book is also useful for M.Com., D.B.M., M.B.A., M.C.M., Diploma in Hotel Management and Diploma in Hospital Management and many other professional courses.

We are very thankful to Shri. Dineshbhai Furia, Shri. Jignesh Furia, Malik Shaikh, Mrs. Nirja Sharma, Prasad Chintakindi and the entire staff of Nirali Prakashan, Pune, for their earnest help in bringing out this book with vigour and accuracy. We have put in maximum efforts to make the text error free. Nevertheless, we do not rule out the possibility of certain shortcomings or misprints still remaining. We will be grateful to the readers, if such errors are being pointed out from time to time.

We must concede that this book would never have been written without the support, encouragement and inspiration of our family members, many, many thanks to them.

Any criticism or valuable suggestion for further improvement of this book will be greatfully acknowledged and highly appreciated.

Sankasthi Chaturthi
21st November, 2013
Pune 411021

Dr. Mahesh Kulkarni
Dr. Suhas Mahajan

BBM (Semester - II)
Cost Accounting
Course Code 201

Syllabus ...

Unit 1 - Introduction (8L)
1.1 Concept of Cost, Costing, Cost Accounting and Cost Accountancy
1.2 Limitations of Financial Accounting
1.3 Origin and Objectives of Cost Accounting
1.4 Advantages and Limitations of Cost Accounting
1.5 Difference between Financial and Cost Accounting
1.6 Cost Unit and Cost Centre

Unit 2 - Elements of Cost (8L)
2.1 Material, Labour and Other Expenses
2.2 Classification of Cost and Types of Costs
2.3 Preparation of Cost Sheet

Unit 3 - Methods of Costing (Theory Only) (12L)
3.1 Job Costing - Meaning, Features, Advantages and Limitations
3.2 Contract Costing - Basic Concepts
3.3 Process Costing - Meaning, Features, Normal and Abnormal Loss or Gains
3.4 Operating Costing - Meaning, Features and Objectives
3.5 Opportunity Costing

Unit 4 - Budget and Budgetary Control (7L)
4.1 Definition
4.2 Meaning and Objectives of Budgetary Control
4.3 Advantages and Disadvantages of Budgetary Control
4.4 Types of Budget

Unit 5 - Marginal Costing (7L)
Meaning and Various Concepts - Fixed Cost, Variable Cost, Contribution, P/V Ratio, Break Even Point, Margin of Safety

Unit 6 - Standard Costing (6L)
Definition and Meaning of Various Concepts, Advantages and Limitations of Standard Costing, Variance Analysis - Material and Labour Variances only.

(48 L)

***

Contents ...

Unit 1 - Introduction	1.1 - 1.20
Unit 2 - Elements of Cost	2.1 - 2.58
Unit 3 - Methods of Costing (Theory Only)	3.1 - 3.34
Unit 4 - Budget and Budgetary Control	4.1 - 4.52
Unit 5 - Marginal Costing	5.1 - 5.48
Unit 6 - Standard Costing	6.1 - 6.66

- **AT A GLANCE**
    - Glossary   G.1 - G.6
    - Formulae   F.1 - F.5
    - Objective Questions
        - True / False Statements   O.1 - O.4
        - Fill in the Blanks   F.1 - F.5
    - Bibliography   B.1 - B.1
- **University Question Papers: 2014 & 2015**   P.1 - P.4

***

List of Figures, Graphs and Charts ...

1.	Cost Concept	1.2
2.	Limitations of Financial Accounting	1.6
3.	Objectives of Cost Accounting	1.10
4.	Advantages of Cost Accounting	1.12
5.	Types of Cost Centres	1.19
6.	Elements of Cost	2.2
7.	Division of Costs	2.8
8.	Need of Cost Classification	2.9
9.	Classification of Cost	2.10
10.	Classification of Cost on the basis of Traceability, Elements and Functions	2.13
11.	Behaviour of Fixed Cost	2.14
12.	Behaviour of Variable Cost	2.14
13.	Behaviour of Semi-variable Cost	2.15
14.	Behaviour of Fixed, Variable and Semi-variable Cost	2.15
15.	Types of Costs	2.18
16.	Composition of Conversion Cost	2.19
17.	Methods of Costing	3.2
18.	Job Order Execution Procedure	3.8
19.	Process Cost Flow	3.23
20.	Costing Techniques	4.2
21.	Budgeting Process	4.12
22.	Components of Revenue Budgets	4.13
23.	Break Even Chart	5.15
24.	Total Cost Variance	6.8

***

Unit ... 1

INTRODUCTION

1.1 Concept of Cost, Costing, Cost Accounting and Cost Accountancy
1.2 Limitations of Financial Accounting
1.3 Origin and Objectives of Cost Accounting
1.4 Advantages and Limitations of Cost Accounting
1.5 Difference between Financial Accounting and Cost Accounting
1.6 Cost Unit and Cost Centre
* Questions for Self-Study

In today's competitive environment, the nature and functioning of business organisations have become very complicated. Various parties viz., owners, creditors, employees, government agencies, tax authorities, investors, management of the business etc. are interested in the functioning of the business. Accounting provides substantial information to all these parties. In order to satisfy their needs, a sound organisation of accounting system is essential. The needs of the majority of the users of accounting information can be satisfied by Financial Accounting. Financial Accounting is mainly concerned with preparation of two important statements, viz. Profit and Loss Account and Balance Sheet. This information serves the needs of all those who are not directly associated with the management of business. To carry out the functions of planning, decision-making and control more efficiently, the management require more analytical information relating to cost. The Financial Accounting system fails to some extent to provide all these required information to management and hence a new system of accounting necessitates, which fulfils all the needs of management. Thus, **Cost Accounting** is developed to offset the limitations of **Financial Accounting**. Broadly speaking, there are three branches of accounting viz., Financial Accounting, Cost Accounting and Management Accounting which are concerned with presenting business data to the users.

The following example clearly indicates the need and importance of Cost Accounting as a separate branch of accounting, which has emerged mainly because of the limitations of Financial Accounting.

| EXAMPLE |

Godrej Ltd.; Gorakhpur a leading soap manufacturer runs three separate divisions viz. Hamam, Rexona and Liril. Their books of accounts for the year 2012-13 discloses the annual results as follows : Actual Turnover ₹ 3,00,000, Expenses incurred ₹ 2,00,000.

Evaluate their business performances.

ANSWER

A) Evaluation of Business Performance by Finance Department.

In the books of Godrej Ltd., Gorakhpur

Profitability Statement for the year ended 31st March, 2013

	Particulars		₹
	Sales		3,00,000
Less :	Expenses	(−)	2,00,000
	∴ Profit		1,00,000
	Percentage of Profit to Sales		33 1/3%

Comments :

During the year 2012-13, the overall company's financial performance is good as the profits are 33 1/3% of sales.

B) Evaluation of Business Performance by Cost Accounting Department.

In the books of Godrej Ltd., Gorakhpur

Profitability Statement for the year ended 31st March, 2013

Particulars		Divisions			Total
		Hamam ₹	Rexona ₹	Liril ₹	₹
Sales		1,50,000	1,00,000	50,000	3,00,000
Less : Costs	(−)	90,000	70,000	40,000	2,00,000
∴ Profit		60,000	30,000	10,000	1,00,000
Percentage of Profit to Sales		40%	33 1/3%	20%	33 1/3%

Comments :

During the year 2012-13, all divisions are working satisfactorily as the overall performance shows a substantial profit of 33 1/3% of actual turnover. Hamam division is earning more profits as compared to Rexona and Liril. As well Rexona division is more profitable as compared to Liril division. It is advisable to exercise additional efforts to control the costs and increase the turnover of particularly Liril division to increase the profit margins substantially.

1.1 CONCEPT OF COST, COSTING, COST ACCOUNTING AND COST ACCOUNTANCY

It is necessary to understand some of the important Cost Concepts used very often in the business world, which are shown in Figure 1.1 as follows.

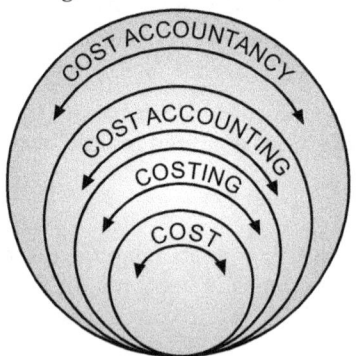

Fig. 1.1 : Cost Concepts

Cost

Meaning and Definitions :
The term "**Cost**" may be defined as a noun or a verb as follows :

1. **As a noun :**
   The amount of expenditure (actual or notional) incurred on or attributable to specified thing or activity.

2. **As a verb :**
   To ascertain the cost of specified thing or activity.

   The term 'Cost' is defined, in different ways by various authorities as follows :

i) *I.C.M.A., London :*
   "Cost is the amount of expenditure (actual or notional) incurred on or attributable to a specified thing or activity".

ii) *Crowningshield :*
   "It is an expenditure made to secure an economic benefit, generally resources that promise to produce revenue. The resources may have tangible substance (material or machinery) or they may take the form of services (wages, rent, power)".

iii) *Shillinglaw :*
   "Cost represents the resources that must be sacrificed to attain a particular objective".

iv) *The Committee on Cost Concepts and Standards of the American Accounting Association :*
   "It is the foregoing, in monetary terms incurred or potentially to be incurred to achieve a specific objective".

v) *Anthony and Welsh :*
   "Cost is a measurement in monetary terms, of the amount of resources used for some purposes".

vi) *A. I. C. P. A. Committee on terminology :*
   "It is the amount measured in money or cash expended or other property transferred, capital stock issued, services performed, or a liability incurred in consideration of goods or services received or to be received".

vii) *W. M. Harper :*
   "It is the value of economic resources used as a result of producing or doing the thing costed".

viii) *Oxford Dictionary :*
   "Cost is the price paid for something".

Again, the general concept of **Cost** which is most widely used is the "money cost" of production. Another concept of cost is the real cost according to Marshall. Again "Opportunity Cost" concept is there which means the sacrifice made for not utilising the other alternatives.

From the above definitions, we can conclude that **Cost** is the total of all expenses incurred, whether paid or outstanding, in the manufacturing and sale of product or those incurred in giving a service. **Costs** are calculated from the point of view of management which expects costs to perform three functions i.e. cost computation, cost control and cost analysis. Thus, the concept of **Cost** depends upon the purpose for which it is used, the conditions under which it is employed and the people who intend to use this concept. From the management point of view, the cost may be direct, indirect, prime, conversion, joint product, period, controllable, out of pocket, imputed, differential, marginal, standard etc. In short, **Cost** is a sacrifice made to achieve something and measured in terms of money and has always been used with some specific objective. It depends upon many factors and it changes with the changes in factors.

Costing

Meaning and Definitions :

Costing is simply 'cost finding'. It is the process, technique and procedure of ascertaining the costs. It includes all the principles, rules and regulations of calculating the costs.

The term **'Costing'** is defined in different ways by various authorities as follows :

i) *I.C.M.A., London :*

"It is the technique and process of ascertaining costs".

ii) *Wheldon :*

"Costing is the classifying, recording and appropriate allocation of expenditure for the determination of the costs of products or services and for the presentation of suitably arranged data for the purposes of control and guidance of the management. It includes the ascertainment of the cost of every order, job, contract, process, service or unit as may be appropriate. It deals with the cost of production, selling and distribution".

iii) *Harold James :*

"Costing is the proper allocation of expenditure, whereby, reliable cost may be ascertained and suitably presented to afford guidance to the producers in control of their business".

From the above definitions we can summarise that, **Costing** is a technique of ascertaining the cost. This technique is however, dynamic and changes with the changes in time. **Costing** can be carried out by the process of arithmetic, memorandum, statements etc. The costs may be either ascertained from the historical records i.e. after they have been incurred or by the pre-determined standards and analysis of variances between the standard and the actuals or by using the marginal costing method i.e. by differentiating the fixed and variable costs.

Cost Accounting

Meaning and Definitions:

Cost Accounting is the process of accounting for costs. It begins with the recording of income and expenditure and ends with the preparation of periodical statements. The term **'Cost Accounting'** is defined in different ways by various authorities as follows :

i) *Kohler :*

"It is that branch of accounting dealing with the classification, recording, allocation, summarisation and reporting of current and prospective costs".

ii) *Wheldon :*

"It is the classifying, recording and appropriate allocation of expenditure for the determination of the costs of products or services, the relation of these costs to sales values and the ascertainment of profitability".

iii) *Van Sickle :*

"Cost Accounting is the science of recording and presenting business transactions pertaining to the production of goods and services, whereby these records become a method of measurement and means of control".

iv) **Shillinglow :**

"Cost Accounting as a body of concepts, methods and procedures used to measure, analyse or estimate the costs, profitability and performance of individual products, departments and other sequences of a company's operations, for either internal or external use or both and to report on these questions to the interested parties".

v) **I.C.M.A., London :**

"It is the process of accounting for cost from the point at which expenditure is incurred or committed to the establishment of its ultimate relationship with cost centres and cost units". In its widest usage, it embraces the preparation of statistical data, the application of cost control methods and the ascertainment of the profitability of activities carried out or planned.

An analysis of the above comprehensive definitions reveals some of the important functions of **Cost Accounting. Cost Accounting** refers to the formal mechanism or a systematic procedure by means of which costs of products and services are computed. This is one of the important aspects which distinguishes **Cost Accounting** from **Costing**.

Cost Accountancy

Meaning and Definition :

It is the application of Costing and Cost Accounting principles, methods and techniques. It is also the science, art and practice of controlling the costs and ascertainment of profitability. **Cost Accountancy** is mainly concerned with the presentation of costing data to the management in a precise form, so that vital decisions can be taken by the management.

- It is a *science* because there are certain definite principles which are followed in cost accountancy.
- It is an *art* because it is the ability and skill of the cost accountant to apply the principles of cost accountancy to solve the intricate and complex problems of the management.
- It is a *practice* because a cost accountant has to keep himself abreast of the latest developments. He has to present the data to the management in a most up-to-date manner with latest techniques and methods for taking various decisions.

The term **'Cost Accountancy'** is defined as follows :

i) **I.C.M.A. London :**

"It is the application of costing and cost accounting principles, methods and techniques to the science, art and practice of cost control and the ascertainment of profitability. It includes the presentation of information derived therefrom, for the purpose of managerial decision-making".

Thus, Cost Accountancy is a comprehensive term and includes the various aspects such as costing, cost accounting, cost control and cost audit and budgetary control.

The Difference between Costing, Cost Accounting and Cost Accountancy can be shown as follows:

Points of Distinction	Costing	Cost Accounting	Cost Accountancy
i) Scope	It is broader in its scope	It is narrow in its scope	It is broadest in its scope
ii) Function	It is concerned with the ascertainment of costs	It is concerned with recording of cost	It is concerned with the formulation of costing principles, methods and techniques to be adopted by a business
iii) Periodicity of functioning	It begins where cost accountancy ends	It begins, where costing ends	It is a starting point
iv) Persons involved	The person involved is cost accountant	The persons involved are cost clerks	The persons involved are experts in the field of cost accountancy such as management accountant.

1.2 LIMITATIONS OF FINANCIAL ACCOUNTING

Financial Accounting is mainly concerned with recording business transactions in the books of accounts for the purpose of presenting final accounts to the Board of Directors, shareholders and tax authorities etc. The objective of Financial Accounting is to present a true and fair view of the company's income, financial position and funds at regular intervals.

In the modern business world, business concerns need some methods and ways by which they can measure their performance. Financial Accounting cannot serve this purpose at all. The indications given by Profit and Loss Account and Balance Sheet are generally inadequate. It is just like thermometer which only indicates the temperature of human body. Only judgements can be made on the basis of such thermometer and a good doctor will have to conduct a number of other checks in order to see what the patient is suffering from. The profit shown by Profit and Loss Account should not be taken as a sign of success because there may be a loss on certain items which might have been compensated by the profit of certain other items. Information regarding wastages and losses is very difficult to be obtained from financial accounts and it is only Cost Accounts which makes such information available to the management. So Cost Accounting, has emerged mainly because of certain **Limitations of Financial Accounting** which are shown in Figure 1.2 as follows.

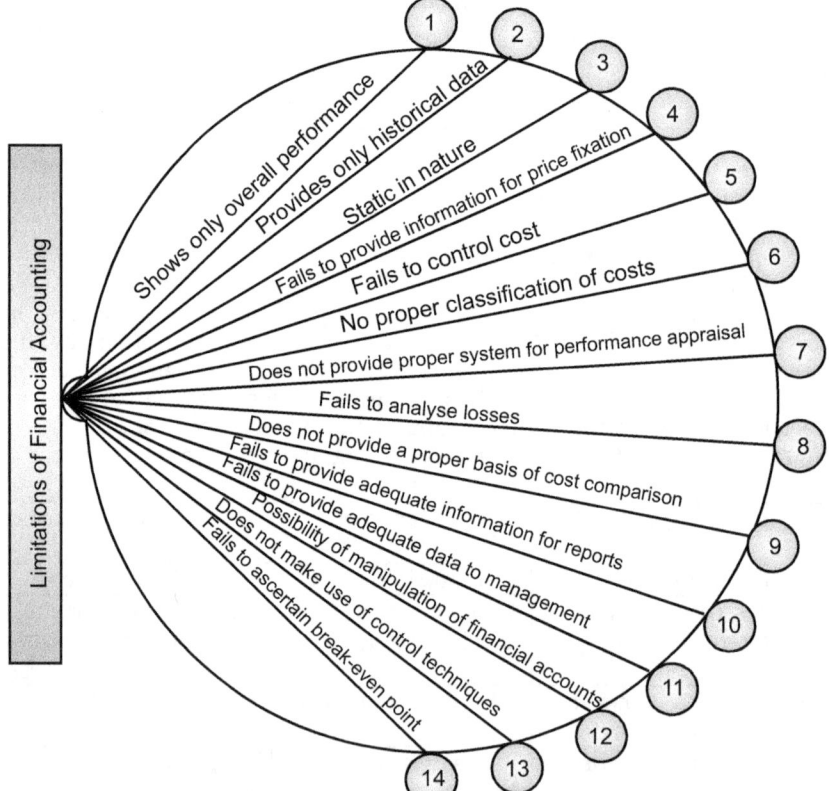

Fig. 1.2 : Limitations of Financial Accounting

i) It shows only Overall Performance :

Financial Accounting provides information about profit, loss, cost etc. of the collective activities of the business as a whole. It does not provide data for each and every product, process, department or operation separately.

ii) It provides only Historical Data :

Financial Accounting is historical in nature and it provides data of past activities. It does not provide current data which management requires for making effective plans for future. So it is rightly said that financial accounts provide only a post-mortem analysis of past activities. It does not help in fixation of selling price.

iii) It is Static in Nature :

Modern business is dynamic and not static. Financial Accounts does not incorporate the changes that takes place within the business.

iv) It fails to provide information for Price Fixation :

In Financial Accounting, costs are not available by division, products, process etc. So, price fixation becomes difficult and estimates cannot be prepared.

v) It fails to Control Cost :

Financial Accounts fail to exercise control over materials, labour and other expenses incurred in a business enterprise. As a result, avoidable wastages and losses remains as it is under this system.

vi) No proper Classification of Costs :

In Financial Accounting, expenses are not classified into direct and indirect, fixed and variable and controllable and uncontrollable. These classifications have utility of their own.

vii) It does not provide proper System for Performance Appraisal :

In Financial Accounting there is no system of developing norms and standards to appraise the efficiency in the use of materials, labour and other costs by comparing the actual performance with what should have been accomplished during a given period of time.

viii) It fails to Analyse Losses :

Financial Accounting does not fully analyse the losses due to idle time, idle plant capacities, inefficient labour, sub-standard materials etc.

ix) It does not provide a Basis of Cost Comparison :

Financial Accounting does not provide cost data regarding operations of the enterprise for the purpose of comparing such data with other periods of operations or other concerns in the industry.

x) It fails to provide Adequate Information for Reports :

It does not provide adequate information for reports to outside agencies like banks, government, insurance companies and trade associations.

xi) It fails to provide adequate Data to Management :

Financial Accounting fails to supply useful data to management for taking various decisions like replacement of labour by machines, introduction of new products, make or buy decisions, selection of the most profitable product mix etc.

xii) Possibility of Manipulation of Financial Accounts :

Very often Financial Accounts are manipulated at the *whim* and *fancies* of the management so as to project a better image in the minds of prospective investors. Financial Accounts may be manipulated by making under or overvaluation of machinery, excessive or inadequate provisions for depreciation, creation of secret reserves etc.

xiii) It does not make use of Control Techniques :

Financial Accounts fail to make use of certain important cost control techniques, such as Budgetary Control, Standard Costing, and so on. Thus, financial accounts do not facilitate in measuring the efficiency of the business with the help of control techniques.

xiv) It fails to ascertain Break-Even Point :

Financial Accounting does not help in ascertaining the break-even point. i.e. the sale or output where the revenue equals the cost. Hence, the point of no profit-no loss cannot be found out under financial accounts.

1.3 ORIGIN AND OBJECTIVES OF COST ACCOUNTING

Origin of Cost Accounting

The science of **Cost Accounting** is of recent origin. The idea of Cost Accounting started in the early years of the 20th century, when the concept of large scale production in the factories started growing. It made the traditional accounting system bulky. The new problems in accounting faced by the factories were numerous. With the increase in the production, different types of costs were found to have different rules on the cost structures of the products. Thus, the variety of expenditures increased and many new items of costs entered the calculations and became vital for taking important decisions by the management.

Costing is a branch of accounting, which has developed because of the limitations of Financial Accounts. It was developed because of certain needs of management which financial account could not meet. The modern industrial requirements were different and to fulfil these requirements some new methods and principles of accounting became necessary over the old traditional method of financial accounting system. This resulted into the outcome of the "Cost Accounting systems". The requirements of management may be summarised as follows :

i)   Measurement of performance and efficiency :

To face severe competition in the business world, a management always needs to maintain their customers. Therefore, to evaluate the present product and market it, it is necessary to measure the performance and business efficiency. Financial accounts cannot serve this purpose at all. In normal times, we can say that profit or loss shown by Profit and Loss account is an indicator of overall efficiency or inefficiency. But in the periods of inflation or depression this may not be true. So the management, would be well advised to ascertain the profit or loss of each product separately. Besides this, management must also try to see that in producing each unit of product there is no unnecessary wastage or loss as regards materials, labour and other expenses. This information is available to the management only under Cost Accounting System. Again a management can know the exact reason of profit or loss by making proper cost analysis which is possible only in cost accounts.

ii) **Pricing:**
For fixing prices of products or services, it is necessary to have information regarding each product or unit of service rather than total expenditure. Only, Cost Accounting system can provide this information to the management.

iii) **Control:**
To maximise profits by minimising costs, it is necessary to set up standards and then compare actual costs with these standards. The reason for the discrepancy may be ascertained and then only possible action can be taken to rectify the situation. Such action is possible only in Cost Accounting.

iv) **Forecasting:**
For planning in future, preparation of budgets are necessary. Budgets are prepared on the basis of forecasts of future costs and revenue. In this field also, Cost Accounting is more capable of helping management than Financial Accounting.

v) **Day-to-Day decisions:**
Besides price fixing decisions, various other decisions have to be taken continuously such as make or buy, whether an old machine should be replaced by a new one, when operational activities be stopped or started, whether an order at concessional rate should be accepted or not etc. Cost accounting is able to provide the necessary information for such decisions.

Thus, the need for Cost Accounting arises because of the management's requirement to know the cost of various activities in various circumstances. Costing has a vital role to play in almost any activity which involves expenditure of money, whether it is a business house or a charitable concern or whether it is a Government Department.

Development of Cost Accounting Phenomenon:

The growth of **Cost Accounting** could be seen during the First World War i.e. 1914-1919 which was rapid, due to the control on the prices imposed by the Government. The Government entered into the "Cost-Plus" contract systems. Cost plus contract provides for the payment by the customers or the contractee of the actual cost of manufacture or of rendering service plus a stipulated profit. This necessitated the maintenance of cost records, ascertainment of cost and cost control for a job or service rendered. Due to increase in competition and rapid growth in the international trade, industries became more cost conscious. In 1929, there was a great depression in the economy during which survival of most of the industries became a problem. Hence, cost reduction techniques had to be adopted for survival.

In today's world of competition, cost consciousness is the key factor for determining the growth of the industrial economy. Ours is a developing country, where we have mixed economy and hence we are having mixed problems. We are facing acute inflation problem, depression in the industries and stagnation in the economy. Hence, cost reduction has become the need of the hour. Therefore, the industrialists must have a perfect knowledge of costs, so that they can take various decisions regarding planning, pricing, budgeting, policy making of the company regarding fixation of wages etc. Thus, the study of **Cost Accounting** is of utmost importance in our country because unless we reduce the costs, we cannot survive in the competitive world and have progress of our economy.

Cost Accounting in Indian Context:

The application of **Cost Accounting** methods in Indian industries was felt from the beginning of the 20th century. The following factors have accelerated the system of Cost Accounting in our country.

i) Increased awareness of cost consciousness by Indian industrialists with a view to ascertain costs more accurately for each product or job.

ii) Growing competition among manufacturers led to fixation of prices at a lower level, so as to attract more customers.

iii) Government economic policy emphasising on planned economy.
iv) Increased Government control over pricing led the Indian manufacturers to give more importance to the installation of cost accounts.
v) The establishment of National Productivity Council in 1958 and a statutory body viz. Institute of Cost and Works Accountants of India.

By realising importance of Cost Accounting techniques, benefits available to the industries, Government of India has made compulsory the maintenance of cost accounts to most of the industries in the corporate sector. For development of cost accounting profession in India, Government passed an Act viz. **"Cost and Works Accountants Act, 1959**, and established a statutory institute styled as **"Institute of Cost and Work Accountant of India"**. The Companies Act, 1956 has been amended and provision has been made to make it obligatory to industries to maintain the Cost Accounting records. Besides this, Government made 'Cost Audit' compulsory to these industries.

During the last 50 years, Cost Accounting emerged as an important tool to the management for improving efficiency and the profitability of the organisation, with increasing complexities in business for efficient management, costing data became important and hence the importance of Cost Accounting is increasing day-by-day.

Objectives of Cost Accounting

The important **Objectives of Cost Accounting** are indicated in Figure 1.3 as follows :

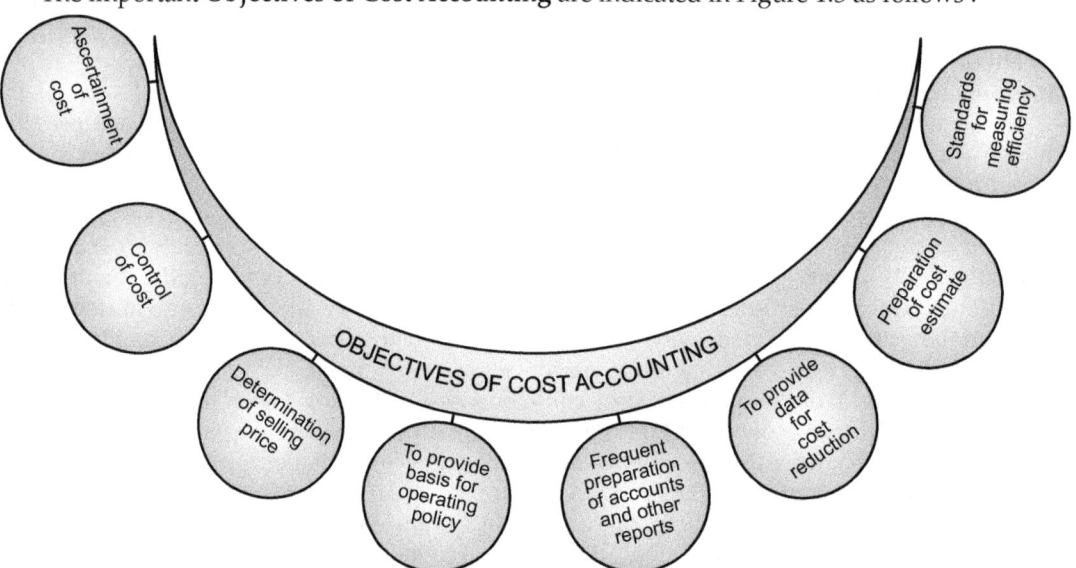

Fig. 1.3 : Objectives of Cost Accounting

i) **Ascertainment of Cost :**

This is the primary objective of Cost Accounting. For the purpose of ascertaining the cost of a product, process or operation, it is necessary to record the expenses incurred, classify them properly and then allocate or apportion it amongst the respective products, processes or departments for calculating total cost of each of these. If there is only one product, cost per unit can be found out by dividing the total expenditure by the total number of units produced. But if there are many products manufactured, then the cost is to be split up between the various products. For this purpose various techniques may be used.

ii) Control of Cost :

Cost control aims at improving efficiency by controlling and reducing cost. Cost control is exercised at different stages in a factory, viz., acquisition of materials, recruiting and deployment of labour force, during production process and so on. As such, we have material cost control, labour cost control, production control, quality control and so on. Control over cost is exercised through the techniques of budgetary control and standard costing. In these techniques, cost is controlled by comparing actual cost with predetermined cost. Cost control is becoming more and more important because of growing competition.

iii) Determination of Selling Price :

Cost accounting provides information on the basis of which selling prices of products or services may be fixed. Total cost of production constitutes the basis on which selling price is fixed by adding a margin of profit. Cost accounting furnishes both the total cost of production as well as cost incurred at each and every stage of production. In fixation of selling price other factors are also important such as market conditions, the area of distribution, volume of sales etc. But no doubt, cost plays the dominating role in price fixation.

iv) To provide a basis for Operating Policy :

Cost data to a great extent helps the management in formulating the policies of a business and in decision-making. Hence, availability of cost data is a must for all levels of management. Some of the decisions which are based on cost data are make or buy decision, manufacturing by mechanisation or automation, whether to close or continue operations, inspite of losses, selling below cost decision, introduction of new products etc.

v) Frequent Preparation of Accounts and Other Reports :

Every concern rely upon the reports on cost data to know the level of efficiency regarding purchase, production, sales and operation results. Financial accounts provide information only at the end of the year because value of closing stock is available at the end of the year. But cost accounts provide the value of closing stock at frequent intervals by adopting, "continuous stock verification" system. Using the value of closing stock it is possible to prepare final accounts and to know the operating results of the business.

vi) To provide Data for Cost Reduction :

For survival in the world of competition, it is necessary to keep the prices of products or services as low as possible. It is only possible when cost of production is less. So the management has to make continuous efforts to reduce the cost. To provide data for cost reduction is one of the important objectives of Cost Accounting. It helps the management in finding out new and improved methods to reduce costs.

vii) Preparation of Cost Estimates :

Many times, it is required to take new jobs by the manufacturing concern or introduce new product as per customer's requirements. Before manufacturing, cost estimates are to be made. Under cost accounting system, preparation of cost estimates is possible. So the preparation of cost estimates is also one of the important objective of Cost Accounting.

viii) Standards for measuring efficiency :

For measuring the performance of various business activities, management requires some base for evaluating the performance. Standard Cost is one of the means for evaluating the performance. So the development of Standard Cost is also an important objective of Cost Accounting.

1.4 ADVANTAGES AND LIMITATIONS OF COST ACCOUNTING

Cost Accounting is a tool with the management for making decisions as regards sales, purchases, production, finance, inventory control etc. If the costing system is sound, it provides the following benefits to the management.

Advantages of Cost Accounting

The Figure 1.4 shows the graphical presentation of **Advantages of Cost Accounting** as follows :

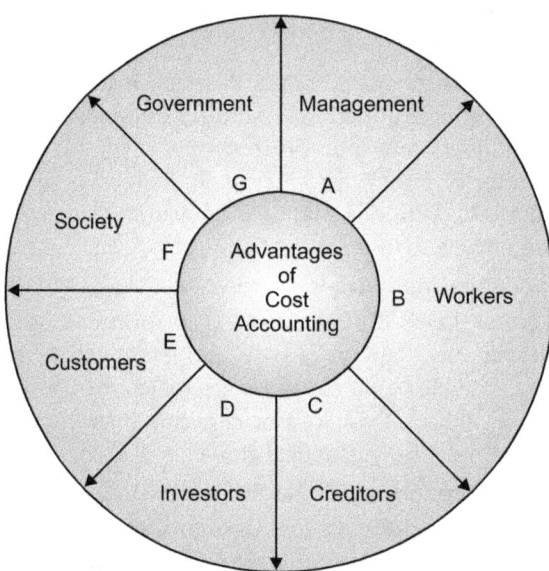

Fig. 1.4 : Advantages of Cost Accounting

A) Advantages to the Management :

i) **Helps in Decision-Making :**

Decision-making is concerned with choosing between alternative courses of action. An important factor involved in the choice is the financial implication of the available alternatives. Cost Accounting is a decision-making tool. It provides suitable cost data and other related information to enable management to evaluate alternative courses of action.

ii) **Supplies detailed Cost Information :**

Cost Accounting classifies cost and revenue by every possible division of the business and supplies management with detailed and regular cost information. Such information is useful for ascertaining the cost of product, process, department, division or unit of service.

iii) **Guides in Price Fixation :**

Cost is one of the most important factor to be considered while fixing prices. It assists the management in fixation of selling price both in normal conditions and during the period of depression. With the help of costing, it is possible to prepare estimates, tenders and quotations.

iv) **It reveals Operating Efficiency :**

Cost information reveals, profitable and unprofitable activities, so that steps may be taken to reduce or eliminate wastages and inefficiencies occurring in any form such as idle time, under-utilisation of plant capacity, spoilage of materials etc.

v) **It Facilitates Planning :**
   It enables the management to know the future costs, so that appropriate plans and decisions can be made.

vi) **It reveals Idle Capacity :**
   A concern may not be working to full capacity due to reasons such as shortage of demand, machine breakdown or other bottlenecks in production. A Cost Accounting system can easily find out the cost of idle capacity so that the management may take immediate steps to improve the position.

vii) **Helps in Inventory Control :**
   Perpetual inventory system which is an integral part of cost accounting, helps in the preparation of interim profit and loss account. Other inventory control techniques like ABC Analysis, Level setting etc., are also used in Cost Accounting.

viii) **Helps in Cost Control :**
   Cost Accounting helps in controlling costs with special techniques like standard costing and budgetary control.

ix) **Helps in Cost Reduction :**
   It helps in the introduction of cost reduction programme and finding out new and improved ways to reduce costs.

x) **Checks the Accuracy of Financial Accounts :**
   Cost Accounting provides a reliable check on the accuracy of financial accounts with the help of reconciliation between the two at the end of the accounting period.

xi) **It Facilitates Cost Comparison :**
   Cost Accounting enables management to make cost comparison of jobs, products, departments, sales territories etc. within the same concern. It provides inter-firm cost comparison also.

xii) **It Prevents Frauds and Manipulation :**
   It helps in preventing manipulation and frauds through cost audit system. Thus, reliable cost data can be furnished to management and others.

B) **Advantages to the Workers :**
From the cost records, we can find out the efficiency of the workers. Thus, the efficient workers are rewarded and the slow workers are given more incentives to come up to a certain level of efficiency. A sound costing system, therefore, increases the profitability and the workers get more wages. Workers are benefited by the introduction of incentive plans which is an integral part of a cost system.

C) **Advantages to the Creditors :**
The creditors feel secured, where there is a good system of costing in a concern because they can verify the creditworthiness of the concern. Thus, the creditors extent credit facilities on a longer term which is beneficial to the business.

D) **Advantages to the Investors :**
The investors also feel secured if there is prosperity in a business as they feel that their money remains secured. Hence, more and more people are attracted to invest in the concern which further increases the prosperity of the business.

E) **Advantages to the Customers :**
The customers always feel that the products which they are buying are the cheapest in the market but at the same time best in quality. Hence, when the prices are quoted in the products to the nearest paisa the customer feel that there is much accuracy in fixing the selling price.

F) **Advantages to the Society :**
As costing removes all the types of wastages, scraps the general public, gets the products at lower prices. Again when a unit grows in size its requirements also grow. For example, more man-power is needed, more raw material requirements arise, more sales are made etc. Hence, it

leads to more employment of the local people, more suppliers of raw materials enter the markets etc. When the sales are more, there can be large sale production and hence the advantages of economies of scale can be achieved, which in turn reduces the prices. Due to reduction in costs, inflation in the economy can be controlled. This is because people will have to pay less price for the products and hence, can save their income.

G) **Advantages to the Government :**

A cost system provides ready figures to use for Government, wage tribunals, trade unions etc. for use in problems relating to price fixing, wage level fixation, settlement of industrial unions disputes etc. The Government can plan its policies based on the techniques and procedures of cost accounting. Cost accounting, therefore, promotes economic development. To reduce cost of production and sales price, the Government has introduced cost audit in most of the industries for e.g., the industries which are engaged in production, processing, manufacturing and mining activities. Such companies are now required to keep certain costing records and have to submit certain statutory returns to the Government periodically. By doing all these, the advantage to the Government is that there can be price stability in the economy.

Limitations of Cost Accounting

Besides the various advantages of Cost Accounting system, it suffers from certain **limitations** which are as follows :

i) **Expensive :**

Highly paid cost accountants and the organisation of costing system involve additional expenditure. However, before installing it, care must be taken to ensure that the benefits derived are more than the investment made on this system of accounting.

ii) **More Complex :**

Cost accounting system involves a number of steps in ascertaining cost such as collection and classification of expenses, allocation and apportionment of expenses etc. These steps are considered as complicated and requires several forms and documents in preparing the reports. This will lead to delay in the preparation of accounts.

iii) **Limited Applicability :**

All business enterprises cannot make use of a single method and technique of costing. It all depends upon the nature of the business and type of product manufactured by it. If a wrong technique and method is used, it misleads the results of the business.

iv) **Not applicable to Small Concerns :**

A cost accounting system is applicable only to large sized business and not suitable for small sized business because it is more expensive.

v) **Lack of Uniformity :**

This is the greatest limitation of cost accounting system. It fails to conform to any uniform procedure. It is possible that two equally competent cost accountants may arrive at different results from the same information. So it is said that all cost accounting results are mere estimates and not reliable.

vi) **Lack of Accuracy :**

Accuracy in Cost Accounting is relative. Certain assumptions are always made while ascertaining cost to suit a particular situation.

vii) **Confusion regarding Non-cost Items :**

There may be confusion regarding non-cost items for e.g., interest in capital, cash discount etc. should be included or to be excluded from cost accounts.

viii) Not useful for Handling Futuristic Situations :

The contribution of Cost Accounting for handling futuristic situations has not been much. For example, Cost Accounting has not evolved any tool so far, for handling inflationary situation.

ix) Failure in many Cases :

It is argued that the adoption of costing system failed to produce the desired results in many cases and so it was not effective.

x) It fails in considering Social Obligations :

Cost Accounting fails to take into account the social obligations of the business. In other words, social accounting is outside the purview of the cost accounts.

Thus, Cost Accounting cannot be termed as an exact science like physics, or mathematics but it is a subjective art which is practised based on the accounting theories, reasoning and most important the common sense. Hence, all the decisions of the management are based upon the best judgement of the cost accountants who take into account the various factors while preparing the cost statements, which may not be the same with other cost accountants.

But apart from the above limitations, Cost Accounting helps the management to take vital decisions with valuable cost figures without which management today, cannot solve the complex business problems.

1.5 DIFFERENCE BETWEEN FINANCIAL ACCOUNTING AND COST ACCOUNTING

Financial Accounting refers to recording of all money transactions on double entry principles in a set of books with an object to prepare final accounts of the business. **Cost Accounting** refers to accumulation, classification, analysis and presentation of costs for managerial control. Both the systems of accounting makes use of the same items of expenditure but in different ways, to serve their own purposes. Due to the complexities of large scale production in the modern business activities, the financial accounting falls short of meeting these challenges. Hence, cost accounting has come into existence to solve all the managerial problems.

The following are the differences between Financial Accounting and Cost Accounting.

Points of Distinction	Financial Accounting	Cost Accounting
i) Coverage	It covers accounts of whole business relating to all commercial transactions.	It covers the transactions relating to certain specific activities only for e.g., production, sales, services etc.
ii) Purpose	Its purpose is external reporting mainly to owners, creditors, tax authorities, Government and prospective investors.	Its purpose is the internal reporting i.e. to the management of every business.
iii) Statutory Requirement	These accounts have to be prepared according to the legal requirements of the Companies Act and Income Tax Act.	These Accounts are generally prepared to meet the requirements of the management. But now it has been made obligatory to keep cost records under the Companies Act.
iv) Recording of transactions	It records, classifies and analyses the transactions in a subjective manner i.e. according to the nature of expenditure.	It records the expenditure in an objective manner i.e. according to the purposes for which cost are incurred.

	Points of Distinction	Financial Accounting	Cost Accounting
v)	Nature of costs	It records only historical costs.	Cost Accounts records both historical and estimated costs.
vi)	Nature of expenses incurred	In **Financial Accounts** expenses are recorded in totals.	In **Cost Accounts**, cost are expressed by proper analysis and classification in order to find out cost per unit.
vii)	Analysis of cost and profit	It disclose profits for the entire business as a whole. It does not show the figures of cost and profit for individual products, departments and processes etc.	It show the profitability or otherwise of each product, process or operation, so as to reveal the areas of profitability.
viii)	Duration of Reporting	The reports are prepared periodically, usually on an annual basis.	It is a continuous process and may be prepared daily, weekly, monthly etc.
ix)	Control aspect	It does not make use of any control techniques. It does not control material and labour cost.	It makes use of some important control techniques such as Standard costing, Marginal costing, Budgetary costing etc. It exercises control over material cost by ABC Analysis, level setting, EOQ etc. and over labour cost by minimising idle time, overtime etc.
x)	Types of Statements prepared	It prepares general purpose statements like Profit and Loss A/c and Balance Sheet.	It generates special purpose statements and reports like Report of Loss of Materials, Idle Time Reports, Variance Report etc.
xi)	Pricing	It fails to guide the formulation of pricing policy.	It provides adequate data for formulating pricing policy.
xii)	Valuation of Stock	Stock is valued at cost price or market price, whichever is less.	Stock is always valued at cost price.
xiii)	Evaluation of Efficiency	The information provided by the Accounts is not sufficient to evaluate the efficiency of the business.	The cost data helps in evaluating the efficiency of the business.
xiv)	Break-up of costs	Costs are not broken up, according to their nature and functions.	The costs are analysed according to their nature and functions for further analysis and control.
xv)	Inter/Intra Firm comparison	Under **Financial Accounting**, Inter-firm or Intra-firm comparison cannot be made.	Under **Cost Accounting** it is possible to make Inter-firm and Intra-firm comparison.
xvi)	Classification of Costs	There is no system of classification of costs into fixed and variable or controllable and uncontrollable.	Since, there is classification of costs into controllable and uncontrollable costs, the management can reduce the controllable costs. The distinction between fixed costs and variable costs also helps the management to take vital decisions.
xvii)	Reference	In **Financial Accounting** reference can be made in case of difficulty to the company law, case decisions and to business ethics.	In **Cost Accounting** no such reference is possible. Guidance can be had only from a body of conventions followed by cost accountants.
xviii)	Dealing of Transactions	It deals with only monetary transactions and it deals only with actual facts and figures.	It deals with monetary as well as non-monetary transactions and it deals partly with the facts and figures and partly with estimates.

1.6 COST UNIT AND COST CENTRE

The entire accounting process of ascertaining the costs accurately and controlling the costs strictly becomes a very simple task only after analysing the important concepts of cost unit and cost centre scientifically and more logically as follows :

Cost Unit

Meaning :

Cost Unit is a quantitative unit of product or service or time in relation to which costs are ascertained or expressed. Cost Units differ from industry to industry. The cost unit selected should be the most natural to the business and accepted by all concerned. Therefore, utmost care should be taken while selecting cost units. It should be neither too small nor too large. If unit is too large, significant cost trends may pass unnoticed, due to averaging of cost. If the unit is too small, it may necessitate detailed and expensive clerical work.

Definition :

C.I.M.A., London has defined Cost Unit as, "a unit of product of service in relation to which costs are ascertained".

Costing means measuring the costs in relation to a unit. Hence, the unit of measurement must be clearly defined and selected. This should be done before ascertainment of costs. For example in a cement factory, the cost per tonne of cement is found out, in a cloth mill, the cost per meter is ascertained in case of machine, the cost per machine hour is found out and so on. Thus here, tonne, metre and machine hour become the cost units. Hence, we can say that a cost unit is nothing, but a unit of measurement of cost.

In case of a service unit, it is difficult to find out and decide a suitable cost unit, for example, in case of a transport undertaking, the costs may be either related to the distance travelled in kilometer, or the weight carried i.e. tonnes. While selecting proper cost unit for the transport both factors i.e. distance and weight should be considered. Hence, tonne kilometer or passenger kilometer will be a proper unit.

Types of Cost Units :

i) **Single Cost Unit :**

It is a cost unit in which only one characteristics is used in measurement of cost e.g. per kilometre, per litre, per passenger, and so on.

ii) **Composite Cost Unit :**

It is a cost unit in which two characteristics are used simultaneously in measurement of cost e.g. per tonne-kilometre, per passenger-kilometre, per kilowatt-hour, per patient-bed, and so on.

Each industry has a different cost units, some of which are given below :

Industry/Product	Cost Unit
Automobile	Number
Bricks	Thousand
Cotton/Jute	Bale
Chemicals	Litre, Gallon, K.G. Tonne
Electricity	KWH
Furniture	Number
Gas	Cubic metre
Hotel or Hospital	Room per day or per bed
Mines	Tonne
Steel	Tonne
Shoes	Pair
Transport	Tonne km/Passenger km
Utensils	KG/Tonne
Cement	Tonne
Cable	Metre or km
Fertiliser	Tonne
TV or Radio or VCR	Set
Building	Sq. ft. or Sq. mtr.
Nuts and Bolts	Gross
Sugar and Flour Mills	Quintal
Timber	Cubic foot
Water Supply	Thousand litres/Gallon

Hence, an appropriate cost unit selected should be :

i) same as being followed throughout the industry.

ii) very simple and easy to understand.

iii) neither to big nor too small.

iv) uniformally maintained over a period of time.

v) most natural to the business.

vi) more suitable to that business.

Cost Centre

Meaning :

For the purposes of administrative control, the entire organisation is divided into a number of sub-units which may be in the form of departments, branches, processes etc., for ascertaining and controlling costs. Because, the costs incurred will be charged initially to these sub-units which are known as **Cost Centres.** A cost centre is therefore, a sub-unit of the organisation for which costs may be collected separately and used for cost ascertainment and control.

Definition :

C.I.M.A., England has therefore defined cost centre as **"a location, person or item of equipment (or group of these) for which costs may be ascertained and used for the purposes of control".** An analysis of this definition reveals that a Cost Centre may be in the form of : a) a location, (such as a department, division, section or process) or b) an item of equipment (like machine) or c) a person (e.g. salesman), or a group of these. However, costs incurred are identified with the cost centres initially (for distribution later amongst cost units). It helps to ascertain the cost centre-wise costs. Divisionalisation of an organisation into a number of cost centres, therefore, assumes importance. The number and size of cost centres differ from one organisation to another depending upon the nature of production activities, size of the organisation, management's informational needs, etc. The Figure 1.5 shows the various **Types of Cost Centres** as follows :

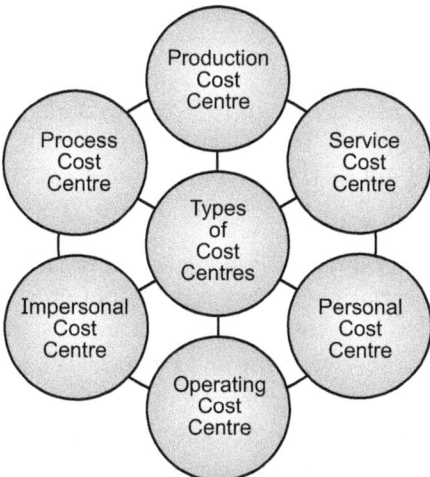

Fig. 1.5 : Types of Cost Centres

Types of Cost Centres :

i) **Production Cost Centre :**

It is a cost centre connected with production i.e. machine shop, welding shop, assembly shop etc. The manufacturing and non-manufacturing costs are charged to product cost centres.

ii) **Service Cost Centre :**

A Service Cost Centre is one which provides services to the other cost centres. Only non-manufacturing costs are charged to service cost centre. Examples of service cost centre are canteen, machinery maintenance, office service etc.

iii) **Personal Cost Centre :**

Personal Cost Centre consists of a person or group of persons. Personal Cost Centre follows the organisational structure of a factory. Under this type of cost centre, the costs are analysed and accumulated by Works Manager, Sales Manager, Store-keeper, Foreman etc.

iv) **Impersonal Cost Centre :**
It consists of a location or item of equipment. A cost centre relating to location may represent a region of sales, a warehouse, or store-room. Cost centre relating to location may represent a region of sales, a warehouse or storeroom. Cost centre relating to an item of equipment could be a machine or group of machines.

v) **Operation Cost Centre :**
It is a cost centre which consists of machines or persons carrying out similar operations i.e. machines and operations engaged in welding, turning or matching.

vi) **Process Cost Centre :**
It is a cost centre which consists of a specific process or continuous sequence of operations.

Whatever may be the type of Cost Centre, it is determined by taking into consideration, the following factors viz. the volume of work to be performed, the extent of cost control that can be exercised, responsibilities to be identified and the uses of cost centres to the cost accounting department.

QUESTIONS FOR SELF-STUDY

I. Theory Questions :
 i) Explain the concept 'Cost'.
 ii) Define the terms :
   a) Cost, b) Costing, c) Cost Accounting, d) Cost Accountancy.
 iii) "Cost Accounting begins where Financial Accounting ends". Discuss.
 iv) What is Financial Accounting ? Explain the limitations of Financial Accounting.
 v) "Cost Accounting has been developed out of the limitations of Financial Accounting". Comment.
 vi) Define 'Cost Accounting'. State the advantages and limitations of Cost Accounting.
 vii) "The scope of the subject of Cost Accounting is not only confined to the ascertainment, but it can be enlarged, so as to cover cost control and cost presentations". Elaborate.
 viii) Differentiate between Cost Accounting and Financial Accounting.
 ix) "Cost Accounting has become an essential tool of management". Elaborate.
 x) What is the difference between Cost Accounting and Cost Accountancy.
 xi) What is 'Cost Unit' ? State the unit of cost in various industries.
 xii) Define the term 'Cost Unit'. State the various types of cost unit giving suitable examples.
 xiii) What is 'Cost Centre' ? Explain the various types of Cost Centres.
 xiv) Write short notes on :
   a) Cost, b) Costing, c) Cost Accounting, d) Cost Accountancy, e) Limitations of Financial Accounting, f) Advantages of Cost Accounting, g) Limitations of Cost Accounting, h) Cost Unit, i) Cost Centre.
 xv) Differentiate between :
   a) Cost Accounting and Financial Accounting
   b) Single Cost Unit and Composite Cost Unit
   c) Production Cost Centre and Service Cost Centre

***

Unit ... 2

ELEMENTS OF COST

2.1 Material, Labour and Other Expenses
2.2 Classification of Cost and Types of Costs
2.3 Preparation of Cost Sheet
* Illustrations
* Questions for Self-Study

The constituent elements which build up the cost of a unit are materials, labour, energy and equipments. These elements are broadly divided into three major groups of **Materials, Labour and Other Expenses**. These three elements of cost or cost factors could then be further classified into direct and indirect categories. The term '**Materials**' refers to all commodities supplied to an undertaking. **Labour** is an essential factor of production. It is a human resource and participates in the process of production. Labour cost is a significant element of cost of a product or service. All costs other then material costs and labour costs are termed as '**Expenses**'. Direct expenditure is one which is identifiable as belonging exclusively to a particular process, product, unit or service. Indirect expenditure is one which, while still being part of the cost of production, is not incurred exclusively for a particular part of the job and must, therefore, be spread over the whole.

2.1 MATERIAL, LABOUR AND OTHER EXPENSES

On the basis of the nature or elements of costs, costs may be classified into three broad categories as **Material Cost, Labour Cost and Other Expenses. Material Cost** denotes the cost of raw materials consumed in the process of manufacturing and marketing a commodity. **Labour Cost** represents the wages, salaries, and so on, payable to the employees of a corporate entity. **Expenses** refer to the costs other than material and labour costs (but including notional costs of the use of owned assets) of other services provided and used in manufacturing and marketing the goods and services of the company. Elementwise classification is important for the purpose of ascertaining the costs of different elements of total cost of a product manufactured or services generated. Further, it also helps to ascertain the relative share and importance of each of the elements of total cost of goods and services.

For the management, it is not just sufficient to have knowledge of total cost control, but for effective control and decision-making the management must know further sub-analysis and classification of costs. Hence, the total cost is analysed according to the elements of cost. There are basically three elements of cost viz. **material, labour and other expenses**. Again they are further analysed into different elements i.e. direct and indirect material, direct and indirect labour and direct and indirect expenses. **Indirect expenses** are termed as **Overheads** or on cost. The Overheads are Factory Overheads, Office and Administrative Overheads and Selling and Distribution Overheads.

The Figure 2.1 indicates the different **Elements of Cost** as follows :

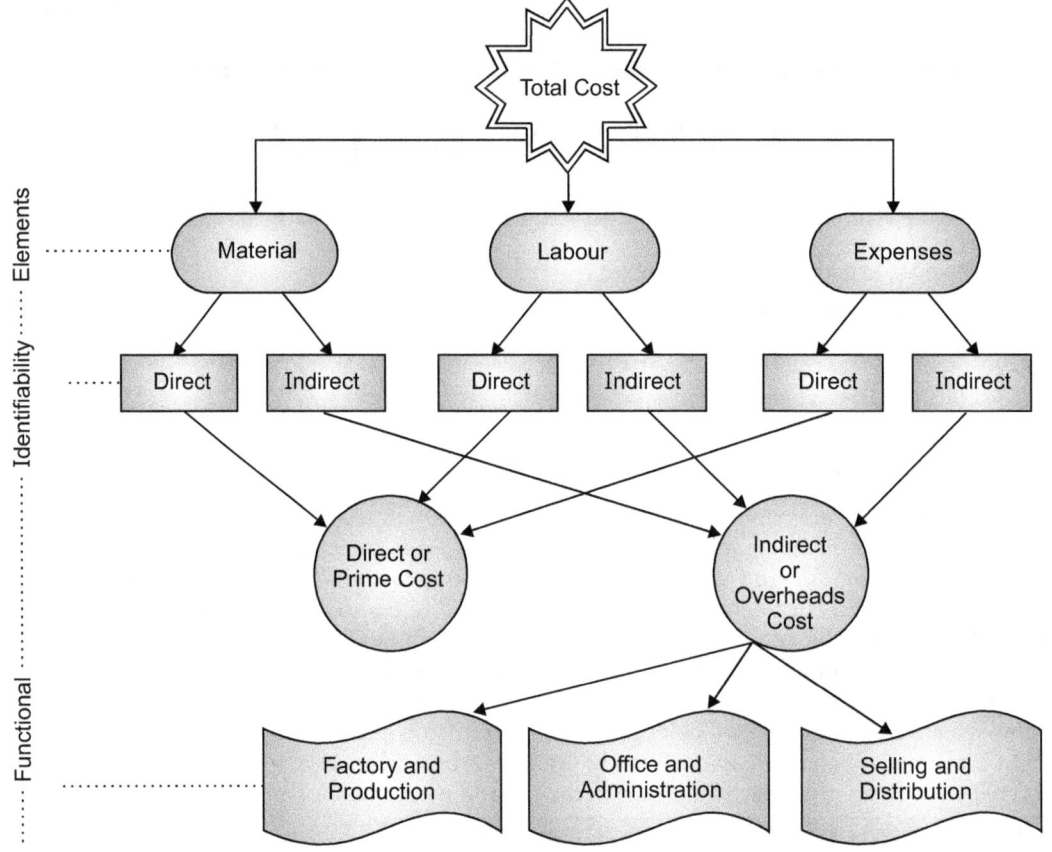

Fig. 2.1 : Elements of Cost

Thus, **Elements of Cost** are the different items or components of cost which are added to get the total cost of any product or service.

According to I.C.M.A., London, Elements of Cost means, "the primary classification of costs according to the factors upon which expenditure is incurred viz. material cost, labour cost and expenses".

Analysis and classification of costs facilitates cost ascertainments, renders it possible to make valid comparisons of the operating efficiency of various departments and assists in locating the responsibility for off-standard performance.

The total cost of a product consists of various elements of cost. These elements are described in detail as under.

Material

According to *I.C.M.A., London-Material Cost* is, "the cost of commodities supplied to an undertaking". Material Cost is further divided into Direct Materials and Indirect Materials as follows :

1) Direct Materials :

Direct Materials are those which can be identified in the product and can be measured. They can also be charged to the product directly. Thus, direct materials enter the product and form a part of finished product. For example, cotton used in a textile mill, timber used in furniture making, pig-iron in foundry etc., are treated as direct materials. The cost of direct material is termed as the 'direct material cost'.

But sometimes, even if some materials go directly into the production, they are not treated as direct materials. For example, thread in dress making, nails in shoe making, glue in binding etc. The reason for this is that the value of these materials is very less and the quantity used is also negligible. Hence, attempt is not made to analyse their costs which will otherwise be time consuming and will add to extra cost because of spending more time on them, with their value being negligible. Thus, such materials should conveniently be treated as indirect materials.

2) Indirect Materials :

Indirect Materials are those which do not form a part of the finished products. It is defined as, "materials which cannot be allocated, but which can be apportioned to or absorbed by cost centres or cost units. For example lubricants, oils, cotton wastes, small tools etc.. Thus, materials which cannot be conveniently identified with individual cost units are termed as indirect materials. These are minor in importance. But sometimes, the cost of small items which have less value like the nails in furniture, thread in the dress manufacturing, paper used in polishing, etc. are treated as indirect materials though they go directly into production. The cost of these indirect materials is termed as 'indirect material cost'.

Generally, the materials are purchased from market or directly from manufacturers. The materials purchased have to be brought to the factory for converting them into finished product. So all the expenses which will be incurred for bringing the materials to the place of production will have to be considered for ascertaining the cost of materials. Materials purchased are stored in godowns, therefrom, they are issued for production. The valuation of material issued for consumption is done by Costing Department. This value of materials consumed is charged as 'Material cost'.

Following are the points of differences between Direct Materials and Indirect Materials :

	Direct Materials		Indirect Materials
i)	They can be conveniently identified with and allocated to cost units.	i)	These are certain materials which cannot be conveniently identified with individual cost units.
ii)	They generally form a part of the finished product. e.g., cotton used in a textile mill, clay in bricks, leather in shoes, timber in furniture, etc.	ii)	These are minor in importance, such as a) small and relatively, inexpensive items which may become a part of finished product e.g., pins, screws, nuts and bolts, thread, etc. b) those items which do not physically become a part of the finished products e.g., coal, lubrication oil and greece, sand paper, etc.
iii)	They directly enter the product and form a part of the finished product.	iii)	The costs which relate to the factory form a part of the factory overhead.

Labour

According to *I.C.M.A., London*, **Labour Cost** is defined as, "the cost of remuneration (wages, salaries, commissions, bonus etc.) of the employees of an undertaking". Generally worker's efforts are necessary for producing any particular thing or giving any service. In spite of computerisation and automation, the importance of labour force in manufacturing a product or giving service is increasing day-by-day. The expenses incurred for obtaining the services of human being are known as labour cost of a Job. Labour Cost is further divided into the following :

1) **Direct Labour :**

All the workers who are directly engaged in a manufacturing activity such as operating machines, doing assembly work etc., are known as direct workers and wages paid to them are known as '**Direct Labour Cost**'. These wages can be conveniently identified with a particular product, job or process. For ascertaining direct labour cost, it is necessary to know how much and what work has been done by an individual worker. For this purpose, various records should be maintained by the management. Wages of skilled and unskilled labour may be included in this item. Examples of direct labour are : Baker, Shoe-maker, Carpenter, Weaver, Tailor, Bus Drivers and Conductors etc.

2) **Indirect Labour :**

It is of a general character and cannot be conveniently identified with a particular cost unit. In other words, indirect labour is not directly engaged in the production operations, but only to assist or help in production operations. Thus, the wages which cannot be allocated but which can be apportioned or absorbed by cost centres or cost unit is known as **Indirect Labour**. Examples of indirect labour are : salaries and wages paid to foreman, supervisors, chargeman, inspectors, clerical staff etc., working in production department, overtime and night shift allowance paid and any other benefits paid to them.

Following are the points of differences between Direct Labour and Indirect Labour.

	Direct Labour		Indirect Labour
i)	It consists of wages paid to workers directly engaged in converting raw materials into finished products.	i)	They are not directly engaged in the production operations but only assist or help in production operations.
ii)	These wages can be conveniently identified with a particular product, job or process.	ii)	They are of a general character and cannot be conveniently identified with a particular cost unit.
iii)	Wages paid to Baker, Shoe-maker, Carpenter, Weaver and Tailor are examples of Direct Labour.	iii)	Wages paid to Supervisor, Inspector, Cleaner, Clerk, Peon, Watchman are examples of Indirect Labour.
iv)	'All labour expended in altering the construction, composition, confirmation or condition of the product' is known as Direct Labour.	iv)	The wages which cannot be allocated, but which can be apportioned to or absorbed by cost centres or cost units is known as Indirect Labour.

Other Expenses

All costs, other than material and labour are termed as **Other Expenses**. According to *I.C.M.A., London,* Expense is defined as, "the cost of services provided to an undertaking and the notional cost of the use of owned assets". Expenses are further divided into the following:

1) **Direct Expenses :**

Direct Expenses include all types of expenses other than direct materials and direct labour which are incurred specifically for a particular product or process. It is defined as "expenses which can be identified with and allocated to cost centres and cost units". Direct expenses are also known as 'chargeable expenses'. Direct expenses form a part of the Prime Cost for e.g. chargeable expenses, Hire of special plant, Royalties, Cost of patents and patterns, Engineers Fees, Cost of special drawings, Designs and layouts, Architect's fees, Direct expenses payable, Surveyor's fees, Productive expenses outstanding, Consultants fees, Process expenses due, but not paid, Prime cost expenses etc.

2) **Indirect Expenses :**

All indirect costs other than indirect material and indirect labour costs are termed as **Indirect Expenses**. These expenses are not charged directly to production. Indirect expenses cannot be allocated, but they can be apportioned to or absorbed by cost centres or cost units. Examples of indirect expenses are : rent, rates and taxes, salary of general manager, staff welfare expenses, canteen expenses, telephone expenses, lighting, power, fuel, depreciation, insurance, bank charges and interest paid, etc.

The aggregate of direct material cost, direct labour cost and direct expenses is termed as "**Prime Cost**" while the aggregate of indirect material cost, indirect labour cost and indirect expenses is termed as "**Overheads**".

Following are the points of differences between Direct Expenses and Indirect Expenses.

	Direct Expenses		Indirect Expenses
i)	"Expenses which can be identified with and allocated to cost centres and cost unit" is known as Direct Expenses.	i)	"All indirect costs other than indirect materials and indirect labour costs, are termed as Indirect Expenses.
ii)	These are those expenses which are specifically incurred in connection with a particular job or cost unit.	ii)	These cannot be directly identified with a particular job, proces or work order and are common to cost units and cost centres.
iii)	These are also known as "chargeable" expenses.	iii)	These are also known as non-chargeable expenses or on costs or overheads.
iv)	These form a part of the Prime Cost.	iv)	They form a part of the Overheads.
v)	Cost of Drawings and Patterns, Royalty paid, Excise Duty, Architect Fees are the examples of Direct Expenses.	v)	Rent and Rates, Depreciation, Light and Power, Advertising, Insurance, Carriage Outward are the examples of Indirect Expenses.

Overheads

Overhead Costs are the operating costs of a business enterprise which cannot be identified with a particular unit of output. Overheads consists of all expenses incurred for in connection with the general organisation of the entire concern or a part of it, i.e. cost of operating supplies and services used by the undertaking. It also include maintenance of capital assets. There are four main types of overheads which are as follows :

1) Factory or Production or Works or Manufacturing Overheads :

These are the overheads which are concerned with the production function. It includes indirect materials, indirect wages and indirect expenses in producing goods or services. Thus, overhead covers all types of indirect expenses incurred by a concern right from the receipt of an order to the final delivery of goods to the customer or for storing the finished goods in the godowns. Examples of factory overheads are : depreciation of plant and machinery, depreciation of factory buildings, insurance charges and repairs on plant and machinery and factory building, power consumption, coal and other fuel charges, wages of indirect workers, welfare services etc.

2) Office or Administration or Establishment or Management Overheads :

These are the indirect expenditure incurred in general administrative function i.e. in formulating policies, planning and controlling the function, directing and motivating the personnel of an organisation in the attainment of its objectives. Examples of office and administration overheads are : Office rent, rates and taxes, salaries of office staff, postage, telegrams and telephone, printing and stationery, office lighting, repairs and depreciation of office building and equipments, legal expenses, audit fees, director's fees, bank charges and interest paid, etc.

3) Selling Overheads :

It is the cost of promoting sales and retaining customers. It is the skill of any business to attract new customers by offering extra facilities and services by giving them free samples etc., so that they get attracted to the company. Similarly, the existing customer should be retained by providing the best services for which certain expenses are incurred. Thus, if a concern wants to expand its business it must incur selling expenses which cannot be avoided. Examples of selling overheads are : salaries of the sales manager and sales staff, commission paid to salesman and selling agents, advertising charges, packing charges, free catalogues, pamphlets and price lists, mail order house expenses, showroom expenses, bad debts, after sales service expenses, travelling expenses etc.

4) Distribution Overheads :

These are the expenses incurred in moving the goods from the company's godowns to the customers premises. It means that distribution overhead starts with all indirect material, indirect wages and indirect expenses incurred upto the point of packing the product, for making available for despatch and ends with making the re-conditioned returned empty packages and tins available for reuse. The actual definition of distribution expenses is "the cost of the sequence of operations, which begins with making the packed product available for despatch and ends with making the re-conditioned returned empty package, if any available for reuse". Examples of distribution overheads are : warehouse rent and insurance, salary of warehouse keeper and other cost of transportation of goods, insurance of goods in transit, cost of maintenance of vehicles, loading expenses, carriage outward, special packing expenses, cost of repairing and re-conditioning of empty packages etc.

Items to be excluded from Cost or Non-cost Items :

There are certain items of expenses which are purely of financial nature and hence they are simply excluded, while recording the business transactions into the books of cost accounts. The following is the summarised list of financial items which are to be excluded from the computation of Total Cost.

1) **Financial Incomes :**
   Capital Profits, Dividend Received, Brokerage and Commision Received, Share Transfer Fees Received, Interest on Investments, Interest on Bank Deposits, Rent Received, Bad Debts Recovery, Interest on Loan given, Discount Received etc.

2) **Financial Charges :**
   Capital Losses, Cash Discount, Trade Discount, Penalties and Fines, Share Transfer Fees Paid, Interest on Bank Loan, Interest on Debentures, Preliminary Expenses, Underwriting Commission, Discount on Issue of Shares and Debentures, Loss on Investments, Capital Expenses, Interest on Capital, Salary or Commission paid to Partners, Income Tax, Wealth Tax, Interest on Debentures, Reconstruction Expenses, Development Expenses, Reorganisation Expenses etc.

3) **Appropriations :**
   Bad Debts Reserve, Dividends or Bonus Paid, Charitable Donations, Transfer to Reserves, General Reserves, Sinking Fund, Debenture Redemption Fund, Machinery Replacement Fund, Investment Fluctuation Fund, etc.

4) **Abnormals :**
   Abnormal Wastage, Abnormal Idle Time, Loss by fire, Loss by Theft, Loss of Stock, etc.

Division of Costs :

The division of costs are obtained with the help of Elements of Cost. The following are the various divisions of costs of an article or a product.

1) **Prime Cost :**
   This is the total of Direct material, Direct labour and Direct expenses.
   Prime Cost = Direct Material + Direct Wages + Direct Expenses.

2) **Works Cost :**
   This consists of Prime cost plus Works overheads.
   Works Cost = Prime Cost + Works Overheads

3) **Cost of Production :**
   This is made up of Works Cost plus Office and Administrative Overheads. Cost of production is termed as "Gross Cost".
   Cost of Production = Works Cost + Office and Administration Overheads.

4) **Total Cost or Cost of Sales :**
   This is the cost of production plus selling and distribution overheads. In other words, it is the total expenditure incidental to production, administration, selling and distribution of commodities manufactured. Total Cost is termed as "Net Cost".
   Total Cost / Cost of Sales = Cost of Production + Selling and Distribution Overheads.

5) **Selling Price =**
   Total Cost / Cost of Sales + Profit (or – Loss).

The **Division of Costs** may be shown in the following chart indicated in Figure 2.2.

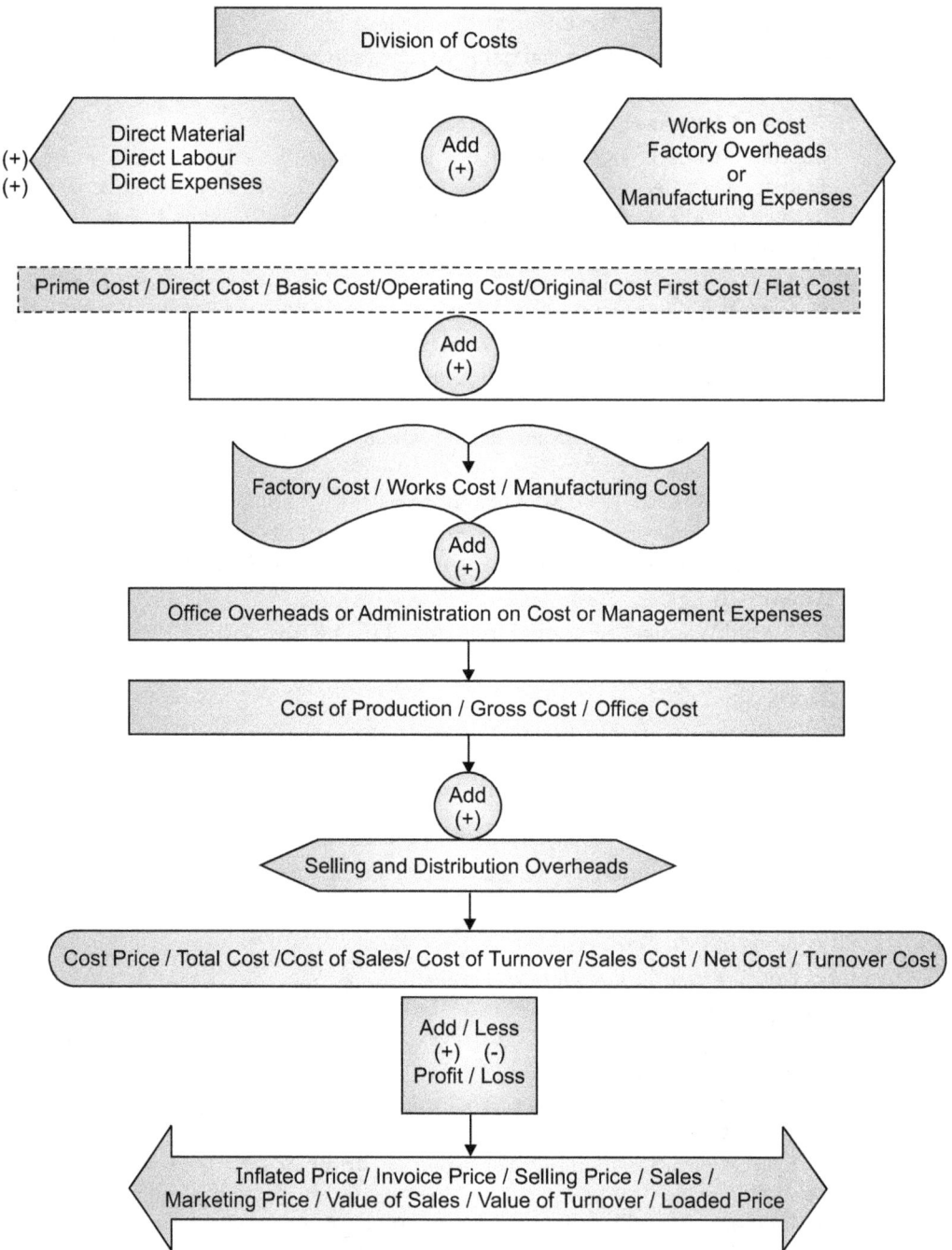

Fig. 2.2 : Division of Costs

2.2 CLASSIFICATION OF COST AND TYPES OF COSTS

Classification of Cost

Meaning and Definition :

Cost Classification means grouping of costs according to their common characteristics. It is the process of grouping the items together which are alike.

According to *Dickey*, "Classification is the process of grouping like facts under a common designation on the basis of similarities of nature, attributes or relations".

The *Committee on National Association of Accountants defines Classification* as, "The identification of each item and the systematic placement of like items together according to their common features".

Items grouped together under common heads are further defined according to their fundamental differences. Suitable classification of costs is of utmost important, so that these costs can be identified with the cost centres or cost units.

Need of Cost Classification :

The need for classification arises having to use cost data for a variety of purposes. For different purposes different kinds of cost informations are required. Therefore, costs must be arranged and classified in such a manner that they can be combined in different ways to serve different purposes. Generally, **Cost Classification** is required for the attainment of the following **purposes** shown in Figure 2.3.

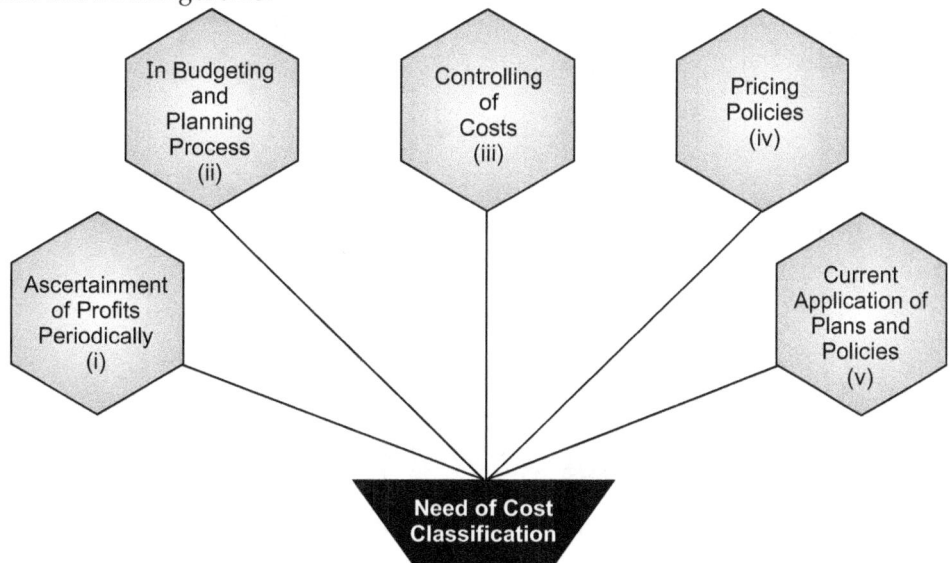

Fig. 2.3 : Need of Cost Classification

Methods of Classification :

Costs are classified in different ways according to their elements i.e. material, labour and expenses. Other basis of cost classification are function, variability, controllability, normality, period, investment etc. The costs may be the same, but the classification of costs are made in different ways depending upon the **specific requirement and the purpose** to be achieved in a particular organisation. The Figure 2.4 shows the graphical presentation of **Classification of Costs** as follows.

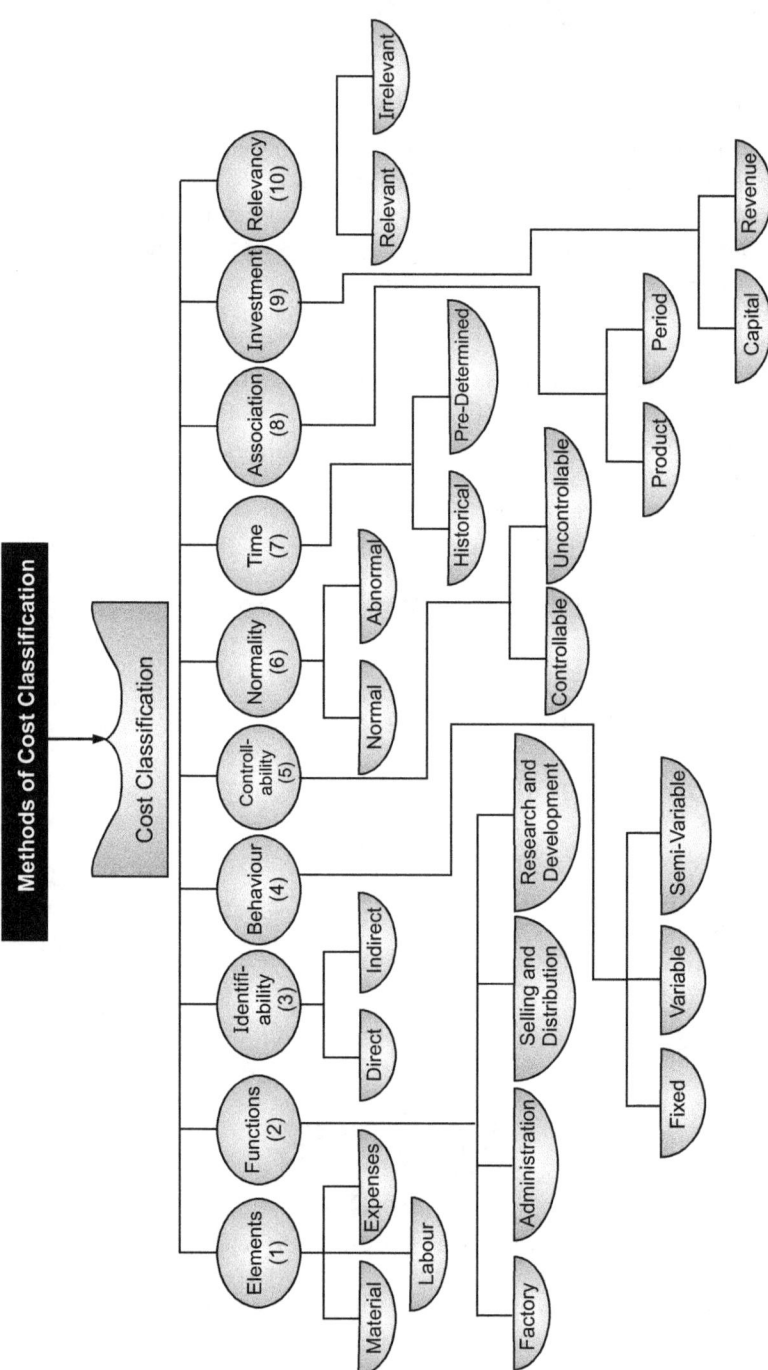

Fig. 2.4 : Classification of Cost

1) Elements :

The **cost elements** of a product are Material, Labour and Expenses.

i) Materials :

The *I.C.M.A., London* defines material cost as, "the cost of commodities, other than fixed assets, introduced into products or consumed in the operation of an organisation. Material cost may be either direct material cost or indirect material cost.

Direct material cost is defined as "the cost of materials entering into and becoming constituent element of a product or saleable service". Thus, materials which can be identified with the production of a product or which can be traced to the finished product are known as direct materials. Examples of direct materials are cotton in cotton textile, timber in furniture making industries, leather in shoe making industries etc.

Indirect material cost has been defined as, "material cost other than direct material cost". In other words, material cost which cannot be identified with a product, job or process or traceable to the same, is known as indirect material cost. Examples of indirect materials are consumable stores such as oil, cotton waste, small tools, works stationery etc.

But in some cases, even direct materials which can be traced to the product concerned may be treated as indirect materials because of time and labour involved in ascertaining their cost for the purposes of a direct charge. For example, thread, buttons, nails, gum, metal strips etc. which are used in production are treated as indirect, although they are direct in nature.

ii) Labour :

Labour is the physical or mental effort expended in production. The remuneration for such efforts is known as wages. Labour cost may be either direct labour cost or indirect labour cost.

Direct labour cost is defined as, "the cost of remuneration for employee's efforts and skills applied directly to a product or saleable service".

Indirect labour cost is defined as, "labour cost other than direct labour cost". Thus, indirect labour is not directly engaged in the production operations, but only to assist or help in production operations. Examples of indirect labour are : salaries and wages paid to foreman, supervisors, chargeman, inspectors, maintenance workers, clerical staff etc. working in production department, overtime and night shift allowance paid and any other benefit paid.

iii) Expenses :

The term 'Expenses' denotes the cost of services provided to an undertaking. Expenses may be direct or indirect.

ICMA, defines direct expenses as "Costs other than materials or wages which are incurred for a specific product or a saleable service". Direct expenses form a part of Prime Cost. Examples of direct expenses are : Cost of drawings and patterns, Repairs and maintenance of plant and equipment taken on hire, Architect's fees, Research expenditure, Excise duty, Royalty etc.

Indirect expenses are "expenses other than direct expenses". These expenses are not charged directly to production. Examples of indirect expenses : Rent and rates, Salary of General Manager, Staff welfare expenses, Canteen expenses, Lighting, Telephone expenses etc.

2) Functions :

Costs may be classified on the **basis of business functions** like manufacturing, administration, selling and distribution, research and development etc. Ascertainment of costs for all these functions is necessary and hence they are classified as follows :

i) Factory Costs :

This is the cost which is incurred for a series of operations i.e. right from the supply of materials, labour and expenses incurred, till the completion of production. Thus, materials, labour and expenses, both direct and indirect, constitute production cost. Examples of manufacturing cost are : material, labour, factory rent rates and taxes, depreciation on factory building and plant and machinery, factory lighting and power, store keeping expenses, insurance of factory building etc.

ii) Administration Costs :

This is the cost of running a concern i.e. for framing the policies, directing and controlling all the activities of the organisation other than manufacturing and selling and distribution expenses. According to *I.C.M.A.*, it defines as, "the sum of these costs of general and management and of secretarial, accounting and administrative services which cannot be directly related to production, marketing, research and development function of the enterprise". Examples of administration cost are : Director's fees and allowances, Salaries of office staff, Audit fees, Legal expenses, Office rent and taxes, Office lighting, Expenses of secretarial and accounting department, Postage and telegram, Printing and stationery etc.

iii) Selling and Distribution Costs :

Selling costs are those costs which are incurred for attracting the potential customers and retaining the existing customers. Thus, demand is created in the market through advertisement and publicity, so that new orders can be secured.

Selling costs include : Advertisement, Hoarding / Neon signs etc. Salaries and commission to salesman and sales staff, Costs of free samples / brochures etc. Showroom expenses, Travelling expenses of salesman etc.

Distribution expenses are incurred for despatching the products which are ready after packing. These expenses include : Carriage outward, Warehouse expenses, Packing costs, Running and maintenance cost of delivery van, Salary of the godown staff etc.

iv) Research and Development Costs :

Research Cost is defined as, "the cost of seeking new or improved products, applications of material or methods". **Development Cost** is defined as, "the cost of process which begins with the implementation of the decision to produce a new or improve methods and ends with the commencement of formal production of that product or by that method.

3) Identifiability :

According to the identifiability with the cost units, jobs or processes the costs are classified into direct and indirect. In costing, Direct and Indirect costs have much significance.

    i)   Direct Costs :

            All the costs which can be conveniently allocated to cost unit or cost centre is known as direct cost. For example, the cost of cotton in case of textile industries, the cost of timber in furniture industries etc.

    ii)   Indirect Costs : It is a cost which is of a general character and which cannot be identified with a particular unit of cost. These cost cannot be allocated, but can be apportioned to cost unit or cost centre. The terms 'direct' and 'indirect' relate to the methods of allocating them because it depends upon whether the same cost should be treated as direct or indirect. Thus, same item may be treated as a direct cost in one case and indirect cost in another case. This bifurcation depends upon the nature of business and also cost unit decided by the management. For example, we can treat depreciation as a direct cost, if there is only one machine or cost centre, but if there are many cost units it becomes difficult to allocate the cost accurately. In this case, it is treated as an indirect cost, for e.g. in cost of construction sites, the depreciation of machinery etc. is taken as direct cost, while in case of a factory where there are many departments which use the same machine, it is treated as an indirect cost.

Identifiability classification is important because,
- it facilitates accurate ascertainment of cost.
- it facilitates controlling of costs.
- it enables in fixing the responsibility to the executives.

Direct Costs are those costs which are incurred for and may easily and conveniently be identified with a particular cost unit or cost centre. Direct costs include direct material cost, direct labout cost and other direct expenses. **Indirect Costs**, on the other hand, represent the costs which are of general nature and which cannot easily and conveniently be identified with a particular cost unit or cost centre. They include indirect material cost, indirect labour cost and other indirect expenses. The indirect costs are therefore called **Overhead Expenses.** These indirect or overhead expenses can further be divided into three sub-categories as factory overhead expenses, administration overhead expenses, and selling and distribution overhead expenses (on the basis of the functions). The Classification of Costs on the basis of Traceability Elements and Functions is shown in Figure 2.5.

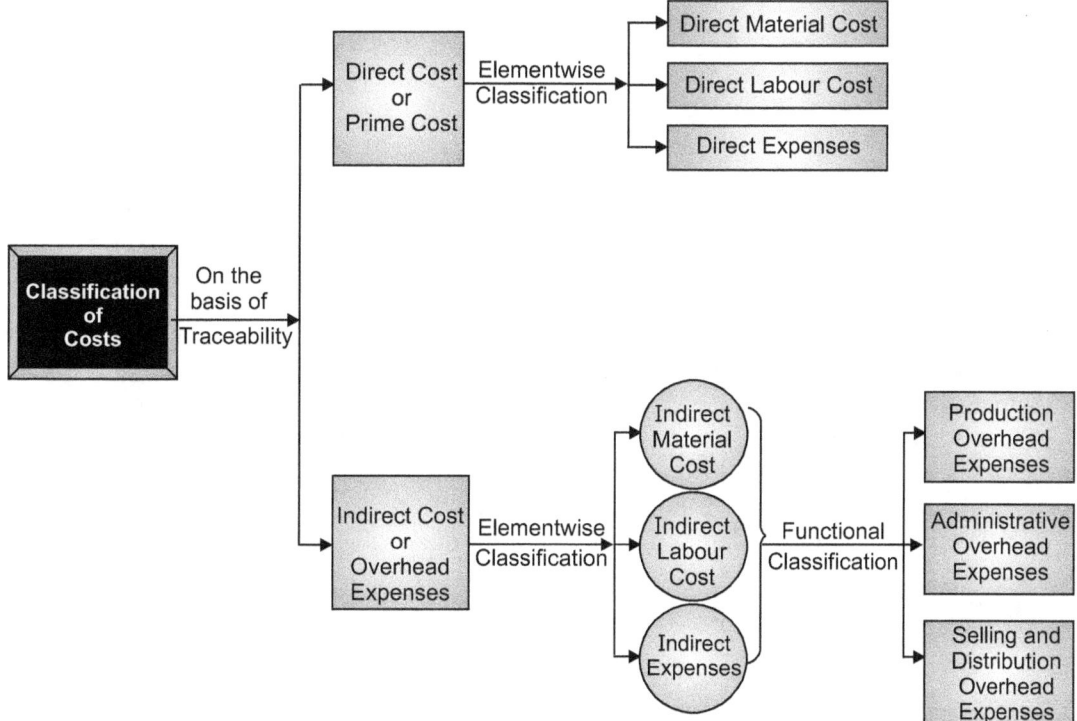

Fig. 2.5 : Classification of Cost on the basis of Traceability, Elements and Functions

4) **Behaviour :**

On the basis of this characteristic, costs are classified a**ccording to their nature or behaviour** in relation to changes in the level of activity or volume of production. On the basis of variability, costs are classified as under :

i) **Fixed Costs :**

According to *I.C.M.A., London* Fixed Cost is defined as, "a cost which accrues in relation to the passage of time and which within certain output or turnover limits tends to be unaffected by fluctuations in volume of output or turnover".

In other words, fixed costs remain fixed in total amount and do not increase or decrease with volume of production. But the fixed cost per unit increases when volume of production decreases, and decreases when the volume of production increases. Thus, fixed costs are constant in total amount, but fluctuate per unit as production changes. The characteristics of fixed cost are :

- fixed total amount within a relevant output range.
- increase or decrease in per unit fixed cost, when volume of production changes.
- fixed costs are apportioned to departments on some equitable basis.
- fixed cost can be controlled mostly by the top level management.

Examples of fixed cost are Rent, Rates, Taxes, Insurance of factory building, Manager's salary, Office staff salaries, Municipal taxes etc.

The following is the graph indicating the Behaviour of Fixed Cost in Figure 2.6.

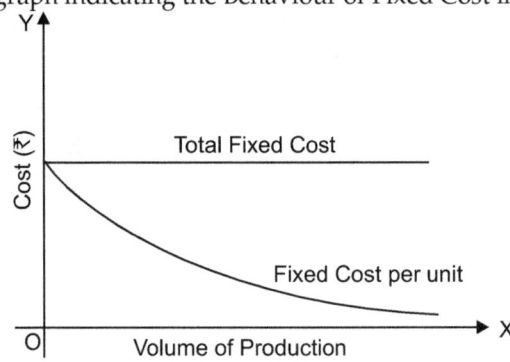

Fig. 2.6 : Behaviour of Fixed Cost

ii) Variable Costs :

I.C.M.A., London defines Variable Cost as, "a cost which in aggregate tends to vary in direct proportions to changes in the volume of output or turnover". In other words, when volume of output increases, total variable cost also increases and vice-versa, when volume of output decreases, total variable cost also decreases. But the variable cost per unit remains fixed.

Example of variable costs are : direct material cost, direct labour cost, direct expenses, power, repairs, royalties, commission of salesman, normal spoilage etc.

The following is the graph indicating the Behaviour of Variable Cost in Figure 2.7.

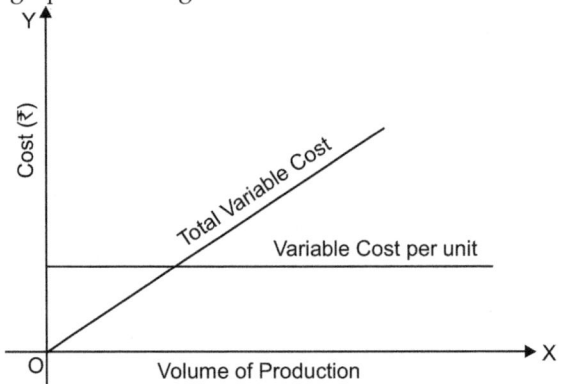

Fig. 2.7 : Behaviour of Variable Cost

Thus, variable costs, in general, indicate the following characteristics:
- they vary in direct proportion to volume of output or turnover.
- the variable cost per unit of product remains constant.
- it is easy for allocation and apportionment to departments.
- such costs can be controlled by departmental heads.

iii) Semi-Variable or Semi-Fixed Costs :

I.C.M.A., London defines **Semi-Variable Cost** as, "a cost containing both fixed and variable elements, which is therefore partly affected by fluctuations in the volume of output or turnover". Thus, these costs are partly fixed and partly variable. A semi-variable cost has often a fixed element below which it will not fall in any level of output. The variable element in semi-variable costs changes either at a constant rate or in lump-sum. For example, if there is additional shift in the factory, it will require additional supervisors and certain costs will increase in lump-sum. In case of telephone charges, there is a minimum rent and after a specified number of calls, the charges are according to the number of calls made. Thus, there is no fixed pattern of behaviour of semi-variable costs. The following is the graph indicating the Behaviour of Semi-Variable Cost in Figure 2.8.

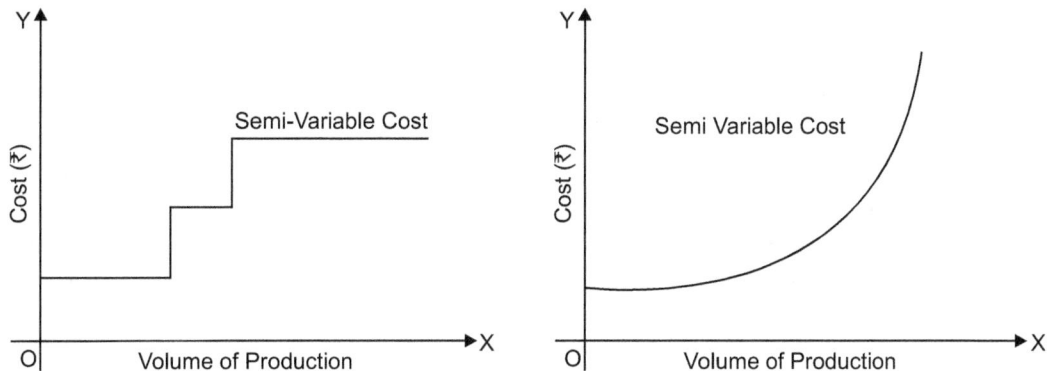

Fig. 2.8 : Behaviour of Semi-Variable Cost

Following is the graph indicating the Behaviour of Fixed, Variable and Semi-Variable Cost in Figure 2.9.

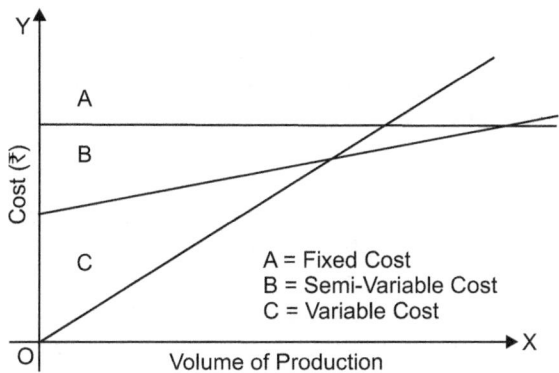

Fig. 2.9 : Behaviour of Fixed, Variable and Semi-Variable Cost

Examples of semi-variable costs are Telephone charges, depreciation, repairs and maintenance of plant and machinery, building, supervision, compensation for accidents, light and power etc.

5) Controllability:

On this basis, costs are classified into two types which are as follows:

i) Controllable Costs:

I.C.M.A., London defines Controllable Costs as, "a cost chargeable to a cost centre, which can be influenced by the actions of the person in whom control of the centre is vested". In other words, these are the costs which may be directly regulated at a given level of management authority. Variable costs are generally controlled by department heads. Practically, all variable costs are controllable cost.

ii) Uncontrollable Costs:

I.C.M.A., London defines Uncontrollable Cost as, "a cost chargeable to a cost centre, which cannot be influenced by the actions of the person in whom, control of the centre is vested". In other words, these are those costs which cannot be influenced by the action of the specified member of an enterprise. It means, these costs are not within the control of management. Practically, all fixed costs are uncontrollable.

6) Normality:

Under this method, costs are classified according to whether these costs are normally incurred at a given level of output in the condition in which that level of activity is normally attained. On this basis, costs are classified into two types which are as follows:

i) Normal Cost:

Normal Cost is defined as, "the cost which is normally incurred to a given level of output in the condition in which that level of output is normally attained". It is a part of the cost of production.

ii) Abnormal Cost:

It is defined as, "a cost which is not normally incurred at a given level of output in the condition in which that level of output is normally attained". It is not a part of cost of production and charged to *Costing Profit and Loss Account*.

7) Time:

On this basis, costs are classified into two types which are as follows:

i) Historical Costs:

It is defined as, "the costs which are ascertained after these have been incurred". Thus, such costs are available only when the production of a particular thing has already been done. Such costs are only of historical value and not useful for cost control purposes. The characteristics of such costs are:

- they are based on recorded facts.
- these costs may be verified with the help of supported documents.
- these are objective in nature because they relate to the past events.

ii) Pre-determined Costs:

It is defined as, "the costs which are ascertained in advance of production on the basis of a specification of all factors affecting cost". These costs are set up from analysis and forecast made before the event and thus, represent not what has happened, but what is expected to happen. Pre-determined cost determined on scientific basis becomes standard cost. Such costs when compared with actual costs determines the reasons of variance. Thus, by these costs, management can fix the responsibility and can take remedial action to avoid its recurrence in future. Pre-determined costs may be in various forms like budgeted cost, estimated cost, standard cost and so on.

8) **Association :**

On this basis, costs are classified into two types which are as follows :

i) **Product Costs :**

It is described as the costs which are directly associated with the product. Thus, unit product is sold, these costs provide no benefit. When the products are sold, the total product costs are recovered as an expense. This expense is called the cost of goods sold. Examples of product costs are : Direct material, Direct labour and Factory overheads.

ii) **Period Costs :**

It is described as the costs which are associated with a particular accounting period. These are not related with the products delivered to the customers. Such costs are charged to Profit and Loss Account of the period. Examples of period costs are : Rent, salaries of office staff, travelling expenses etc. These costs are inventoried i.e. these are not included in the value of closing stocks.

This classification is important for ascertainment of profit. Product cost can be carried forward to the next accounting period as a part of unsold finished stock, whereas period cost is written off in the accounting period in which it is incurred.

9) **Investment :**

On this basis, costs are classified into two types which are as follows :

i) **Capital Costs :**

It is defined as, "a cost which is intended to benefit in future period". Capital cost is treated as purchase of an asset. Examples of capital cost are purchase of premises, plant and machinery, furniture etc.

ii) **Revenue Costs :**

It is defined as, "a cost which is incurred to benefit the current period". Revenue cost is treated as an expense. Examples of revenue costs are : salaries, postage, printing and stationery, rent, rates and taxes, insurance etc.

10) **Relevancy :**

On the basis of whether the cost items are relevant or irrelevant to the decisions under the consideration of the management, costs may broadly be classified into two types which are as follows :

i) **Relevant Costs :**

Relevant costs are those costs which have a bearing, or which have an effect on the decisions under the consideration of the management. That means, they are the most pertinent costs and therefore their effects are to be reckoned before taking a decision.

ii) **Irrelevant Costs :**

Irrelevant costs represent the costs which have no effect on the decisions under the consideration of the management. For instance, marginal cost is an example to relevant costs. It may be noted here that the marginal costs represents the extra cost for an additional unit. On the other hand, sunk cost is a good example to irrelevant costs. Because, sunk cost represents the costs incurred in the past. They are therefore called **past costs.** Since they represent the costs which have already been incurred, no present or future decision is able to alter them. Hence, they are irrelevant.

Types of Costs

These costs are not used for recording purposes, but mostly used for decision-making. From this point of view, Types of Costs may be classified as indicated in Figure 2.10 as follows.

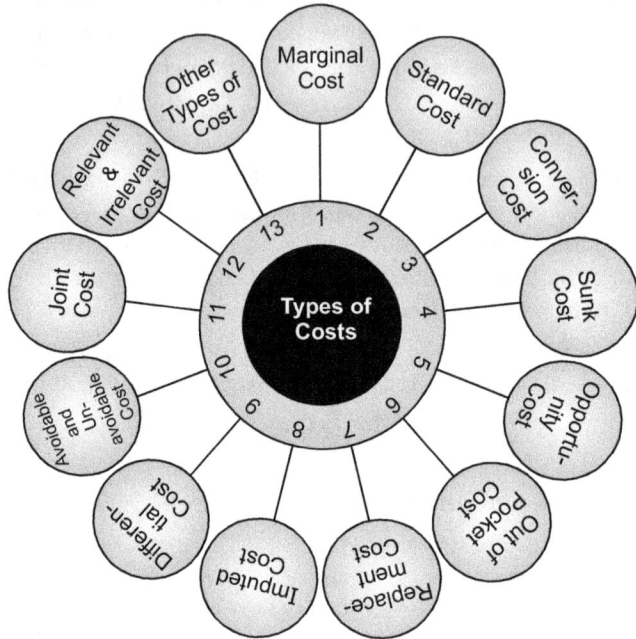

Fig. 2.10 : Types of Costs

1) Marginal Cost :

Marginal Costs are the sum total of variable costs. *I.C.M.A., London* defines it as, "the variable cost of one unit of product or a service i.e. a cost which would be avoided if the unit was not produced or provided". It consists of all direct costs and variable overheads. It is based on the distinction between fixed and variable costs. Fixed costs are ignored and only variable costs are taken into consideration for determining the cost of products and value of work in progress and finished goods. Thus, marginal cost is the additional cost of producing additional units. It remains the same per unit irrespective of the volume of output.

For example, if the cost of producing 50 T.V. sets is given as follows :

			₹
	Variable Costs		1,00,000
Add :	Fixed Costs		(+) 25,000
∴	**Total Costs**		**1,25,000**

If the output is increased by 10 units of T.V. sets, the cost will be as follows :

			₹
	Variable Cost		1,20,000
	(60 T.V. set × ₹ 2,000)		
Add :	Fixed Cost		(+) 25,000
∴	**Total Cost**		**1,45,000**

Thus, the additional costs of producing 10 units of T.V. sets is ₹ 20,000 which is known as the 'Marginal cost or Variable cost'.

2) Standard Cost :

This is a pre-determined estimated cost which an organisation tries to attain under standard normal conditions. Thus, estimates of costs are made before incurring them and then the actual results are compared with the standards to find out the efficiency of a business.

3) Conversion Cost :

It is the term used to denote the sum total of Direct Labour, Direct Expenses and Overhead Costs in the production of a certain product where Material Cost is negligible as in the case of Brick Manufacturing Business. Hence, 'Conversion Cost' is the total of Direct Labour Cost, Direct Expenses and Overhead Costs incurred to convert raw materials – input into finished goods – output. As it includes only the conversion of raw materials from one stage of production to another, it does not consider the negligible Direct Material Cost. Under these circumstances, Labour Cost becomes the major part of Prime Cost as well as Total Cost i.e. Conversion Cost. The composition of Conversion Cost is shown in Figure 2.11 as follows :

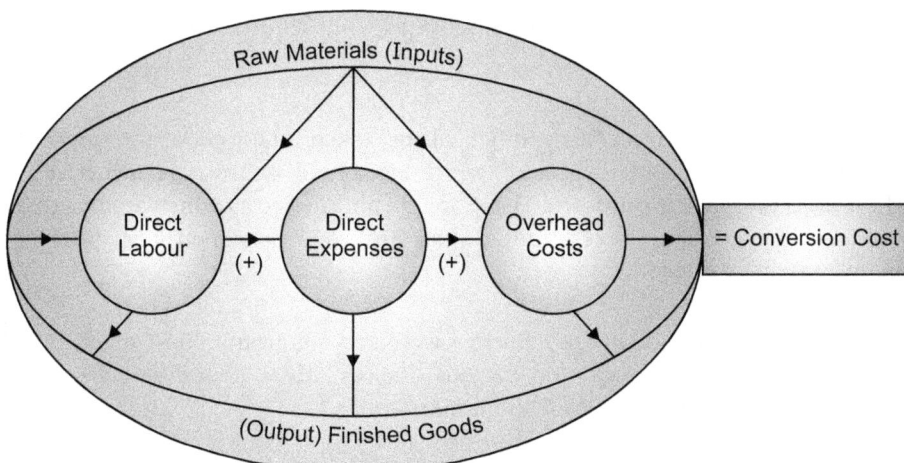

Fig. 2.11 : Composition of Conversion Cost

4) Sunk Cost :

The **National Association of Accountants**, defines a sunk cost as, "an expenditure for equipment or productive resources which has no economic relevance to the present decision-making process". As the name implies it is historical in nature. It is a cost which has been created by a decision that was made in the past which cannot be changed by any decision that will be made in the future. These costs are not relevant for decision-making about the future. Thus, the book value of an asset currently being used is not relevant in making the decision to replace it.

5) Opportunity Cost :

I.C.M.A., London defines it as, "the value of benefit sacrificed in favour of an alternative course of action". *Edward Hermanson and Salmonson* defines it as "the benefit lost by rejecting the best competing alternatives to the one chosen". Thus, Opportunity cost is the sacrifice involved in accepting the alternative under consideration. This concept is used in the problems of alternative choices. Opportunity cost is a pure decision-making cost and is not entered in the books of account. Suppose a company owns a building which is proposed to be used for a special project, the likely rent of the building is the Opportunity Costs, which should be taken into consideration that evaluates the profitability of the project.

6) Out of Pocket Cost :

These are the costs which require cash payments to be made (such as wages, rent etc.) whereas many costs do not require cash outlay (such as depreciation). Out-of-pocket costs are those costs that involve cash outlays or require the utilisation of current resources. Out-of-pocket cost may be either fixed (such as manager's salary) or variable (such as raw material, direct wages etc.) This cost is frequently used as an aid in make or buy decisions, price fixation during recession and many other vital decisions.

7) Replacement Cost :

It is the current market price of replacing an existing asset. The present market price is always considered for taking any decision for buying a machine and not the original cost at which it was bought.

8) Imputed Cost :

I.C.M.A., London defines it as, "a hypothetical cost taken into account to represent a benefit enjoyed by the undertaking in respect of which no actual expense is incurred". They are computed for decision-making purposes. These are the built-up costs which are imaginary. These are the non-cash items. Examples of imputed costs are : rent of owned land, salary of owner, interest on owned capital etc.

9) Differential Cost :

It is the increase or decrease in the total cost which results from taking alternative decisions by the management from amongst the various choices. Thus, the difference between two alternative course of action is known as 'Differential Cost'.

10) Avoidable and Unavoidable Cost :

Avoidable costs are those which can be eliminated if a particular product or department with which they are directly related, is discontinued. For example, salary of the clerks employed can be eliminated if a particular department in which they are employed is decided to discontinue. Unavoidable costs are those costs which cannot be eliminated with the discontinuation of a particular product or department. Such costs are merely allocated if the product or department is discontinued. For example, salary of factory manager or factory rent cannot be eliminated even if a product is eliminated.

11) Joint Cost :

When two or more products are produced from the use of a single raw material, we get either two main products from it, or one may be a main product and the other a by-product. But the cost to produce these are the combined costs. Then the management can take decisions whether to take up manufacture of joint products or to go in for processing of the by-products further, so that the total costs can be reduced.

12) Relevant and Irrelevant Cost:

Relevant costs are those costs that would be changed by the decision. Irrelevant costs are those costs that would not be affected by the decision. It means a relevant cost is a cost whose magnitude will be affected by a decision being made. Management is concerned only with those things which it can affect. For example, management cannot change the cost of equipment purchased in 1980. It can change future costs by its current decisions. Hence, relevant costs are future costs that will differ depending on the action of the management. For each decision the management must decide which costs are relevant. For example, when a manufacturer decides to close a certain unit, the wages associated with the maintenance of such unit is relevant cost as wage payment cease if the unit is closed. But rent which was already paid under lease agreement which cannot be recovered is irrelevant cost.

13) Other Types of Cost:

Other types of costs are described as under:

i) Discretionary Cost:

These are also called managed costs or programmed costs and consist of fixed costs that arise from periodic appropriation decisions that directly reflect top management policies.

ii) Engineered Cost:

These are costs which vary directly with the level of production. These are opposed to managed or discretionary costs.

iii) Shut Down Cost:

A cost which is still incurred although a plant is shut down temporarily, for e.g., rent, rates, depreciation, maintenance of plant, etc.

iv) Traceable Cost:

These are cost which can be easily identified with cost unit or cost centres. The term is used to distinguish it from joint or common costs.

2.3 PREPARATION OF COST SHEET

Meaning

A **Cost Sheet** is an important document prepared by the costing department which shows the analysis for the different elements of cost of the job or a product. The cost data incorporated in Cost Sheet are collected from various statements of accounts which have been recorded in cost accounts, either on day-to-day basis or regular basis. It analyses and classifies the various expenses on different items for a particular period in a tabular form. It may be prepared for a day, a week, a month or so on, as per the specific requirement for a particular period.

Definitions

The term 'Cost-sheet' is defined by various authorities as follows:

i) **C.I.M.A., London** defines Cost-Sheet as, *"a document which provides for the assembly of the estimated detailed cost in respect of a cost centre or a cost unit"*.

ii) **W. W. Bigg :**

"the expenditure which has been incurred upon production for a particular period is extracted from the financial books and stores records and set out in a memorandum statement. If the statement is confined to the disclosure of the cost of the units produced during the period, it is termed as 'Cost-Sheet' but where the statement records cost, sales and profit, it is usually known as 'Production Statement'.

But nowadays, the practice is to prepare the 'Cost-Sheet to show the profit and sales also, hence it is termed as Statement of 'Cost and Profit'.

Thus, **Cost Sheet** is a statement usually prepared to present the analytical cost of total production during a particular period. There is no fixed form for preparation of cost sheet but, in order to make the cost sheet more useful, it is generally presented in columnar form. A Cost Sheet may include as many columns as is desired to show in detail e.g. cost per unit of product, total cost for all the units produced, total cost and per unit cost for the previous year, estimated cost for the future period and so on. A **Cost Sheet** not only shows the total cost but also the various components of total cost. Thus, a cost sheet is a statement prepared to show the detailed analysis of the total cost of production and cost of sales.

Purposes

A Cost Sheet serves the following **purposes** :

i) It discloses the cost per unit as well as the total cost of output.

ii) It discloses the various elements of cost.

iii) It is useful for calculation of tender price as selling price may be fixed in advance.

iv) It helps the management to find out the causes of variations and take steps to eliminate the factors which are responsible for increasing total cost. It is possible by making comparative study of the current cost with the past results and standard costs.

v) It enables a manufacturer to keep a close watch and control over the cost of production.

vi) It helps the management in formulating a definite useful production policy.

Thus, a Cost Sheet is a statement prepared by showing the items of cost of production and services which are analysed by their nature, elements, functions and behaviour. It should also be noted that the non-cost items like the dividends and income-tax paid should not be included in the cost sheets, because they are the appropriations of profits.

A Cost Sheet, including sale, and profit is also known as **Production Account**. Like expanded form of Cost Sheet, the product account consists of two parts. The first part shows the cost of production in total and break-up of costs and the second part known as the 'Statement of Profit' shows sales and profit. Thus, a Cost Sheet is a statement which shows the break-up and built-up of costs. It is a basic document that provides for the assembly of the detailed cost centre or a cost unit.

Proforma of Cost Sheet

(A) Simple Cost Sheet

In the books of a Company

Cost Sheet for the period ended ......

Name of the Product .... Units Produced .... Units Sold ....

	Particulars		Total Cost ₹	Unit Cost ₹
	Direct Materials		–	–
Add :	Direct Labour	(+)	–	–
Add :	Direct Expenses	(+)	–	–
∴	**Prime Cost**	i)	–	–
Add :	Factory Overheads	(+)	–	–
∴	**Factory Cost / Works Cost**	ii)	–	–
Add :	Office Overheads	(+)	–	–
∴	**Cost of Production / Office Cost**	iii)	–	–
Add :	Selling and Distribution Overheads	(+)	–	–
∴	**Total Cost / Cost of Sales**	iv)	–	–
Add :	Profit /	v) (+)	–	–
Less :	Loss	(–)		
	Sales		–	–

(B) Cost Sheet with Stock Adjustments

In the books of a Company

Cost Sheet for the period ended ......

Name of the Product ...... Units Produced ...... Units Sold ......

	Particulars		Total Cost ₹	Unit Cost ₹
	Opening Stock of Raw Materials		–	–
Add :	Purchases of Raw Materials	(+)	–	–
Add :	Expenses on Purchases of Raw Materials	(+)	–	–
			–	–
Less :	Closing Stock of Raw Materials	(–)	–	–
Less :	Purchases Returns	(–)	–	–
Less :	Sale of Scrap or Defectives of Raw Materials	(–)	–	–

Particulars		Total Cost ₹	Unit Cost ₹
∴ **Cost of Materials Consumed** i)	–	–
Add : Direct Labour (+)	–	–
Add : Direct Expenses (+)	–	–
∴ **Prime Cost** ii)	–	–
Add : Factory Overheads (+)	–	–
Add : Opening Stock of Work-in-Progress (+)	–	–
	–	–
Less : Closing Stock of Work-in-Progress (–)	–	–
Less : Sale of Scrap or Defectives of Work-in-progress (–)	–	–
∴ **Factory Cost / Works Cost** iii)	–	–
Add : Office Overheads (+)	–	–
∴ **Cost of Production / Office Cost** iv)	–	–
Add : Opening Stock of Finished Goods (+)	–	–
	–	–
Less : Closing Stock of Finished Goods (–)	–	–
∴ **Cost of Goods Sold** v)	–	–
Add : Selling and Distribution Overheads (+)	–	–
∴ **Total Cost / Cost of Sales** vi)	–	–
∴ Add Profit or vii) (+)	–	–
Less Loss (–)	–	–
Sales	–	–

In present day practice, a 'Cost-Sheet' is prepared in columnar form to show the actual cost details for current period, historical costs for previous period and cost estimations for future period with total cost and unit cost calculations shown separately. The comparative analysis of the cost helps the management to make use of such analytical cost sheet as an instrument of cost planning and cost control. The Proforma of such Analytical Cost Sheet is as follows :

(C) Analytical Cost Sheet

In the books of a Company
Cost-Sheet for the period ended ......

Name of the Product ....   Units Produced ....   Units Sold ....

Previous Period		Particulars	Current Period		Future Period		Remarks
Historical Costs			Actual Costs		Estimated Costs		
Total Cost ₹	Unit Cost ₹		Total Cost ₹	Unit Cost ₹	Total Cost ₹	Unit Cost ₹	
		Direct Materials **Add :** Direct Labour **Add :** Direct Expenses ∴ **Prime Cost** i) **Add :** Works Overheads ∴ **Works Cost** ii) **Add :** Office Overheads ∴ **Cost of Production** iii) **Add :** Selling and Distribution Overheads ∴ **Cost of Sales** iv) **Add :** Profit or v) **Less :** Loss ∴ **Sales**					

Thus, **Cost Sheet** is an analytical statement of cost prepared periodically to show the details of cost incurred during a particular period, on production of a specific unit of cost. It gives cost details regarding total cost, various components of total cost and unit cost. The actual cost built up and the details of cost components are as follows :

i) **Cost of Materials Consumed :**

= Opening Stock of Raw Materials (+) Purchases of Raw Materials (+) Expenses for Purchases of Raw Materials (–) Closing Stock of Raw Materials (–) Purchases Returns (–) Sale of Scrap of Raw Materials.

ii) **Prime Cost :**

= Direct Materials (+) Direct Labour (+) Direct Expenses.

iii) **Works Cost :**

= Prime Cost (+) Factory Overheads (+) Opening Stock of Work-in-Progress (–) Closing Stock of Work-in-Progress

iv) **Cost of Production :**

    =   Works Cost (+) Office Overheads

v) **Cost of Goods Sold :**

    =   Cost of Production (+) Opening Stock of Finished Goods (–) Closing Stock of Finished Goods

vi) **Cost of Sales :**

    =   Cost of Goods sold (+) Selling and Distribution Overheads

vii) **Sales :**

    =   Cost of Sales (+) Profit or Loss

Summary List

Following is the summary list of various items of cost included in the major group of cost and the synonymous terms used for the same in the simplified preparation of a Cost Sheet, Tender, Quotation and Estimates.

(DM) Direct Materials :

Viz. Direct Materials Cost, Prime Cost Materials, Cost of Materials Consumed, Process Materials, Cost of Materials Purchased, Operating Materials, Value of Raw Materials Used, Basic Materials, Productive Materials Cost.

e.g. **Opening Stock of Raw Materials**

Add : Purchases of Materials

Add : Primary Packing Charges

Add : Expenses for Purchases of Raw Materials, e.g. Carriage Inward, Freight Inward, Carriage and Cartage, Octroi Duty and Customs, Excise Duty, Dock Charges, Clearing Charges, Forwarding Charges, Loading and Unloading, Transportation Charges etc.

Less : Closing Stock of Raw Materials

Less : Sale of Scrap or Defectives of Raw Materials

Less : Returns Outward or Purchases Returns or Returns to Suppliers or Defective Materials Returned to Creditors.

(DL) Direct Labour :

Viz. Direct Labour Cost, Prime Cost Labour, Direct Wages, Process Labour, Operating Labour, Basic Labour, Productive Labour.

e.g. Productive Wages, Wages paid to direct Workers, Outstanding Wages etc.

(DE) Direct Expenses :

Viz. Chargeable Expenses, Prime Cost Expenses, Productive Expenses, Basic Expenses.

e.g. Royalty, Hire of Special Plant, Cost of Patterns, Layout, Designs or Drawings, Architects Fees, Engineers Fees, Surveyors Fees, Licence Fees, Outstanding Direct Expenses etc.

| Cost Accounting | 2.27 | Elements of Cost |

(PC) **Prime Cost :**

viz. Direct Cost, Basic Cost, Operating Cost, First Cost, Productive Cost, Flat Cost.

(F) **Factory Overheads :**

viz. Works on Cost, Manufacturing Expenses, Factory Burden.

e.g. Indirect Materials, Factory Lighting Expense, Materials, Motive Power, On Cost Materials, Factory Rent, Rates, Taxes and Insurance, Indirect Labour, Property Tax on Factory Premises, On Cost Wages, Electric Power, Indirect Expenses, Rent of Raw Material Stores, On Cost Expenses, Workshop Rent, Heating and Lighting, Coal and Coke, Steam, Gas and Water, Power and Fuel, Wages to Indirect Labourers i.e. Shop Floor Helpers, Supervisors, Cleaners, Oilers etc. Remunerations to Watch and Ward Staff, Instructors, Factory Clerical Staff, Works Manager, Production Engineer, etc., Technical Directors Fees, Labour Welfare and Amenities to Production Staff, Expenses on Workers Canteen, Entertainment Room, Creches etc., Consumable Stores, Cotton, Oil and Wastes, Haulage, Lubricants, Expenses of Testing Labs., Laboratory Expenses, Drawing Office Salaries, Repairs, Maintenance, Renewals and Depreciation on Plant and Machinery, Tools and Equipments, Fixtures and Patterns, Factory Buildings etc. Cost of Factory Supervision, General Works Overheads, Sundry Factory Expenses, Other Manufacturing on Cost, Factory Cleaning Charges, Storekeeping Expenses, Upkeep of Raw Materials Stores, Time-keeping Expenses, Time Office Expenses, Normal Wastage and Spoilage, Miscellaneous Production Expenses, Works Stationery, Idle Time Wages, Subscription of Technical Journals and Magazines, Works Office Expenses, Internal Transport, Materials Handling Charges, Unproductive Wages, Wages and Salaries, Power and Lighting etc.

(FC) **Factory Cost :**

Viz. Works Cost, Manufacturing Cost, Production Cost.

(O) **Office Overheads :**

Viz. Administration Expenses, Management on Cost, Establishment Overheads.

e.g. Indirect Materials, Indirect Labour and Indirect Expenses of Administrative Office, Office Rent, Rates, Taxes, Insurance, Lighting Expenses , Petrol and Maintenance on Vehicles etc. Property Tax on Office Premises, Office Salaries, Salaries and Wages, Directors Fees, General Managers Salaries and Allowances, Counting House Salaries, Directors Travelling Expenses, General Office Overheads, Electric Lighting, Electricity and Lighting Charges, General on Cost, Sundry Expenses, Other Adminstrative Charges, Miscellaneous Office Expenses, Expenses of Management, Branch Office Expenses, Office Cleaning Charges, Repairs, Maintenance, Renewals and Depreciation on Office Furniture, Office Buildings, Office Equipments, Office Appliances, etc. Renovation of Administrative Office, Lighting and Power, Salaries and Wages, Printing and Stationery, Postage and Telegrams, Telephone Charges, Legal Fees, Audit Fees, Accountancy Charges, Office Conveyance, General Fees, Air-conditioning to Administrative Office, Office Supplies and Expenses, Bank Charges, General Establishment Charges, Office Lighting, Subscription of Trade Journals, Public Relation Expenses, Petrol and Maintenance of Office Vehicles etc.

(COP)	**Cost of Production :**

Viz. Gross Cost, Office Cost.

(S)	**Selling and Distribution Overheads :**

viz. Selling Expenses, Distribution on Cost, Marketing Overheads.

e.g. Indirect Materials, Indirect Labour and Indirect Expenses of Sales Office, Salaries and Allowances to Sales Manager, Marketing Executive, Publicity Officer, Travelling Salesmen, Sales Office Staff, etc.; Travelling Salesmen Salaries and Commission, Selling Agents Salaries and Commission, Carriage on Sales, Commission on Sales, Travelling Expenses, Carriage and Cartage Outward, Freight Outward, Loading and Unloading of Finished Goods, Recurring Expenses of Delivery Vans, Show-room Expenses, Sales Branches and Sales Depot Expenses, Packing Charges, Secondary Packing Charges, Advertisement, Publicity Charges, Cost of Special Advertisement, After Sales Service Expenses, Distribution of Free Samples and Gifts, Diaries and Calendars, Gift Articles and Folders, etc., Bad Debts, Debts Collection Charges, Cash Discount Allowed, Catalogue Expenses, Tendering Expenses, Repairs, Maintenance, Renewals and Depreciation on Delivery Vans, Sales Depots, Show-rooms, Sales Premises etc., Delivery Van Running Expenses, Upkeep of Delivery Vans, Warehouse Expenses, Sales Promotion Expenses, Rent, Rates, Taxes, Insurance and Lighting of Sales Office, Selling on Cost, Warehouse Labour Charges, Other Expenses for Handling of Finished Goods in Stores, Sales Printing and Stationery, Market Research Expenses, Estimating Expenses, Demonstration Expenses, Loading and Unloading of Finished Goods, Price List, Catalogue, Banners, Hand Bills, Posters, etc. Export Duty, Drivers, Conductors, Cleaners Salaries and Wages, Cost of Mailing Literature, Sales Promotion Expenses etc.

(TC)	**Total Cost :**

Viz. Cost of Sales, Cost Price, Cost of Turnover, Sales Cost, Turnover Cost, Net Cost.

(P)	**Profit :**

Viz. Net Margin

(L)	**Loss :**
(S)	**Sales :**

Viz. Selling Price, Value of Sales, Market Price, Value of Turnover, Invoice Price, Inflated Price, Loaded Price.

(NCI)	**Non Cost Items :**

Viz. Items to be excluded from Cost.

e.g.

(1) Financial Incomes :

Capital Profits, Dividend Received, Brokerage and Commission Received, Share Transfer Fees Received, Interest on Investments, Interest on Bank Deposits, Rent Received, Bad Debts Recovery, Interest on Loan given, Discount Received etc.

(2) Financial Charges :

Capital Losses, Cash Discount, Trade Discount, Penalties and Fines, Share Transfer Fees Paid, Interest on Bank Loan, Interest on Debentures, Preliminary Expenses, Underwriting Commission, Discount on Issue of Shares and Debentures, Loss on Investments, Capital Expenses, Interest on Capitals, Salary or Commission paid to Partners, Income Tax, Wealth Tax, Interest on Debentures, Reconstruction Expenses, Development Expenses, Reorganisation Expenses etc.

(3) Appropriations :

Bad Debts Reserve, Dividends Paid, Charitable Donations, Transfer to Reserves, Sinking Fund, Debenture Redemption Fund, Machinery Replacement Fund, Investment Fluctuation Fund, etc.

(4) Abnormals :

Abnormal Wastage, Abnormal Idle Time, Loss by fire, Loss by Theft, Loss of Stock, etc.

EXAMPLE

Prepare a Statement of Cost from the following information relating to Mumbai Traders, Mumbai for the year ended 31st March, 2013.

	₹
Cost of Direct Materials	2,00,000
Sales	4,00,000
Direct Wages	1,00,000
Office Indirect Materials	5,000
Cost of special patterns	40,000
Postage and Telegrams	2,000
Factory Rent and Insurance	5,000
Outstanding Chargeable Expenses	2,000
Carriage Outward	2,500
Interest on Loan	2,150
Printing and Stationery	500
Factory Indirect wages	3,000
Selling on cost	4,000
Travelling salesman's salary	4,000
Factory Indirect Material	1,000
Royalties	8,000
General Works Overheads	2,000
Bad debts written-off	1,000

Also calculate the percentage of profits earned to sales.

ANSWER

In the books of Mumbai Traders, Mumbai
Statement of Cost for the year ended 31st March, 2013

	Particulars		Amount ₹	Amount ₹
	Cost of Direct Materials		2,00,000	
Add :	Direct Wages	(+)	1,00,000	
Add :	**Direct Expenses :**			
a)	Cost of Special Patterns		40,000	
b)	Outstanding Chargeable Expenses		2,000	
c)	Royalties	(+)	8,000	
	Prime Cost	i)	3,50,000	3,50,000
Add :	**Factory Expenses :**			
a)	Factory Rent and Insurance		5,000	
b)	Factory Indirect Wages		3,000	
c)	Factory Indirect Material		1,000	
d)	General Works Overheads	(+)	2,000	
	Factory Cost	ii)	3,61,000	3,61,000
Add :	**Office Expenses :**			
a)	Office Indirect Materials		5,000	
b)	Postage and Telegrams		2,000	
c)	Printing and Stationery	(+)	500	
	Cost of Production	iii)	3,68,500	3,68,500
Add :	**Selling and Distribution Expenses :**			
a)	Carriage Outward		2,500	
b)	Selling on Cost		4,000	
c)	Travelling Salesman's Salary		4,000	
d)	Bad Debts written-off	(+)	1,000	
	Total Cost	iv)	3,80,000	3,80,000
Add :	Profit for the year	v) (+)	20,000	20,000
	Sales		4,00,000	4,00,000

Working Notes :

i) Calculation of percentage of profits earned to sales :

   For ₹ 4,00,000 Sales = ₹ 20,000 Profits.

   ∴ 100 = ?

   $= \dfrac{100 \times ₹\,20{,}000}{₹\,4{,}00{,}000}$

   = 5%

ii) Interest on Loan is an item of financial nature hence it should be excluded from cost.

ILLUSTRATIONS

ILLUSTRATION 1

From the following particulars relating to M/s Rajchand Rayon Manufacturers, Chinchwad, prepare a Simple Cost-Sheet showing a) Prime Cost, b) Works Cost, c) Cost of Production, d) Cost of Sales, e) Profit or Loss for the period, for six months ended 31st March, 2013.

	₹
Cost of Materials Consumed	40,000
Oil and Waste	100
Operating Labour	9,000
Wages of Foreman	1,000
Direct Expenses	2,000
Store keepers Wages	500
Sales – Cash and Credit	1,00,000
Commission paid to the partner, Chandmal	350
Electric Power	200
Salary paid to the partner, Rajmal	650
Consumable Stores	1,000
Direct Wages Payable	1,000
Lighting :	
• Factory Plant	500
• Office Establishment	200
Carriage Outward	150
Rent :	
• Administrative Office	1,000
• Workshop	2,000
Warehouse Charges	200
Repairs and Renewals :	
• Factory Plant	500
• Machinery	1,000
• Office Premises	200
• Warehouse	100
Interest on Bank Overdraft	340
Advertising	400
Depreciation :	
• Office Buildings	500
• Machinery	200
Travelling Expenses	200
Office Manager's Salary	2,250
Salesmen's Commission and Salaries	500
Director's Fees	500
Printing and Stationery	200
Telephone Charges	50
Postage	100
Bad Debts	450

SOLUTION

In the books of M/s Rajchand Rayon Manufacturers, Chinchwad
Cost-Sheet for the six months ended 31st March, 2013

		Particulars		Amount ₹	Amount ₹
		Cost of Materials Consumed		40,000	
Add :		Direct Labour :		10,000	
	a)	Operating Labour	9,000		
	b)	Direct Wages Payable	(+) 1,000		
Add :		Direct Expenses	(+)	2,000	
	∴	**Prime Cost**	i)	52,000	52,000
Add :		**Factory Overheads :**		7,000	
	a)	Oil and Waste	100		
	b)	Wages of Foreman	1,000		
	c)	Storekeepers Wages	500		
	d)	Electric Power	200		
	e)	Consumable Stores	1,000		
	f)	Lighting – Factory Plant	500		
	g)	Rent – Workshop	2,000		
	h)	Repairs and Renewals - Factory Plant	500		
	i)	Repairs and Renewals - Machinery	1,000		
	j)	Depreciation - Machinery	(+) 200		
			(+)		
	∴	**Works Cost**	ii)	59,000	59,000
Add :		**Office Overheads :**		5,000	
	a)	Lighting – Office Establishment	200		
	b)	Rent – Administrative Office	1,000		
	c)	Repairs and Renewals – Office Premises	200		
	d)	Depreciation – Office Buildings	500		
	e)	Office Manager's Salary	2,250		
	f)	Director's Fees	500		
	g)	Printing and Stationery	200		
	h)	Telephone Charges	50		
	i)	Postage	(+) 100		
			(+)		
	∴	**Cost of Production**	iii)	64,000	64,000
Add :		**Selling and Distribution Overheads :**		2,000	
	a)	Carriage Outward	150		
	b)	Warehouse Charges	200		
	c)	Repairs and Renewals – Warehouse	100		
	d)	Advertising	400		
	e)	Travelling Expenses	200		
	f)	Salesmen's Commission and Salaries	500		
	g)	Bad Debts	(+) 450		
			(+)		
	∴	**Cost of Sales**	iv)	66,000	66,000
Add :		Profit for the period	v) (+)	34,000	34,000
		Sales – Cash and Credit		1,00,000	1,00,000

Cost Accounting 2.33 Elements of Cost

Working Notes :

i) Commission paid to the partner Chandmal, salary paid to the partner Rajmal and Interest on Bank Overdraft are the items to be excluded from cost.

ILLUSTRATION 2

The Cost of Sale of product 'Butnol' is made up as follows :

Particulars	₹
Royalties	1,000
Materials used in Production – Direct	12,000
Carriage on Sales	1,250
Materials used in Primary Packing	9,000
Carriage on Purchases	5,000
Materials used in Secondary Packing	1,500
Bad Debts	3,250
Materials used in Factory Workshop	750
Coal and Coke	1,750
Materials used in Administrative Office	1,250
Administration on Cost	750
Labour required in Manufacturing – Direct	9,500
General Overheads	1,000
Purchases of Raw Materials	44,000
Labour required for Works Supervision	2,500
Motive Power	1,000
Productive Wages Payable	500
Chargeable Expenses	4,000

Assuming that all products manufactured in Peterson Chemicals Ltd., Bhosari are sold, what should be the Invoice Price to obtain a profit of 20% on Selling Price ?

SOLUTION

In the books of Peterson Chemicals Ltd., Bhosari
Cost Sheet for the period ended ……   **Product : Butnol**

Particulars		Amount ₹	Amount ₹
Direct Materials :			
a) Materials used in Production – Direct	12,000		
b) Materials used in Primary Packing	9,000		
c) Purchases of Raw Materials	44,000		
d) Carriage on Purchases	(+) 5,000	70,000	
Add : Direct Labour :			
a) Labour required in Manufacturing – Direct	9,500		
b) Productive Wages Payable	(+) 500	10,000	
Add : Direct Expenses :			
a) Royalties	1,000		
b) Chargeable Expenses	(+) 4,000	5,000	
∴ **Prime Cost**	i)	85,000	85,000

Particulars			Amount ₹	Amount ₹
Add :	Factory Overheads :			
	a) Materials used in Factory Workshop	750		
	b) Coal and Coke	1,750		
	c) Labour required for Works Supervision	2,500		
	d) Motive Power	(+) 1,000	6,000	
	∴ **Factory Cost**	ii)	91,000	91,000
Add :	Office Overheads :			
	a) Materials used in Administrative Office	1,250		
	b) Administration on Cost	750		
	c) General Overheads	+ 1,000	3,000	
	∴ **Cost of Production**	iii)	94,000	94,000
Add :	Selling and Distribution Overheads :			
	a) Carriage on Sales	1,250		
	b) Materials used in Secondary Packing	1,500		
	c) Bad Debts	(+) 3,250	6,000	
		(+)		
	Total Cost	iv)	1,00,000	1,00,000
Add :	Profit	v)	25,000	25,000
	(20% on Selling Price)	(+)		
∴	**Invoice Price**		1,25,000	1,25,000

Working Notes :

i) Calculation of Profit i.e. 20% on Selling Price

    Selling Price = Total Cost + Profit
        100   80   20

    If 80 TC = 20 P

∴ ₹ 1,00,000 TC = ?

$$= \frac{₹\,1,00,000 \times 20}{80}$$

= ₹ 25,000

ILLUSTRATION 3

Prepare a Statement of Cost from the following information relating to Cotton Textiles Ltd., Mumbai, for the year ended 31st March, 2013.

	₹
Cost of Direct Materials	2,00,000
Sales	4,00,000
Direct Wages	1,00,000
Office Indirect Materials	5,000
Cost of Special Patterns	40,000
Postage and Telegram	2,000
Bad Debts Recovered	250
Factory Rent and Insurance	5,000
Outstanding Chargeable Expenses	2,000

Carriage Outward		2,500
Interest on Loan		2,150
Printing and Stationery		500
Factory Indirect wages		3,000
Selling on Cost		4,000
Travelling Salesman's Salary		4,000
Works Indirect Material		1,000
Royalties		8,000
General Works Overheads		2,000
Bad Debts written-off		1,000

Also calculate the percentage of profits earned to sales.

SOLUTION

In the books of Cotton Textiles Ltd., Mumbai
Statement of Cost for the year ended 31st March, 2013

	Particulars			Amount ₹	Amount ₹
	Cost of Direct Materials			2,00,000	
Add :	Direct Wages		(+)	1,00,000	
Add :	Direct Expenses :			50,000	
	a) Cost of Special Patterns	40,000			
	b) Outstanding Chargeable Expenses	2,000			
	c) Royalties	(+) 8,000			
			(+)		
	∴ **Prime Cost**		i)	3,50,000	3,50,000
Add :	Factory Overheads :			11,000	
	a) Factory Rent and Insurance	5,000			
	b) Factory Indirect Wages	3,000			
	c) Works Indirect Material	1,000			
	d) General Works Overheads	(+) 2,000			
			(+)		
	∴ **Factory Cost**		ii)	3,61,000	3,61,000
Add :	Office Overheads :			7,500	
	a) Office Indirect Materials	5,000			
	b) Postage and Telegram	2,000			
	c) Printing and Stationery	(+) 500			
			(+)		
	∴ **Cost of Production**		iii)	3,68,500	3,68,500
Add :	Selling and Distribution Overheads :			11,500	
	a) Carriage Outward	2,500			
	b) Selling on Cost	4,000			
	c) Travelling Salesman's Salary	4,000			
	d) Bad Debts written-off	(+) 1,000			
			(+)		
	∴ **Total Cost**		iv)	3,80,000	3,80,000
Add :	Profits for the year		v) (+)	20,000	20,000
	Sales			4,00,000	4,00,000

Working Notes:

i) Calculation of percentage of profits earned to sales

If ₹ 4,00,000 Sales = ₹ 20,000 Profit

∴ 100 = ?

$$= \frac{100 \times ₹20,000}{₹4,00,000}$$

= 5%

ii) Bad Debts recovered and Interest on Loan are the items to be excluded from cost.

ILLUSTRATION 4

Majestic Furnitures Ltd., Manmad, manufactures Cots, Tables, Chairs and Cupboards. The following are the cost details available for the year ended 31st March, 2013.

Particulars	Prime Cost Materials ₹	Process Labour ₹	Productive Expenses ₹	Value of Turnover ₹
Cots	50,000	30,000	16,000	1,50,000
Tables	45,000	20,000	19,000	1,20,000
Chairs	70,000	40,000	18,000	2,00,000
Cupboards (+)	28,000	50,000	2,000	1,30,000
Total	1,93,000	1,40,000	55,000	6,00,000

Additional Information:

- Works on Cost ... 80% of Direct Wages   ₹
- Bad Debts Provision   ...   600
- Administrative Overheads   ...   15,000
- Bad Debts Recovery   ...   250
- Selling and Distribution Expenses ...   12,000
- Book Debts   ...   41,000

Allocate Management on Cost on the basis of Works Cost and Selling and Distribution Overheads on the basis of Actual Sales. You are required to prepare a Simple Cost Statement showing the following in case of each of the product in the columnar form.

a) Direct Cost, b) Factory Cost, c) Cost of Production, d) Cost of Sales and e) Profit or Loss for the year.

SOLUTION

In the books of Majestic Furnitures Ltd., Manmad
Cost Statement for the year ended 31st March, 2013

Particulars		Cots ₹	Tables ₹	Chairs ₹	Cupboards ₹	Total ₹
Prime Cost Materials		50,000	45,000	70,000	28,000	1,93,000
Add : Process Labour		30,000	20,000	40,000	50,000	1,40,000
Add : Productive Expenses	(+)	16,000	19,000	18,000	2,000	55,000
∴ **Direct Cost**	i)	96,000	84,000	1,28,000	80,000	3,88,000
Add : Works on Cost (80% of Direct Wages i.e. Process Labour)	(+)	24,000	16,000	32,000	40,000	1,12,000
∴ **Factory Cost**	ii)	1,20,000	1,00,000	1,60,000	1,20,000	5,00,000
Add : Administrative Overheads	(+)	3,600	3,000	4,800	3,600	15,000
∴ **Cost of Production**	iii)	1,23,600	1,03,000	1,64,800	1,23,600	5,15,000
Add : Selling and Distribution Expenses	(+)	3,000	2,400	4,000	2,600	12,000
∴ **Cost of Sales**	iv)	1,26,600	1,05,400	1,68,800	1,26,200	5,27,000
Add : Profits for the year	v) (+)	23,400	14,600	31,200	3,800	73,000
Value of Turnover		1,50,000	1,20,000	2,00,000	1,30,000	6,00,000

Working Notes :

i) Allocation of Management on Cost (i.e. Administrative Overheads) on the basis of Works Cost (i.e. Factory Cost).

Particulars		Cots	Tables	Chairs	Cupboards
Factory Cost	₹	1,20,000	1,00,000	1,60,000	1,20,000
∴ Ratio		6	5	8	6
Allocation of Administrative Overheads (₹ 15,000 / 6 : 5 : 8 : 6)	₹	3,600	3,000	4,800	3,600

ii) Allocation of Selling and Distribution Overheads (i.e. Selling and Distribution Expenses) on the basis of Actual Sales (i.e. Value of Turnover).

Particulars		Cots	Tables	Chairs	Cupboards
Value of Turnover	₹	1,50,000	1,20,000	2,00,000	1,30,000
∴ Ratio		15	12	20	13
Allocation of Selling and Distribution Expenses (₹ 12,000 / 15 : 12 : 20 : 13)	₹	3,000	2,400	4,000	2,600

iii) Bad Debts Provision, Bad Debts Recovery and Book Debts are the items to be excluded from cost.

ILLUSTRATION 5

Sudarshan Chemicals Ltd., Satana, produces a standard product, the cost data relating to the same for April, 2013 is given below. You are required to prepare a Cost Sheet showing separately
  i) Cost of Materials Consumed, ii) Prime Cost, iii) Works Cost,
  iv) Cost of Production v) Total Cost, vi) Net Profit and vii) Market Price.

	₹
Purchases of Materials – Cash	4,000
Establishment Overheads : 20% of Factory Cost	
Wages Payable	800
Purchases of Materials – Credit	12,000

Works Overheads : 80% of Direct Wages
Cost of Special Designs — 850
Clearing Charges on Purchases — 1,200
Productive Wages — 3,200
Selling on Cost : ₹ 4 per unit sold
Chargeable Expenses Payable — 150
Defective Materials Returned — 400
Distribution Overheads : ₹ 1 per unit despatched
Trade Discount — 785

During the month of April, 2013, units sold and despatched were 1,300 units only. Also find out the market price per unit on the basis that profit mark-up is uniformly made to yield a profit of 4% on Cost of Sales.

SOLUTION

In the books of Sudarshan Chemicals Ltd., Satana

Cost Sheet for the month ended 30th April, 2013

Units Produced – 1,300
Units Sold – 1,300

	Particulars			Amount ₹	Amount ₹
	Purchases of Materials		16,000		
	a) Cash	4,000			
	b) Credit	(+) 12,000			
Add :	Clearing Charges on Purchases		(+) 1,200		
			17,200		
Less :	Defective Materials Returned		(−) 400		
	∴ **Cost of Materials Consumed**		i)	16,800	16,800
Add :	**Direct Labour :**				
	a) Wages Payable		800		
	b) Productive Wages		(+) 3,200	4,000	
Add :	**Direct Expenses :**				
	a) Cost of Special Designs		850		
	b) Chargeable Expenses Payable		(+) 150	1,000	
	∴ **Prime Cost**		ii)	21,800	21,800
Add :	**Works Overheads :**				
	(80% of Direct Wages i.e. ₹ 4,000)			3,200	
	∴ **Works Cost**		iii)	25,000	25,000
Add :	**Establishment Overheads :**				
	(20% of Factory Cost i.e. ₹ 25,000)			5,000	
	∴ **Cost of Production**		iv)	30,000	30,000
Add :	**Selling and Distribution Overheads :**				
	a) Selling on Cost			5,200	
	(₹ 4 × Units Sold – 1,300 = ₹ 5,200)				
	b) Distribution Overheads –			1,300	
	(Re. 1 × Units Despatched 1,300 = ₹ 1,300)				
	∴ **Total Cost**		v)	36,500	36,500
Add :	**Net Profit**		vi)		
	(4% on Cost of Sales i.e. ₹ 36,500)			1,460	1,460
	∴ **Market Price**		vii)	37,960	37,960

Working Notes :

i) Calculation of Net Profit i.e. 4% on Cost of Sales.
   = 4% of ₹ 36,500 i.e. Cost of Sales
   = ₹ 1,460

ii) Calculation of Market Price per unit.
   = $\dfrac{\text{Market Price}}{\text{Number of Units Sold}}$
   = $\dfrac{₹ 37,960}{\text{Units } 1,300}$
   = ₹ 29.20 per unit.

ILLUSTRATION 6

The accounts of Dorabjee Manufacturers, Deolali for the year ended 31st March, 2013 shows the following.

	₹
Stock of Raw Materials as on 1-4-2012	67,200
Bad Debts written-off	9,100
Raw Materials Purchased	2,59,000
Motive Power	320
Traveller's Commission	10,780
Depreciation on Office Equipments	420
Carriage Inwards	720
Interest on Bank Loan	380
Factory Taxes	11,900
Productive Wages	1,76,400
Directors Travelling Expenses	8,400
Coal and Coke	560
General Overheads	4,760
Gas and Water - Factory	1,680
Packing Charges	940
Sales of Finished Goods	6,00,000
Manager's Salary (Factory - $2/3$, Office - $1/3$)	15,000
Delivery Van Expenses	4,060
Depreciation on Factory Buildings	18,200
Publicity Charges	2,000
Repairs to Plant	6,340
Carriage Outward	7,120
Hire Charges of Special Machinery	9,010
Office Rent	2,800
Surveyor's Fees	590
Legal Charges	620
Stock of Raw Materials as on 31-3-2013	87,920

Prepare a Cost Statement giving the following details for the year ended 31st March, 2013.

i) Cost of Material Consumed ii) Prime Cost
iii) Works Cost iv) Cost of Production
v) Total Cost vi) Net Profit for the year.

SOLUTION

In the books of Dorabjee Manufacturers, Deolali
Cost Statement for the year ended 31st March, 2013

	Particulars			Amount ₹	Amount ₹
	Stock of Raw Materials as on 1-4-2012		67,200		
Add :	Raw Materials purchased		2,59,000		
Add :	Carriage inward	(+)	720		
			3,26,920		
Less :	Stock of Raw Materials as on 31-3-2013	(−)	87,920		
	∴ **Cost of Materials Consumed**	i)		2,39,000	2,39,000
Add :	Productive Wages	(+)		1,76,400	
Add :	Direct Expenses :				
a)	Hire Charges of Special Machinery		9,010		
b)	Surveyor's Fees	(+)	590	9,600	
	∴ **Prime Cost**	ii)		4,25,000	4,25,000
Add :	Factory Overheads :				
a)	Motive Power		320		
b)	Factory Taxes		11,900		
c)	Coal and Coke		560		
d)	Gas and Water - Factory		1,680		
e)	Manager's Salary – Factory ($2/3 \times$ ₹ 15,000)		10,000		
f)	Depreciation on Factory Buildings		18,200		
g)	Repairs to Plant	(+)	6,340	49,000	
	∴ **Works Cost**	iii)		4,74,000	4,74,000
Add :	Office Overheads :				
a)	Depreciation on Office Equipments		420		
b)	Director's Travelling Expenses		8,400		
c)	General Overheads		4,760		
d)	Manager's Salary – Office ($1/3 \times$ ₹ 15,000)		5,000		
e)	Office Rent		2,800		
f)	Legal Charges	(+)	620	22,000	
	∴ **Cost of Production**	iv)		4,96,000	4,96,000
Add :	Selling and Distribution Overheads :				
a)	Bad Debts written-off		9,100		
b)	Traveller's Commission		10,780		
c)	Packing Charges		940		
d)	Delivery Van Expenses		4,060		
e)	Publicity Charges		2,000		
f)	Carriage Outward	(+)	7,120	34,000	
	∴ **Total Cost**	v)		5,30,000	5,30,000
Add :	Net Profit for the year	vi)		70,000	70,000
	Sales of Finished Goods			**6,00,000**	**6,00,000**

Working Notes :
i) Interest on Bank Loan is an item to be excluded from cost.

Cost Accounting   2.41   Elements of Cost

ILLUSTRATION 7

Following details have been obtained from the cost records of Colgate Ltd., Kolkata, for the year ended 31st March, 2013.

	₹
Stock of Operating Materials as on 1-4-2012	30,000
Wages paid to Direct Workers	55,000
Interim Dividend paid	12,000
Purchases of Raw Materials	87,000
Heating and Lighting	6,000
Counting House Salaries	20,000
Carriage and Cartage on Purchases of Raw Materials	3,000
Commission on Sales	5,000
Wages Payable	5,000
Technical Director's Fees	10,000
Stock of Operating Material as on 31-3-2013	40,000
Showroom Expenses	7,000
Establishment on Cost	12,000
Share Transfer Fees	2,000
Expenses of Testing Labs.	4,000
Branch Office Expenses	8,000
After-Sales Service Expenses	8,000
Selling Price	2,50,000

Prepare a Cost-Sheet showing :

i) Cost of Raw Materials Consumed, ii) Prime Cost, iii) Works Cost, iv) Cost of Production, v) Total Cost and vi) Profit or Loss

Also calculate the percentage of :

i) Factory Overheads to Direct Wages, ii) Office on-Cost to Works Cost and iii) Selling and Distribution Expenses to Cost of Production.

SOLUTION

In the books of Colgate Ltd., Kolkata
Cost-Sheet for the year ended 31st March, 2013

	Particulars			Amount ₹	Amount ₹
	Stock of Operating Material as on 1-4-2012		30,000		
Add :	Purchases of Raw Materials		87,000		
Add :	Carriage and Cartage on Purchases of Raw Materials		(+) 3,000		
			1,20,000		
Less :	Stock of Operating Material as on 31-3-2013		(−) 40,000		
	∴ **Cost of Raw Materials Consumed**	i)		80,000	80,000
Add :	**Direct Labour :**				
a)	Wages paid to Direct Workers		55,000		
b)	Wages Payable		(+) 5,000	60,000	
	∴ **Prime Cost**	ii)		1,40,000	1,40,000
Add :	**Factory Overheads :**				
a)	Heating and Lighting		6,000		
b)	Technical Director's Fees		10,000		
c)	Expenses of Testing Labs.		(+) 4,000	20,000	
	∴ **Works Cost**	iii)		1,60,000	1,60,000
Add :	**Office Overheads :**				
a)	Counting House Salaries		20,000		
b)	Establishment on Cost		12,000		
c)	Branch Office Expenses		(+) 8,000	40,000	
	∴ **Cost of Production**	iv)		2,00,000	2,00,000
Add :	**Selling and Distribution Overheads :**				
a)	Commission on Sales		5,000		
b)	Show Room Expenses		7,000		
c)	After Sales-Service Expenses		(+) 8,000	20,000	
	∴ **Total Cost**	v)		2,20,000	2,20,000
Add :	Profit	vi)		30,000	30,000
	Selling Price			**2,50,000**	**2,50,000**

Working Notes :

i) Calculation of percentage of Factory Overheads to Direct Wages.

If ₹ 60,000 D.W. = ₹ 20,000 F.O.

∴ 100 = ?

$$= \frac{100 \times ₹ 20,000}{₹ 60,000}$$

= 33.33%

ii) Calculation of percentage of Office on Cost to Works Cost.

If ₹ 1,60,000 W.C. = ₹ 40,000 O.O.C.

∴ 100 = ?

Cost Accounting 2.43 Elements of Cost

$$= \frac{100 \times ₹\, 40{,}000}{₹\, 1{,}60{,}000}$$

$$= 25\%$$

iii) Calculation of percentage of Selling and Distribution Expenses to Cost of Production.
If ₹ 2,00,000 C.O.P. = ₹ 20,000 S. & D.E.
∴   100 = ?

$$= \frac{100 \times ₹\, 20{,}000}{₹\, 2{,}00{,}000}$$

$$= 10\%$$

iv) Interim Dividend and Share Transfer Fees etc., are the items to be excluded from cost.

ILLUSTRATION 8

The following is the Trading and Profit and Loss Account of Sarabhai Chemicals Ltd. Surat, for the year ended 31st March, 2013.

Dr. Trading and Profit and Loss Account **Cr.**
for the year ended 31st March, 2013

Particulars		₹	Particulars		₹
To Stock of Raw Materials 1-4-2012		18,000	By Sales	5,10,000	5,00,000
To Purchases of Raw Materials	2,52,000	2,50,000	Less : Returns Inward (–)	10,000	
Less : Returns Outward (–)	2,000		By Stock of Raw Materials on 31-3-2013		10,000
To Productive Wages		1,02,000			
To Carriage on Purchases		25,000	By Sale of Scrap Materials		1,000
To Royalty		7,200			
To Gas and Water		19,000			
To Customs and Duty		8,000			
To Chargeable Expenses due, but not paid		2,800			
To Wages Outstanding		8,000			
To Heating and Lighting		11,000			
To Gross Profit C/D		60,000			
		5,11,000			5,11,000
To Carriage on Sales		5,000	By Gross Profit B/D		60,000
To Underwriting Commission		4,500	By Interest on Investment		1,000
To Commission on Sales		7,600			
To Sales Depot Expenses		2,400			
To Salaries		16,000			
To Bad Debts Provision		1,500			
To Property Tax on Office Premises		2,000			
To Depreciation on Office Equipments		2,000			
To Net Profit C/D *		20,000			
		61,000			61,000

You are required to prepare a Cost Statement for the year ended 31st March, 2013 showing i) Cost of Materials Consumed, ii) Flat Cost, iii) Manufacturing Cost, iv) Gross Cost, v) Cost of Turnover, vi) Profits for the year.

Also calculate the percentage of profit on sales.

SOLUTION

In the books of Sarabhai Chemicals Ltd., Surat
Cost Statement for the year ended 31st March, 2013

Particulars			Amount ₹	Amount ₹
Stock of Raw Materials on 1-4-2012		18,000		
Add : Purchases of Raw Materials		2,52,000		
Add : Expenses on Purchases of Raw Materials :				
a) Carriage on Purchases		25,000		
b) Customs and Duty		8,000		
		3,03,000		
Less : Stock of Raw Materials on 31-3-2013		10,000		
Less : Returns Outward		2,000		
Less : Sale of Scrap Materials		1,000		
∴ **Cost of Materials Consumed**	i)		2,90,000	2,90,000
Add : Direct Labour :				
a) Productive Wages		1,02,000		
b) Wages Outstanding	(+)	8,000	1,10,000	
Add : Direct Expenses :				
a) Royalty		7,200		
b) Chargeable Expenses due, but not paid	(+)	2,800	10,000	
∴ **Flat Cost**	ii)		4,10,000	4,10,000
Add : Factory Overheads :				
a) Gas and Water		19,000		
b) Heating and Lighting	(+)	11,000	30,000	
∴ **Manufacturing Cost**	iii)		4,40,000	4,40,000
Add : Office Overheads :				
a) Salaries		16,000		
b) Property Tax on Office Premises		2,000		
c) Depreciation on Office Furniture	(+)	2,000	20,000	
∴ **Gross Cost**	iv)		4,60,000	4,60,000
Add : Selling and Distribution Overheads :				
a) Carriage on Sales		5,000		
b) Commission on Sales		7,600		
c) Sales Depot Expenses	(+)	2,400	15,000	
∴ **Cost of Turnover**	v)		4,75,000	4,75,000
Add : Profits for the year	vi)		25,000	25,000
Sales			5,00,000	5,00,000

Working Notes :

i) Calculation of percentage of Profit on Sales.

If ₹ 5,00,000 Sales = ₹ 25,000 Profit

∴ 100 = ?

$$\frac{100 \times ₹ 25,000}{₹ 5,00,000} = 5\%$$

ii) Underwriting Commission, Bad Debts Provision, and Interest on Investment are the items to be excluded from cost.

ILLUSTRATION 9

Following information of Finolex Ltd., Faizpur, relates to a commodity for the year ended 31st March, 2013.

	₹
Opening Stock as on 1-4-2012	
• Raw Materials	5,000
• Work-in-Progress	1,200
• Finished Goods (1,000 Tons)	4,000
Closing Stock as on 31-3-2013	
• Raw Materials	3,000
• Work-in-Progress	3,200
• Finished Goods (2,000 Tons)	9,000
Purchases of Raw Materials	35,000
Prime Cost Labour	25,000
Excise Duty on purchases of Raw Materials	2,000
Administration Overheads	8,000
Cost of Factory Supervision	12,000
Income Tax	5,000
Carriage and Cartage	1,000
Management Expenses	1,000
Accountancy Charges	1,000
Preliminary Expenses	3,200
Sale of Finished Goods	1,17,500

Advertising, Bad Debts and Selling on Cost amounted to 50 paise per ton sold. 16,000 tons of commodities were produced during the year 2012-2013.

Prepare a Cost-Sheet showing

i) Cost of Materials Consumed, ii) Prime Cost, iii) Works Cost, iv) Cost of Production, v) Cost of Goods Sold, vi) Cost of Sales, vii) Profits for the period, viii) Profits per ton of commodity sold.

SOLUTION

In the books of Finolex Ltd. Faizpur
Cost-Sheet for the year ended 31st March, 2013

Units Produced – 16,000 Tons
Units Sold – 15,000 Tons

Particulars		Amount ₹	Amount ₹
Opening Stock as on 1-4-2012 of Raw Materials	5,000		
Add: Purchases of Raw Materials	35,000		
Add: **Expenses for purchases of Raw Materials :**			
a) Excise Duty on Purchases of Raw Materials	2,000		
b) Carriage and Cartage	(+) 1,000		
	43,000		
Less: Closing Stock as on 31-3-2013 Raw Materials	(–) 3,000		
∴ **Cost of Materials Consumed** i)		40,000	40,000

Particulars		Amount ₹	Amount ₹
Add : Prime Cost Labour (+)		25,000	
∴ **Prime Cost** ii)		65,000	65,000
Add : Cost of Factory Supervision 12,000		13,200	
Add : Opening Stock as on 1-4-2012 Work-in-Progress (+) 1,200			
		78,200	
Less : Closing Stock as on 31-3-2013 Work-in-Progress (−) 3,200		3,200	
∴ **Works Cost** iii)		75,000	75,000
Add : Office Overheads :			
a) Administration Overheads	8,000		
b) Management Expenses	1,000		
c) Accountancy Charges	(+) 1,000	10,000	
∴ **Cost of Production** iv)		85,000	85,000
Add : Opening Stock as on 1-4-2012 Finished Goods		4,000	
		89,000	
Less : Closing Stock as on 31-3-2013 Finished Goods		9,000	
∴ **Cost of Goods Sold** v)		80,000	80,000
Add : Advertising, Bad Debts and Selling on Cost			
(50 Ps. × 15,000 Tons)		7,500	
∴ **Cost of Sales** vi)		87,500	87,500
Add : Profits for the period vii)		30,000	30,000
Sales of Finished Goods		1,17,500	1,17,500

Working Notes :

i) Calculation of Units Sold during the year 2012-2013

	Tons
Opening Stock of Finished Goods as on 1-4-2012	1,000
Add : Production during the year	(+) 16,000
	17,000
Less : Closing Stock of Finished Goods as on 31-3-2013	(−) 2,000
∴ Units Sold	15,000

ii) Calculation of profits per ton of commodity sold −

If 15,000 Tons = Profit ₹ 30,000

∴ 1 Ton = ?

$$= \frac{1 \text{ ton} \times ₹\, 30{,}000}{15{,}000 \text{ Tons}}$$

= ₹ 2 per ton

iii) Income Tax, Preliminary Expenses etc. are the items to be excluded from Cost.

Cost Accounting — Elements of Cost

ILLUSTRATION 10

The following information has been obtained from the records of Quality Manufacturing Co. Ltd., Bharatpur, for the year ended 31st March, 2013.

Summary of Stock Position

Type of Stock	As on 1-4-2012 ₹	As on 31-3-2013 ₹
Finished Goods-Stock	50,000	75,000
Raw Materials	20,000	25,000
Stock of Work-in-Progress	5,000	7,000

Additional Information

	₹
Purchases of Raw Materials	1,30,000
Wages Outstanding	3,000
Indirect Material	12,000
Discount on issue of Debentures	8,000
Freight Inward	15,000
Property Tax on Factory Buildings	8,000
Director's Travelling Expenses	8,000
Carriage on Sales	5,000
Defective Raw Materials Returned	5,000
Direct Chargeable Expenses	2,000
Workshop Rent	7,000
Expenses for participating in Industrial Exhibition	3,000
Value of Sales	3,00,000
Office Cleaning Charges	2,000
Sales Promotion Charges	6,000
Miscellaneous Overheads	7,000
Upkeep of Delivery Vans	1,000
Motive Power	5,000
Productive Wages	60,000
Postage and Telegrams	3,000

Prepare a Statement of Cost showing:

i) Value of Raw Materials Consumed, ii) Direct Cost, iii) Manufacturing Cost, iv) Cost of Production, v) Cost of Goods Sold, vi) Cost of Turnover, vii) Profit.

Also calculate the percentage of Profit on Cost Price and on Selling Price separately.

SOLUTION

In the books of Quality Manufacturing Co. Ltd., Bharatpur
Statement of Cost for the year ended 31ˢᵗ March, 2013

	Particulars			Amount ₹	Amount ₹
	Raw Materials as on 1-4-2012	20,000			
Add :	Purchases of Raw Materials	1,30,000			
Add :	Freight Inward	(+) 15,000			
		1,65,000			
Less :	Raw Materials as on 31-3-2013	(–) 25,000			
Less :	Defective Raw Materials returned	(–) 5,000			
	∴ **Value of Raw Materials Consumed**		i)	1,35,000	1,35,000
Add :	**Direct Labour :**			63,000	
a)	Productive Wages	60,000			
b)	Wages Outstanding	(+) 3,000			
Add :	Direct Chargeable Expenses			2,000	
	∴ **Direct Cost**		ii)	2,00,000	2,00,000
Add :	**Factory Overheads :**				
a)	Indirect Material	12,000			
b)	Property Tax on Factory Buildings	8,000			
c)	Workshop Rent	7,000			
d)	Motive Power	(+) 5,000		32,000	
Add :	Work-in-Progress as on 1-4-2012			5,000	
				2,37,000	
Less :	Work-in-Progress as on 31-3-2013			7,000	
	∴ **Manufacturing Cost**		iii)	2,30,000	2,30,000
Add :	**Office Overheads :**				
a)	Director's Travelling Expenses	8,000			
b)	Postage and Telegrams	3,000			
c)	Miscellaneous Overheads	7,000			
d)	Office Cleaning Charges	(+) 2,000		20,000	
	∴ **Cost of Production**		iv)	2,50,000	2,50,000
Add :	Finished Goods - Stock as on 1-4-2012			50,000	
Less :	Finished Goods - Stock as on 31-3-2013			75,000	
	∴ **Cost of Goods Sold**		v)	2,25,000	2,25,000
Add :	**Selling and Distribution Overheads :**				
a)	Carriage on Sales	5,000			
b)	Expenses for participating in Industrial Exhibition	3,000			
c)	Upkeep of Delivery Vans	1,000			
d)	Sales Promotion Charges	(+) 6,000		15,000	
	∴ **Cost of Turnover**		vi)	2,40,000	2,40,000
Add :	**Profits**		vii)	60,000	60,000
	Value of Sales			**3,00,000**	**3,00,000**

Working Notes:

i) Calculation of percentage of Profit on Cost Price.

If ₹ 2,40,000 CP = ₹ 60,000 P

∴ 100 = ?

$$= \frac{100 \times ₹ 60,000}{₹ 2,40,000}$$

$$= 25\%$$

ii) Calculation of percentage of Profit on Sales.

If ₹ 3,00,000 SP = ₹ 60,000 P

∴ 100 = ?

$$= \frac{100 \times ₹ 60,000}{₹ 3,00,000}$$

$$= 20\%$$

iii) Discount on issue of Debentures is an item to be excluded from cost.

ILLUSTRATION 11

Jindal Cables and Conductors Ltd., Jalgaon, provides the following cost data relating to the manufacture of a standard product during the month of May, 2013.

	₹
Carriage and Cartage	200
Units Sold – 900 units @ ₹ 40 per unit	
Raw Materials Stock as on 31st May, 2013	2,850
Monthly Production – 1,000 units	
Sale of Raw Materials Scrap	150
Selling and Distribution on Cost : ₹ 3.60 per unit	
Operating Wages Payable	600
Operation of Machine Hours – 1,600	
Stock of Raw Materials as on 1st May, 2013	1,200
Administration Overheads : 10% of Works Cost	
Hire of Special Machinery	1,500
Machine Hour Rate	2.50
Raw Materials Purchases	14,600
Productive Wages	4,400
Cost of Layout	500

You are required to prepare a Cost-Sheet showing Total Cost Unit and Unit Cost for the month ended 31st May, 2013. Also calculate Profit earned for the month and Profit per unit sold.

SOLUTION

In the books of Jindal Cables and Conductors Ltd., Jalgaon
Cost-Sheet for the month ended 31st May, 2013

Units Produced — 1,000 units
Units Sold — 900 units

Particulars		Total Cost ₹	Unit Cost ₹
Stock of Raw Materials as on 1-5-2013	1,200		
Add : Raw Materials Purchases	14,600		
Add : Carriage and Cartage	(+) 200		
	16,000		
Less : Raw Materials - Stock as on 31-5-2013	(–) 2,850		
Less : Sale of Raw Materials Scrap	(–) 150		
∴ **Cost of Materials Consumed** i)		13,000	13.00
Add : Direct Labour :		5,000	5.00
a) Operating Wages Payable	600		
b) Productive Wages	(+) 4,400		
Add : Direct Expenses :		2,000	2.00
a) Hire of Special Machinery	1,500		
b) Cost of Layout	(+) 500		
	(+)		
∴ **Prime Cost** ii)		20,000	20.00
Add : Factory Overheads :	(+)	4,000	4.00
∴ **Works Cost** iii)		24,000	24.00
Add : Administration Overheads :	(+)	2,400	2.40
∴ **Cost of Production** iv)		26,400	26.40
Add : Stock of Finished Goods on 1-5-2013	(+)	–	
Less : Stock of Finished Goods on 31-5-2013	(–)	2,640	–
∴ **Cost of Goods sold** v)		23,760	26.40
Add : Selling and Distribution on Cost			
(900 Units × ₹ 3.60)	(+)	3,240	3.60
∴ **Total Cost** vi)		27,000	30.00
Add : Profits for the month	vii) (+)	9,000	10.00
Sales (900 Units × ₹ 40)		36,000	40.00

Working Notes :

i) Calculation of Factory Overheads :

Operation of Machine Hours × Machine Hour Rate = Factory Overheads
1,600 Hrs. ₹ 2.50 ₹ 4,000

ii) Calculation of Administration Overheads i.e. 10% of Works Cost :
= 10% of ₹ 24,000
= ₹ 2,400.

iii) Valuation of Closing Stock of Finished Goods on the basis of Cost of Production :

		Units
	Monthly Production	1,000
Less :	Units Sold	(−) 900
	∴ Closing Stock	100

If 1,000 Units = ₹ 26,400 Cost of Production
∴ 100 Units = ?

$$= \frac{100 \text{ Units} \times ₹ 26,400}{1,000 \text{ Units}}$$

= ₹ 2,640.

Illustration 12 :

Mafatlal Cotton Textiles Ltd., Bhandup, submits the following information for the year ended 31st March, 2013.

	₹
Inventories as on 31st March, 2012 :	
• Raw Materials	12,500
• Work-in-Progress	16,400
• Finished Goods	17,300
Inventories as on 31st March, 2013 :	
• Raw Materials	9,300
• Work-in-Progress	6,400
• Finished Goods	5,300
Additional Information :	
Special Trade Discount	275
Annual Turnover :	
a) Cash	45,000
b) Credit	1,55,000
Excise Duty on Purchases	3,200
Defective Materials Returned	1,400
Materials Inventory Purchases	62,700
Prime Cost Labour	29,400
Raw Materials Scrap Sold	200
Hire of Cutting Machinery	10,800
Dock Charges	1,400
Carriage Inward	1,100
Productive Wages Payable	10,600
Preliminary Expenses	1,300
Cost of Patterns	5,200
Productive Expenses	4,000

Factory Overheads – 50% of Basic Wages
Management on Cost – 5% of Sales Value
Selling Expenses – 3% of Invoice Price
Distribution Overheads – 1% of Loaded Price

You are required to prepare a Statement of Cost showing –
i) Cost of Raw Materials Consumed, ii) Prime Cost,
iii) Works Cost, iv) Cost of Production,
v) Cost of Goods Sold, vi) Cost of Sales and vii) Profits for the year.

SOLUTION

In the books of Mafatlal Cotton Textiles Ltd., Bhandup
Statement of Cost for the year ended 31st March, 2013

Particulars		Amount ₹	Amount ₹
Inventories of Raw Materials as on 1-4-2012	12,500		
Add: Materials Inventories Purchases	62,700		
Add: Expenses for Purchases of Raw Materials			
a) Excise Duty on Purchases	3,200		
b) Dock Charges	1,400		
c) Carriage Inward	(+) 1,100		
	80,900		
Less: Inventories of Raw Materials as on 31-3-2013	9,300		
Less: Defective Materials Returned	1,400		
Less: Raw Materials Scrap Sold	(–) 200		
∴ **Cost of Raw Materials Consumed** i)		70,000	70,000
Add: Direct Labour:			
a) Prime Cost Labour	29,400		
b) Productive Wages Payable	(+) 10,600	40,000	
Add: Direct Expenses:			
a) Hire of Cutting Machinery	10,800		
b) Cost of Patterns	5,200		
c) Productive Expenses	(+) 4,000	20,000	
∴ **Prime Cost** ii)		1,30,000	1,30,000
Add: Factory Overheads		20,000	
(50% of Basic Wages i.e. Direct Labour ₹ 40,000)			
Add: Inventories of Work-in-Progress as on 1-4-2012		16,400	
		1,66,400	
Less: Inventories of Work-in-Progress as on 31-3-2013		6,400	
∴ **Works Cost** iii)		1,60,000	1,60,000
Add: Management on Cost		10,000	
(5% of Sales Value i.e. Annual Turnover ₹ 2,00,000)			
∴ **Cost of Production** iv)		1,70,000	1,70,000
Add: Inventories of Finished Goods as on 1-4-2012		17,300	
		1,87,300	
Less: Inventories of Finished Goods as on 31-3-2013		5,300	
∴ **Cost of Goods sold** v)		1,82,000	1,82,000
Add: Selling and Distribution Overheads:			
(i) Selling Expenses	6,000		
(3% of Invoice Price i.e. Annual Turnover ₹ 2,00,000)			
(ii) Distribution Overheads			
(1% of Loaded Price i.e. Annual Turnover ₹ 2,00,000)	(+) 2,000	8,000	
∴ **Cost of Sales** vi)		1,90,000	1,90,000
Add: Profits for the year vii)		10,000	
Annual Turnover		**2,00,000**	2,00,000
(Cash ₹ 45,000 + Credit ₹ 1,55,000)			

Working Notes:

i) Special Trade Discount, Preliminary Expenses etc. are the items to be excluded from cost.

QUESTIONS FOR SELF-STUDY

I. Theory Questions:

i) Define the term 'Cost'. Explain the various Elements of Cost.

ii) Define the term Elements of Cost. State the different elements of costs with suitable examples.

iii) What is 'Material Cost'? State the importance of Material Cost in total cost structure.

iv) Explain briefly the various elements of cost. Give suitable examples for the same.

v) What is 'Labour Cost'? State the importance of Labour Cost in total cost structure.

vi) Explain the importance of 'Other Expenses' as the elements of cost.

vii) What do you understand by the term 'Element of Cost'? What is the important basis of such Classification of Cost?

viii) "Direct Costs and Controllable Costs are not necessarily the same". Explain.

ix) What is Cost? How would you classify the cost? Give suitable examples.

x) What is Cost Classification? Explain the need for Cost Classification. State the various methods of Cost Classification with suitable examples.

xi) Distinguish between Fixed Costs and Variable Costs with suitable examples.

xii) "Costing systems are classified according to the nature of operation". Explain.

xiii) "Fixed Costs are Variable per unit while Variable costs are fixed per unit". Comment.

xiv) What is Fixed Cost? Explain the important characteristics of Fixed Cost.

xv) What is Variable Cost? Explain the important characteristics of variable cost.

xvi) What is Semi-variable Cost? Explain the important characteristics of Semi-variable Cost.

xvii) Explain the various costs used in decision-making and their characteristics.

xviii) What is 'Cost-Sheet'? Explain the various purposes for preparing a 'Simple Cost Sheet'.

xix) Why a 'Cost Sheet' is to be prepared? Give the specimen of a 'Simple Cost Sheet'.

xx) Define the terms 'Direct Costs' and 'Indirect Costs'. A particular cost may be a direct cost in one situation and indirect in the other. Illustrate.

xxi) 'Variable Costs may be direct or indirect'. Discuss giving suitable examples.

xxii) 'Variable costs are constant on per unit basis, while fixed costs are constant in total'. Explain.

xxiii) Importance of Fixed Cost lies in decision-making, due to their special characteristics'. Discuss.

xxiv) Explain the importance of Decision-Making Costs.

xxv) Write short notes on:

a) Material Cost, b) Labour Cost, c) Direct Expenses, d) Cost Classification, e) Types of Cost, f) Need for Classification of Cost, g) Semi-fixed Costs, h) Types of Cost, i) Decision-Making Costs, j) Functional Classification of Cost, k) Avoidable Cost, l) Purposes of a Cost Sheet, m) Shut-Down Costs, n) Opportunity Cost, o) Out of Pocket Costs, p) Sunk Costs, q) Fixed Costs.

xxvi) Differentiate between :
- a) Direct Material and Indirect Material
- b) Direct Labour and Indirect Labour
- c) Direct Expenses and Indirect Expenses
- d) Fixed Costs and Variable Costs
- e) Variable Costs and Semi-variable Costs
- f) Controllable Costs and Non-Controllable Costs
- g) Capital Costs and Revenue Costs
- h) Period Costs and Product Costs
- i) Factory Costs and Administration Costs
- j) Normal Costs and Abnormal Costs
- k) Cost Estimation and Cost Ascertainment
- l) Cost of Goods Sold and Cost of Sales
- m) Prime Cost and Factory Cost
- n) Sunk Costs and Out-of-Pocket Costs
- o) Office Cost and Selling Cost
- p) Simple Cost Sheet and Estimated Cost Sheet.

II. Practical Problems :

i) Tata Cement Co., Badalapur, furnishes you with the following cost data. You are required to prepare a Cost Sheet for the year ended 31st March, 2013, showing therein the Prime Cost, Works Cost, Cost of Production and Cost of Sales alongwith cost per unit and the percentage of each element of cost to total cost.

	₹
Units Produced - 10,000	
Material Consumed	10,00,000
Wages paid to Workers	40,000
Power and Fuel (Factory)	20,000
Repairs to Machines	8,000
Depreciation - Machinery	6,000
Depreciation - Office Furniture	1,000
Supervision Expenses (Factory)	2,000
Hire Charges for machines of special purposes	4,000
Wages paid to Maintenance Workers	20,000
Audit Fees	1,500
Director's Fees	7,500
Bad Debts	2,500
Office Expenses	3,500
Salaries	2,000
Rent, Rates and Taxes (Factory)	5,000
Sales	3,00,000
Salesman Salary	8,000
Advertising Expenses	2,000
Delivery Van Expenses	8,000
Warehouse Rent	6,000
Printing and Stationery	1,000
Direct Expenses	8,000

ii) From the following particulars of Goldstar Cement Ltd., Chalisgaon, prepare a Cost Sheet showing : i) Prime Cost, ii) Factory Cost, iii) Total Cost of Production and iv) Cost of Sales for the period ended 31st March, 2013.

	₹
Raw Material Consumed	50,000
Wages paid to Workers	20,000
Direct Expenses incurred for production	2,500
Consumable Stores	500
Supervisor's Wages	2,000
Wages paid to shop floor helper	600
Electric Power (Factory)	800
Electric Power (Office)	500
Rent (Factory)	5,000
Rent (Office)	2,000
Repairs and Renewals Plant and Machinery	5,000
Renovation of Office Buildings	1,000
Depreciation on Plant and Machinery	500
Depreciation on Office Buildings	200
Manager's Salary	3,000
Telephone Charges	200
Printing and Stationery	400
Postage and Telegrams	150
Director's Fees	800
Advertisement	800
Travelling Expenses	300
Salesmen's Salary and Commission	1,000
Warehouse Rent	900
Delivery van Expenses	1,000

iii) Atlas Cycle Co. Ltd., Dombivili, produce auto parts. From the following particulars prepare Cost Sheet for the period ended 31st March, 2013.

	₹
Opening Stock of Raw Materials	20,000
Raw Material purchased	70,000
Closing Stock of Raw Materials	15,000
Direct Labour Cost (20% of Factory on Cost)	
Factory on Cost	30,000
Administrative Overhead (10% of Works Cost)	
Selling and Distribution Expenses	10,000
Details of the Finished Goods are as follows :	
Opening Stock of Finished Goods 2,000 units	25,000
Finished Goods produced during the period	20,000 units
Closing Stock of Finished Goods	4,000 units

You are required to find out the profit made during the year @ 10% on the Selling Price.

Note : i) There was no balance of Opening or Closing Stock of Work-in-Progress.

ii) Show the working of calculating the profit.

iv) The accounts of MRF Ltd., Fatehpur for the year ended 31st March, 2013, shows the following:

	₹
Drawing Office Salaries	6,500
Counting-House Salaries	12,600
Cash-Discount Allowed	2,900
Carriage and Cartage Outwards	4,300
Carriage and Cartage Inwards	7,150
Bad Debts written off	6,500
Repairs of Plant, Machinery and Tools	4,450
Rent, Rates, Taxes and Insurance - Factory	8,500
Rent, Rates, Taxes and Insurance - Office	2,000
Sales	4,61,100
Stock of Materials – 1st April, 2012	62,800
Stock of Materials – 31st March, 2013	48,000
Materials purchased	1,85,000
Travelling Expenses	2,100
Traveller's Salaries and Commission	7,700
Productive Wages	1,26,000
Depreciation – Plant, Machinery and Tools	6,500
Depreciation – Furniture	300
Director's Fees	6,000
Gas and Water – Factory	1,200
– Office	400
Manager's Salary ($\frac{3}{4}$ Factory and $\frac{1}{4}$ Office)	10,000
General Expenses	3,400
Income-Tax	1,000
Dividend	2,000

Prepare a statement giving the following information:
i) Materials Consumed; ii) Prime Cost; iii) Factory on-Cost and the percentage on Wages; iv) Factory Cost; v) General on Cost and percentage on Factory Cost; vi) Total Cost; vii) Net Profit.

v) The following details have been obtained from the cost records of Cement India Ltd., Manmad for April, 2013.

	₹
Stock of Raw Materials on 1st April, 2013	75,000
Stock of Raw Materials on 30th April, 2013	91,500
Direct Wages	52,500
Indirect Wages	2,750
Sales	2,11,000
Work-in-Progress 1st April, 2013	28,000
Work-in-Progress 30th April 2013	35,000
Purchases of Raw Materials	66,000
Factory Rent, Rate, Power	15,000

Depreciation on Plant and Machinery	3,500
Expenses on Purchases	1,500
Carriage Outward	2,500
Advertising	3,500
Office Rent and Taxes	2,500
Travellers Wages and Commission	6,500
Stock of Finished Goods 1st April, 2013	54,000
Stock of Finished Goods 30th April, 2013	31,000

Prepare Cost-Sheet for the month ended 30th April, 2013.

vi) Following information has been obtained from the records of a Caustic Soda Manufacturing Co., Gurgaon.

	1st April, 2012 ₹	31st March, 2013 ₹
Stock of Raw Materials	40,000	50,000
Stock of Finished Goods	1,00,000	1,50,000
Stock of Work-in-Progress	10,000	14,000

Other Particulars :

	₹
Indirect Labour	50,000
Lubricants	10,000
Insurance on Plant	3,000
Purchase on Raw Materials	4,00,000
Sales Commission	60,000
Salaries of Salesmen	1,00,000
Administrative Expenses	1,00,000
Carriage Outward	20,000
Power	30,000
Direct Labour	3,00,000
Depreciation on Machinery	50,000
Factory Rent	60,000
Property Tax on Factory Buildings	11,000
Sales	12,00,000

Prepare a statement of cost and profit showing :
i) Value of Raw Materials Consumed   ii) Prime Cost
iii) Factory Cost   iv) Cost of Production
v) Cost of Sales   vi) Profit

vii) The following information is received from the books of ABC Co. Ltd., Hinjewadi, for the year ending 31st March, 2013.

	₹
Stock of Materials 31-3-2013	75,000
Purchases of Material	7,95,000
Stock of Material on 1-4-2012	1,05,000
Travelling Expenses	5,100
Carriage Inward	8,290
Carriage Outward	9,150
Labour Welfare Expenses	14,200
Depreciation on Plant	18,000
Factory Rent	11,200
Office Rent	29,100

	₹
Bad Debts	9,000
Productive Wages	2,27,000
Travellers' Salary and Commission	9,000
Expenses regarding Purchase of Materials	4,500
Director's Fees	8,700
Fuel, Gas and Water	17,900
Manager's Salary (He devotes 2/3 of his time to factory)	18,000
Airconditioning Charges of Office	9,000
Outstanding Productive Wages	33,000
Sales	14,29,500

Prepare Cost-Sheet giving
i) Prime Cost, ii) Works Cost, iii) Cost of Production, iv) Total Cost

viii) The following data have been extracted from the books of Birla Tractors Ltd., Pune, for the year 2012-2013.

	₹
Opening Stock of Raw Materials	25,000
Purchase of Raw Materials	85,000
Closing Stock of Raw Materials	40,000
Carriage Inward	5,000
Wages – Direct	75,000
Wages – Indirect	10,000
Other Direct Charges	15,000
Rent and Rates –	
Factory	5,000
Office	500
Indirect Consumption of Material	500
Depreciation –	
Plant and Machinery	1,500
Office Furniture	100
Salary –	
Office	2,500
Salesmen	2,000
Other Factory Expenses	5,700
Other Office Expenses	900
Manager's Remuneration	12,000
Bad Debts written off	1,000
Advertisement Expenses	2,000
Travelling Expenses of Salesmen	1,100
Carriage and Freight Outward	1,000
Sales	2,50,000
Advance Income Tax	15,000
Cash Discount	5,000

The manager has the overall charge of the company and his remuneration is to be allocated ₹ 4,000 to Factory, ₹ 2,000 to Office and ₹ 6,000 to the Selling.

From the above particulars prepare a Cost Statement showing :
i) Prime Cost, ii) Factory Cost, iii) Cost of Production, iv) Cost of Sales, and v) Net Profit.

***

Unit ... 3

METHODS OF COSTING

3.1 Job Costing
    3.1.1 Meaning
    3.1.2 Features
    3.1.3 Advantages
    3.1.4 Limitations
3.2 Contract Costing
    3.2.1 Basic Concepts
3.3 Process Costing
    3.3.1 Meaning
    3.3.2 Features
    3.3.3 Normal and Abnormal Loss or Gain
3.4 Operating Costing
    3.4.1 Meaning
    3.4.2 Features
    3.4.3 Objectives
3.5 Opportunity Costing
✱ Questions for Self-Study

    The **method of cost accumulation** and identifying them to products and services depending upon the nature of operations in an enterprise. Therefore, cost accounting procedure varies from one company to another. For example, a non-manufacturing enterprise may not follow the procedure of accumulating costs with specific customer orders. Similarly, a hospital may prefer to accumulate costs in a manner so as to provide the cost of outpatient treatment or a specific medical treatment; a concern organising exhibitions and fairs may be interested in knowing the cost of an exhibition to be organised in a particular season. On the contrary, a contractor accumulates costs for each separate contract. Although the procedure of accumulating costs may differ among different types of organisations, the basic principles underlying cost accumulating procedures are applicable to all types of organisations. Each cost accounting procedure or system aims to provide information that is needed by the management.

Need of Costing Methods :

    Methods of Costing indicates a systematic procedure established for ascertaining cost of a product, job process or services by using the principles of costing. A Cost Accounting method is merely the process of 'collating and presenting costs". The nature of industries differs. Some are very simple and produce only one product for e.g., brick-making. Some industries may produce only one product but it may be an assembly of numerous components for e.g., bicycle, motor car etc. Again there may be a homogeneous product, but involving many distinct stages and processes such as vegetable oil. In some case, there may be important by-products or joint products for e.g., petroleum products, sugar etc. It is therefore, natural that the exact method employed to ascertain cost per unit should depend on the nature of the industry. The general principle of ascertaining cost of production per unit are the same, but the methods ascertaining and presenting the costs vary with the type of production. Hence, various methods are required for ascertaining the costs because every business is different in its nature, in its type of products, in methods of production etc.

Methods of Costing :

In manufacturing organisations, the principles of cost accumulation and their identification with products are more clear and visible and therefore the principles used by a manufacturing enterprise is often used by other organisations also for accumulating costs. In manufacturing concerns, costs are accumulated and assigned to products on the basis of the following cost accounting methods viz. Specific Order Costing and Operation Costing.

But according to **Mr. Batty**, "Many costing systems do not fall neatly into the category of either job or process costing. Often, systems use some features of both the main costing systems". It is, for this reason, that he uses the term "hybrid costing systems" for all those methods that combine the features of the basic costing methods. The Figure 3.1 indicates different **methods of costing** as follows :

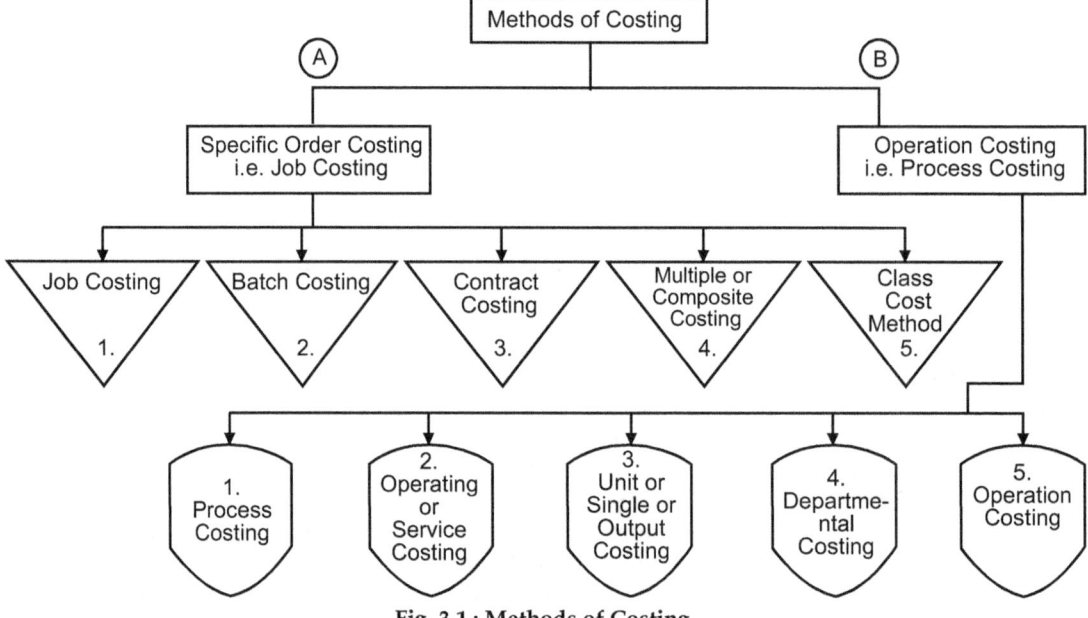

Fig. 3.1 : Methods of Costing

(A) Specific Order Costing

The terminology of I.C.M.A., defines **Specific Order Costing** as *"the category of basic costing methods applicable where the work consists of separate contracts, jobs or batches each of which is authorised by a special order or contract"*. This method is adopted in made-to-order type of products which depends entirely on the specification of customers. As such there is no standardisation in the production process for want of uniformity. This method may take any of the following :

1) **Job Costing :**

   The terminology of I.C.M.A., defines **Job Costing** as *"that form of specific order costing which applies where work is undertaken to customers' special requirements"*. Under this method, costs are collected and accumulated for each job, work order or project separately. Each job can be separately identified, so it becomes essential to analyse the cost, according to each job. A Job Card is prepared for each job for cost accumulation. This method is applicable to printers, machine tool manufacturers, foundries and general engineering workshops, interior decorator, painters, repair shops etc.

2) **Batch Costing :**

   The terminology of I.C.M.A. defines **Batch Costing** as *"that form of specific order costing which applies where similar articles are manufactured in batches either for sale or use within the undertaking"*. This method is a variation of Job Costing. In this method, the cost of a batch or group of identical products is ascertained and, therefore, each batch of products is a unit of cost for which costs are accumulated. This method is used in biscuit factories, bakeries, ready-made garments, hardwares like nuts, bolts, screws, shoes, toys, drugs and pharmaceuticals etc.

3) **Contract Costing :**

   The terminology of I.C.M.A., defines **Contract Costing** as *"that form of specific order costing which applies where work is undertaken to customers' special requirements and each order is of long duration"*. The cost unit here is a contract which is of a long duration and may continue over for more than one financial year. A separate account is kept for each contract. This method is used by builders, civil engineering contractors, constructional and mechanical engineering firms etc.

4) **Multiple or Composite Costing :**

   It is an application of more than one method of cost ascertainment in respect of the same product. This method is used in industries where a number of components are separately manufactured and then assembled into a final product. In such industries each component differs from the others as to price, material used and process of manufacture undergone. So it will be necessary to ascertain the cost of each component. For this purpose, process costing may be applied. To ascertain the cost of the final product, batch costing may be applied. This method is used in factories manufacturing cycles, automobiles, engines, radios, TVs, typewriters, aeroplanes etc. This method has been completely dropped from the latest I.C.M.A. Terminology.

5) **Class Cost Method :**

   It is the method of Job Costing, where the costing of goods is done by classes instead of the unit or price. Instead of the cost being separately accumulated for each article or piece, the cost will cover a group of orders of the same class of a product.

(B) Operation Costing

The terminology of I.C.M.A., defines **Operation Costing** as *"the category of basic costing methods applicable where standardised goods or services result from a sequence of repetitive and more or* *less continuous operations or process to which costs are charged before being averaged over the units produced during the period".*

The following are the different methods of costing which fall under this category.

1) **Process Costing :**

   The terminology of I.C.M.A. defines **Process Costing** as *"that form of operation costing which applies where the standardised goods are produced"*. It is a method of costing where cost is ascertained at the stage of every process and also after completing the finished production. It is used in concerns where production follows a series or sequential process. Process type of industries do not manufacture individual items to the specific requirements of customers. As such, production is not intermittent but continuous. Each process represents a distinct stage of manufacture and the output of one process becomes the input of the following process. The unit cost is arrived at by averaging the cost over the units produced, and cost per unit of each process is ascertained. Process Costing is used in a variety of industries such as chemicals, oil refining, paper making, flour milling, cement manufacturing, sugar, rubber, textiles, soap, glass, food processing etc.

2) **Operating or Service Costing :**

   The terminology of I.C.M.A., defines **Service Costing** as *"that form of Operation Costing which applies where – standardised services are provided either by an undertaking or by a service cost centre within an undertaking"*. This method of costing is used by those undertakings which render services as against manufacturing and supply of tangible products. It is an essential method of costing, where only the services are rendered. It ascertains the cost of one unit of service rendered. This method is applicable to transport undertakings, electricity supply undertakings, hospitals, hotels, canteen, water works, gas companies, educational institutions etc. The cost unit depends upon the service provided. Usually, a composite cost unit is used. For example, tonne km., passenger km, patient day or bed day, kWH, meal served, student hours etc.

3) **Unit or Single or Output Costing :**

   It is a method of costing by the unit of production, where manufacturing is continuous and the units are identical. In some cases, the units may differ in terms of size, shape, quality etc. This method is also called as 'Single Costing' because only one type of product alone is manufactured. Examples of industries where this method is applicable are : Collieries, quarries, flour-mills, paper mills, textile mills, brick-making, radio, cameras, pencils, slates, diary products etc. No separate set of books is generally required and costing information is presented in the form of a statement known as Cost Sheet.

4) **Departmental Costing :**

   A factory may be divided into a number of departments and sometimes good results are obtained by allocating expenditure first to different departments and then to different products manufactured in that department. Under this method, the cost incurred in maintaining a particular department is ascertained. There are two objectives for using this method viz., to control the cost of department and to charge the cost of a department or to the finished product.

5) **Operation Costing :**

It is a special type of Process Costing. It refers to the determination of cost of operations, the cost unit is the 'operation' instead of the process. The per unit cost is arrived at by dividing the cost of an operation by the number of units completed in the operation centre. For large undertakings, it is frequently necessary to ascertain the cost of various operations. Cost control can be exercised more effectively with operation costing.

3.1 JOB COSTING

3.1.1 Meaning

The industries which manufacture articles or products or render services against specific orders, use the Job costing method for ascertaining the cost per job or service. e.g., specific requirement of a customer, fabrication, repairs etc. Each job has a separate identity. Under this method, individual jobs are identifiable and each job becomes a separate cost centre. I.C.M.A. London, defines **Job Costing** as *"it is that category of basic costing method which is applicable where the work consists of separate contract, jobs or batches each of which is authorised by specific order or contract"*. Examples of job order industries are printing press, construction of buildings, bridges, ship-building, furniture-making, machine tool manufacturing repair shops, painting works etc.

3.1.2 Features

The important **features of Job Costing** are as follows :
i) Production is made or services are rendered against specific orders.
ii) A Job is clearly identifiable throughout the production process.
iii) Each job has its own characteristics and requires special attention.
iv) A distinguishing number is allotted to each Job order undertaken.
v) Each of the job becomes a separate cost centre.
vi) Costs are charged directly to individual job orders.
vii) The manufacturing cost of a Job order can be found out only after the Job order is completed, irrespective of the time taken for the same.
viii) Production is not made in anticipation of demand and for storing purpose.

3.1.3 Advantages

The important **Advantages of Job Costing** are as follows :
i) Cost of each job as per order is ascertained separately. This helps in finding out the profit or loss on each individual job.
ii) It enables the management to detect those jobs which are more profitable and those which are not profitable.
iii) It provides a basis for determining the cost of similar jobs undertaken in future. It thus helps in future production planning.
iv) It enables the management to know the trends in costs.
v) Profitability ratio of different jobs can be found out.
vi) It helps the management to fix selling price of specific job on the basis of costs.
vii) It enables the management to provide quotations for similar type of jobs.
viii) Spoilage and defective work can be easily identified with specified jobs or products.
ix) It enables the management to take corrective steps for improving the efficiency in future.
x) It is essential for cost plus contracts.

3.1.4 Limitations

The important **Limitations of Job Costing** are as follows :

i) Calculations are more and hence there is possibility of errors which may cause a serious loss.

ii) A system of budgetary control may not be used effectively.

iii) The system does not indicate any standard of performance efficiency.

iv) Comparison of cost of a job over any period of time cannot be made if certain economic changes takes place in between.

v) It is expensive to operate as there is increase in clerical works.

vi) Job costing comes under historical costing which ascertains the cost of job or product after it has been manufactured.

Procedure followed in Job Costing :

Job Costing is designed to show in detail their cost components of the total cost executing a job. A Job Cost sheet is prepared for every job which is undertaken. Material Cost is accounted for in the job cost sheet on the basis of material requisition concerned. Labour cost on the basis of time clocked in respect of the job with the help of time tickets and factory overheads are added to those cost components, according to some reasonable methods of overhead absorption. Thus, the total cost of the job consists partly of direct cost and partly of costs arrived at by assignments, allocation, apportionment and finally by absorption. Thus, the **procedure for Job Order Cost System** may be summarised as follows :

i) **Receiving an Enquiry :**

Before placing an order with the manufacturer, usually the customer will enquire about the price, quality to be maintained, the duration within which the order is to be executed and other specifications of the job.

ii) **Estimation of the price of the job :**

The cost accountant estimates the cost of Job after considering the various elements of costs and keeping in mind the specification of customers. This is based on the cost of execution of similar Job in the previous year and considering the possible changes in the various element of costs. The estimated cost of the job is then communicated to the prospective customer.

iii) **Receiving of Order :**

If the prospective customer accepts the quotation, the intention of acceptance is forwarded to the respective departments, so that preparation work may begin even before the issue of the formal Production Order. The production control department receives the order.

iv) **Job Number :**

When an order has been accepted, an individual work order number must be assigned to each such Job, so that separate orders are capable of being identified at all stages of production. Assignment of Job numbers also facilitates reference for costing purposes in the ledger and convenient for use in various forms and documents.

v) Production Order :

Once the job is accepted the Planning department prepares Production Order. The Production Order is nothing, but a form of instructions issued to the foreman to proceed with the manufacture of the articles. Several copies of Production Order are prepared and passed on to the following :

- All departmental foremen connected with the job.
- Store-keeper for issuance of materials.
- Tool room – an advance notification of tools required.

A Production Order contains all the information that is relevant to the job or products or service. It gives information about the following :

- Particulars of job, product or service.
- Quantity to be produced.
- Date of starting and required date of completion of the job.
- Particulars of materials required.
- Particulars of various operations involved in the performance and execution of the job.

The Figure 3.2 shows a specimen form of Production Order for a job which is as follows :

PRODUCTION ORDER

Name of Customer	....	Job No.	....
Date of Commencement	....	Date	....
Date of Completion	....	Bill of Material No.	....
Special Instructions	....	Drawing attached-Yes/No.	....

Quantity (Units)	Description	Machines to be used	Tools required

sd./-
....
Production Authorised by :
Head of Production Control Dept.

Production Order for a Job

The columns provided in the Production Order differ widely, depending largely upon the nature of production. Some orders are accompanied by the blue prints and contain a bill of materials and detailed instructions as to which tools and machineries are to be used.

(vi) Recording of Costs :

There are various costs required for the job. The raw materials, the labour costs, overhead charges etc., are directly chargeable to that particular production order number. General Job Cost Sheet is prepared for each job.

The basis of collection of costs are :
- **Materials :** Materials Requisition, Bills of Materials or Material Issue Analysis Sheet.
- **Wages :** Operation Schedule, Job Card or Wages Analysis Sheet.
- **Direct Expenses :** Direct Expenses Vouchers.
- **Overheads :** Standing Order Number or Cost Account Number.
- **Completion of Job :** On completion of the Job, report is sent to the Costing Department. The expenditure under each element of cost is totalled and the total Job cost is ascertained.

(g) Profit or Loss on Job : It is determined by comparing the actual expenditure of costs with the price obtained.

The Figure 3.2 is a diagram showing **Job Order Execution Procedure** which is as follows.

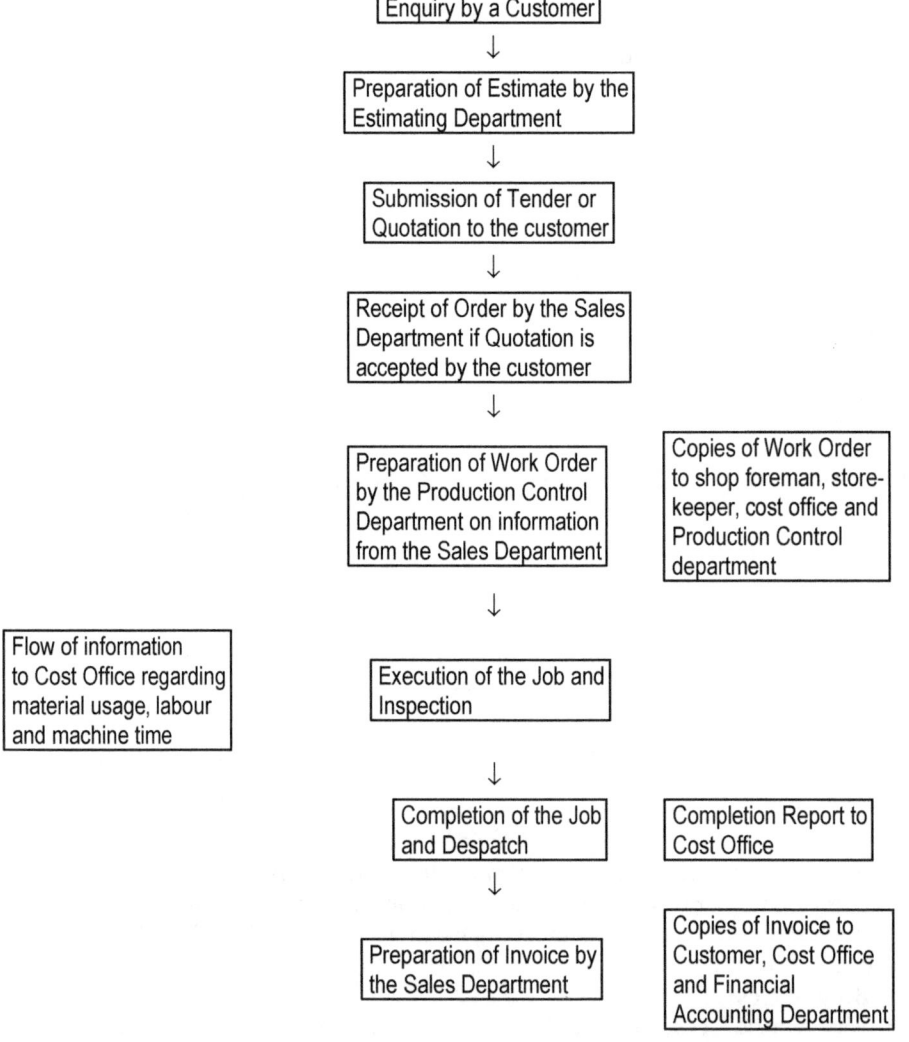

Fig. 3.2 : Job Order Execution Procedure

Preparation of Job Cost Sheet :

A **Job Cost Sheet** is a cost statement prepared to analyse and ascertain the actual cost incurred with respect to the individual jobs. Thus, a card for each Job is maintained where in the total cost of the job is accumulated. A separate Job Cost Sheet is prepared to find out profit or loss on each job. It records the actual costs incurred on direct material, direct labour, direct expenses and overheads on the Job passing through the factory. The total constitutes the cost of the Job Order or operation. **Cost of Material Consumed** is collected from invoices and material requisition note. **The Direct Labour Cost** is found out by operating each workmen's wages according to the time he spends on each job, as recorded on job sheets. **Overheads** may be allocated as a simple percentage of material cost or by some other method as is appropriate and practicable for the organisation concerned. On completion of a job the various elements of costs are summed together and the total cost is ascertained. The total cost is then divided by the number of jobs completed or units produced to ascertain the cost per job or unit.

The specimen of Job Cost Sheet which is as follows :

JOB COST SHEET

Customer .... Job No. ....
Date of Commencement .... Date of Completion ....

Material Cost			Labour Cost				Factory Overheads (Absorbed)			
Date	Material Req. No.	Amount ₹	Date	Hours	Rate ₹	Amount ₹	Date	Hours	Rate ₹	Amount ₹
Total			**Total**				**Total**			

Profit or Loss		Cost Summary		
	₹			₹
Price Quoted	......	Material		
Less : Cost	......	**Add :** Labour	(+)	
	------	**Add :** Factory Overhead	(+)	
		Add : Administration Overhead	(+)	
Profit or Loss	......	**Add :** Selling Overhead	(+)	
	------		**Total Cost**	———

Job Cost Sheet

Forms used in Job Costing :

Following are the various forms used in Job Costing method :

- **Production Order :** It is a written authority to factory foreman to proceed with the job.
- **Bill of Materials :** It is a complete schedule of materials, parts etc., required for a particular Job or Production order.

- **Operation Schedule :** There are various operations of a Job for e.g., turning, drilling, milling, assembling etc. It contains name of Job, Name of operation, Description of operation, Starting time and Completion time etc.
- **Tool List :** It is a list of all types of tools required for a particular job. It is given alongwith the schedule and instruction cards.
- **Planning Board :** It is nothing, but a time-table of a particular job to be done. It sets the time for processing the various jobs.
- **Move Tickets :** There are various steps in completion of the job. There is a progress of each job which is checked off on the operations schedule. The move tickets are sent alongwith each lot at the time of transfer to the next department.

3.2 CONTRACT COSTING

Meaning

Contract Costing is a special type of Job Costing where the unit of cost is a single contract. It is a further development of Job Costing. In this method, it is desired to find out the cost of carrying out a complete contract for a customer involving numerous jobs and batches of jobs. The costs are ascertained and analysed with respect to the contract accepted for execution. This method of costing is adopted by those concerns undertaking definite contracts for e.g., builders, contractors and civil engineers who undertake long-term projects like construction of roads, bridges, houses, large estates, irrigation schemes etc. It is also adopted by the concerns where the unit of output is heterogeneous for e.g., ship building companies, turbines and boilers manufacturing company motion pictures etc. The terminology of I.C.M.A., defines Contract Costing as *"that form of specific order costing which applies where work is undertaken to customers special requirements and each order is of long duration"*. It is also known as 'Terminal Costing' because when the work is terminated, the Job Cost sheet has to be completed.

Features

The important **Features of Contract Costing** are as follows :

i) The work is carried out away from the contractor's premises.

ii) A contract is usually of long-duration and may continue for over more than one accounting period.

iii) As the contracts are of large size, a contractor usually carries out a small number of contracts in the course of a year.

iv) Cost unit in contract costing is a contract.

v) A separate account is prepared for each contract to ascertain profit or loss on each contract.

(vi) Most of the materials are specially purchased for each contract.

vii) Expenses chargeable to contracts are direct in nature, for e.g., electricity, telephone charges, insurance etc.

viii) Specialist sub-contractors may be employed for say, electrical fittings, welding works, glass work, plumbing work etc.

ix) Plant and equipment may be purchased or hired for the duration of the contract.

x) Nearly all labour will be direct.

xi) The payment is received depending on the stage of completion of work.

xii) A contract usually includes clause for 'penalty' for delayed completion.

xiii) A contract usually includes 'Escalation Clause' under which the contractor is compensated for increase in costs on account of inflation.

xiv) A percentage of the value of work done is deducted from the progress payment as 'Retention Money'.

Difference between Job Costing and Contract Costing

	Job Costing		Contract Costing
i)	A job is small in size.	i)	A contract is big in size.
ii)	Work under job costing is performed in the premises of the manufacturer.	ii)	A contract is executed generally in the premises of the customer i.e. (contractee).
iii)	A job usually takes less time to complete.	iii)	A contract takes more time to complete.
iv)	The selling price is paid after completing the job in full.	iv)	The price is paid in various instalments depending upon the progress of work.
v)	Job Costing involves heavy investment on assets initially.	v)	Investment on assets in Contract costing is less than compared to Job costing.
vi)	Expenses under job costing takes the form of both direct and indirect.	vi)	Under contract costing, most of the expenses are direct in nature.
vii)	Profit carried on Job is entirely taken to Profit and Loss Account.	vii)	In case of incomplete contract, only proportionate profit is taken to Profit and Loss Account.
viii)	The number of Jobs in hand may be large.	viii)	Number of contract that may be undertaken at a time may be few.

Procedure of preparing Contract Account :

The preparation of Contract Account is the essence of Contract Costing. The Contract Account is prepared by the contractor in his books. In addition to this account, he prepares Contractee's Account also. A separate account is opened for each contract. The purpose of Contract Account is to know the profit or loss on every contract executed. The basic procedure for costing of contract is as follows :

i) **Contract Account Number :**

Each contract is allotted a distinct number in order to distinguish it from other contracts. A separate account is opened for each contract.

ii) **Direct Costs :**

Most of the costs of a contract can be allocated direct to the contract. All such direct costs are **debited** to the Contract Account.

Direct costs for contracts include Materials, Labour Cost, Direct Expenses, Depreciation of Plant and Machinery and Sub-Contract Costs.

iii) **Indirect Costs :**

Contract Account is also **debited** with overheads which tends to be small in relation to direct costs. Such costs are often absorbed on some arbitrary basis as a percentage of prime cost, materials, wages etc. Overheads are normally restricted to head office and storage costs.

iv) **Transfer of Materials or Plant :**

When materials, plant or other items are transferred from the contract, the Contract Account is **credited** by that amount.

v) **Contract Price :**

The Contract Account is also credited with the contract price. In some of incomplete contract, the Contract Account is **credited** with the value of work-in-progress as on that date.

vi) **Profit or Loss on Contract :**

The balance of Contract Account represents profit or loss which is transferred to Profit and Loss Account. In case of incomplete contract, only a part of profit arrived is taken into account and remaining profit is kept as reserve to meet any contingent loss on the incomplete portion of the contract.

3.2.1 Basic Concepts

The **basic concepts used in Contract Costing** are as follows :

i) **Material Cost :**

The material required for the contract are **debited to Contract Account** which includes :

- Materials specifically purchased for the contract.
- Materials issued from stores against requisition.
- Materials urgently required transferred from another contract.

On completion of the contract, the following types of materials should be **credited to Contract Account**.

- Materials returned to store.
- Materials in hand on site at the end of the accounting period.
- Materials transferred to another contract.
- Sale of materials.

Any profit or loss arising out of such materials transactions must be recorded from Profit and Loss Account. Following are certain items of losses which should be **debited to Profit and Loss Account** and should be **credited to Contract Account**.

- Loss on sale of materials.
- Materials which are stolen destroyed by fire.
- Materials lost in accidents.
- Cost of defective materials.

ii) **Labour Cost :**

All labour actually engaged at contract site is regarded as direct labour, irrespective of the nature of the tasks performed by the workers concerned and charged to the contract. The exact labour cost that should be **debited to Contract Account**, thus includes the total remuneration paid and payable to all workers engaged on contract at the end of the accounting period.

iii) **Other Direct Expenses :**

All other expenses incurred directly for the contract should be **debited to Contract Account**. for e.g., Architect's or Surveyors fee, Sub-contract costs, hire charges of Plant and Machinery etc.

iv) **Overhead Costs :**

There are some common indirect expenses incurred for various contracts, which cannot be charged directly to the individual contract. These expenses are divided into works expenses, office expenses and are distributed to various contracts on some appropriate basis. The ultimate proportionate industry expenses paid or payable should be **debited to Contract Account** i.e. head office expenses, expenses of central stores, establishment charges etc.

v) **Plant and Machinery Costs :**

In every Contract work, some special plant, heavy machines and special tools are usually employed. The Plant and Machinery cost represents the cost for the use of Plant and Machinery and tools for the contract. These costs are treated in Contract Account with the following alternative methods.
- If Plant and Machinery and tools are used for the contract only for **a short period**, **Contract Account may be debited** with the amount of depreciation on it.
- If Plant and Machinery and tools are used for the contract for **a long period**, the full amount of it may be **debited to Contract Account** at the end of the accounting period or on completion of the contract, the residual or written down value of it may be **credited to the Contract Account**.

vi) **Sub-Contract Cost :**

If the contractor has entrusted some special work to some expert sub-contractor, the costs incurred for such sub-contract is treated as a direct charge to the contract and hence should be **debited to Contract Account**. For e.g., A building contractor may entrust the following types of specialised jobs to the sub-contractors such as task of digging foundations, electrical installation, specialised flooring, installation of lifts, painting work, plumbing work etc.

vii) **Cost of Additional Work :**

If a contractor is asked to do some extra work or alteration in the work which is not included in the original contract, the cost of such additional work may be charged separately to the contract as follows :
- If the additional work is substantial and the amount involved is large, it is better to treat the same as a subsidiary contract and a **separate Contract Account** should be operated for the same.
- If the additional work is not substantial, its cost should be **debited to Contract Account** and should be added to the contract price.

viii) **Escalation Clause :**

Normally, a contract takes fairly a long period to complete the same. Due to the ever increasing tendency of rising prices, it becomes necessary to incorporate a clause in the contract to cover up likely charges in the price or utilisation of material and labour.

Hence, an "**Escalation Clause**", is inserted in the contract agreement to avoid the element of risk and to protect the interests of both the parties against unfavourable changes in prices. It is also provided where the material quantities or labour time cannot be properly assessed, unless the actual work is sufficiently advanced. Under this clause the contractor is authorised to increase the contract price if the prices of materials, labour, plant increases beyond a specific point or if there is a change in the utilisation factors of production. Also there may be a reverse clause providing for reduction in the contract price in case of falling prices to protect the interest of the contractee viz. **de-escalation clause.**

ix) **Architect's Certificate :**
In case of a large contract which takes a long period, it is a normal practice for the contractor to get interim advanced payments against the actual portion of contract completed by him. The contractee appoints the architect or surveyor or engineer who works as a technical assessor and issues the certificate as to the value of work so far performed. Thus, as per the contract agreement the periodical payment is made to the contractor on the basis of such an architects certificate.

x) **Retention Money :**
It is a common practice to include the clause of retention money in the contract agreement. Under this clause, the contractee will not make payment of the work certified by the architect, but a certain portion thereof shall be retained by him which is called retention money. The object of this retention money is to place the contractee in a favourable position in case of faulty work or penalty payable by the contractor. This amount will be paid to the contractor after the satisfactory completion of the work depending upon the terms of the contract.

xi) **Work Certified :**
It is the cost of that part of the contract work which is being completed by the contractor for which a completion certificate has been issued by the contractee's architect. The amount of work certified is **debited to Contractee Account** and **credited to Contract Account.**

xii) **Work Uncertified :**
It is the cost of that part of the contract work which is being completed by the contractor, but not certified by the architect because of the faulty work or the work not according to the specifications. In respect of such work, there will be no payment from the contractee. The cost price of each work is **debited to Work-in-Progress Account** and **credited to Contract Account.**

xiii) **Profit on Incomplete Contracts :**
If contracts are started and completed during the same accounting year, there is no problem as regards profit computation. But in case of those contracts which take more than one accounting year, a problem arises whether profit on such contracts should be worked out only on the completion of the contract or at the end of each accounting year on the partly completed work. If profit is computed only on the completion of the contract, profit will be high in the year of completion of the contract, whereas in other years of working on contract, profit will be nil. This would result not only in distorted profit patterns, but also higher tax liability became income tax at higher rates may have to be paid. Hence, when contracts extends beyond a year, it becomes necessary to take into account the profit earned (or loss incurred) on the work performed during each year. This helps in avoiding distortion of the year to year profit trend of the business.

There are two aspects of profit computation.
a) Computation of estimated or notional profit at the end of the year when contract is not complete.
b) Computation of the portion of such profit to be transferred to Profit and Loss A/c.

The amount of profit that is to be credited to Profit and Loss Account depends upon the fact that how far the contract has advanced.

There are no hard and fast rules in this regard. However, the following are the conventional norms for determining the profit to be taken to the Profit and Loss Account at different stages of completion.

a) It should be noted that the profit should be considered in respect of work certified only. Work certified should always be valued at cost.
b) If a very small portion of the work has been done, it is neither desirable nor sound to take into account profit on the work done and the Contract Account must then be **closed by balance.** In such a case, the amount expended on account of the contract to the date of balancing will be shown as **Work-in-Progress** on the asset side of the Balance Sheet and any cash received from the contractee on account of work will be shown by way of **deduction** therefrom.

No definite rule can be laid down as to what stage of the work it would be safe to take credit for the profit on incomplete contract. But the general rule may be laid down is that **no profit should be ascertained, unless at least one fourth or less of the whole work has been completed.**

c) When the work certified is **25% or more, but less than 50%** of the contract price, profit to be taken to the credit of Profit and Loss Account will be computed as follows :

$$= \text{Notional Profit} \times \frac{1}{3} \times \frac{\text{Cash Received}}{\text{Work Certified}}$$

d) When the work certified is **50% or more but not less than 90%** of the contract price, profit to be taken to the credit of Profit and Loss Account will be computed as follows :

$$= \text{Notional Profit} \times \frac{2}{3} \times \frac{\text{Cash Received}}{\text{Work Certified}}$$

e) When contract is **near completion**, then the estimated profit should be calculated as the whole contract. This is computed as follows :

	₹
Contract Price	....
Less : Total Expenditure to date	
Less : Estimated Additional Expenditure	....
Estimated Profit	....

The profit to be taken to the credit of Profit and Loss Account will be computed by applying any of the following formula :

- $\text{Estimated Profit} \times \dfrac{\text{Work Certified}}{\text{Contract Price}}$

- $\text{Estimated Profit} \times \dfrac{\text{Work Certified}}{\text{Contract Price}} \times \dfrac{\text{Cash Received}}{\text{Work Certified}}$

OR

$\text{Estimated Profit} \times \dfrac{\text{Cash Received}}{\text{Contract Price}}$

- Estimated Profit × $\dfrac{\text{Cost of Work to date}}{\text{Estimated Total Cost}}$

- Estimated Profit × $\dfrac{\text{Cost of work to date}}{\text{Estimated Total Cost}} \times \dfrac{\text{Cash Received}}{\text{Work Certified}}$

f) **For Loss on incomplete contracts :** If the cost of work certified exceeds the value of certificate loss is incurred. The whole amount of such loss is to be charged to Profit and Loss Account. The entry will be passed as follows :

Profit and Loss A/c   ... Dr.

     To Contract A/c

xiv) **Cost Plus Contracts :**

This is a modified method of Contract Costing. Under this the contractee agrees to pay to the contractors the actual cost of work done plus an agreed percentage, thereof, to cover overhead expenses and profits. Cost plus contract method is generally employed in those cases.

- Where the estimated cost of contract cannot be ascertained accurately because of the frequent changes in the prices of materials and labour rates.
- Where the work to be done is not fixed at the time of placing the contract.
- When the contract is totally new to the contractor.
- Where the contract requires fairly a long period to complete the same.

This method is commonly used in the manufacturing of exceptional articles produced very rarely, for e.g., aircraft component, urgent repairing of power house, constructions during war time etc.

Advantages to the Contractor :

- The Contractor will not suffer any risk of loss as he will receive the contract price as is assured by the contractee.
- There is bargain in the contract price in future under this type of contract.
- The contractor is relieved from the botheration of preparing quotation price for the sake of submitting it to the contractee.

Advantages to the Contractee :

- Since the contract price is governed by the contract, the contractee will also not suffer from any risk of loss.
- The contractee also stands to benefit in a period of uncertain market condition as he is expected to pay only a reasonable price after satisfying the ruling prices.

Disadvantages to the Contractor :

- No efforts are taken by the contractor for cost reduction. Hence, it leads to inefficiencies.
- The profit percentage, though fixed, will necessarily vary in amount, since it depends upon the increase in cost.
- The percentage of profit may either be excessive or inadequate to cover the overhead expenses also.

Disadvantages to the Contractee :

- This method is not desirable from the point of view of the contractee because the price to be paid depend upon the cost of contract.
- Till complete execution of the contract, he cannot estimate his commitment accurately.

xv) **Valuation of Work-in-Progress :**

Contracts in progress mean contracts which have not yet, been completed. Such incomplete contracts are also referred to as 'Work-in-Progress'. All the expenditure incurred on such inomplete contracts should be shown on the asset side of the Balance Sheet under the heading 'Work-in-Progress'. Where profit is taken in respect of incompleted contract, the work-in-progress stated in the Balance Sheet should also include the profit i.e. valuation of work-in-progress is done by adding the profit to the cost of the contract. It should be shown as follows :

Balance Sheet – Asset Side

Work-in-Progress :

Cost of Contract till date –

- Cost of Work Certified ......
- Cost of Work Uncertified ......

......

Add : Profit taken to Profit and Loss Account (+) ......

......

Less : Cash Received from the contractee (−) ....

OR

Work-in-Progress Account :

- Cost of Work Certified (+) ......
- Cost of Work Uncertified (−) ....

Less : Reserve for unrealised profit (−)
Less : Cash received from contractee (−) ....

|Journal Entries|

i) **For materials issued to Contract :**
　　Contract A/c　　　　　　... Dr.
　　　　To Materials A/c

ii) **For surplus materials transferred to another Contract :**
　　Receiving Contract A/c　　... Dr.
　　　　To Supplying Contract A/c

iii) **For expenses incurred or payable on contract :**
　　Contract A/c　　　　　　... Dr.
　　　　To Expenses A/c
　　　　To Outstanding Expenses A/c

iv) **For Plant and Machinery and Equipments (at cost) issued to contract :**
    Contract A/c   ... Dr.
        To Plant and Machinery/Equipment A/c

v) **For share of apportioned Overhead Expenses :**
    Contract A/c   ... Dr.
        To Overhead A/c

vi) **For sub-contract cost :**
    Contract A/c   ... Dr.
        To Sub-contract A/c

vii) **For materials at site at the end / materials returned to stores/supplier :**
    Materials A/c or Material Returned A/c   ... Dr.
        To Contract A/c

viii) **For Plant and Machinery and Equipment at site at the end at written down value :**
    Plant and Machinery A/c/Equipment A/c   ... Dr.
        To Contract A/c

ix) **For Work Certified :**
    Contractee's A/c   ... Dr.
        To Contract A/c

x) **For Work Uncertified :**
    Work-in-Progress A/c   ... Dr.
        To Contract A/c

xi) **For cash received against Work-Certified from Contractee :**
    Bank A/c   ... Dr.
        To Contractee's A/c

xii) **For materials / plant sold at site at profit :**
    Bank A/c   ... Dr.
        To Contract A/c (cost of material/plant)
        To Profit and Loss A/c (with Profit on sale)
    If there is a loss, the above entry will be reversed.

xiii) **For materials stolen or lost and Insurance Co. admitted claim for certain account :**
    Bank A/c   ... Dr.   (Recovery for Insurance Co).
    Profit and Loss A/c   ... Dr.   (Loss on material)
        To Contract A/c

xiv) **For Abnormal Loss of materials, Plant etc. on site :**
    Profit and Loss A/c   ... Dr.
        To Contract A/c

xv) **For Sale of scrap :**
    Bank A/c   ... Dr.
        To Contract A/c

xvi) **For Profit transferred to Profit and Loss A/c / Profit to be reserved :**
    Contract A/c   ... Dr.
        To Profit and Loss A/c   (with profit credited)
        To Work-in-Progress/Profit Reserve A/c   (with profit kept as Reserve)

Ledger Accounts

In the Books of a Contractor

Dr. Contractee's Account **Cr.**

Particulars	₹	Particulars	₹
		By Balance B/D	
		By Bank (Part payment)	
To Contract (Contract Price)			
To Balance C/D		By Bank (Final Payment)	

Contract Account

Particulars	₹	Particulars	₹
To Work-in-Progress (Opening): • Work-Certified • Work uncertified • Plant at Site • Materials at Site **Less:** Reserve **To Materials:** • From Stores • From outside (purchases) • From Other Contracts To Wages (including Outstanding) To Direct Expenses (including Outstanding) To Plant at Cost/Tools at Cost To Overheads (including outstanding) To Sub-contract costs To Cost of extra-work done To Profit and Loss A/c (Profit on sale, if any) To Notional Profit C/D * To Profit and Loss A/c $\left(\frac{1}{3} \text{ or } \frac{2}{3} \times \text{Notional Profit} \times \frac{\text{Cash Received}}{\text{Work Certified}}\right)$ To Work-in-Progress A/c (Reserve)		**By Materials:** • Returned to Store • Transferred to other contracts By Profit and Loss A/c (Loss on Sale, if any) By Plant returned to stores **Less** Depreciation By Profit and Loss (For items stolen/lost) **By Work-in-Progress A/c (Closing):** • Work Certified • Work Uncertified • Plant at site • Materials at site **OR** By Contractee's (with total contract price) (in case of contracts completed) By Notional Profit B/D	

3.3 PROCESS COSTING

3.3.1 Meaning

Process Costing refers to a method of accumulating cost of production by process. It represents a method of cost procedure applicable to continuous or mass production industries producing standard products. Costs are compiled for each process or department by preparing a separate account for each process.

According to I.C.M.A., Process Costing is *"that form of operating costing which applies where standardised goods are produced"*.

Kohler defines Process Costing as *"a method of cost accounting whereby costs are charged to processes or operations and averaged over units produced"*.

Like unit costing, Process costing is also a form of Operation costing as distinguished from Specific order costing. In case of Unit costing, production of a single product is brought about by setting up a separate plant. In the case of Process costing, however, production follows a series of sequential processes for either a single product or a limited range of product. The aim of process costing is to determine the total cost of each operation and to apply this cost to the product at each state of process. It will then be possible to ascertain cost per unit for each operation or process and in total. Process costing is suitable for a large number of industries like mines and quarries, cotton, wool and jute textiles, chemicals, soap-making, paper plastics, distilleries, oil refining, screws, bolts and revets, food products, dairy, breweries, sugar works, confectionaries, cement, flour mill or gas etc. In short, **Process Costing** is easily applicable to these industries where manufacture of product is of uniform standards and there is continuous production.

3.3.2 Features

The **important features of Process Costing** are as follows :
i) Each plant is divided into a number of process cost centres or departments and each such division is a stage of production or a process.
ii) The finished products are uniform in all respects such as shape, size, weight, quality, colour, chemical content etc. so unit cost is calculated by dividing the total cost by the number of units produced.
iii) Output of one process is the input of the next process.
iv) It is not possible to distinguish finished products, while they are in the stage of processing.
v) Costs follow the flow of production i.e. costs incurred in the earlier process are transferred to the later process alongwith the output.
vi) Total cost of the finished product in the last process is cumulative i.e. it comprises of costs of all processes.
vii) The cost of any particular unit is the average cost of manufacture over a period.
viii) Production of one article may give rise to two or more by-products.
ix) Occurrence of process losses, for e.g., evaporation, shrinkage, chemical reaction etc.
x) The semi-finished products are expressed in terms of complete products. This is technically termed as equivalent production.
xi) Production accumulated and reported by process.
xii) Production process is predetermined and a definite sequence of production is followed.
xiii) The unit of cost is the "process" under this method of costing.
xiv) The production is continuous and on large scale basis, in anticipation of demand.

Difference between Job Costing and Process Costing

	Job Costing		Process Costing
i)	Production is against specific orders and instructions from the customers.	i)	Production is in continuous flow and is for stocks.
ii)	Cost are determined separately for each unit or job.	ii)	Costs are compiled for each process or department and unit cost is the average cost.
iii)	Jobs are independent of each other.	iii)	Products loose their individual identity because of continuous flow.
iv)	Unit cost of a job is calculated by dividing the total costs incurred into the units produced in the lot or batch.	iv)	The unit of cost of a process is computed by dividing the total cost for the period into the output of the process during that period.
v)	Costs are ascertained when a job is complete.	v)	Costs are calculated at the end of the cost period.
vi)	Cost of a job is not transferred to another.	vi)	The cost of process is transferred to the next process.
vii)	There may or may not be work-in-progress at the beginning or at the end of the accounting period.	vii)	Due to continuous production, work-in-progress is a regular feature.
viii)	Cost control is comparatively difficult and needs more attention.	viii)	Production is standardised, making it comparatively easier to exercise cost control.
ix)	It requires more forms and documents.	ix)	It requires less paper work.
x)	Diversification is possible in Job Costing.	x)	Diversification is not possible under process costing unless altogether a new set of machineries are installed.
xi)	In Job Costing, reporting is after completion of job.	xi)	In Process Costing, reporting is progresswise and in respect of time.
xii)	Investment of capital is less.	xii)	Investment of capital is more.

Advantages

The **advantages of Process Costing** are as follows :
  i) It helps in computation of costs of the process as well as of the end product at short intervals.
  ii) Average costs of homogeneous products can easily be computed.
  iii) Allocation of expenses can be easily made and this results into more accurate costing.
  iv) It involves less clerical labour because of the simplicity of cost records.
  v) Quotation can be submitted more promptly with standardisation of processes.
  vi) Managerial control is possible by evaluating the performance of each process and by ascertaining the abnormal losses.
  vii) It is easier to establish the standards in case of continuous production. Hence, Standard costing system can be followed easily in process costing.
  viii) As cost of production is ascertained periodically, management is in a position to receive various reports periodically and review the progress and efficiency of the production process.

Disadvantages

The **disadvantages of Process Costing** are as follows :

i) The average cost ascertained under this method is not true cost per unit. As such, it conceals weaknesses and inefficiencies in processing.

ii) Since, it is based on historical costs, it has all the weaknesses of historical costing.

iii) The valuation of work-in-progress on the basis of the degree of completion may sometimes, be more of a guess work.

iv) The emergence of joint products may present the problem of apportionment of joint costs and if apportionment is not properly done cost results may not be accurate.

v) It may not always be possible to indicate the suitable units for showing quantity figures in process cost statements.

vi) It is very difficult to estimate the normal quantity loss in process.

vii) The method does not permit evaluation of efforts of individual workers or supervisors.

viii) It involves difficulty in ascertaining closing stock value when output of one process is transferred to another process at transfer price or market price.

Collection of Costs

The whole industry is divided into distinct processes to which all assets of direct material, direct labour, direct expenses and overheads are debited.

i) **Direct Materials :**
With the help of material requisition, costs of raw materials are **debited** to the process concerned.

ii) **Direct Labour :**
Wages paid to the labourers and other staff engaged in particular process are charged to the concerned process. Sometimes, many workers are engaged in more than one process, the gross wages paid concerned are to be allocated on the basis of time spent.

iii) **Direct Expenses :**
There are certain expenses chargeable to the process concerned for e.g., electricity bill, depreciation etc.

iv) **Overheads :**
There are many expenses which are incurred for more than two processes the total of such expenses may be apportioned either on a suitable basis or at a predetermined rate based on direct labour charges or prime cost etc.

Accounting Procedure

i) For the purpose of cost accounting, process industries are divided into departments, each department representing a particular process. A process may consist of a separate operation or series of operations. A foreman or supervisor is appointed for each department. He is responsible for efficient functioning of his department.

ii) A separate account is maintained for each process and it is **debited** with the value of raw material, labour and overheads relating to the process.

iii) Output is recorded in terms of units (e.g. tons, litres, kg., etc.) on daily, weekly or suitable periodical basis depending upon the processing time.

iv) Average cost per unit is found out by dividing the total cost of each process by total production of that process. In arriving at average unit costs / costs normal loss in production and incomplete units in the beginning and at the end of the period, are taken into consideration.
(v) Cost of previous process is transferred to the subsequent process, so that the total cost and unit cost of products are accumulated.
(vi) Products remaining unfinished in the process at the close of the period are to be assessed in terms of equivalent completed units on the basis of percentage/degree of completion.

In making process accounts, columns are generally provided on both debit side and credit side for total cost, per unit cost and for material quantities.

The Figure 3.3 indicates the diagram showing **Process Cost Flow** as follows.

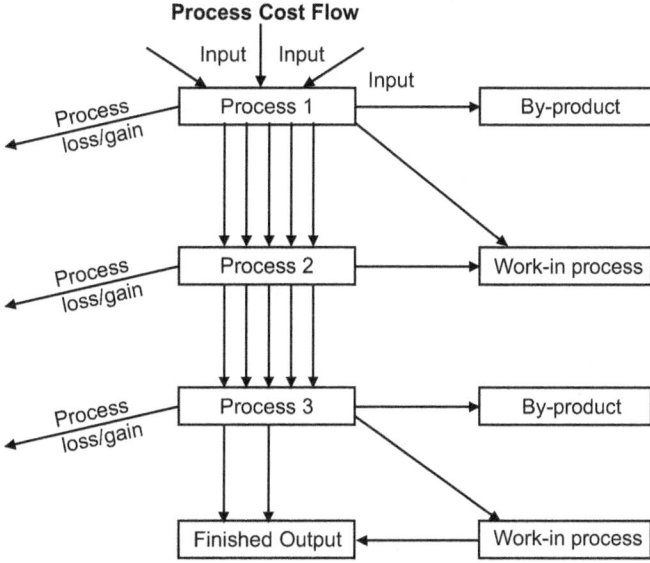

Fig. 3.3 : Process Cost Flow

3.3.3 Normal and Abnormal Loss or Gain

In many of the industries which employ Process Costing, a certain amount of loss or wastage occurs at various stages of production. This loss may be due to evaporation, chemical change, change in moisture content, carelessness, accident or any other reason. It is therefore, necessary to keep accurate records for both input and output of each process. Where loss occurs at a last stage of manufacture it is apparent that financial loss is greater than the mere cost of raw materials. This is because more and more labour and overhead are expanded in process as the products move towards completion stage.

The term **"Process loss"** may be defined *as the difference between the input quantity of raw material and the output quantity.*

The I.C.M.A., defines 'waste' and 'scrap' from the recovery value point of view as follows :

Waste : "Discarded substances having no value".

Scrap : "Discarded material having some recovery value which is usually disposed of without further treatment or re-introduced into the production process in the place of raw material".

Process losses and wastages are of two types viz. Normal Process Loss and Abnormal Process Loss.

Normal Loss

Normal Process Loss represents the loss which is expected under normal conditions. This type of loss is unavoidable and is inherent in the process of manufacture. It is often caused by factors such as evaporation, chemical change, withdrawals for test or sampling, unavoidable spoilage quantities or other physical reasons. It often includes scrap and waste. This type of losses can be estimated from the nature of materials, nature of operation, previous experience or technical data. Normal loss is generally calculated at a certain percentage of the input of units introduced in the respective process.

Accounting Treatment :

The normal process cost is borne by the good units produced.

$$\text{Unit Cost} = \frac{\text{Total Process Cost} - \text{Value of Normal Wastage}}{\text{Good Units Produced}}$$

The units of normal wastage are recorded on the credit side of a process account in quantity column only. The value of normal wastage, if any, should be included in the amount column on the credit side as saleable value. This reduces the cost of normal output. Process loss is shared by saleable units.

The accounting entries in respect of normal loss may be passed as follows :

- **For arising normal loss :**
  Normal Loss A/c   ... Dr.
      To Process A/c
- **For adjustment of the deficiency in the sale of normal loss :**
  Abnormal Gain A/c   ... Dr.
      To Normal Loss A/c
- **For sale of scrap, if any :**
  Costs A/c   ... Dr.
      To Normal Loss A/c

Abnormal Loss

Where the loss is caused by unexpected or abnormal conditions and if it is beyond limit, it is called "**Abnormal Loss**". In other words, any wastage arising in excess of the normal wastage is known as "Abnormal Wastage". It arises due to abnormal causes or unforseen factors. Use of defective materials, carelessness, fire, machine-breakdown, power failure, strike etc., may give rise to abnormal process losses.

Abnormal loss is avoidable. It can be controlled by the management by taking proper care. Units of abnormal loss is calculated as follows :

Units Introduced (entered)	......
Less : Normal loss in units	......
Normal Output	......
Less : Actual Output	......
Units of Abnormal Loss	......

Thus, in short, the difference between the normal output and the actual output is the abnormal loss where Normal Output = Units entered – Normal loss in units.

Accounting Treatment :

Accounting procedure for abnormal loss is different. Abnormal loss (wastage) is valued at the end at which the good units would be valued if there were only normal loss (wastage). The amount of abnormal loss is credited to a process concerned. A separate Abnormal Loss A/c is opened and the scrap value, if any, is credited to Abnormal Loss A/c and the balance on it ultimately transferred to Costing Profit and Loss Account. The value of abnormal wastage is calculated as follows :

$$\text{Value of Abnormal Loss (Wastage)} = \frac{\text{Normal Cost of Normal Output}}{\text{Normal Output}} \times \text{Units of Abnormal Loss}$$

[where,   Normal Cost   =   Total Process Cost − Value of normal loss, if any
                Normal Output   =   Units entered − Normal loss in units]

The Accounting entries may be passed as follows :

- **For the value of Abnormal Loss :**
  Abnormal Loss A/c   ... Dr.
       To Concerned Process A/c
- **If any amount is received from sale of scrap :**
  Cash/Bank A/c   ... Dr.
       To Abnormal Loss A/c
- **For Closing Abnormal Loss A/c**
  Costing Profit and Loss A/c   ... Dr.
       To Abnormal Loss A/c

Abnormal Gain

The Normal Loss is an estimated figure. The actual loss may be more or less than the normal loss. If the actual loss is more than the normal loss, it is treated as abnormal loss. But if the actual loss is less than the normal loss, it is known as **abnormal gain or abnormal effectives**. The abnormal gain is calculated in a similar manner as an abnormal loss.

Units of Abnormal Gain is to be calculated as under :

           Actual Output   ....
Less :   Normal Output   ....
           Units of Abnormal Gain   ....

           Normal Output   =   Units entered (Introduced) − Normal loss in units

Accounting Treatment :

Like Abnormal loss, Abnormal gain also does not affect the cost of normal output as this is also valued in the same manner as abnormal loss. The process account is **debited** with the quantity and value of Abnormal Gain, and Abnormal Gain A/c is credited. Finally, it is seen that the Process account is credited with the quantity and value of normal scrap. But the actual quantity is less. Hence, the difference is credited to Normal Loss Account by debiting the Abnormal Gain Account. Then, the balance to the credit of Abnormal Gain A/c is transferred to Costing Profit and Loss Account as Abnormal Gain.

The value of Abnormal Gain is calculated as follows :

$$\frac{\text{Value of}}{\text{Abnormal Gain}} = \frac{\text{Total Process Cost} - \text{Value of Normal Wastage}}{\text{Normal Units Produced}} \times \text{Units of Abnormal Gain}$$

The Accounting entries may be passed as follows :

- **For value of Abnormal gain :**
  Concerned Process A/c   ... Dr.
       To Abnormal Gain
- **For adjustment of scrap value of Abnormal gain :**
  Abnormal Gain A/c   ... Dr.
       To Normal Loss A/c

- **For Closing Abnormal Gain Account :**
    Abnormal Gain A/c
        To Costing Profit and Loss A/c

Dr.   Process Account   Cr.

Particulars	Quantity units	Cost per unit ₹	Amount ₹	Particulars	Quantity units	Cost per unit ₹	Amount ₹
To Earlier Process A/c (in the case of later Process A/c)	……….	……….	……….	By Normal Loss A/c (% of input)	……….	……….	……….
To Raw Materials	……….	……….	……….	By Loss in Weight		……….	
To Direct Labour (Wages)		……….	……….	By Scrap Value			……….
To Direct Expenses		……….	……….	By Sale of by-product	……….		……….
To Indirect Exp. (Overheads)	……….		……….	By Abnormal Loss A/c	……….	……….	……….
To Abnormal Gain	……….		……….	By Next Process A/c or Finished Stock A/c (In the case of last process)			
	……….	……….	……….		……….	……….	……….

Dr.   Normal Loss Account   Cr.

Particulars	Quantity Units	Amount ₹	Particulars	Quantity Units	Amount ₹
To Process A/c	…….	…….	By Abnormal Gain A/c	…….	…….
			By Cash (Sale)		…….
	…….	…….		…….	…….

Dr.   Abnormal Loss Account   Cr.

Particulars	Quantity Units	Amount ₹	Particulars	Quantity Units	Amount ₹
To Process A/c	…….	…….	By Cash (Sale)	…….	…….
			By Costing P & L A/c		
	…….	…….		…….	…….

Dr.   Abnormal Gain Account   Cr.

Particulars	Quantity Units	Amount ₹	Particulars	Quantity Units	Amount ₹
To Normal Loss A/c	…….	…….	By Process A/c	…….	…….
To Costing Profit and Loss A/c		…….			
	…….	…….		…….	…….

3.4 OPERATING COSTING

3.4.1 Meaning

Operating Costing is a method of costing to ascertain the cost of providing or operating a service. The cost of providing a service is termed as "Operating Cost". Operating Costing which is also known as "Service Costing" is defined by I.C.M.A., as, *"that form of operation which applies where standardised services are provided either by an undertaking or by a service cost centre within an undertaking"*. This method may be used where service is not completely standardised but where it is convenient to regard it as such, and to calculate average cost per period in relation to the standardised list of measurement. Thus, it is the cost of producing and maintaining a service.

Operating Costing should not be confused with Operation Costing. Operating Costing is applied to determine the cost of providing a service whereas Operation Costing is a refinement and more detailed application of Process Costing.

A Manufacturing process may sometimes be sub-divided into a number of parts, each of which is known as an Operation. **Operating Costing** is the determination of the cost of each operation which is a part of a process.

3.4.2 Features

The important **Features of Operating Costing** are as follows :
i) A uniform service is rendered to the customers.
ii) Many processes and stages are involved in converting the basic materials and facilities to the ultimate service rendered. These processes and operations are standardised, repetitive and continuous.
iii) Usually large plants are involved and the concerns are either large monopolistic units or public utility undertakings.
iv) The distinction between direct and indirect cost is largely unnecessary. The costs and expenses are traced to the individual plants or facilities which render the services. The cost of plant, transport vehicles and facilities is distributed to the volume of services rendered on a pro-rata basis.
v) The distinction between fixed cost and variable cost is extremely important as the economies of state of operations considerably affect the unit cost of the services.
vi) Optimum efficiency is considered by factors related to usage and idle capacity cost. This initially affects the pricing system of such services.
vii) Costs are usually computed periodwise. However, under special circumstances costs are computed orderwise in the case of utilisation of vehicles, use of road-roller etc.
viii) No difficulty arised in respect of valuation of work-in-progress or closing stock as compared to other industries.
ix) This method requires a more detailed, but simpler statistical data for proper costing.
x) Selection of cost unit is difficult in Operating Costing.

3.4.3 Objectives

The important **Objectives of Operating Costing** are as follows :
i) To calculate the cost of uniform service rendered to the customers.
ii) To ascertain cost of all services produced within an undertaking viz. internal and external services.

iii) To keep the operating cost at the optimum level.

iv) To make a comparative analysis of operating cost incurred for different periods.

v) To make proper evaluation of different alternatives available.

vi) To determine whether to produce a service or buy it from outside.

vii) To ascertain whether the cost incurred on maintenance is excessively incurred or not.

Applicability

Operating Costing is applied to those organisations which render service externally (i.e. to public at large) or internally (i.e. to various departments of the same organisation). Some examples of services rendered to outsiders are electricity supply, water supply, gas supply, lodging and boarding and so on. While services such as repairs and maintenance, purchasing and storage, internal transport etc. constitute services rendered internally. There is a point of difference in respect of accounting of services rendered. Whereas the objective of accounting external service is to know the total cost of manufacturing and profit on provision of such service, the object of internal service is to facilitate apportionment of service department cost to various other departments. Generally, Operating Costing is applied to the following undertakings :

- Transport undertakings such as Roadways, Railways, Tramways and Airways.
- Municipal services such as supply of water, street light etc.
- Steam and Electricity Undertakings.
- Hotels covering lodging and boarding.
- Hospitals.
- Educational Institutions.
- Public Libraries.
- Service departments in big factories.
- Cinemas.
- Distribution of gas, air compressor, air conditioning.
- Sports and Recreational clubs.
- Services such as supply cranes, road-roller, water pumping, fire, extinguishers etc.

The following steps are usually involved in Operating Costing.

I. Determination of Cost Unit :

A basic problem in Operating Costing is the adoption of the suitable cost units. A cost unit should be one which is related to the service rendered. Selection of cost unit depends upon the nature of business. Each undertaking is free to determine the cost unit most appropriate for its own purpose. However, a common cost unit by similar undertakings facilitates valuable cost comparisons. Selection of suitable cost unit depends on,

i) Management's need and requirement.

ii) Efforts involved in ascertainment of costs.

iii) Practice followed by other similar concerns.

iv) Practical use of the data for effective cost control.

Basics of Cost Accounting — Methods of Costing

Generally, the following are the two types of cost units :

i) **Simple Cost Unit :** In this type, one unit is considered for measurement of cost.

Undertaking	Cost Unit
• Transport	• Per km or Per passenger or Per tonne
• School or College	• Per student
• Hospital	• Per Bed
• Canteen	• Cup of tea sold / Meals served
• Electricity undertakings	• KWH
• Water supply	• A Gallon
• Gas supply	• Cubic Metre of Gas
• Boiler Home	• Quantity of Steam raised (kg.)
• Cinemas	• A seat per show

ii) **Composite Cost Unit :**

In this type, more than one units are combined together for measurement of cost.

Undertaking	Cost Unit
• Transport	• Per passenger km. or Per tonne
• Hospital	• Per bed per day
• Cinemas	• Per seat per show
• Electricity	• Per killowatt hour
• Canteen	• Per meal / Per cup of tea sold

II. Compilation of Costs :

In Operating Costing, costs are classified and compiled as follows :

A) Fixed Costs (Standing charges) :

These are constant costs and are incurred irrespective of the extent of service rendered. These include Garage Rent, Insurance, Road licence, Depreciation, Interest on capital, General supervision, Vehicle tax, Salary of Operating Manager, Establishment expenses of the work-shop and office, Wages of drivers and cleaners (if it is fixed on period basis) etc.

B) Maintenance Costs :

These are semi-variable in nature and include spare parts, repairs and maintenance, tyres and tubes, overheads, paintings etc.

C) Operating and Running Costs :

These are variable in nature and include cost of petrol and diesel, lubricating oil, grease, wages of drivers, conductors and cleaners (if payment is according to distance or trips), transit insurance, allowances to staff etc.

III. Determination of the cost per unit of service :

To ascertain cost per unit of service, it is necessary to divide total cost by the number of units of service.

Transport Costing :

In Transport undertaking, costing consists of the determination of the operating cost of each vehicle and the application of the cost, thus, determined to find out the cost per unit of service rendered by a vehicle. Transport includes Air, Water, Road, Railways and Motors. Motor transport includes private cars and carriers for owners, buses, taxies, carrier's lorries, etc.

Purposes :

Determination of Operating Costs for each vehicle serves the following **important purposes** :

i) Determining the price at which a vehicle should be hired out.

ii) Cost of running own vehicles may be compared with hired or other forms of transport.

iii) Comparison between owned transport and hired transport to decide whether it is economical to go in for a hired one.

iv) Determining the basis for charging departments using the service.

v) Control of operating and running costs and avoidance of waste of fuel and other consumable material.

vi) Suitable information is obtained for efficient routing of vehicles.

vii) Cost of idle vehicles and lost running time are easily obtained.

viii) The operational efficiency of transport services can be judged by utilisation ratio.

(ix) Determining the basis for quotations and fixing of rates.

x) Comparison between the cost of maintaining of one group of vehicles with another group.

xi) For deciding at what price the use of vehicle can be charged.

Classification of Costs :

The Operating costs of a transport undertaking composed of various items are classified under the following three categories :

A) Standing Charges :

Standing charges represent expenses which have to be incurred whether the vehicle operates or not. The vehicle may be idle, but even then its expenses have to be met. These are more or less fixed in nature in a transport company. The typical items of standing charges are : Road licence fees, Insurance premium, interest on capital, garage rent, depreciation, general supervision, vehicle tax, salary of operating manager establishment costs of workshop and head office, wages of drivers, conductors and cleaners etc.

B) Maintenance Charges :

These expenses are incurred on the repairs and maintenance of vehicles as to keep them in proper condition. They are semi-variable in nature and include the cost of tyres and tubes, repairs and maintenance, spares and accessories, overheads, painting etc.

C) Operating and Running Charges :

These are just the opposite of standing charges. These expenses are incurred on the actual running of vehicles. These vary from day-to-day and come to zero when the vehicles are off the road. These are variable in nature and include the cost of petrol and diesel, lubricating oil, grease, wages of drivers, conductors and attendants etc. (if payment is related to distance run or trips made or when drivers and cleaners are specially deployed to man specific vehicles, operating and running costs may be easily allocated to each vehicle).

Collection of Cost :

Cost accumulation procedure in operating costing is the same as in Job Order Costing. Each vehicle is given a distinct number and all the basic documents bear the assigned numbers. For cost ascertainment and cost control a separate Log Book is maintained for each vehicle. The Log Book gives performance statistics of each vehicle the details shown in the log book enable the management to make suitable allocation of vehicles, to avoid unnecessary or duplicate trips and to avoid waste or idle running capacity. It is usually divided into three parts. The first part gives the full description of the vehicle, for e.g., the name, its registration number, date of purchase, cost capacity, insurance policy number, amount of premium, taxes paid, estimated life and scrap value. These details facilitate – collection of fixed charges in respect of the vehicle.

The second part contains details relating to names and address of the driver, conductor, cleaner and mechanic, their salaries and wages, repairs and maintenance charges garage rent, renewals of tyres, batteries etc. these details facilitates collection of maintenance charges.

The third part of the Log Book contains - particulars of operating expense such as the number of trips made, number of kilometers run, petrol, oil, the ratio of kilometers run per litre of petrol hours lost due to the vehicle remaining idle, exceptional delays such as loading delays, traffic delays and accidents. Thus, this part gives the essential information for the computation and control of the operating costs.

The daily log sheet contains the same particulars as those in the third part of the log book. It is handed over to the transport manager. A specimen of Daily Log Sheet is given as under.

Daily Log Sheet

Vehicle No. ....
Route No. ....
Name and No. of Driver :
Registration/Licence No. : TRIP PARTICULARS
Date :
Time of leaving the garage :
Time of returning :

Trip No.	From	To	Tonnes or Packages — Out / Collected in route	Kilometres	Time — Out In	Remarks

Supplies	Worker's Time	Exceptional Delays
Petrol	Driver	Loading and Unloading
Oil	Conductor	Traffic delays
Grease etc.	Cleaner	Accidents
	Mechanic	Others

Daily Log Sheet

Operating Cost Sheet :

It is said that, "a well-designed cost sheet is the heart of transport costing". For collecting and controlling costs, costs are classified and accumulated under the three heads stated as above, suitably analysed and presented periodically in the form of an operating cost sheet. A specimen of Operating Cost Sheet is given as follows.

Roadways Transport Co., Ltd.
Operating Cost Sheet

Vehicle No. .... No. of Trips : Period :
Registration No. .... Kms. run : Capacity :
Route No. .... Total weight carried : No. of Cost units.
Cost : .... Total hours operated :
Estimated Life : ....

	Particulars		Total	Per Unit
A)	**Fixed Costs :**			
	Garage Rent			
	Licences and Taxes			
	Insurance			
	Interest on Capital			
	Supervision Charges			
	Establishment and General Charges	(+)		
	Sub-Total (A)		....	....
B)	**Maintenance Costs :**			
	Tyres and Tubes			
	Repairs and Maintenance			
	Spare Parts and Accessories			
	Overhauling			
	Painting	(+)		
	Sub-Total (B)		....	....
C)	**Operating and Running Costs :**			
	Depreciation			
	Petrol and Diesel			
	Oil and Grease			
	Transit Insurance			
	Wages of Drivers, Cleaners and Conductors	(+)		
	Sub-Total (C)	(+)	....	....
	Grand Total (A + B + C)		....	....
D)	Ton Km/Passenger Km. run			
E)	Cost per ton Km/passenger Km.			

Operating Cost Sheet

3.5 OPPORTUNITY COSTING

It refers to **Opportunity Cost** which may be assessed in the decision-making process of production. The **New Oxford American Dictionary** defines it as, "the loss of potential gain from other alternatives when one alternative is choosen". Thus, **opportunity costs** are not restricted to monetary or financial costs : the real cost of output forgone, lost time, pleasure or any other benefit that provides utility should also be considered opportunity cost.

The cost of an alternative that must be forgone in order to pursue a certain action. Put another way, the benefits you could have received by taking an alternative action. The formal definition of opportunity cost describes it as "the value of a benefit sacrificed in favour of a alternative course of action". It can be further described as "the amount earned or forgone by applying a unit of the resource under consideration in its next best alternative use.

Opportunity cost is what you have to forgo when you choose to do 'A' rather than 'B'. Opportunity cost is primarily on economic-based concept that emphasises the importance of the economic value attached to alternative courses of action - an approach which lies at the very root of management decision-making. The most important element of opportunity cost provides a further complement to the **relevant cost approach** developed in cost accounting.

In short, **opportunity cost** is a benefit sacrificed or the value of a resource in its next best alternative use i.e. the value of the displaced alternative. The sacrifice of a return or benefit from a rejected alternative is known as the opportunity cost of the alternative accepted. Opportunity cost are not entered in accounting records while, they are used in decision-making. For example,

i) The difference in return between a choosen investment and one that is necessarily passed-up. Say 'X' invest in a stock and it returns a partly 2% over the year. In placing his money in the stock, he has an opportunity of another investment - say a risk-free government (bond yielding 5%). In this situation, 'X' is opportunity costs are 3% (i.e. 5%-2%).

ii) Say, there may be an **opportunity** to make only one of the two different products with the available facilities. It may be estimated that product 'X' will contribute ₹ 36,000 a year to profits and on the other hand the product 'Y' will contribute ₹ 42,000, a year to profit. Here, product 'Y' should be selected and the opportunity cost of selecting product 'Y' is the sacrifice of ₹ 36,000 that could be earned by product X.

iii) Implicit cost are the opportunity costs in factors of production that a producer already owns.

iv) Explicit cost are the opportunity costs that are involved in direct monetary payment by producers.

QUESTIONS FOR SELF STUDY

I. **Theory Questions :**
   i) How a system of costing can be installed ?
   ii) Explain the basic need of various methods of ascertaining cost ?
   iii) "A standard method of costing cannot be used for all types of industries". Discuss.
   iv) What are the principal methods of costing ?
   v) What is 'Specific Order Costing' ? Explain the various methods classified under Specific Order Costing.
   vi) What is Job Costing ? Explain the important features of Job Costing.
   vii) What are the advantages and limitations of Job Costing ?
   viii) Explain the procedure involved in Job Costing.
   ix) Define 'Job Costing'. For what types of concerns is this method suitable ?
   x) Describe Job Costing System. Give a specimen of Job Cost Sheet.
   xi) Explain the various forms used in Job Costing Method.
   xii) Define 'Contract Costing'. Explain the distinguishing features of Contract Costing.
   xiii) What are the similarities and dissimilarities between Job Costing and Contract Costing ?
   xiv) Explain the basic procedure for costing of contract.
   xv) How would you treat the profit on incomplete contract ?
   xvi) Explain in detail the method of contract costing.
   xvii) How would you deal with the cost of additional work in Contract Costing ?
   xviii) What is 'Retention Money' ? Explain the objective of Retention Money.
   xix) Explain briefly the different methods of computing profits on contract, where work is not completed at the close of the accounting year.

xx) Is it desirable to take into account the profit on incomplete contracts in the Balance-Sheet ? If so, why and to what extent ?

xxi) What is Notional Profit ? Explain the rules for transfer of Notional Profit to Profit and Loss Account in Contract Costing.

xxii) What is 'Cost-plus-contract' ? Explain the main features of cost-plus-contract.

xxiii) What is work-in-progress ? How it is calculated in a Contract Account shown in the Balance-Sheet ?

xxiv) What is cost plus contract ? Explain the advantages and disadvantages to the contractor.

xxv) What is cost plus contract ? Explain the advantages and disadvantages to the contractee.

xxvi) "Both Job Costing and Contract Costing are forms of Specific Order Costing". Discuss.

xxvii) What is Sub-contract Cost ? How it is treated in Contract Account ?

xxviii) Define 'Process Costing' ? Describe the main features of Process Costing.

xxix) What is 'Process Costing' ? Mention the types of industries where process costing is applicable.

xxx) In what way does Process Costing differ from Job Costing ?

xxxi) Explain the advantages and disadvantages of Process Costing.

xxxii) Define 'Normal Loss'. Explain the accounting treatment of Normal Loss in Process Costing.

xxxiii) Define 'Abnormal Loss'. Explain the accounting treatment of Abnormal Loss in Process Costing.

xxxiv) Define 'Abnormal Gain'. Explain the accounting treatment of Abnormal Gain in Process Costing.

xxxv) Define 'Operating Costing'. Give the name of industries where it can be applied.

xxxvi) What is Operating Costing ? Explain the features of Operating Costing.

xxxvii) What is Transport Costing ? How costs are compiled in Transport Costing ?

xxxviii) What is Transport Costing ? What purposes are served in determination of the operating costs for each vehicle ?

xxxix) What is Operating Costing ? Prepare a proforma of operating cost sheet in Transport costing.

xxxx) Write short notes on :

a) Installation of costing system, b) Need of costing methods, c) Methods of costing, d) Job order costing, e) Features of job costing, f) Advantages of job order, g) Limitations of job costing, h) Production job order, i) Job cost sheet, j) Features of contract costing, k) Sub-contract cost, l) Cost of additional work, m) Escalation clause, n) Retention money, o) Architect's Certificate, p) Profit on incomplete contracts, q) Cost plus contracts, r) Work-in-progress, s) Features of Process costing, t) Advantages of Process costing, u) Abnormal loss, v) Abnormal gain, w) Notional profit, x) Features of operating costing, y) Transport costing, z) Opportunity costing.

xxxxi) Distinguish between :

a) Job Costing and Contract Costing, b) Work Certified and Work Uncertified, c) Escalation Clause and De-escalation Clause, d) Job Costing and Process Costing, e) Normal Loss and Abnormal Loss. f) Abnormal Loss and Abnormal Gain.

***

Unit ... 4

BUDGET AND BUDGETARY CONTROL

4.1 Meaning and Definitions

4.2 Objectives

4.3 Advantages and Disadvantages

4.4 Types of Budget

* Illustrations

* Questions for Self-Study

The **costing techniques** are generally considered as a basic requirement for many of the planning, control and decision-making activities, a manager faces. These techniques provide useful insights and guidelines for internal managerial tasks and purposes. For the purpose of cost control, costs should be pooled into separate variable and fixed totals. Separation of variable and fixed costs supports the use of standards, budgets and responsibility reporting to help management in controlling costs. Management requires knowledge of cost behaviour under various operating conditions and business decisions. The identification and classification of costs as either fixed or variable, with semi-variable expenses properly sub-divided into their fixed and variable components, provides useful framework for the accumulation and analysis of costs and further for making decisions. Budgeting acts as a tool of both planning and control. Standard Costing is also an important tool in planning, operating and control of a business enterprise. On the other hand, variable costing provides more useful information to management for pricing policies. Thus, costing techniques contributes significantly to management decision-making in different areas.

Figure 4.1 indicates certain important **techniques of costing** used by the management in the process of planning, controlling and decision-making which are as follows :

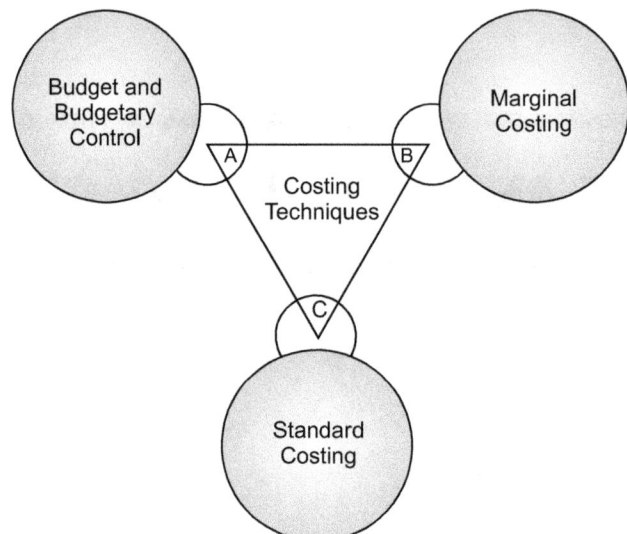

Fig. 4.1 : Costing Techniques

4.1 MEANING AND DEFINITIONS

A) Budget :

With growing complexity of business problems, new tools, techniques and procedures came to be evolved to aid managers in handling these problems effectively. **Budget** is one such managerial tool employed to chart future course of action and to co-ordinate and control business operations, so that financial objectives are accomplished. Budget is a short-term plan expressed in monetary terms, prepared and approved prior to a defined period of time, usually showing planned income to be generated and/or expenditure to be incurred during that period and the capital to be employed to achieve a given objective. It is a plan containing the strategies to be pursued during the budget and is prepared before the commencement of the budget period. Thus, plan is expressed mainly in financial terms, but also at times it incorporates many non-financial quantitative measures as well.

Hence, **Budget** is a written statement of plan which shows the policy and programme to be followed in future. It spells out goals laid down in advance by the top management for the business as a whole and for different departments as well as plan of operations. It is a statement of planned allocation of resources expressed in financial or numerical terms.

The term '**Budget**' refers to a statement showing the quantities and monetary values, relating to a specific period prepared in advance and indicating the future policy to be pursued by the organisation. Precisely, it is a plan of operation expressed in monetary terms covering a stipulated period. Policies are relatively clear guidelines or criteria for managerial decision-making, on major or day-to-day matters. The budget portrays a particular course of action contemplated by the management in carrying on the business. Generally speaking, these budgets are formulated on the basis of the forecasts prepared in the light of the past and present achievements. They are prepared to accomplish the desired objectives or goals. They serve as tools by means of which the management is able to obtain all the facts required for efficient management of the business.

The Institute of Cost and Management Accountants (UK) defines **Budget** as, *"a financial and/or quantitative statement, prepared and approved prior to a defined period of time, of the policy to be pursued during that period for the purpose of attaining a given objective. It may include income, expenditure and the employment of capital".*

In the words of **Cecil Gillespie**, *"a plan of operations, integrated and co-ordinated, comprising all phases of business activities and summarised to show the financial results of carrying out the plan".*

George R. Terry has defined the **Budget** as, *"an estimate of future needs arranged according to an orderly basis, covering some or all the activities of an enterprise for a definite period of time".*

B) Budgeting :

One of the primary objectives of management accounting is to provide information to management for planning and control. Budgeting acts as a tool of both planning and control. Budgeting is a formal process of financial planning using estimated financial and accounting data.

Budgeting is the process of designing, implementing and operating budgets. It is the managerial process of budget planning and preparation, budgetary control and the related procedures. Budgeting is the highest level of accounting in terms of future which indicates a definite course of action and not merely reporting. It is an integral part of such managerial policies as long-route planning, cash flow, capital expenditure and project management.

The National Association of Accountants (USA) defines **Budgeting** as, *"the process of planning all flows of financial resources into, within, and from an entity during some specified future period".* Budgeting is a means of co-ordinating the combined intelligence of an entire organisation into a plan of action based on past performances and governed by a rational judgement of factors that will influence the course of business in future.

Budgeting and Forecasting :

It must be remembered that **Budgeting is not Forecasting**. It is true that budgeting does involve some sort of forecasting, particularly in the area of sales budget. But the process is physically one of detailed analysis and planning, not merely prognosticating future results. Forecasting is a process of predicting the future state of world in connection with those aspects of the world which are relevant to and likely to affect future activities. Any organised business cannot avoid anticipating or calculating future conditions and trends for the framing of its future policy and decisions. Forecasting is concerned with probable events, whereas budgeting relates to planned events. Budgeting should be preceded by forecasting, but forecasting may be done for purpose other than budgeting.

Thus, in **forecasting** an estimate of what is likely to happen, is made, whereas budgeting is the process of stating policy and programme to be followed in future. Further, forecasting does not connote any sense of control, while budgeting is a tool of control, since it represents actions which can be shaped according to will so that it can be suited to the conditions which may or may not happen.

In sum, **budget** is an operating and financial plan spelling out a target which the management seems to attain on the basis of the forecasts made. A **forecast** denotes some degree of flexibility, while a budget denotes a definite target. The term **'budgeting'** refers to the process of preparing the budgets. The purpose of budgeting is to assess the extent of success of the management in their planning and the actions to be launched, in case of deviations. The budget system is both a "plan" as well as a "control", since it invariably includes in its fold "budgetary control".

(c) Budgetary control :

Budgetary control is the process of laying down in monetary and quantitative terms, what exactly has to be done and how exactly it has to be done in future and ensuring that actual results do not diverge from the planned course. Thus, budgetary control is concerned with the comparison of the actuals with the targets and reporting the results of the comparison. The budget reports form the basis for action.

Floyd H. Rowland and William H. Bann have defined **Budgetary Control** as, *"a tool of management used to plan, carry out and control the operations of business. As a further explanation it establishes pre-determined objectives and provides the basis for measuring performance against these objectives".*

4.2 OBJECTIVES

The important basic **objective of the technique of budgetary control** is to exercise managerial control over the different activities of the organisation through effective planning, proper co-ordination and strict control. However, the other **Objectives of Budgetary Control** are as follows :

i) to identify the overall aims of the business enterprise.
ii) to determine specific targets of performance for each division of the business.
iii) to fix up the responsibilities of the top executives and other personnel.
iv) to provide a basis for comparison of actual performance with the predetermined targets.
v) to analyse the variances more carefully for maximisation of quality production.
vi) to ensure the best use of the available resources for maximisation of quality production.
vii) to co-ordinate the overall activities of the business for centralising control and decentralising responsibilities.
viii) to delegate authority for increasing efficiency.
ix) to provide a suitable basis for necessary revision of current and future policies.
x) to draw long-term plan with absolute accuracy.
xi) to provide a suitable standard performance with which actuals can be compared.
xii) to find out capital requirements for achieving planned targets.

4.3 ADVANTAGES AND DISADVANTAGES

Advantages of Budgetary Control:

A system of **Budgetary control is more advantageous** because,

i) It locates the inefficient areas and persons in the business.
ii) It helps to increase the efficiency, reduce wastages and control costs.
iii) It helps to co-ordinate the activities of the various employees, departments and thus helps to achieve the goal of the management.
iv) With the help of budgeting, the responsibilities of the managers can be fixed for planning, so that they can think ahead, anticipate and be prepared to meet the challenges ahead.
v) Maximisation of profits is possible through budgeting.
vi) It helps to introduce the standard costing technique.
vii) It helps to ensure cash flow and hence bank credit can be obtained.
viii) It creates cost consciousness in the minds of all the employees in the organisation.
ix) Authority can be delegated and responsibilities fixed.

x) It rewards the efficient workers and the managers can show their efficiency by achieving the goals fixed by the management through the budgets.

xi) It ensures that the capital of the firm is utilised in a proper way and that there is no misutilisation of funds.

xii) Vital decisions can be taken by the management based on the budgets.

xiii) Actual results can be compared with the budgets, so that corrective action can be taken in time.

xiv) It is like a barometer which enables us to study the changes in the business conditions.

Disadvantages of Budgetary Control:

Though there are many advantages of Budgetary Control it suffers from many defects also. Hence, the persons using the budgets should be careful and should be fully aware of the limitations. The following are the important **disadvantages of Budgetary Control System**.

i) **Budgetary Control does not replace management :**

It cannot replace the management because in business all vital decisions have to be taken by the management.

ii) **Too much reliance on budgets is harmful :**

Budgetary control is only a technique and tool in the hands of the management. To execute the budget, all the employees must take active part and co-operate with one another, so that the budgetary goal can be achieved. But the budgets should not be taken as the only means through which the business should run. Though sometimes, through budgetary control it is possible to achieve success in business, it should not be depended upon totally.

iii) **Less Flexibility :**

A Budgetary control system should be more flexible and should be changed, according to the changing circumstances. The alternative systems should be added, deleted, improved, replaced or compared with the present system of budgetary control.

iv) **Budgets are based on estimated figures :**

Budgets are prepared in anticipation of various factors. These factors are estimated by seeing the past and forecasting for the future. Hence, forecasting is done which may or may not happen in actual life. Thus, it is not an exact prediction of figures, but based on estimates.

v) **Costly System :**

The installation of the system and its execution is an expensive affair. This is because specialised persons have to be appointed and extra costs have to be incurred for carrying out the operations. Hence, small scale units cannot go in for budgetary control system.

vi) **Budgetary Control deals with quantitative data only :**

In Budgetary control system, only the figures are considered and hence quantitative i.e. the facts are not considered. For example, if a worker is inefficient. We should analyse the various reasons for his inefficiency as he may be inefficient because of the conditions (environment) where the works are not suitable for his health. Here, budgets are of no use because, budgets will only measure his efficiency in terms of quantity produced and will not consider other factors.

Budgetary Control Organisation :

Budgets provide relevant control information to the management for future decisions and actions. With the budgetary system in existence, control of performance and evaluation of results become more purposeful and goal-oriented. The budgetary system should be organised for maximising the benefits of such a system. A budget centre is invariably located without the framework of the organisation. Budget centre must be clearly demarcated to facilitate the formulation of various budgets with the help of the heads of the departments concerned. A 'chart of accounts' in conformity with budget centres should be maintained so as to facilitate recording and analysis of information required for the operation of the 'feedback' for the management. An organisation chart highlighting the functional responsibilities of each member of the management team helps a member to know his position in the organisational hierarchy vis-a-vis his relationship to other members. Each official in the organisation knows precisely whom he should obey and whom he can command in the day-to-day administration.

4.4 TYPES OF BUDGETS

There may be different types of budgets depending upon the various basis adopted by a team. The following are the four principal bases adopted generally by organisations:

A) Classification According to Time :

Based on time factors budgets can be classified into three types, such as long-term budgets, short-term budgets and current budgets.

  i) Long-term Budgets :

  These budgets are related to planning the operations of an organisation for a period of 5 to 10 years. They are usually expressed in physical quantities.

  ii) Short-term Budgets :

  These budgets are drawn usually for a period of one or two years. They are usually quantified and expressed in monetary terms.

  iii) Current Budgets :

  These budgets cover a period of one month or more and the short-term budgets are modified according to current conditions or prevailing situations.

B) Coverage :

According to this basis, budgets can be categorised in terms of various activities in the organisation. Budgets prepared for individual activities are called *'Functional Budgets'*. All these activities have to be consolidated to know their total effect on the organisation. A consolidated statement based on the functional budgets is termed as *'Master Budget'*. A master budget consists of a projected income statement (planned operating budget) and a projected balance sheet (financial budget) showing the organisation's objectives and proposed ways of achieving them.

C) Classification According to Flexibility :

Budgets based on flexibility can be divided into fixed budgets and flexible budgets.

A **Fixed Budget** is one which rigidly specifies the targets for a particular level of activity. The targets are not revised during the budget period, irrespective of the fact that the actual level of activity attained is much different from the budgeted figure. Consequently, the variances are violent and it becomes difficult to isolate the reasons for variances due to change in the level of activity. **Fixed Budgets** can serve the purpose only if the budgets can be prepared with high degree of accuracy and budget period is short because the forecast for short period can be made with reasonable degree of accuracy. On the other hand, a **Flexible Budget** is one which permits the change in accordance with the changes in the level of activity. According to **Flexible Budgeting**, budgets for different levels of activity are prepared and the management enjoys the benefit of adopting any one of them according to changes in the attainment of the level of activity. Thus, the **Flexible Budget** has a series of fixed budgets for different levels of activity. It is always preferable to prepare flexible budget particularly, when the economic conditions frequently change and it is difficult to forecast with any fair degree of accuracy.

i) **Fixed Budget :**

Meaning and Definition :

Fixed Budgets are prepared for only one level of activity under the same conditions. It is unchangeable, is drawn on the assumption that the level of activity will remain the same. Hence, the changes in the expenses due to changes in the conditions are not provided for in this budget. Thus, a fixed budget becomes useful when the actual level of activity is equal to the budgeted level of activity. However, in real life, the level of activity and business conditions due to the internal constraints as well as external factors like changes in the demand, price, shortage of materials, cut in the electricity, etc. go on changing. Thus, a fixed budget is not that successful because it does not consider the variable, semi-variable and fixed costs as separate items and also does not consider change in costs due to the change in the level of activity.

I.C.M.A., London, defines **Fixed Budget** as, *"a budget which is designed to remain unchanged irrespective of the volume of output or turnover achieved".*

The reasons why fixed budgets are not considered to be useful are given below :

i) In fixed budgets the manager becomes helpless as they cannot do anything beyond the budget.

In case of Fixed Budgets, if the actual level differs widely as compared to the fixed budget, we find large variances.

ii) In real life, we find that the cost of material, labour and overheads go on changing. Hence, fixed budgets are not useful because these changes do not have any effect on the budgeted figures.

iii) Since, it is fixed in nature, it is not suitable for long-term planning.

2) **Flexible Budget :**

Meaning and Definition :

A **Flexible Budget** is one which is designed to change, according to the level actually achieved. The budgeted figures can be changed according to the changing conditions. Hence, a Flexible Budget is just the opposite of a fixed budget. Thus, it is more elastic, practical and useful in the real life. These budgets are prepared for the purpose of cost control.

I.C.M.A., London, Terminology defines a **Flexible Budget** as, *"one which by recognising the difference between fixed, semi-fixed and variable costs, is designed to change in relation to the level of activity attained".*

Generally, Flexible budget are prepared under the following situations :

i) Where the business depends upon some scarce material.

ii) Where the exact demand cannot be estimated, for e.g., in new business.

iii) Where the business depends upon nature, for e.g., rainfall.

iv) In some business, where the sales cannot be predicted.

v) Where sufficient labour force is necessary for running the business smoothly.

Distinction between Fixed Budget and Flexible Budget :

Fixed Budget	Flexible Budget
i) It is prepared for a particular level of activity.	i) It is designed to change in accordance with the level of activity actually attained.
ii) It is prepared only for one level of activity.	ii) It is prepared for any level of activity.
iii) It is static and does not change with the changes in the level of activity attained.	iii) It is variable and can change on the basis of activity level to be achieved.
iv) Here, costs are not classified according to behaviour.	iv) Here, costs are classified according to the behaviour i.e. fixed, variable and semi-variable.
v) Formation of budget equation is not necessary.	v) Budget equation is formed for each and every cost.
vi) It is difficult to ascertain the cost under changing circumstances.	vi) It is possible to ascertain cost at different levels of activity.
vii) Fixation of price do not give a correct picture.	vii) It facilitates fixation of selling price.
viii) It has very limited use in controlling costs.	viii) It is a more useful technique for cost control.
ix) Tendering quotations do not give correct picture.	ix) It helps a lot in tendering quotations.
x) It is not useful for performance evaluation.	x) It is useful for performance evaluation.

Methods of Preparing Flexible Budgets :

A Flexible Budget can be prepared in the following manner :

At first, a number of fixed budgets are prepared for each manufacturing budget centre. Within the limits of these budgets, the flexible budgets are prepared. In Flexible budgets, clear differences are drawn between fixed, semi-fixed and variable costs.

There are three methods of preparing Flexible Budgets which are as follows :

i) **Tabular Method :**

In this method, a table is prepared wherein different capacities are shown in horizontal columns and the budget, the budgeted figures are shown against different capacities in the vertical columns. The expenses are recorded as variable, semi-variable and fixed. Various capacity levels showing different volumes of production are shown in the flexible budgets.

ii) **Charting Method :**

In this method, the expenses are analysed, according to their nature or behaviour i.e. variable, semi-variable and fixed. The budgeted expenses are prepared and these are plotted on a graph paper against different levels of activity. The budgeted expenses relating to the level of activity actually attained can be read from this chart.

iii) **Ratio Method :**

If the activities of a company are standardised and the expenses are of uniform nature, most of the expenses can be worked out as a percentage level of activity. The method is that the common cost are estimated. For the normal production, i.e. the normal level of activity. From this we can work out various ratios which show the relationships of each expenses with each increase in the level of activity. Then, the budgeted cost for any level of activity can be ascertained by using these ratios.

Uses :

The flexible budget is more useful as,

i) it is more realistic and has great practical utility in the business.
ii) the efficiency of the managers can be measured.
iii) it helps to control the costs.
iv) it is more realistic than a fixed budget because a fixed budget deals with only one level of activity of condition.
v) the figures in a flexible budget can be changed according to the change in the volume of activity.

Proforma of Flexible Budget

In the books of a Company
FLEXIBLE BUDGET

Normal Activity : Units
Capacity : %

Production		Units	–		–		–	
Capacity		%	–		–		–	
Particulars			Unit Cost ₹	Total Cost ₹	Unit Cost ₹	Total Cost ₹	Unit Cost ₹	Total Cost ₹
A)	**Fixed Expenses :** • Salaries • Depreciation • Insurance • Rent							
B)	**Variable Expenses :** • Direct Material • Direct Labour • Direct Expenses • Indirect Material/Labour/Expenses • Variable Overheads							
C)	**Semi-variable Expenses :** • Electricity • Repairs and Maintenance • Administrative Expenses • Selling Expenses • Distribution Expenses	(+)						
	∴ **Total Cost**							
Add :	Profit	(+)						
Less :	Loss	(–)						
	∴ **Sales**							

D) Nature of Activity :

Business activity involves two processes, viz., Creation of the infrastructure for doing the business; and Actual carrying out of the operations. Therefore, planning is done for both kinds of activities. Depending on the nature of the activities, budgets can, therefore, be grouped into capital and Revenue Budgets.

'Capital Budget' is a statement of estimated receipts and expenditure to be incurred on creation of manufacturing facilities, repair facilities etc.

'Revenue Budget' involves the formulation of targets and the allied process in respect of routine functions, viz., sales, production, finance and other allied activities.

Types of Functional Budgets :

When budgets are classified on the basis of functions they are called 'functional budgets'. They correspond and remain co-terminous with a particular function of the business. They are integrated with the master budget of the business. The number of the functional budgets depends on the size and nature of the business concern. The functional budgets which are commonly found in a business concern are as follows :

1) **Sales Budget :**

    This represents the forecast of the total sales classified according to the types of products, salesmen and the geographic locations. The sales budget holds the key for the success of all other budgets and hence, great care and caution are taken at the time of formulation of this budget ensuring accuracy in the estimated figures.

2) **Selling and Distribution Cost Budget :**

    It relates to estimates of cost of selling and distribution of goods. This is prepared on the basis of past experience taking into consideration a variety of a factors such as future trends, economic conditions and competition.

3) **Production Budget :**

    This represents a forecast based on sales and production capacity. When the budget is expressed in terms of physical quantity, it is called production budget. But when the same is expressed in financial terms covering direct materials, direct labour and expenses – fixed, variable and semi-variable – it becomes production cost budget. This enables the management to minimise the cost of production and maximise the output. This also forms the most important part of the budgetary control system.

    i) *Materials Cost Budget* shows expected cost of materials required for budgeted production and sales purpose. Determination of material cost involves quantities to be used and the rate per unit. The task of determining the quantities required is that of the Production engineering department while the purchase department has the responsibility of deciding the rate.

    ii) *Labour Cost Budget* prognosticates the direct labour cost expected to be spent on carrying into effect the targeted production. Preparation of this budget requires information regarding the time required to do one unit of work and the wages to be paid for it.

iii) *Overhead Budget* is a statement of expected overheads (comprising fixed and variable overheads) which the firm will have to incur during the budget period. This budget is prepared on the basis of the centres of overhead forecasts of all the departments of the firm.

Once material cost budget, labour cost budget and overheads budget are under preparation, a full production cost budget can be drawn. This budget is generally presented in the form of a Cost Sheet.

4) **Materials Budget :**

This is a by-product of Production Budget. This is expressed in terms of physical quantities and values of materials to be issued from the stores for production purpose. This budget ensures that right materials of right quantity and quality are procured.

5) **Labour Budget :**

This represents the utilisation of labour force employed in productive activity. The standard time required for production by employees of various skills is fairly estimated.

6) **Cash Budget :**

This represents the sum total of the requirements of cash in respect of various functional budgets and of estimated cash receipts for a stipulated period.

(7) **Research Budget :**

This includes the salaries of the research assistants and technical expenses of the research department. This concerns improvement in the quality of the products or introduction of new products.

8) **Plant Utilisation Budget :**

This includes the plant and machinery requirements to meet the budgetary production within the stipulated period. Various schedules are prepared indicating the available load in each department expressed in standard hours or units.

9) *Administrative Expenses Budget :*

This comprises the salaries and expenses of the administrative office and management for a stipulated period. All administrative expenses such as staff salaries including that of directors and managing director and expenses of office management like rents, insurance, lighting, and so on, are all included in this budget.

10) *Capital Budget :*

This represents the forecast of the total financial outlay on acquisition of fixed assets such as plant and machinery, building, and furniture and fixtures as also of different sources of capital required. The budget period, contemplated in this case which differs from that of other budgets, is a fairly long period.

11) *Master Budget :*

The final integration of all functional budgets by the accountant provides the master budget. This reflects the estimated profit and loss account, for the future period and balance sheet at the end thereof. Summarised figures are indicated for each item in the budget. This portrays the overall plan for the budget period. This highlights the information relating to sales, production, direct and indirect cost, profits and appropriation of profits.

The Budgeting Process:

The **budgeting process** usually begins when managers receive top management's economic forecasts and marketing project objectives for the coming year, alongwith a time-table stating when budgets must be completed. The forecasts and objectives provided by top management represent guidelines within which the departmental budgets are prepared.

Once separate budgets for sales, production, finance and other activities have been prepared and finalised and the targeted sales, cost of sales, expenses are determined, the targeted profit and loss account and balance sheet are drawn. These statement together are known as *'Master Budget'*. The Budgeting Process is indicated in Figure 4.2 as follows.

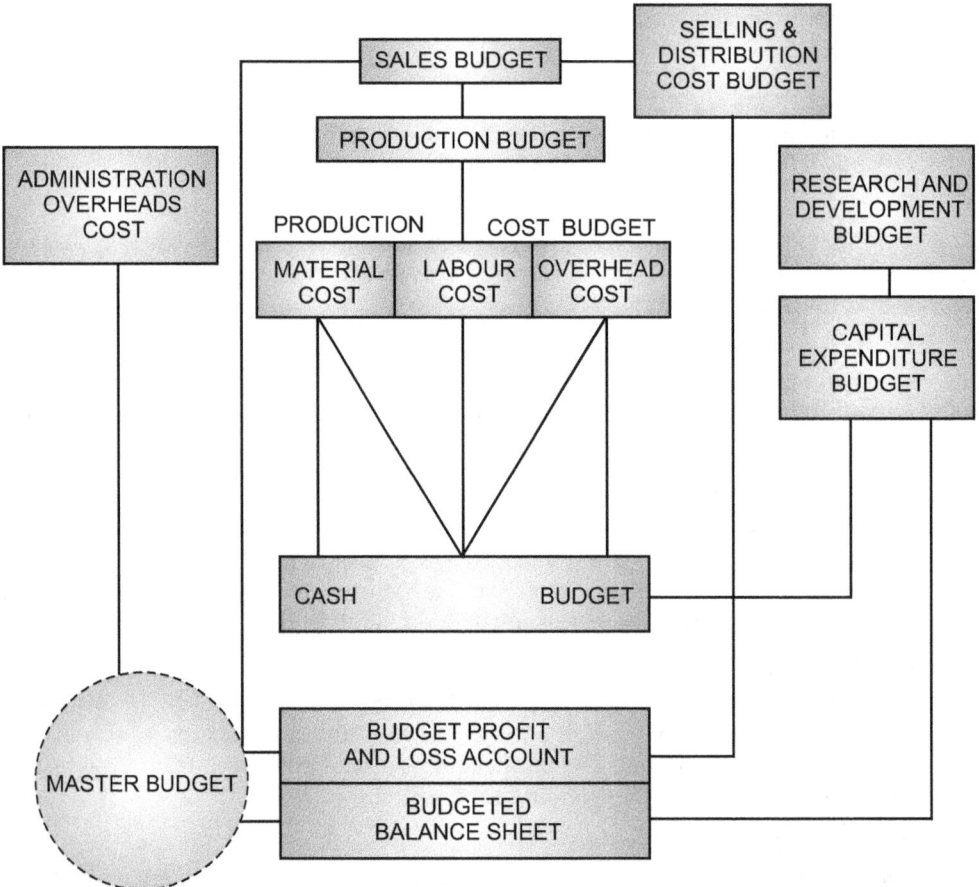

Fig. 4.2 : Budgeting Process

Revenue Budgets :

The components of Revenue Budgets are shown in Figure 4.3 as follows.

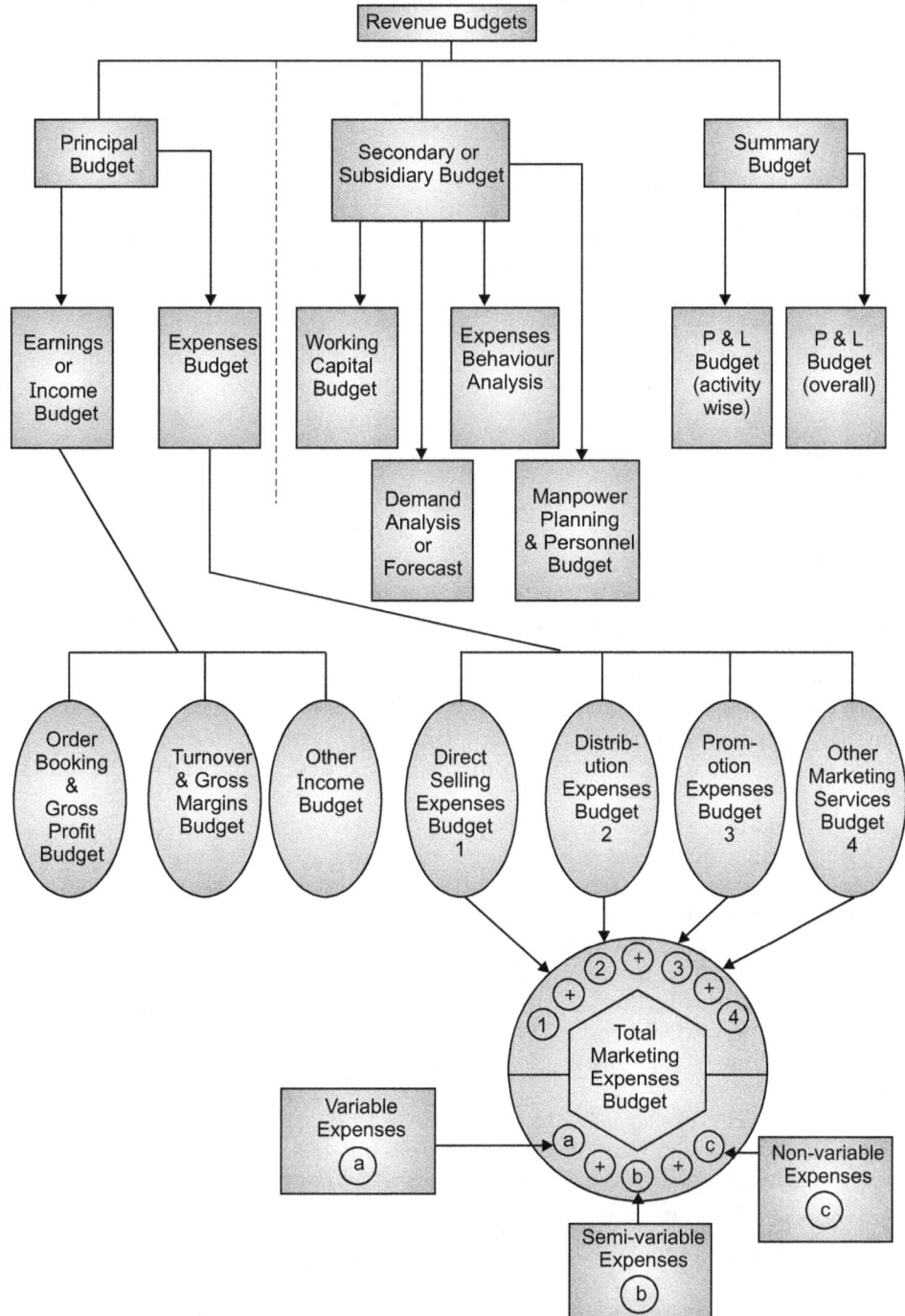

Fig. 4.3 : Components of Revenue Budgets

Principal Budgets :

Principal Budget is that factor, the extent of whose influence must first be assessed in order to ensure that functional budgets are reasonably capable of fulfilment.

A) Revenue Earning or Income Budget :

   i) **Order Booking and Gross Profit Budgets :**
   These budgets are specially applicable to industrial marketing or other such situations where there is a distinct time lag between the booking of order and effecting actual delivery and sales. This budget is a statistical budget and not an accounting one.

   ii) **Turnover and Gross Margin Budgets :**
   This is the main revenue income budget and is in line with the financial accounting definition of sales and gross margin. This budget has to be in conformity with the order booking and gross margin. This budget can be prepared productwise.

   iii) **Other Income Budgets :**
   This would cover income from scrap sales, commission on third party sales, income out of after sales services beyond warranty period, commission on imports and exports on behalf of others, recovery of bad debts, income from brand name, non operating incomes etc.

B) Marketing Expense Budgets :

   i) **Direct Selling Expense Budget :**
   This will cover direct expenses on salesmen such as, salesmen's commission, salesmen's stationery, salesman postage and telegram, bad debts etc.

   ii) **Distribution Expense Budget :**
   This includes expenses on maintenance of sales depots and branches, expenses on transportation of goods and expenses on outside transport and owned transport housing expenses, licences and instance of such other expenses related to distribution.

   iii) **Promotional Expense Budget :**
   This covers all expenses connected with advertisement and sales promotion including media advertisement, payments to advertising agencies and commerce. However company's prestige or image advertisement expenses should not be included in this budget.

   iv) **Other Marketing Service Budgets :**
   These include all expenses relating to marketing director's office, market planning activities, marketing research and such other general marketing services. This also includes budget for special sales (i.e. new areas being tapped, new lines being introduced, special advertising campaign etc.).

   v) **Total Marketing Expenses Budget :**
   This budget can be further classified on the basis of cost behaviour approach viz. fixed, semi-fixed and variable costs. This budget includes all marketing expenses which are mentioned above (i.e. i + ii + iii + iv as above).

Secondary Budgets :

There are various types of subsidiary budgets intended to provide supporting data and analysis is with regard to the framing of the principal budgets mentioned above, including the various expenses budgets. Following are the examples of various types of subsidiary budgets.

   1) **Working Capital Budget :**
   Initial working capital budget is prepared to show the expected fund during the "take of" period or gestation period. This in turn, helps in the determination of interest cost to be included in the expense budget and also the budgeted "Return on Investment" in the marketing operations.

2) **Personnel Budget :**

Personnel budget is prepared with reference to production budget. If wages are paid according to piece rate systems in all the departments preparation of personnel budget is comparatively easy, when payment are made according to time rate or piece rate-cum time rate, production in terms of ordinary units should be converted into standard hours of production in different departments. In other cases, requirements for skilled and unskilled labour time shall be budgeted. This budget depends on the decisions taken by the management. While taking such decisions the management attempts to meet simultaneously the goals of the organisation and the needs and value of their employees.

3) **Expense Behavioural Analysis :**

This requires isolation of fixed, semi-fixed and variable expenses of marketing operations. The expenses are grouped as : Variable, Semi-variable and Fixed. The first is directly related with production, the second is partly related and the third is not related with the level of activity. Apart from variability with production, likely change in rate of expenses should be considered. If expenses for each department are to be shown separately, expenses are to be departmentalised in the light of allocation of factory over-heads. An analysis of expenses in this manner facilitates precise estimates of various heads of expenses covered under expense budgets. It would be obvious that expense behaviour analysis made and used at the time of preparing budgets not only puts the budget estimation on a sounder footing, but also helps in reviewing the various budget estimates. It also forms a systematic basis for subsequent comparison between budgeted expenses and actual expenses for the purpose of effective control. As the main purpose of budgeting is control of expenses by pin pointing responsibility, no useful purpose is served by allocating expenses incurred under one responsibility over various departments which have no control on them.

4) **Sales forecasting or demand analysis :**

Sales forecast may be made in different ways. Best result is achieved when there is arrangement of 'Market Research'. Market Research may be conducted continuously by marketing research department or may be taken up periodically with the help of specialised consultancy firms, when such services are available. Whatever be the system followed, nature of the demand i.e. whether local or restricted, whether it is within a state or national or international in character, must be determined. The pattern of demand for different products, and how it is affected by the substitutes, should be considered. In this connection now, price, design quality and packing influence, consumer preference should be studied in the context of price and of the products of the competitors. The type of customers (i.e. whether one industry or group of industries, or whether public at large, or particular sections of the public or any part of community etc.) require serious study. The trend and seasonal influences in sales should be brought to light by mathematical, statistical or other techniques. In short, this analysis establishes a systematic basis for budgeting order bookings as well as turnover in respect of scientific products or services.

Summary Budgets :

We have seen how each revenue budget is prepared. After budgeting all business functions, the owner is obviously eager to know the summarised result of these revenue budgets. This result may be net business profit of net business loss. So all the revenue budgets along with the development and finance budgets have to integrated and summary budget are to be prepared.

These are actually summary profit and loss or revenue statement budgets prepared separately for each important division or activity group, and also for the organisation's total operations.

In short, with the help of the above revenue budgets, a summary budget is prepared.

A summary budget is a budget which is prepared from, and summarises, all the functional budgets. The end products of summary budgets are :

i) **The Budgeted Profit and Loss Account :**

Summarising the budgeted income from the sales budget and the budgeted costs from other functional budgets, a budgeted profit and loss account is built up.

ii) **The Budgeted Balance-Sheet :**

The summary budget thus prepared are reviewed, re-adjusted and re-budgeted in order to get the maximum benefit from budgetary control. It will be observed that once a summary is approved, it ceases to be merely a plan, it becomes the target for the concern during the budget period to be achieved by the executive directors.

Cash Budget :

Meaning and Definition :

Cash Budget is the forecast of cash position for a particular period. It represents the cash requirements of the business during the budget period. It is a financial budget prepared after the preparation of all the functional budgets.

A Cash Budget is usually defined as, "an estimate of receipts and payments for each month or any other relevant period forming part of the entire budget period".

Thus, it is the future plan of receipts and payment of cash for the budget period, analysed to show the monthly flow of cash drawn up in such a way that the balance can be forecasted at regular intervals. It is a 'means budget' prepared by the chief accountant in terms of money value. It may be prepared for a short period or a long period depending on the requirements, for e.g., weekly, fortnightly, monthly, quarterly, half yearly, annually, etc. A company may have divisional and departmental cash budgets in addition to a cash budget for the overall organisation.

Purpose :

Generally, a **Cash Budget** is prepared to achieve the following **purposes** :

i) to obtain necessary working capital easily from the banks and financial institutions for smooth running of the business.

ii) to enable the top management to make necessary arrangements of cash in case of emergency situations,

iii) to ensure that sufficient cash is made available throughout the financial period to meet the required payments,

iv) to ascertain any expected shortage of cash and to make it available through bank loan or sale of fixed assets.

v) to ascertain any expected surplus of cash and to make its proper investment,

vi) to know the exact amount of cash required for the business operations,

vii) to present the budget to the banks at the time of applying for bank loans,

viii) to serve as a sound basis for cash control,
ix) to know budgeted cash balance at the beginning and at the end of the period,
x) to know the cash generations to be made through probable capital and revenue receipts,
xi) to know the cash payments to be made through probable capital and revenue payments.

Following are the **important points to be considered while preparing a Cash Budget.**

i) cash and bank opening position.
ii) statement showing cash budgets for previous period.
iii) minimum requirement of cash during the period.
iv) expected change in the level of activities.
v) necessary changes in the credit policy of business.
vi) estimated capital expenses.
vii) available sources of raising funds.
viii) likely changes in the nature of production
ix) expected changes in the credit policy of suppliers.
x) profitable investment opportunities available in the business world.

Uses :

A **Cash Budget is more useful** to the organisation in the following manner.

i) in co-ordinating activities of different divisions of a corporate sector.
ii) it helps the company to plan for dividend and interest payments.
iii) in proper planning for long-term capital requirement.
iv) it helps the management to know the type of capital required to be raised.
v) it helps the management to raise the finance from economical sources.
vi) is useful in knowing the flow of funds and their requirements.
vii) it helps in providing sufficient information on the probable profits to be realised during the budgeted period.
viii) is useful in analysing the estimated changes in the receipts and planned payments in the budget period.
ix) it highlights the fluctuations in cash, due to various financial transactions.
x) it indicates the surplus or deficiency of cash at the end of every budgeted period.

Methods of preparing Cash Budget :

Generally, a Cash Budget can be prepared by any one of the three methods viz. Receipts and Payments Method, Cash Flow Statement Method and the Balance Sheet Method.

But a Receipts and Payments Method seems to be more popular because of its own advantages as well as, the Receipts and Payments Method is useful for short-term cash budget whereas the other two methods are used for long-term cash budgets.

1) Receipts and Payments Method :

According to this method, Cash Budget includes all the cash receipts whether they are on revenue account or capital account. Similarly, all expected capital and revenue expenditures are brought in a cash budget. The accruals i.e. income earned, but not received and expenditure due but not paid are excluded from the cash budget. Thus, a cash budget is a sort of cash account which records cash receipts and cash payments and shows expected cash balance at the end of the budget period. The informations for cash budget are derived from other budgets. For example, the sales budget will provide the amount of sales and the receipts from sales and realisation from debtors can be estimated by taking into account the terms of sales. The raw materials purchase budget, labour budget and overheads budget will provide information relating to payments for raw materials, wages and overhead charges. The management can forecast payments on account of capital expenditure, tax, dividend etc. The difference of cash receipts and cash payments for a period is either positive or negative, which is carried to the next period.

In this method, all the cash receipts which are expected and all the cash payments which are expected to be made are taken into account. Thus, the cash balance will represent the difference between the total cash receipts expected (including the opening cash balance) and the total cash payments to be made.

The following are the sources and application of cash.

Sources :

i) **Collection from debtors i.e. credit customers :** This can be ascertained from the Sales Budget. The terms and conditions of sale, lag in payments and other factors should be considered, while estimating the cash receipts.

ii) Cash receipts from other sources viz. Dividends received interest on investments, rent received, sale of investments, sale of fixed assets etc.

Applications :

i) Cash payments for purchase of raw materials, payment of wages and other expenses are estimated from the various budgets viz. Purchase budgets personnel budget and overhead/expenses budget. The suppliers credit period, terms and conditions of purchases, cash discount allowed, law in payment of wages, etc. should be considered.

ii) Cash payments for capital expenditure can be ascertained from the capital expenditure budget.

iii) Cash payments for dividends income tax etc.

EXAMPLE

From the following budgeted data relating Zenith Industries Ltd., Amravati, prepare Cash Budget for three months from February to April 2013.

2013 Months	Sales ₹	Purchases ₹	Wages ₹	Overheads ₹
January	85,000	48,000	10,000	12,500
February	90,000	52,000	11,000	13,500
March	1,20,000	60,000	14,000	15,000
April	1,30,000	62,000	14,000	16,000

Other Informations :
i) 20% sales is for cash and the remaining amount is realised in the month following that of sales.
ii) Suppliers supply raw materials at one months credit.
iii) Wage-bill is paid in the first week of next month.
iv) Overheads are paid in cash in the same month.
v) Monthly rent payment is ₹ 1,000.
vi) Advance Income Tax of ₹ 15,000 is payable in April.
vii) Bonus of ₹ 10,000 is payable to workers in February.
viii) Plant costing ₹ 80,000 is due to be installed in February. The part of the bill will be paid in March amounting to ₹ 18,500.
ix) Half year interest on 12% ₹ 50,000 Debentures is to be received in February and August every year.
x) Cash at Bank on 1st February, estimated at ₹ 5,000.

ANSWER

In the books of Zenith Industries Ltd., Amravati
Cash Budget for the three months ended 30th April, 2013

Particulars		Feb. ₹	March ₹	April ₹
Opening Cash (A)		(+) 5,000	(+) 11,500	(+) 10,000
Add : Receipts :				
i) Cash Sales i.e. 20% of Sales		18,000	24,000	26,000
ii) Collection from Debtors i.e. 80% of Sales - One month credit		68,000	72,000	96,000
iii) Interest on Debentures received @ 12% p.a. on ₹ 50,000 for six months		3,000	–	–
∴ **Actual Receipts** (B)		89,000	96,000	1,22,000
∴ **Total Receipts (A + B)** (C)		94,000	1,07,500	1,32,000
Less : Payments				
i) To suppliers for purchase of raw materials – One month credit		48,000	52,000	60,000
ii) Wage bill – One month credit		10,000	11,000	14,000
iii) Overheads – Paid on same month		13,500	15,000	16,000
iv) Monthly Rent		1,000	1,000	1,000
v) Advance Income Tax Payable		–	–	15,000
vi) Plant installation and payment of bill		–	18,500	–
viii) Bonus to workers		10,000	–	–
∴ **Total Payments** (D)		82,500	97,500	1,06,000
∴ **Cash Bank Closing (C – D)** (E)		(+) 11,500	(+) 10,000	(+) 26,000

2) Adjusted Profit and Loss Method

Under this method, the profits as shown in the Profit and Loss Account prepared in the conventional manner forms the basis for cash forecast. The profit is adjusted by adding back to it the non-cash items such as depreciation, outstanding expenses, other provisions etc. The other items which increase the total cash inflows are the increase in share capital, debenture and loans, current liabilities (creditors) and decrease in fixed assets, debtors and stock etc. Out of the total cash-inflows calculated as above, the items which results in cash outflow are subtracted to arrive at the cash position at the end of the period. The items which reduce the cash position are accrued incomes, advance payments, dividend payment, redemption of debentures and loans, decrease in creditors, payment for fixed assets, increase in debtors and stock etc. This method of cash forecast may also be called as the Cash Flow Statement method as the net income as per the conventional income statement is converted into a cash flow forecast. The main sources of information for cash forecast as per this method are the profit and loss account and balance sheet. This method is suitable to prepare cash budget for long period.

EXAMPLE

From the following Balance Sheet and Projected Profit and Loss Account of Aptech Ltd., Ahmedabad, prepare the Cash Budget according to Adjusted Profit and Loss Account method for the year ended 31st December, 2012.

Balance Sheet as at 31st December 2011

Liabilities	₹	Assets	₹
Share Capital	1,50,00,000	Land and Buildings	1,25,00,000
General Reserve	50,00,000	Plant and Machinery	80,00,000
Profit and Loss	25,00,000	Furniture and Fixtures	15,00,000
Debentures	80,00,000	Sundry Debtors	75,00,000
Creditors	1,00,00,000	Stock	50,00,000
Bills Payable	20,00,000	Bills Receivable	10,00,000
Outstanding Salaries	30,00,000	Prepaid Rent	3,00,000
		Cash at Bank and in hand	70,00,000
	4,55,00,000		4,28,00,000

Dr. Projected Profit and Loss Account for the year ended 31st December 2012 Cr.

Particulars		₹	Particulars	₹
To Opening Stock		50,00,000	By Sales	3,00,00,000
To Purchases		2,25,00,000	By Closing Stock	45,00,000
To Gross Profit C/D		70,00,000		
		3,45,00,000		3,45,00,000
To Salaries	10,00,000		By Gross Profit B/D	70,00,000
Less : Last years Outstanding	(–) 3,00,000			
	7,00,000			
Add : Outstanding for current year	(+) 1,00,000	8,00,000		
To Commission		1,50,000		
To Rent	9,00,000			
Add : Last years prepaid	(+) 3,00,000	12,00,000		
To Interest		8,00,000		
To Establishment Charges		2,50,000		
To Advertising Expenses		2,00,000		

To Depreciation :				
i) Plant and Machinery 8,00,000				
ii) Land and Building 6,00,000				
iii) Furniture (+) 1,50,000	15,50,000			
To Net Profit C/D	20,50,000			
	70,00,000			70,00,000
To Dividend	30,00,000	By Net Profit B/D		20,50,000
To General Reserve	10,00,000	By Profit and Loss A/c		25,00,000
To Balance C/D	5,50,000			
	45,50,000			45,50,000

On 31st December, 2012, the position of some of the items was as under :

	₹
Share Capital	2,00,00,000
Debentures	1,00,00,000
Creditors	80,00,000
Debtors	90,00,000
Bills Payable	25,00,000
Bills Receivable	8,00,000

Purchase of Plant and Machinery during, 2012, amounted to ₹ 28,00,000 and Purchase of Furniture and Fixtures ₹ 21,50,000.

ANSWER

In the books of Aptech Ltd., Ahmedabad
Cash Budget (Adjusted Profit and Loss Method) for the year ended 31st December, 2012

Particulars	₹	₹	₹
Cash Balance as on 31st December, 2011			70,00,000
Add :			
i) Net Profit for 2011		20,50,000	
ii) Depreciation :			
• Plant and Machinery	8,00,000		
• Land and Building	6,00,000		
• Furniture	1,50,000	15,50,000	
iii) Decrease in Prepaid Rent		3,00,000	
iv) Decrease in Stock		5,00,000	
v) Decrease in Bills Receivable		2,00,000	
vi) Increase in Bills Payable		5,00,000	
vii) Issue of Share Capital		50,00,000	
viii) Issue of Debentures		(+) 20,00,000	1,21,00,000
			1,91,00,000
Less :			
i) Purchase of Plant and Machinery		28,00,000	
ii) Purchase of Furniture and Fixtures		21,50,000	
iii) Dividend		30,00,000	
iv) Decrease in Outstanding Salaries		2,00,000	
v) Increase in Debtors		15,00,000	
vi) Decrease in Creditors		20,00,000	1,16,50,000
∴ Cash Balance as on 31st December, 2012			74,50,000

3) **Balance Sheet Method :**

As per this method, a projected Balance Sheet is prepared in which cash balance is not an estimated item, but a difference between total projected assets and total estimated liabilities. In other words, the excess of projected assets over projected liabilities, represents cash balance. If the liabilities are more than the assets, the balance shows the overdraft.

EXAMPLE

Using the data of previous example of Aptech Ltd., Ahmedabad, prepare a projected Balance Sheet as on 31st December, 2012 to show the cash position as on that date :

ANSWER

In the books of Aptech Ltd., Ahmedabad
Projected Balance Sheet as on 31st December, 2012

Liabilities	₹	Assets		₹
Share Capital	2,00,00,000	Land and Buildings	1,25,00,000	
Debentures	1,00,00,000	**Less** : Depreciation	(–) 6,00,000	1,19,00,000
General Reserve	60,00,000	Plant and Machinery	80,00,000	
Profit and Loss A/c	5,50,000	**Less** : Depreciation	(–) 8,00,000	
Creditors	8,00,000		72,00,000	
Bills Payable	25,00,000	**Add** : Purchases	(+) 28,00,000	1,00,00,000
Outstanding Salaries	1,00,000	Furniture and Fixtures	15,00,000	
		Less : Depreciation	(–) 1,50,000	
			13,50,000	
		Add : Purchases	(+) 21,50,000	35,00,000
		Debtors		90,00,000
		Bills Receivable		8,00,000
		Stock		45,00,000
		Cash and Bank Balance (Balancing figure)		74,50,000
	3,99,50,000			4,71,50,000

Proforma of Cash Budget :

The proforma of Cash Budget can be shown by two methods as follows :

I) Proforma of Cash Budget under Rolling Period Basis :

Budget Actual Comparison Month – I		Particulars		Month 1	Month 2	Month 3
Budget	Actual					
		A)	Sales Receipts :			
		i)	Cash Sales and Advances			
		ii)	Sundry Debtors Collection			
		iii)	Cash Subsidies, Rebate etc. (+)			
			Total (A)			
		B)	Operations Distribution			
		i)	Cash Purchases and Advances			
		ii)	Sundry Creditors Payment			
		iii)	Wages, Salaries etc.			
		iv)	Rent, Electricity etc.			
		v)	Selling Expenses			
		vi)	Administrative Expenses			
		vii)	Income Tax paid			
			Total (B)			

		C)	Cash Flow Through Operations (A – B)			
		D)	Miscellaneous Receipts : (Interest, Rent, Royalties etc.)			
		E)	Capital Receipts :			
		i)	Debenture Issues			
		ii)	Term Loans			
		iii)	Issue of Share Capital			
		iv)	Sales of Assets			
			Total (E)			
		F)	Non-Operating Distributions			
		i)	Interest and Financial Cost			
		ii)	Donations			
		iii)	Dividends			
		iv)	Capital Expenditures			
		v)	Debt redemption			
			Total (F)			
		G)	Net Cash Flow (C + D + E – F)			
		Add :	Opening Balance Cash Position (+)			
		Less :	Minimum Cash Required			
			Bank Loan (Increase)/ decrease			
			Cumulative Bank Position			
			(Drawing Power) (–)			

II) **Proforma of a Cash Budget :**

In the books of a company
Cash Budget for the period ended

Particulars	January ₹	February ₹	March ₹	Total ₹
Opening Balance of Cash	....	....	....	....
Add : Receipts :				
• Cash Sales	....	....	....	....
• Receipts from Debtors	....	....	....	....
• Issue of Shares and Debentures	....	....	....	....
• Dividends etc.				
Total (A)	....	....	....	....
Less : Payments :				
• Cash Purchases	....	....	....	....
• Creditors	....	....	....	....
• Wages	....	....	....	....
• Capital Expenditure	....	....	....	....
• Dividend Payable	....	....	....	....
• Interest Payable	....	....	....	....
• Income-Tax Payable	....	....	....	....
Total (B)	....	....	....	....
∴ Closing Cash Balance : (A – B)	....	....	....	....

ILLUSTRATIONS

CASH BUDGET

ILLUSTRATION 1

Prepare a Cash Budget for three months ended 31-3-2013, from the following particulars relating to Bharat Forge Co. Ltd., Bengaluru.

2012-2013 Months	Credit Sales ₹	Purchases ₹	Wages ₹
November, 2012	1,00,000	80,000	5,000
December, 2012	90,000	70,000	6,000
January, 2013	1,10,000	1,00,000	4,500
February, 2013	60,000	95,000	5,500
March, 2013	80,000	1,30,000	7,000

40% of the credit sales will be realised in the month following the sales and the remaining 60% in the second month following. The creditors will be paid in the month following the purchases. Interest of ₹ 5,000 will have to be paid in the month of February, 2013. Income-tax of ₹ 15,000 will have to be paid in the month of March, 2013. Wages are paid in the same month. The opening balance of cash as on 1st January, 2013 was ₹ 20,000.

SOLUTION

In the Books of Bharat Forge Co. Ltd., Bengaluru

Cash Budget for the three months ending 31st March, 2013

Particulars		January ₹	February ₹	March ₹
Cash Balance (Opening) :	(A)	20,000	41,500	29,000
Add : Receipts :				
1) Collection from Debtors				
a) 40% of Credit Sales - one month credit		36,000	44,000	24,000
b) 60% of Credit Sales - two months credit		60,000	54,000	66,000
∴ Actual Receipts	(B)	96,000	98,000	90,000
∴ Total Receipts (A + B)	(C)	1,16,000	1,39,500	1,19,000
Less : Payments :				
1) Creditors for purchases one month credit		70,000	1,00,000	95,000
2) Interest		–	5,000	–
3) Income-tax		–	–	15,000
4) Wages		4,500	5,500	7,000
∴ Total Payments	(D)	74,500	1,10,500	1,17,000
Closing Cash Balance (C – D)	(E)	41,500	29,000	2,000

ILLUSTRATION 2

Cadbury India Ltd., Cochin, wants to avail overdraft facility with Bank of India for the period October - December 2012 for meeting the orders. From the following particulars, prepare a cash budget and find out the amount of overdraft facility required.

2012 Months	Credit Sales ₹	Purchases ₹	Wages ₹
July	1,30,000	1,60,000	14,000
August	2,10,000	1,55,000	15,000
September	2,20,000	1,80,000	18,000
October	3,00,000	3,20,000	15,000
November	1,50,000	2,20,000	17,000
December	1,50,000	3,50,000	16,000

The credit sales are realised as below :
- 50% of the amount in the second month following, the sales two months or
- 50% of the amount in the third month following the sales three months

The creditors for purchases are paid in the month following the month of purchase.

The bank pass book showed a balance in the current account as on 30th September, 2012, as ₹ 10,000.

SOLUTION

In the Books of Cadbury India Ltd., Cochin
Cash Budget for the three months ending 31st December, 2012

Particulars		October ₹	November ₹	December ₹
Cash at Bank (Opening) : A)		(+) 10,000	(–) 15,000	(–) 1,37,000
Add : Receipts :				
1) Collection from Debtors				
a) 50% of Credit Sales - two months credit		1,05,000	1,10,000	1,50,000
b) 50% of Credit Sales - three months credit		65,000	1,05,000	1,10,000
∴ Actual Receipts	B)	1,70,000	2,15,000	2,60,000
∴ Total Receipts (A + B)	C)	1,80,000	2,00,000	1,23,000
Less : Payments :				
1) Wages		15,000	17,000	16,000
2) Creditors for purchases one month credit		1,80,000	3,20,000	2,20,000
∴ Total Payments	D)	1,95,000	3,37,000	2,36,000
Cash at Bank (Closing) (C – D)	E)	(–) 15,000	(–) 1,37,000	(–) 1,13,000

ILLUSTRATION 3

Eskay Ltd., Ernakulam, wishes to prepare a Cash Budget from January. Prepare a cash budget for the first six months from the following estimated revenue and expenses of 2013.

2013 Months	Total Sales ₹	Materials ₹	Wages ₹	Overheads Production ₹	Overheads Selling and Distribution ₹
January	20,000	20,000	4,000	3,200	800
February	22,000	14,000	4,400	3,300	900
March	24,000	14,000	4,600	3,300	800
April	26,000	12,000	4,600	3,400	900
May	28,000	12,000	4,800	3,500	900
June	30,000	16,000	4,800	3,600	1,000

Cash balance on 1st January 2013, was ₹ 10,000. A new machine is to be installed at ₹ 30,000 on credit to be repaid by two equal instalments in March and April 2013. Sales commission @ 5% on total sales is to be paid within the month following actual sales. ₹ 10,000 being the amount of 2nd call may be received in March, 2013. Share premium amounting to ₹ 2,000 is also receivable with 2nd call.

- Period of credit allowed by suppliers – 2 months.
- Period of credit allowed to customers – 1 month
- Delay in payment of overheads – 1 month
- Delay in payment of wages – 1/2 month.

Assume cash sales to be 50% of total sales.

SOLUTION

In the Books of Eskay Ltd., Ernakulam
Cash-Budget for the six months ending 30th June, 2013

Particulars		Jan. ₹	Feb. ₹	March ₹	April ₹	May ₹	June ₹
Cash Balance – Opening	A)	10,000	18,000	29,800	20,000	6,100	8,800
Add : Receipts :							
1) Share 2nd Call		–	–	10,000	–	–	–
2) Share Premium		–	–	2,000	–	–	–
3) Cash Sales : 50% of Total Sales		10,000	11,000	12,000	13,000	14,000	15,000
4) Collection from Debtors 50% of Total Sales 1 month credit			10,000	11,000	12,000	13,000	14,000
∴ Actual Receipts	B)	10,000	21,000	35,000	25,000	27,000	29,000
∴ Total Receipts (A + B)	C)	20,000	39,000	64,800	45,000	33,100	37,800
Less : Payments							
1) Purchase of Machine				15,000	15,000		
2) Sales Commission @ 5% on Total Sales			1,000	1,100	1,200	1,300	1,400
3) Payment to Suppliers for purchase of material (2 months credit)				20,000	14,000	14,000	12,000
4) Payment of Production Overheads (1 month credit)			3,200	3,300	3,300	3,400	3,500
5) Payment of Selling and Distribution (1 month credit)			800	900	800	900	900
6) Payment of Wages (1/2 month credit)		2,000	4,200	4,500	4,600	4,700	4,800
∴ Total Payment	(D)	2,000	9,200	44,800	38,900	24,300	22,600
∴ Cash Balance Closing (C – D)	(E)	18,000	29,800	20,000	6,100	8,800	15,200

ILLUSTRATION 4

Summarised below are the income and expenditure forecasts for the month of March to August, 2013, of Flex Industries Ltd., Faridabad.

2013 Month	Credit Sales ₹	Credit Purchases ₹	Wages ₹	Manufacturing Expenses ₹	Office Expenses ₹	Selling Expenses ₹
March	60,000	36,000	9,000	4,000	2,000	4,000
April	62,000	38,000	8,000	3,000	1,500	5,000
May	64,000	33,000	10,000	4,500	2,500	4,500
June	58,000	35,000	8,500	3,500	2,000	3,500
July	56,000	39,000	9,000	4,000	1,000	4,500
August	60,000	34,000	8,000	3,000	1,500	4,500

You are given the following further information :
(a) Plant costing ₹ 16,000 is due for delivery in July, 2008, payable 10% on delivery and balance after three months.
(b) Advance Tax of ₹ 8,000 each is payable in March and June, 2008.
(c) Period of credit allowed
   i) by suppliers 2 months and
   ii) to customers one month
(d) Lag in payment of manufacturing expenses half month.
(e) Lag in payment of all other expenses one month.

You are required to prepare a Cash Budget for three months starting on 1st May, 2013, when there was a cash balance of ₹ 8,000.

SOLUTION

In the Books of Flex Industries Ltd., Faridabad
Cash-Budget for the three months ended on 31st July, 2013

Particulars		May ₹	June ₹	July ₹
Cash Balance Opening :	(A)	8,000	15,750	12,750
Add Receipts :				
1) Collection from customers for credit sales (1 month credit)		62,000	64,000	58,000
∴ Actual Receipts	(B)	62,000	64,000	58,000
∴ Total Receipts (A + B)	(C)	70,000	79,750	70,750
Less : Payments :				
1) Purchase of Plant		–	–	1,600
2) Advance-Tax		–	8,000	–
3) Payment to suppliers for credit purchase (2 months credit)		36,000	38,000	33,000
4) Payment of Manufacturing Expenses (half month credit)		3,750 (1,500 + 2,250)	4,000 (2,250 + 1,750)	3,750 (1,750 + 2,000)
5) Wages (one month credit)		8,000	10,000	8,500
6) Office expenses (one month credit)		1,500	2,500	2,000
7) Selling Expenses (one month credit)		5,000	4,500	3,500
∴ Total Payments	(D)	54,250	67,000	52,350
∴ Cash at Bank Closing (C – D)	(E)	15,750	12,750	18,400

ILLUSTRATION 5

From the following information relating to Gesco Ltd., Gurgaon, prepare a Cash Budget for the half year ended 30th June, 2013.

2008 Months	Sales ₹	Materials ₹	Wages ₹	Selling Expenses ₹	Works Overheads ₹	Manufacturing Expenses ₹
January	72,000	25,000	10,040	4,000	6,000	1,500
February	97,000	31,000	12,190	5,000	6,300	1,700
March	86,000	25,500	10,620	5,500	6,000	2,000
April	88,600	30,600	25,042	6,700	6,500	2,200
May	1,02,500	37,000	22,075	8,500	8,000	2,500
June	1,08,700	38,800	23,039	9,000	8,200	2,500

The Cash balance on 1-1-2013, is ₹ 2,500. Assume that 50% of the total sales are cash sales. Assets are to be acquired in the month of February and April 2013, hence, provision should be made for the payment of ₹ 8,000 and ₹ 25,000 respectively for the same. An application has been made to the bank for the grant of a loan of ₹ 30,000 and it is expected that it will be received in May, 2013. It is also anticipated that a dividend of ₹ 35,000 will be paid in June. Debtors are allowed one months credit, whereas creditors, for goods or overheads, grant one months credit. Sales commission @ 3% on total sales is to be paid in the same month.

SOLUTION

In the Books of Gesco Ltd., Gurgaon
Cash-Budget for the six months ended on 30th June, 2013

Particulars		Jan. ₹	Feb. ₹	March ₹	April ₹	May ₹	June ₹
Cash Balance – Opening	(A)	2,500	26,300	51,200	85,500	81,100	1,35,500
Add Receipts :							
1) Cash Sales – 50% of Total Sales		36,000	48,500	43,000	44,300	51,250	54,350
2) Collection from Debtors – 50% of Total Sales one months credit		–	36,000	48,500	43,000	44,300	51,250
3) Grant of Bank Loan						30,000	
∴ Actual Receipts	(B)	36,000	84,500	91,500	87,300	1,25,550	1,05,600
∴ Total Receipts (A + B)	(C)	38,500	1,10,800	1,42,700	1,72,800	2,06,650	2,41,100
Less : Payments							
1) Credit for purchase of materials One month credit			25,000	31,000	25,500	30,600	37,000
2) Wages		10,040	12,190	10,620	25,042	22,075	23,039
3) Creditors for selling expenses One month credit		–	4,000	5,000	5,500	6,700	8,500
4) Creditors for Works Overheads One month credit		–	6,000	6,300	6,000	6,500	8,000
5) Creditors for Office on Cost One month credit		–	1,500	1,700	2,000	2,200	2,500
6) Purchase of Asset		–	8,000	–	25,000	–	–
7) Dividend		–	–	–	–	–	35,000
8) Sales Commission @ 3% on Total Sale		2,160	2,910	2,580	2,658	3,075	3,261
∴ Total Payments	(D)	12,200	59,600	57,200	91,700	71,150	1,17,300
Cash Balance Closing (C – D)	(E)	26,300	51,200	85,500	81,100	1,35,500	1,23,800

Cost Accounting 4.29 Budget and Budgetary Control

ILLUSTRATION 6

Prepare a Cash Budget of India Nippon Ltd., Indore, for the three months ended 30th June, 2013, in a columnar form using the following cost data.

2013 Months	Total Sales ₹	Total Purchases ₹	Wages ₹	Overheads ₹
January - Actual	80,000	45,000	20,000	5,000
February - Actual	80,000	40,000	18,000	6,000
March - Actual	75,000	42,000	22,000	6,000
April - Budgeted	90,000	50,000	24,000	7,000
May - Budgeted	85,000	45,000	20,000	6,000
June - Budgeted	80,000	35,000	18,000	5,000

Additional Information :

i)   10% of the Purchases and 20% of the Sales are for cash.

ii) The average collection period of the company is half a month and the credit purchases are paid-off regularly after one month.

iii) Wages are paid off half monthly and the taxes of ₹ 500 included in Overheads are paid off on monthly basis.

iv) Cash balance on 1st April, 2013, was ₹ 15,000 and the company has decided to maintain it at the end of every month at the same amount, the excess cash if any, be deposited into fixed deposit account.

SOLUTION

In the books of India Nippon Ltd., Indore
Cash Budget for the three months ending 30th June, 2013

Particulars		April ₹	May ₹	June ₹
Cash Balance Opening : A)		15,000	15,000	15,000
Add : Receipts				
i) Cash Sales i.e. 20% of Total Sales		18,000	17,000	16,000
Credit Sales i.e. 80% of Total Sales –				
Average collection period half a month		66,000	70,000	66,000
		(30,000 +	(36,000 +	(34,000 +
		36,000)	34,000)	32,000)
∴ **Actual Receipts** B)		84,000	87,000	82,000
∴ **Total Receipts : (A + B)** C)		99,000	1,02,000	97,000
Less : Payments :				
1) Cash Purchases i.e. 10% of Total Purchases		5,000	4,500	3,500
2) Payment to Creditors from Credit Purchases i.e. 90% of Total Purchases – One month credit		37,800	45,000	40,500
3) Wages - Half a month credit		23,000	22,000	19,000
		(11,000 +	(12,000 +	(10,000 +
		12,000)	10,000)	9,000)
4) Overheads - Monthly basis		6,500	5,500	4,500
5) Taxes - Monthly basis		500	500	500

Particulars		April ₹	May ₹	June ₹
∴ Total Payments :	D) (–)	72,800	77,500	68,000
∴ Actual Cash Balance Closing (C – D)	E)	26,200	24,500	29,000
Less : Excess cash deposited into Fixed Deposit Account	(–)	11,200	9,500	14,000
∴ Required Cash Balance Closing :		15,000	15,000	15,000

ILLUSTRATION 7

From the following forecast of income and expenditures of Forex Engineering Co. Ltd., Faizpur, prepare a Cash Budget for the three months ended 31st August, 2013.

2013 Months	Total Turnover ₹	Purchases ₹	Prime Cost Labour ₹	Works Overhead ₹	Selling on Cost ₹
April	50,000	39,700	5,000	20% of Direct Wages	5% of market price
May	80,000	49,600	5,000	20% of Direct Wages	5% of market price
June	60,000	51,050	6,000	20% of Direct Wages	5% of market price
July	70,000	38,340	6,000	20% of Direct Wages	5% of market price
August	60,000	28,910	7,000	20% of Direct Wages	5% of market price

The additional information made available is as follows :

i) One-fifth of the sales are on cash basis. Of the remaining credit sales, fifty percentage are to be recovered in the next month, whereas, fifty percentage are recovered after two months. Cash sales are made at five percentage cash discounts.

ii) All Purchases are credit and the payment to suppliers is made after two months.

iii) Wages are paid fifteen days in arrears.

iv) Overheads are paid in the same month.

v) A Texmo machine costing ₹ 60,000 is to be purchased in July, 2013. Fifty percentage of the total amount is to paid in the same month as down payment whereas the remaining balance is to be paid in three equal instalments together with interest at eighteen percentage per annum.

vi) On 31st May, 2013, cash balance is estimated at ₹ 36,000.

SOLUTION

In the books of Forex Engineering Co. Ltd., Faizpur
Cash Budget for the three months ending 31st August, 2013

Particulars		June ₹	July ₹	August ₹
Cash Balance Opening :	A)	36,000	50,000	29,000
Add : Receipts				
1) Cash Sales i.e. 20% of Total Sales				
Less : 5% Cash Discounts		11,400	13,300	11,400
2) Collection from Debtors - from Credit Sales				
i.e. 80% of Total Sales		52,000	56,000	52,000
∴ Actual Receipts :	B)	63,400	69,300	63,400
∴ Total Receipts : (A + B)	C)	99,400	1,19,300	92,400
Less : Payments :				
1) Payment to Creditors from Credit Purchases - Two months credit		39,700	49,600	51,050
2) Prime Cost labour i.e. Wages - 15 days in arrears		5,500 (2,500 + 3,000)	6,000 (3,000 + 3,000)	6,500 (3,000 + 3,500)
3) Works Overhead - in the same month i.e. 20% of Direct Wages (i.e. actual Prime Cost Labour)		1,200	1,200	1,400
4) Selling on Cost - in the same month i.e. 5% of market price (i.e. Total Turnover)		3,000	3,500	3,000
5) Purchase of Machine and payment of 'down payment' and payment of equal instalment together with interest of 18% p.a.		– –	30,000 –	– 10,450
∴ Total Payments	D)	49,400	90,300	72,400
∴ Cash Balance Closing (C – D)	E)	50,000	29,000	20,000

Working Notes :

1. **Calculation of Net Cash Sales :**

Particulars		June ₹	July ₹	August ₹
Actual Cash Sales (i.e. 20% of Total Sales)		12,000	14,000	12,000
Less : Cash Discount (i.e. 5% of Cash Sales)	(–)	600	700	600
∴ Net Cash Sales		11,400	13,300	11,400

2. **Calculation of Net Cash Collection from Debtors - from Credit Sales i.e. 80% of Total Sales:**

	Particulars	June ₹	July ₹	August ₹
i)	50% of Credit Sales - One month credit	32,000	24,000	28,000
ii)	50% of Credit Sales - Two months credit	20,000	32,000	24,000
	∴ Net Cash Sales	52,000	56,000	52,000

3. **Calculation of instalment amount to be paid on purchase of machine:**

	₹
• Cost price of 'Texmo' machine - July, 2013	60,000
• Down Payment i.e. 50% of total amount	30,000
• Total Amount due on 31st July, 2013	30,000
• To be paid in three equal instalments of	10,000
• Togetherwith interest @ 18% p.a. (i.e. 18% of ₹ 30,000 or one month)	450
Hence, total instalment to be paid in August will be (i.e. ₹ 10,000 + ₹ 450).	10,450

ILLUSTRATION 8

Prepare a Cash Budget for the three months ending 30th September 2013, based on the following cost data relating to Hikal Industries Ltd., Himmatpur.

i) Cash balance as on 1st July, 2013, was ₹ 25,000.
ii) Monthly salaries estimated to be ₹ 10,000.
iii) Interest payable in August, 2013, amounted to ₹ 5,000.

Other estimated cost details are as follows:

Particulars	June ₹	July ₹	August ₹	September ₹
Cash Turnover	–	1,40,000	1,52,000	1,21,000
Purchases - Credit	1,60,000	1,70,000	2,40,000	1,80,000
General Expenses	–	20,750	22,500	21,250
Sales Credit	1,00,000	80,000	1,40,000	1,20,000

Credit Sales are collected 50% in the month of sales made and remaining 50% in the following month. Collection from Credit Sales are subject to 5% cash discount if payment is received during the month of Sales and $2^1/_2$% if payment is received in the following month of Sales. Creditors are paid either on a prompt or 30 days credit basis. It is estimated that 10% of the Total Creditors are in the prompt category.

SOLUTION

Working Notes:

i) **Calculation of Total Collection from Debtors:**

Particulars	July ₹	July ₹	August ₹	August ₹	September ₹	September ₹
a) 50% of Credit Sales in the same month	40,000	38,000	70,000	66,500	60,000	57,000
Less: Cash Discount	(–) 2,000		(–) 3,500		(–) 3,000	
b) 50% of Credit Sales – One month credit	50,000	48,750	40,000	39,000	70,000	68,250
Less: 2½% Cash Discount	(–) 1,250	(+)	(–) 1,000	(+)	(–) 1,750	(+)
∴ Total		86,750		1,05,500		1,25,250

ii) **Calculation of Total Payment to Creditors:**

	Particulars		July ₹	August ₹	September ₹
a)	90% of Credit Purchases 30 days credit basis (i.e. one month)		1,44,000	1,53,000	2,16,000
b)	10% of Credit Purchases – Prompt basis	(+)	17,000	24,000	18,000
∴	Total		1,61,000	1,77,000	2,34,000

In the books of Hikal Industries, Ltd., Himmatpur
Cash Budget for the three months ending 30th September, 2013

Particulars		July ₹	August ₹	September ₹
Cash Balance Opening: (A)		25,000	60,000	1,03,000
Add: Receipts				
1) Cash Turnover		1,40,000	1,52,000	1,21,000
2) Total Collection from Debtors		86,750	1,05,500	1,25,250
∴ **Actual Receipts:** (B)		2,26,750	2,57,500	2,46,250
∴ **Total Receipts (A + B)** (C)		2,51,750	3,17,500	3,49,250
Less: Payments				
1) Monthly Salaries		10,000	10,000	10,000
2) Interest Payable		–	5,000	–
3) Total payment to Creditors		1,61,000	1,77,000	2,34,000
4) General Expenses		20,750	22,500	21,250
∴ **Total Payments** (D)		1,91,750	2,14,500	2,65,250
∴ **Cash Balance Closing (C – D)** (E)		60,000	1,03,000	84,000

Cost Accounting   4.34   Budget and Budgetary Control

ILLUSTRATION 9

Prepare a Cash Budget for three months ending 30th June, 2013, from the following particulars relating to Atlas Cycle Co., Ajmer.

2013 Months	Total Sales ₹	Material Purchases ₹	Salary ₹	Selling on Cost ₹
January	80,000	40,000	6,000	3,800
February	1,00,000	80,000	8,000	4,200
March	60,000	80,000	8,000	6,100
April	1,20,000	1,00,000	10,000	3,800
May	1,60,000	1,43,000	12,000	4,300
June	1,40,000	1,00,000	10,000	6,800

Additional Information :

i) 30% of Credit Sales will be realised in the second month following, whereas remaining 70% of Credit Sales will the realised in the month following the sales.
ii) The Materials Purchases will be on credit and the Creditors to be paid in the month following the purchases.
iii) Delay in payment of salary is half a month.
iv) Selling on costs are to be paid in the same month.
v) The proportion of cash turnover to credit turnover is 1 : 3 in total turnover.
vi) Advance income tax is to be paid in the month of April, amounting to ₹ 4,000.
vii) The Cash at Bank on 1st April, 2013, estimated at ₹ 40,000.

SOLUTION

In the books of Atlas Cycle Co., Ajmer
Cash Budget for the three months ended 30th June, 2013

Particulars		April ₹	May ₹	June ₹
Cash Balance Opening : (A)		(+) 40,000	(+) 26,000	(+) 26,000
Add : Receipts				
1) Cash Sales i.e. 1/4th of Total Sales(+)		30,000	40,000	35,000
2) Collection from Debtors - from Credit Sales i.e. 3/4th of Total Sales				
(a) 70% of Credit Sales - One month credit		31,500	63,000	84,000
(b) 30% of Credit Sales - Two months credit		22,500	13,500	27,000
∴ **Actual Receipts** (B)		84,000	1,16,500	1,46,000
∴ **Total Receipts (A + B)** (C)		1,24,000	1,42,500	1,72,000
Less : Payments				
1) Purchase of materials and payment to Creditors - One month credit		80,000	1,00,000	1,43,000
2) Delay in payment of salary - half a month		9,000 (4,000 + 5,000)	11,000 (5,000 + 6,000)	11,000 (6,000 + 5,000)

Particulars		April ₹	May ₹	June ₹
3) Selling on Cost - Payment in same month)		3,800	4,300	6,800
4) Advance Income Tax		4,000	–	–
5) Carriage on Sales		1,200	1,200	1,200
	(+)			
∴ Total Payments	(D)	98,000	1,16,500	1,62,000
	(–)			
∴ Cash Bank - Closing (C – D)	(E)	(+) 26,000	(+) 26,000	(+) 10,000

ILLUSTRATION 10

Intel Co. Ltd., Indapur, expects to have ₹ 37,500 cash at bank opening on 1st April, 2013, and requires you to prepare an estimate of cash position during the three months ended 30th June, 2013. The cost data is made available to you is as follows :

2013 Months	Sales ₹	Purchases ₹	Wages ₹	Works Overhead ₹	Management on Cost ₹	Selling Expenses ₹
February	75,000	45,000	3,000	7,500	6,000	4,500
March	84,000	48,000	9,750	8,250	6,000	4,500
April	90,000	52,500	10,500	9,000	6,000	3,500
May	1,20,000	60,000	13,500	11,250	6,000	2,250
June	1,35,000	60,000	14,250	14,000	7,000	7,000

Additional information is as follows :
i) Period of credit allowed by suppliers is two months.
ii) 20% of Total Sales are for cash and period of credit allowed to customers for credit sales is one month.
iii) Delay in payment of all other expenses is one month.
iv) Preference share dividend amounting to ₹ 57,500 is to be paid on 1st June, 2013.
v) The company is to pay bonus to workers of ₹ 22,500 in the month of April.
vi) Plant has been ordered to be received and paid in May, which will cost ₹ 1,20,000.
vii) Income-tax of ₹ 15,700 is due to be paid in April, 2013.

SOLUTION

In the books of Intel Co. Ltd., Indapur
Cash Budget for the three months ended 30th June, 2013

Particulars		April ₹	May ₹	June ₹
Cash Balance Opening :	A)	(+) 37,500	(+) 11,000	(–) 90,000
Add : Receipts				
1) Cash Sales i.e. 20% of Total Sales		18,000	24,000	27,000
2) Collection from Debtors - from Credit Sales i.e. 80% of Total Sales - One month credit		67,200	72,000	96,000
∴ **Actual Receipts :**	B)	85,200	96,000	1,23,000

Particulars			April ₹	May ₹	June ₹
∴ Total Receipts (A + B)		C)	1,22,700	1,07,000	33,000
Less : Payments :					
1)	Payment to suppliers on credit purchases - Two months credit		45,000	48,000	52,500
2)	Wages - One month delay		9,750	10,500	13,500
3)	Works Overhead - One month delay		8,250	9,000	11,250
4)	Management on Cost - One month delay		6,000	6,000	6,000
5)	Selling Expenses - One month delay		4,500	3,500	2,250
6)	Preference Share Dividend		–	–	57,500
7)	Bonus to Workers		22,500	–	–
8)	Purchase of Plant		–	1,20,000	–
9)	Income-tax		15,700	–	–
∴ Total Payments		D)	1,11,700	1,97,000	1,43,000
∴ Cash at Bank Closing (C – D)		E)	(+) 11,000	(–) 90,000	(–) 1,10,000

ILLUSTRATION 11

Snowwhite Ltd., Surat, provides following cost details from which you are required to prepare a Cash Budget for three months ended 30th September, 2013.

Particulars	June ₹	July ₹	August ₹	September ₹
Cash Sales - actuated	1,20,000	1,40,500	1,52,000	81,000
Credit Sales - estimated	1,00,000	80,000	1,40,000	1,20,000
Total Purchases	1,60,000	1,70,000	2,40,000	1,80,000
Selling Overheads	18,000	20,000	22,000	21,000

Additional Information :

i) Cash at Bank on 1st July, 2013 estimated, to be ₹ 25,000.

ii) Credit Sales are collected 50% in the month of sale, subject to 10% discount and 50% in the month following subject to 5% discount.

iii) Wages, Salaries and all other revenue charges have been estimated at ₹ 10,000 per month, including depreciation on Fixed Assets of ₹ 4,000 per month.

iv) 10% of Total Purchases are in cash and balance is paid in next month.

v) The company intends to replace an asset at a cost of ₹ 1,08,000 during September, 2013.

vi) Delay in payment of selling overheads in one month.

Also suggest necessary measures for better management of cash under the prevailing situation.

SOLUTION

Working Notes :

i) **Calculation of Collection from Debtors :**

Particulars	July ₹	July ₹	August ₹	August ₹	September ₹	September ₹
a) 50% in the month of sales	40,000	36,000	70,000	63,000	60,000	54,000
Less : Cash Discount	(–) 4,000		(–) 7,000		(–) 6,000	
b) 50% in the month following Sales	50,000	47,500	40,000	38,000	70,000	66,500
Less : 5% Cash Discount	(–) 2,500	(+)	(–) 2,000	(+)	(–) 3,500	(+)
∴ Total		83,500		1,01,000		1,20,500

ii) As Depreciation Expense is the expired cost of an asset during the accounting period and has nothing to do with cash payment, hence it is to be excluded from monthly payment of wages, salaries and all other revenue charges as follows :

		₹
•	Wages, Salaries and other revenue charges (estimated)	10,000
Less :	Depreciation on Fixed Assets	(–) 4,000
∴	Actual Payment per month	6,000

In the books of Snowwhite Ltd., Surat
Cash Budget for the three months ended 30th September, 2013

Particulars		July ₹	August ₹	September ₹
Cash Balance Opening :	A)	(+) 25,000	(+) 64,000	(+) 1,14,000
Add : Receipts				
1) Cash Sales		1,40,500	1,52,000	81,000
2) Collection from Debtors		83,500	1,01,000	1,20,500
3) Realisation of Old Asset		–	–	4,500
∴ **Actual Receipts :**	B)	2,24,000	2,53,000	2,06,000
∴ **Total Receipts (A + B)**	C)	2,49,000	3,17,000	3,20,000
Less : Payments				
1) Wages, Salaries and other Revenue Charges		6,000	6,000	6,000
2) Cash Purchases (10% of Total Purchases)		17,000	24,000	18,000
3) Credit Purchases - One month credit (90% of Total Purchases)		1,44,000	1,53,000	2,16,000
4) Selling Overheads - One month credit		18,000	20,000	22,000
5) Purchase of Asset		–	–	1,08,000
∴ **Total Payments**	D)	1,85,000	2,03,000	3,70,000
∴ **Cash at Bank Closing (C – D)**	E)	(+) 64,000	(+) 1,14,000	(–) 50,000

FLEXIBLE BUDGET

ILLUSTRATION 1

The statement given below gives the Flexible Budget at 60% capacity of Finolex Cable Ltd., Faizpur. Prepare a tabulated statement giving the budget figures at 75% and 90% capacity where no indication has been given. Make your own classification of expenses between fixed, variable and semi-variable expenses.

Particulars	60% capacity ₹
Prime Cost Materials	1,60,000
Depreciation	60,000
Productive Wages	40,000
Rent	12,000
Indirect Materials	48,000
Insurance of Machinery	12,000
Indirect Labour	40,000
Electric Power (40% Fixed)	8,000
Repairs and Maintenance (60% Fixed)	20,000

SOLUTION

In the books of Finolex Cable Ltd., Faizpur
Flexible Budget

Normal Activity : Units
Capacity : 60%

Production	Units			–	–	–
Capacity	%			60	75	90
Particulars				Total Cost ₹	Total Cost ₹	Total Cost ₹
A) Fixed Expenses :						
i) Depreciation				60,000	60,000	60,000
ii) Rent				12,000	12,000	12,000
iii) Insurance of Machinery				12,000	12,000	12,000
B) Variable Expenses :						
i) Prime Cost Materials				1,60,000	2,00,000	2,40,000
ii) Productive Wages				40,000	50,000	60,000
iii) Indirect Materials				48,000	60,000	72,000
iv) Indirect Labour				40,000	50,000	60,000
C) Semi-Variable Expenses						
i) Electric Power			8,000			
• Fixed – 40%		3,200		3,200	3,200	3,200
• Variable – 60%		(+) 4,800		4,800	6,000	7,200
ii) Repairs and Maintenance			20,000			
• Fixed – 60%		12,000		12,000	12,000	12,000
• Variable – 40%		(+) 8,000		8,000	10,000	12,000
∴ Total				4,00,000	4,75,200	5,50,400

ILLUSTRATION 2

The expenses budgeted for production at 100% capacity of Infosys Ltd., Islampur, are given below.

Particulars	At 100% capacity ₹
Direct Materials	6,00,000
Variable Works Overheads	2,00,000
Basic Wages	2,00,000
Fixed Production Overheads	80,000
Productive Expenses – Marginal	40,000
Administrative Expenses – Rigid	40,000
Selling Overheads (10% Fixed)	1,20,000
Distribution on Cost (80% Variable)	60,000

Prepare a Flexible Budget for the production at 60% and 80% capacity showing separately –
i) Prime Cost, ii) Works Cost, iii) Cost of Production, iv) Cost of Turnover.

SOLUTION

In the Books of Infosys Ltd., Islampur
Flexible Budget

Normal Activity : Units
Capacity : 100%

Production Capacity	Particulars		Units %	60 Total Cost ₹	80 Total Cost ₹	100 Total Cost ₹
	Direct Materials			3,60,000	4,80,000	6,00,000
Add :	Basic Wages			1,20,000	1,60,000	2,00,000
Add :	Productive Expenses – Marginal			24,000	32,000	40,000
	Prime Cost		i)	5,04,000	6,72,000	8,40,000
Add :	Factory Overheads					
	• Variable Works Overheads			1,20,000	1,60,000	2,00,000
	• Fixed Production Overheads			80,000	80,000	80,000
	Works Cost		ii)	7,04,000	9,12,000	11,20,000
Add :	Administrative Expenses – Rigid			40,000	40,000	40,000
	Cost of Production		iii)	7,44,000	9,52,000	11,60,000
Add :	Selling and Distribution Overheads					
	• Selling Overheads –		1,20,000			
	• Fixed – 10%	12,000		12,000	12,000	12,000
	• Variable – 90%	(+) 1,08,000		64,800	86,400	1,08,000
	• Distribution on Cost –		60,000			
	• Fixed – 20%	12,000		12,000	12,000	12,000
	• Variable – 80%	(+) 48,000	iv)	28,800	38,400	48,000
	Cost of Turnover			8,61,600	11,00,800	13,40,000

ILLUSTRATION 3

From the following information relating to Castrol Ltd., Cochin, prepare a Flexible Budget at 60% and 80% capacity.

Particulars	70% Capacity ₹
A) Variable Overheads :	
• Indirect Material	5,000
• Indirect Labour	15,000
B) Semi-variable Overheads :	
• Electricity	50,000
Variable – 60%	
Fixed – 40%	
• Repairs and Maintenance	5,000
Variable – 65%	
Fixed – 35%	
C) Fixed Overhead :	
• Salaries to Staff	10,000
• Depreciation on Machines	14,000
• Insurance on Machines	(+) 6,000
∴ Total	1,05,000

The company estimated the direct labour hours to be worked at 70% capacity as 70,000 hours. Also calculate the overhead recovery rate at 60%, 70% and 80% capacities.

SOLUTION

In the Books of Castrol Ltd., Cochin
Flexible Budget

Normal Activity : Units
Capacity : 70%

Production Capacity		Units %			– 60 Total Cost ₹	– 70 Total Cost ₹	– 80 Total Cost ₹
	Particulars						
A)	**Variable Overheads :**						
	i) Indirect Material				4,286	5,000	5,714
	ii) Indirect Labour				12,857	15,000	17,143
B)	**Semi-variable Overheads :**						
	i) Electricity			50,000			
	• Variable – 60%		30,000		25,714	30,000	34,286
	• Fixed – 40%		20,000		20,000	20,000	20,000
	ii) Repairs and Maintenance			5,000			
	• Variable – 65%		3,250		2,786	3,250	3,714
	• Fixed – 35%		1,750		1,750	1,750	1,750
C)	**Fixed Overheads :**						
	i) Salaries to Staff				10,000	10,000	10,000
	ii) Depreciation on Machines				14,000	14,000	14,000
	iii) Insurance on Machines				6,000	6,000	6,000
	∴ Total				97,393	1,05,000	1,12,607

Calculation of Overhead Recovery Rate on the basis of Direct Labour Hours :

$$= \frac{\text{Total Overheads}}{\text{Direct Labour Hours}}$$

$= \dfrac{₹\,97,393}{60,000 \text{ Hrs.}}$ $= \dfrac{₹\,1,05,000}{70,000 \text{ Hrs.}}$ $= \dfrac{₹\,1,12,607}{80,000 \text{ Hrs.}}$

$= ₹\,1.62$ $= ₹\,1.50$ $= ₹\,1.41$

ILLUSTRATION 4

Dupont Chemicals Ltd., Delhi, has submitted the actual cost data working on two capacity levels as follows :

Particulars	Capacity –	60%	70%
	Cost – Amount –	Total ₹	Total ₹
Distribution on Cost		30,000	40,000
Prime Cost Labour		3,00,000	3,50,000
Factory Overheads		2,00,000	2,20,000
Chargeable Expenses		1,20,000	1,40,000
Raw Materials		3,60,000	4,20,000
Selling Expenses		60,000	70,000
Office on Cost (Rigid)		1,00,000	1,00,000

Prepare a Flexible Budget at 80%, 90% and 100% capacity showing clearly i) Direct Cost, ii) Works Cost, iii) Cost of Production, and iv) Total Cost.

The costs have a rising tendency, according to the change in the capacity levels.

SOLUTION

Working Notes :
i) Raw Materials Cost increases by ₹ 60,000 per 10% increase in capacity.
ii) Prime Cost Labour increases by ₹ 50,000 per 10% increase in capacity.
iii) Factory Overheads increases by ₹ 20,000 per 10% increase in capacity.
iv) Office on Cost are rigid, hence remain fixed at various capacity levels.
v) Selling Expenses and Distribution on Cost increases by ₹ 10,000 per 10% increase in capacity.

In the books of Dupont Chemicals Ltd., Delhi
Flexible Budget

Normal Activity : Units
Capacity : 60% and 70%

Production Capacity %	Units	– 60	– 70	– 80	– 90	– 100
Particulars		Total Cost ₹	Total Cost ₹	Total Cost ₹	Total Cost ₹	Total Cost ₹
Raw Materials		3,60,000	4,20,000	4,80,000	5,40,000	6,00,000
Add : Prime Cost Labour		3,00,000	3,50,000	4,00,000	4,50,000	5,00,000
Add : Chargeable Expenses		1,20,000	1,40,000	1,60,000	1,80,000	2,00,000
∴ Direct Cost	i)	7,80,000	9,10,000	10,40,000	11,70,000	13,00,000
Add : Factory Overheads		2,00,000	2,20,000	2,40,000	2,60,000	2,80,000
Works Cost	ii)	9,80,000	11,30,000	12,80,000	14,30,000	15,80,000
Add : Office-on-Cost		1,00,000	1,00,000	1,00,000	1,00,000	1,00,000
Cost of Production	iii)	10,80,000	12,30,000	13,80,000	15,30,000	16,80,000
Add : Selling Expenses		60,000	70,000	80,000	90,000	1,00,000
Add : Distribution on Cost		30,000	40,000	50,000	60,000	70,000
Total Cost	iv)	11,70,000	13,40,000	15,10,000	16,80,000	18,50,000

Cost Accounting — Budget and Budgetary Control

ILLUSTRATION 5

From the following cost data made available by Ambuja Metals Co. Ltd., Ahmednagar, for a quarterly period, forecast the results by preparing a Flexible Budget at 70%, 80% and 90% capacity level, where the estimated turnover amounted to ₹ 1,26,000, ₹ 1,34,000 and ₹ 1,42,000 respectively. It is assumed that –

i) Marginal expenses varies due to change in production capacity level,
ii) Rigid expenses remains constant at various production capacity level and
iii) Semi-fixed expenses are constant between 55% and 75% capacity, increases by 10% between 75% and 85% capacity and increases by 20% between 85% and 90% capacity.

The expenses and sales at 60% capacity level are as under :

Particulars	₹
A) Fixed Expenses :	
i) Workshop Salary	9,300
ii) Office Rent	6,100
iii) Machinery Depreciation	8,600
B) Variable Expenses :	
i) Basic Materials	24,000
ii) Direct Labour	9,000
iii) Productive Expenses	3,000
C) Semi-Variable Expenses :	
i) Repairs and Maintenance	10,000
ii) Telephone Charges	6,000
iii) Indirect Labour	(+) 4,000
∴ **Total Cost of Sales**	80,000
Value of Sales	1,10,000

Also find out the percentage of profit to sales and submit a report to the management indicating your critical comments on the position at various production capacity level.

SOLUTION

In the books of Ambuja Metals Co. Ltd., Ahmednagar
Flexible Budget

Normal Activity : Units
Capacity : 60%

Production Capacity	Units %	– 60	– 70	– 80	– 90
Particulars		Total Cost ₹	Total Cost ₹	Total Cost ₹	Total Cost ₹
A) Fixed Expenses :					
i) Workshop Salary		9,300	9,300	9,300	9,300
ii) Office Rent		6,100	6,100	6,100	6,100
iii) Machinery Depreciation		8,600	8,600	8,600	8,600
B) Variable Expenses					
i) Basic Materials		24,000	28,000	32,000	36,000
ii) Direct Labour		9,000	10,500	12,000	13,500
iii) Productive Expenses		3,000	3,500	4,000	4,500

| Production | Units | – | – | – | – |
| Capacity | % | 60 | 70 | 80 | 90 |
Particulars		Total Cost ₹	Total Cost ₹	Total Cost ₹	Total Cost ₹
C) Semi-Variable Expenses :					
i) Repairs and Maintenance		10,000	10,000 (constant)	11,000 (increases by 10%)	12,000 (increases by 20%)
ii) Telephone Charges		6,000	6,000 (constant)	6,600 (increases by 10%)	7,200 (increases by 20%)
iii) Indirect Labour		4,000	4,000 (constant)	4,400 (increases by 10%)	4,800 (increases by 20%)
∴ Total Cost of Sales	i) (+)	80,000	86,000	94,000	1,02,000
Add : Forecast Profits	ii) (+)	30,000	40,000	40,000	40,000
Total Turnover		1,10,000	1,26,000	1,34,000	1,42,000
Percentage of Profit to Sales	iii)	27.27	31.75	29.85	28.17

Reporting to the Management :

A critical analysis of the forecasted results as shown above in the flexible budgets reveals that at 70% production capacity level, the percentage of profit to sales (i.e. 31.75%) is more as compared to other production levels. Hence, it is suggested to the management that,

i) the company should increase their production as capacity level from 60% to 70%.

ii) additional efforts are necessary to reduce the cost substantially by introducing effective technique to control variable cost.

iii) the company should concentrate on increasing the turnover sizeably.

ILLUSTRATION 6

In Burma Plastics Co., Badalpur, the cost of an article at a capacity level of 5,000 units is given under 'A' below for a variation of 25% in capacity above or below this level, the individual vary as indicated 'B' below.

Particulars	'A' ₹	'B' Variation
Raw Materials	25,000	100% varying
Direct Labour	15,000	100% varying
Stores Overhead	1,000	100% varying
Productive Expenses	10,000	100% varying
Repairs and Maintenance	2,000	75% varying
Power	1,250	80% varying
Inspection	500	20% varying
Office Overheads	5,000	25% varying
Selling on Cost	3,000	25% varying

Prepare a flexible budget at production levels of 4,000 units and 6,000 units.

SOLUTION

In the books of Burma Plastic Co., Badalpur
Flexible Budget

Normal Activity : Units 5,000
Capacity :

Production Units				4,000		5,000		6,000	
Capacity %				–		–		–	
Particulars			Nature of Cost	Unit Cost ₹	Total Cost ₹	Unit Cost ₹	Total Cost ₹	Unit Cost ₹	Total Cost ₹
A)	Variable Expenses :								
	i) Raw Materials		Variable	5.00	20,000	5.00	25,000	5.00	30,000
	ii) Direct Labour		Variable	3.00	12,000	3.00	15,000	3.00	18,000
	iii) Stores Overhead		Variable	0.20	800	0.20	1,000	0.20	1,200
	iv) Productive Expenses		Variable	2.00	8,000	2.00	10,000	2.00	12,000
B)	Semi-Variable Expenses :		Semi-variable						
	i) Repairs and Maintenance	2,000							
	• Fixed : 25%	500		0.13	500	0.10	500	0.08	500
	• Variable : 75%	1,500		0.30	1,200	0.30	1,500	0.30	1,800
	II) Power	1,250	Semi-variable						
	• Fixed : 20%	250		0.06	250	0.05	250	0.04	250
	• Variable : 80%	1,000		0.20	800	0.20	1,000	0.20	1,200
	III) Inspection	500	Semi-variable						
	• Fixed : 80%	400		0.10	400	0.08	400	0.07	400
	• Variable : 20%	100		0.02	80	0.02	100	0.02	120
	iv) Office Overheads,	5,000	Semi-variable						
	• Fixed : 75%	3,750		0.94	3,750	0.75	3,750	0.63	3,750
	• Variable : 25%	1,250		0.25	1,000	0.25	1,250	0.25	1,500
	v) Selling on Cost	3,000	Semi-variable						
	• Fixed : 75%	2,250		0.56	2,250	0.45	2,250	0.38	2,250
	• Variable : 25%	750		0.15	600	0.15	750	0.15	900
	∴ Total			12.91	51,630	12.55	62,750	12.32	73,870

ILLUSTRATION 7

Thomas Cook Ltd., Talegaon, provides the following cost data for a 60% working capacity, from which you are required to prepare a Flexible Budget for the production at 80% and 100% capacity level.

Current Production	Units 600
Selling Price (Fixed) per unit	₹ 300
Process Material Cost per unit	₹ 100
Productive Wages per unit	₹ 40
Prime Cost Expenses	₹ 10
Total Works Overheads (40% Fixed)	₹ 40,000
Total Office, Selling and Distribution Overheads ₹ 30,000 (50% Variable)	

SOLUTION

In the books of Thomas Cook Ltd., Talegaon
Flexible Budget

Normal Activity : Units 600
Capacity : 60%

Production Units			600		800		1,000	
Capacity %			60		80		100	
Particulars			Unit Cost ₹	Total Cost ₹	Unit Cost ₹	Total Cost ₹	Unit Cost ₹	Total Cost ₹
Process Material Cost			100.00	60,000	100.00	80,000	100.00	1,00,000
Add : Productive Wages			40.00	24,000	40.00	32,000	40.00	40,000
Add : Prime Cost Expenses			10.00	6,000	10.00	8,000	10.00	10,000
∴ **Prime Cost**		i)	150.00	90,000	150.00	1,20,000	150.00	1,50,000
Add : Works Overheads		40,000						
• Fixed : 40%	16,000		26.67	16,000	20.00	16,000	16.00	16,000
• Variable : 60%	24,000		40.00	24,000	40.00	32,000	40.00	40,000
∴ **Works Cost**		ii)	216.67	1,30,000	210.00	1,68,000	206.00	2,06,000
Add : Office, Selling and Distribution Overheads		30,000						
• Fixed : 50%	15,000		25.00	15,000	18.75	15,000	15.00	15,000
• Variable : 50%	15,000		25.00	15,000	25.00	20,000	25.00	25,000
∴ **Total Cost**		iii)	266.67	1,60,000	253.75	2,03,000	246.00	2,46,000
Add : Profit		iv)	33.33	20,000	46.25	37,000	54.00	54,000
Selling Price			300.00	1,80,000	300.00	2,40,000	300.00	3,00,000

ILLUSTRATION 8

Activa Co. Ltd., Anand, produces computer hardware. The estimated unit cost is as under:

Particulars	₹
Direct Material	15
Direct Wages	10
Direct Expenses	4
Variable Overheads	(+) 6
∴ Total	35

The Fixed Overheads are estimated at ₹ 1,00,000. The semi-Variable Overheads are ₹ 50,000 at 100% capacity i.e. 10,000 units. The semi-variable expenses vary in stages of ₹ 4,000 for each change in output of 1,000 units. Selling Price per unit is ₹ 70. You are required to prepare a Flexible Budget at 50%, 70%, 90% and 100% capacities and determine the profit at each level.

SOLUTION

In the Books of Activa Co. Ltd., Anand
Flexible Budget

Normal Activity : 10,000 units
Capacity : 100%

Production Units		5,000		7,000		9,000		10,000	
Capacity %		50		70		90		100	
Particulars		Unit Cost ₹	Total Cost ₹	Unit Cost ₹	Total Cost ₹	Unit Cost ₹	Total Cost ₹	Unit Cost ₹	Total Cost ₹
Direct Material		15.00	75,000	15.00	1,05,000	15.00	1,35,000	15.00	1,50,000
Add : Direct Wages		10.00	50,000	10.00	70,000	10.00	90,000	10.00	1,00,000
Add : Direct Expenses		4.00	20,000	4.00	28,000	4.00	36,000	4.00	40,000
Prime Cost	i)	29.00	1,45,000	29.00	2,03,000	29.00	2,61,000	29.00	2,90,000
Add : Variable Overheads		6.00	30,000	6.00	42,000	6.00	54,000	6.00	60,000
Add : Fixed Overheads		20.00	1,00,000	14.29	1,00,000	11.11	1,00,000	10.00	1,00,000
Add : Semi-Variable Overheads		6.00	30,000	5.43	38,000	5.11	46,000	5.00	50,000
Total Cost	ii)	61.00	3,05,000	54.72	3,83,000	51.22	4,61,000	50.00	5,00,000
Add : Profit	iii)	9.00	45,000	15.28	1,07,000	18.78	1,69,000	20.00	2,00,000
Selling Price	iv)	70.00	3,50,000	70.00	4,90,000	70.00	6,30,000	70.00	7,00,000

ILLUSTRATION 9

The expenses for the production at 5,000 units at 50% capacity in Baroda Chemicals Ltd., Bhavnagar, are given as follows:

	Unit Cost ₹
Materials	50
Labour	20
Variable Overheads	15
Fixed Overheads (₹ 50,000)	10
Administrative Expenses (5% Variable)	10
Selling Expenses (20% Fixed)	6
Distribution Expenses (10% Fixed)	(+) 5
Total Cost of Sales	116

You are required to prepare a budget for 70% and 90% production capacity, assuming that 90% capacity cost of materials will increase by 10% whereas labour cost will decrease by 5%.

SOLUTION

In the Books of Baroda Chemicals Ltd., Bhavnagar
Flexible Budget

Normal Activity : 5,000 units
Capacity : 50%

	Production Capacity			Units %	5,000 50		7,000 70		9,000 90	
	Particulars				Unit Cost ₹	Total Cost ₹	Unit Cost ₹	Total Cost ₹	Unit Cost ₹	Total Cost ₹
A)	Fixed Expenses :									
	i) Fixed Overheads				10.00	50,000	7.14	50,000	5.56	50,000
B)	Variable Expenses :									
	i) Materials				50.00	2,50,000	50.00	3,50,000	55.00 (50 + 10% i.e. ₹ 5)	4,95,000
	ii) Labour				20.00	1,00,000	20.00	1,40,000	19.00 (20 – 5% i.e. ₹ 1)	1,71,000
	iii) Variable Overheads				15.00	75,000	15.00	1,05,000	15.00	1,35,000
C)	Semi-Variable Expenses :									
	i) Administrative Expenses			10.						
	(a) Fixed	95%		9.50	9.50	47,500	6.79	47,500	5.28	6,000
	(b) Variable	5%	(+)	0.50	0.50	2,500	0.50	3,500	0.50	4,500
	ii) Selling Expenses			6.						
	(a) Fixed	20%		1.20	1.20	6,000	0.86	6,000	0.67	6,000
	(b) Variable	90%	(+)	4.80	4.80	24,000	4.80	33,600	4.80	43,200
	iii) Distribution Expenses			5.						
	(a) Fixed	10%		0.50	0.50	2,500	0.36	2,500	0.28	2,500
	(b) Variable	90%	(+)	4.50	4.50	22,500	4.50	31,500	4.50	40,500
∴	Total Cost of Sales				116.00	5,80,000	109.95	7,69,600	110.59	9,53,700

ILLUSTRATION 10

Dabur Chemicals Ltd., Delhi has given you the following information at 50% capacity of the production of 5,000 units during the month of March, 2008.

Particulars	Unit Cost ₹
Materials	50
Labour	30
Variable Overheads	20
Fixed Overheads (₹ 50,000)	10
Administrative Overheads	10
Selling Expenses (25% Fixed)	8
Distribution Expenses (20% Fixed)	5
Total Cost	**133**

You are required to prepare Flexible Budgets at 60%, 70% and 80% capacity presuming that at 80% capacity, material cost will be less by 5% and variable selling expenses will increase by 10%.

SOLUTION

In the Books of Dabur Chemicals Ltd., Delhi
Flexible Budget

Normal Activity : 5,000 units
Capacity : 50%

Production Units			5,000		6,000		7,000		8,000	
Capacity %			50		60		70		80	
Particulars			Unit Cost ₹	Total Cost ₹	Unit Cost ₹	Total Cost ₹	Unit Cost ₹	Total Cost ₹	Unit Cost ₹	Total Cost ₹
A) Fixed Expenses										
i) Fixed Overheads			10.00	50,000	8.33	50,000	7.14	50,000	6.25	50,000
B) Variable Expenses										
i) Materials			50.00	2,50,000	50.00	3,00,000	50.00	3,50,000	47.50 (₹ 50 – 5%)	3,80,000
ii) Labour			30.00	1,50,000	30.00	1,80,000	30.00	2,10,000	i.e. ₹ 2.50) 30.00	2,40,000
iii) Variable Overheads			20.00	1,00,000	20.00	1,20,000	20.00	1,40,000	20.00	1,60,000
C) Semi-Variable Expenses :										
i) Administration Overheads		10.								
• Fixed	90%	9.	9.00	45,000	7.50	45,000	6.43	45,000	5.62	45,000
• Variable	10%	(+) 1.	1.00	5,000	1.00	6,000	1.00	7,000	1.00	8,000
ii) Selling Expenses		8.								
• Fixed	25%	2.	2.00	10,000	1.67	10,000	1.43	10,000	1.25	10,000
• Variable	75%	(+) 6.	6.00	30,000	6.00	36,000	6.00	42,000	6.60 (₹ 6 + 10% i.e. 0.60)	52,800
iii) Distribution Expenses		5.								
• Fixed	20%	1.	1.00	5,000	0.83	5,000	0.71	5,000	0.62	5,000
• Variable	80%	(+) 4.	4.00	20,000	4.00	24,000	4.00	28,000	4.00	32,000
Total Cost			133.00	6,65,000	129.33	7,76,000	126.71	8,87,000	122.84	9,82,800

ILLUSTRATION 11

Crysta Ltd., Cochin, is currently working at 50% capacity and produces 1,000 units at a cost of ₹ 180 per unit as per the details shown below.

Particulars	Unit Cost ₹
Direct Material	100
Direct Labour	30
Factory Overhead (40% Fixed)	30
Administrative Overhead (50% Fixed)	20

The current selling price is ₹ 200 per unit. At 60% working capacity, raw material cost increases by 2% and selling price falls by 2%. At 80% working capacity, material cost increases by 5% and selling price falls by 5%. Estimate profits of the company at 60% and 80% capacity by preparing Flexible Budgets and offer your critical comments.

SOLUTION

In the Books of Crysta Ltd., Cochin
Flexible Budget

Normal Activity : 1,000 units
Capacity : 50%

Production Capacity	Units %	1,000 50		1,200 60		1,600 80	
Particulars		Unit Cost ₹	Total Cost ₹	Unit Cost ₹	Total Cost ₹	Unit Cost ₹	Total Cost ₹
Direct Material		100.00	1,00,000	102.00 (100 + 2% i.e. ₹ 2)	1,22,400	105.00 (100 + 5% i.e. ₹ 5)	1,68,000
Add : Direct Labour		30.00	30,000	30.00	36,000	30.00	48,000
Prime Cost i)		130.00	1,30,000	132.00	1,58,400	135.00	2,16,000
Add : Factory Overheads	30						
• Fixed 40%	12	12.00	12,000	10.00	12,000	7.50	12,000
• Variable 60%	18	18.00	18,000	18.00	21,600	18.00	28,800
Add : Administrative Overheads	20						
• Fixed 50%	10	10.00	10,000	8.33	10,000	6.25	10,000
• Variable 50%	10	10.00	10,000	10.00	12,000	10.00	16,000
∴ **Total Cost** ii)		180.00	1,80,000	178.33	2,14,000	176.75	2,82,800
Add : Profits iii)		20.00	20,000	17.67	21,200	13.25	21,200
Selling Price iv)		200.00	2,00,000	196.00 (200 − 2% i.e. ₹ 4)	2,35,200	190.00 (200 − 5% i.e. ₹ 10)	3,04,000

Comments :
After making a critical analysis, it is suggested that production capacity should not be increased as profit remain constant at 60% and 80% capacity level.

ILLUSTRATION 12

Sudarshan Co., Satara, is engaged in manufacturing Full Scape Note Books is working currently at 40% capacity and produces 10,000 note books per month. The cost and price details for one note book is as under :

Particulars	Unit Cost and Price ₹
On Cost (40% Variable)	5
Productive Expenses	1
Direct Labour Cost	2
Basic Materials Cost	10
Market Price	20

You are required to prepare a Flexible Budget showing separately the profit at 50% and 90% capacities and the break-even points at the production capacity levels assuming that –
 i) at 50% capacity the invoice price falls by 3% and
 ii) at 90% capacity the selling price falls by 5%
accompanied by a similar fall in the price of Direct Material.

SOLUTION

In the books of Sudarshan Co., Satara
Flexible Budget

Normal Activity : Units 10,000
Capacity % : 40

Production Capacity	Units %	10,000 40		12,500 50		22,500 90	
Particulars		Per Unit ₹	Total ₹	Per Unit ₹	Total ₹	Per Unit ₹	Total ₹
Sales		20.00	2,00,000	19.40 (fall by 3%)	2,42,500	19.00 (fall by 5%)	4,27,500
Less : Variable Cost							
i) Basic Material Cost		10.00	1,00,000	10.00	1,25,000	9.50 (fall by 5%)	2,13,750
ii) Direct Labour Cost		2.00	20,000	2.00	25,000	2.00	45,000
iii) Productive Expenses		1.00	10,000	1.00	12,500	1.00	22,500
iv) On Cost (40% of ₹ 5.00)	(−)	2.00	20,000	2.00	25,000	2.00	45,000
∴ Contribution where, (C = S − V)		5.00	50,000	4.40	55,000	4.50	1,01,250
Less : Fixed Cost							
i) On Cost (60% of ₹ 5.00)	(−)	3.00	30,000	2.40	30,000	1.33	30,000
∴ **Profit**		2.00	20,000	2.00	25,000	3.17	71,250
where, (P = C − F) ∴ Break Even Point (Units) where, BEP (Units) = Total Fixed Cost / Contribution per unit		= ₹ 30,000 / Rs. 5.00 = 6,000 units		= ₹ 30,000 / Rs. 4.40 = 6,818 units		= ₹ 30,000 / Rs. 4.50 = 6,667 units	

QUESTIONS FOR SELF-STUDY

I. Theory Questions :
 i) Clearly bring out the meaning of Budget, Budgeting and Budgetary Control.
 ii) What do you mean by Budgetary Control ? Suggest a suitable organisation for efficient Budgetary Control System.
 iii) Discuss the objective, advantages and limitations of Budgetary Control System.
 iv) What are the different types of functional budgets which are prepared by a large scale manufacturing concern ? Explain the method of preparation of a Sales Budget or a Cash Budget.
 v) What do you understand by a Flexible Budget ? How does fixed cost per unit vary in case of a budget for varying levels of activity ?
 vi) Define Cash Budget. Show neatly with the help of a proforma how it is prepared ?
 vii) Explain the various types of Budget.
 viii) Write short notes on :
  a) Sales Budget b) Purchase Budget
  c) Production Budget d) Cost of Production Budget
  e) Cash Budget f) Flexible Budget

g) Fixed Budget
i) Types of Budget
k) Programme Budgeting
m) Objectives of Budgetary Control
h) Sales Budget
j) Zero Base Budgeting
l) Performance Budgeting

II. Practical Problems

i) The following budget estimates are available from Monica Industries Ltd., working at 50% capacity.

	₹
Variable Costs	50,000
Semi-variable Costs	25,000
Fixed Costs	10,000

You are required to prepare a budget for 80% capacity assuming that semi-variable expenses increases by 10% for every 20% increases in capacity.

ii) In a factory, a cost centre works at 60% capacity and the following overhead expenses are incurred.

Particulars	₹
Salary of Supervisor	2,000
Salary of Assistant Supervisor	1,000
Wages of workers	5,000
Repairs of machines	8,000
Spoiled Work	2,500
Spoiled Work	2,500
Oils and Lubricants	2,000
Depreciation of Machine	10,000
∴ Total	33,000

Prepare a Flexible Budget for 75%, 100% and 125% capacities.

iii) Kumaran Mohan Ltd., Kurla, produces a consumer product. The estimated costs per unit are given below :

Raw Material	₹	500
Direct Labour	₹	300
Factory Overhead	₹	400 (30% fixed)
Administrative Overheads	₹	200 (60% fixed)
Cost per unit	₹	1,400

The selling price per unit is ₹ 1,800. At 50% capacity it produces 5,000 units. Find out the profits when it works at 60% and 80% capacity.

Notes :
a) The cost per unit of ₹ 1,400 is at 50% capacity.
b) At 60% capacity, raw material cost increases by 3% and selling price falls by 3%.
c) At 80% capacity, raw material cost increases by 4% and selling price falls by 5%.

Draw a proforma of a Flexible Budget using imaginary figures for 50%, 60% and 70% capacity levels.

iv) From the following particulars, prepare a Cash Budget for January, February and March 2013 in a tabular form.

Months 2012-13	Sales ₹	Purchases ₹	Wages ₹	Expenses ₹
October 2012	1,00,000	50,000	15,000	6,000
November 2012	90,000	45,000	19,000	5,000
December 2012	80,000	40,000	24,000	7,000
January 2013	85,000	42,500	22,000	5,000
February 2013	95,000	50,000	18,000	6,000
March 2013	90,000	45,000	20,000	5,000

Further information :
a) 5% of the purchases and 10% of the sales are for cash.
b) Credit allowed to customers is 1/2 months.
c) Credit for purchases are paid following the month of purchases.
d) Wages are paid every 15 days.
e) Opening Balance of cash as on 1st January, 2013, is ₹ 15,000.

v) From the following particulars, prepare a Cash Budget for the quarter ended 30th June, 2013.

Particulars	Actual			Budgeted		
	January ₹	February ₹	March ₹	April ₹	May ₹	June ₹
Sales	1,00,000	1,00,000	95,000	1,20,000	1,15,000	1,10,000
Purchases	50,000	45,000	48,000	50,000	45,000	30,000
Wages	30,000	25,000	28,000	30,000	25,000	20,000
Expenses	4,000	5,000	5,000	8,000	6,000	40,000

Further Information :
i) 50% of the purchases and sales are for cash
ii) Debtors realised after one month
iii) Creditors paid after two months
iv) Payment of wages made after one week
v) Expenses are paid after one month
vi) Rent of ₹ 5,000 per month not considered in expenses
vii) Income-tax payable in April ₹ 1,500
viii) Cash balance as on 1st April, 2013, was ₹ 1,500.

vi) The following is the estimated data for six months from March, 2013, to August, 2013, of a Rotex Ltd., Rameshwar.

Months 2013	Credit Sales ₹	Credit Purchases ₹	Wages ₹	Manufacturing Expenses ₹	Office Expenses ₹	Selling Expenses ₹
March	50,000	35,000	9,000	5,000	1,500	1,500
April	54,000	39,000	8,500	4,000	2,000	4,000
May	58,000	32,000	9,500	4,500	3,500	4,500
June	50,000	35,000	8,000	3,000	1,000	3,500
July	55,000	38,000	7,900	5,500	1,500	4,500
August	60,000	36,000	8,200	4,400	2,500	4,000

Other Information :
a) A machine valued at ₹ 20,000 will be supplied in June, 2013, when 20% will have to be paid against delivery and the remaining balance to be paid after 4 months.
b) Credit Period .... Allowed to Customers .... 1 month
   Allowed by Suppliers .... 2 month
c) Tax to be paid in advance ₹ 10,000 in March, 2013
d) Lag in payments .... Manufacturing expenses 15 days
   .... All other expenses 30 days

Prepare a Cash Budget for the six months ended 31st August, 2013.

***

Unit ... 5

MARGINAL COSTING

5.1 Meaning
5.2 Various Concepts
    5.2.1 Fixed Cost
    5.2.2 Variable Cost
    5.2.3 Contribution
    5.2.4 Profit Volume Ratio (P/V Ratio)
    5.2.5 Break Even Point
    5.2.6 Margin of Safety
* Illustrations
* Questions for Self-Study

Every manufacturing concern would like to increase its profits by increasing volume of production, which will automatically involve additional cost. Such a decision would require a detailed analysis of additional costs and its behaviour as it has a direct bearing on the profitability of the concern. Any increase in the level of operation will diminish the firm's marginal profit, if it is already at its optimum level of existing operation. However, such a decision would definitely prove financially worthy, if there exists any unutilised operational capacity. Thus, to reach at an accurate decision, management must know how costs will react to changes in activity.

The analysis of cost behaviour reveals that the cost of a product can be divided into two major categories, the first is fixed cost and the second is variable cost.

As we know that, fixed cost remains constant up to a particular level of output, whereas variable cost has a tendency to change proportionally with a change in the level of output. The following example will further clarify the concept.

ABC Co., invited sale of 20,000 units @ ₹ 1000 per unit during the year 2012-2013 with the following details of expenditure on production.

- Raw Material required to produce one unit of finished product 2 kg @ ₹ 2 per kg.
- Wages ₹ 200 per unit.
- Rent of factory ₹ 50,000 p.a.
- Salary of executive ₹ 5,00,000 p.a.

In the above-mentioned example, the costs of raw-material and wages change proportionately with the change in the level of output and, therefore are known as **variable costs**. Whereas the rent of factory and salary of executive are such costs that are not subject to change with the change in output. They remain constant at every level of output and as such are known as **fixed costs**. On account of this reason, it is unlogic to apportion fixed costs to production. Marginal costing is the technique which deals with the concept of variable cost.

Marginal costing which is otherwise known as "**Variable Costing**" is used as a tool for decision-making by the management. Marginal Costing is also known as "**Direct Costing**" and this new concept is gaining wide popularity in the field of accounting. Marginal costing is a technique through which variable costs are taken into account for the purposes of product costing, inventory valuation and other important management decisions. The term "marginal costing" is commonly used in U.K. and other European countries, while the same is denoted as "direct costing" or "variable costing" is U.S.A.

Thus, **Marginal Costing** is also known as 'variable' or 'direct' or 'differential costing'. The term "marginal costing' seems to be inappropriate, since is has an exclusive meaning in Economics. Under the above circumstances, the term 'Variable Costing' seems to be more appropriate and acceptable.

5.1 MEANING

The term "marginal cost" is derived from the word "margin" which is a well known terminology in economics. As it is used in economic parlance, the term "marginal cost" connotes the cost which arises from the production of additional increment of output.

Marginal Cost:

The **Institute of Cost and Works Accounts, London**, in its publication *"A Report of Marginal Costing" defines **marginal cost** as "the amount at any given volume of output by which aggregate costs are changed if the volume of output is increased or decreased by one unit"*.

"Marginal Cost", according to the **Institute of Chartered Accountants, England**, *"is the very expense (whether of production, selling or distribution) incurred by the taking of a particular decision"*.

Blocker and **Weltmore** defines **Marginal Cost** as *"the increase or decrease in total cost which results from producing or selling additional or fewer units of a product or from a change in the method of production or distribution such as the use of improved machinery, addition or exclusion of a product or territory, or selection of an additional sales channel"*. Thus, marginal cost is the cost incurred by a company for the additional output.

Viewed from this angle, marginal costs in the short run will be synonymous with variable costs, i.e., prime costs and variable overheads; but in the long run the marginal costs will include fixed costs in planning production activities involved in increase in the production capacity. It is clear that the marginal costs are related to change in output under certain conditions.

Marginal Costing :

Marginal Costing is an accounting technique which ascertains marginal cost by differentiating between fixed or period, and variable costs. This technique aims to charge only those costs of the cost of the product that vary directly with sales volumes. Those costs would be direct material, direct labour, and factory overhead expenses such as supplies, some indirect labour, and power. The cost of the product would not include fixed or non-variable expenses such as depreciation, factory insurance, taxes and supervisory salaries.

Marginal costing is defined by the **National Association of Accountants**, as follows :

"This method proposes that fixed factory expenses be classified as period expenses and be written off currently as is generally done with selling and administration expenses, and that only the variable costs become the basis of inventory value and profit determination".

According to the **Institute of Cost and Management Accounts,** London, **Marginal Costing** is *"the ascertainment of marginal costs and of the effect on profit of changes in volume or type of output by differentiating between fixed costs and variable costs. In this technique of costing only variable costs are charged to operations, processes or products, leaving all indirect costs to be written off against profits in the period in which they arise".*

In a nutshell, we can say that marginal costing is a costing technique that considers only the costs that vary directly with volume - direct materials, direct labour, and variable factory overheads and ignores fixed cost in additional output decisions. Thus, the technique of marginal costing lies in differentiation between fixed and variable costs, ascertainment of marginal costs, and, finding out the effect on profit due to a change in volume or type of output.

Features of Marginal Costing

The concept of marginal costing is evolved on the main distinction between product cost and period cost. While product cost relates to the volume of output, the period cost is mainly concerned with the period of time. Marginal costing considers all those manufacturing costs which vary directly with the volume of output as product costs. This is in contradiction to the traditional system of costing under which all manufacturing costs - fixed as well as variable - are treated as product costs. It should also be remembered that variability with the volume of production is the basis for the classification of costs into product and period costs.

Thus, marginal costing necessitates classification of costs into fixed and variable. Even the semi-variable costs have to be closely examined, so as to separate fixed and variable components thereof depending upon the increase or decrease in the volume of output. Thus, the marginal costs focuses the effect of costs on the varying of output.

Hence, a pure marginal costing has the following four important features :

i) Under **Marginal costing**, all types of **operating costs i.e.** factory, selling and administrative are separated into fixed and variable components and are recorded separately.

ii) **Variable Cost** elements are handled as product costs i.e. they are charged to the product at the appropriate moments and follow the product through the inventory accounts, and thus are treated as expenses when the product is sold. Variable distribution costs normally are chargeable to product at or near the moment of sale, and thus do not become inclined in inventory values.

iii) **Fixed costs** (including fixed factory overheads) are handled as period costs; i.e., they are written off as expenses in the period in which they are incurred. They do not follow the inventories through the accounts, but rather are treated in the way which is traditional for selling and general administrative expenses.

iv) Marginal costing is a **method of recording as well as reporting** costs. Unlike differential cost analysis and break-even analysis which utilise traditional records, variable costing requires a unique method of recording cost transactions as they originally take place.

Therefore, marginal costing is a technique which deals with the effect on profits of changes in volume or type of output.

Importance of Marginal Costing

Marginal Costing is the extension of cost accounting methodology to the dynamics of an economic situation. Any business may be conceived as an infinite series of decisions and actions, of which each one throws its impact over a period of time with diminishing emphasis. Thus, once a decision is taken and management action is implemented at a given point of time, the resulting situation constitutes a datum subject to room for correction for subsequent management decision and action. From this point of view, every decision reached and action taken at any given time is marginal in character.

It is generally recognised that business decisions are made on the basis of margins.
It means emphasis has been shifted from absolute total cost to marginal cost or differential cost in making policy decisions such as,

- Whether the current rate of production should be continued or stepped up or retarded ?
- Whether to produce certain requirements, the concern for e.g., raw materials, spare parts, capital equipment etc. within organisation or to buy them from outside ?
- Whether it would pay to reduce the prices of certain products during time of trade depression to the point where such reduced price would cover variable expenses through net total cost ?

In answering such questions the technique of marginal costing is used in which emphasis is on the rate of change rather than overall changes. Marginal Costing techniques aims at finding out the effect of changes in the levels of activity on sales prices and cost and consequently on profits.

Following are the different types of Uses of Marginal Costing which indicates the importance of Marginal Costing :

i) **Relative Profitability :**

In case of multi-product and multi-line of business activities, Marginal Costing facilitates the study of relative profitability of different products. It will show where the sales efforts should be concentrated.

ii) **Basis for pricing :**

Marginal Costing furnishes a better and more logical basis for fixation of selling prices and tendering for contract particularly, when business is dull.

iii) **Valuable adjunct to other techniques :**

Marginal Costing is a valuable adjunct to budgeting and standard costing techniques.

iv) **Simple to understand and application :**

Marginal Costing method is simple in application and it is easy for exercise of cost control. It is more informative and simple to understand.

v) **Cost Analysis Possible :**

Profit-volume analysis is facilitated by the use of break-even charts and profit-volume graphs, and so on.

vi) Responsibility Accounting becomes more effective :

Responsibility accounting is more effective when based on marginal costing because managers can identify their responsibilities more clearly when fixed overhead is not charged arbitrarily to their departments or divisions.

vii) Consistency :

The Marginal Cost per unit of output remains the same irrespective of the volume of output.

viii) Realistic Valuation of Stock :

In Marginal Costing, stocks of finished goods and work-in-progress are valued at their variable cost only. Therefore, it is more realistic and uniform. No fictitious profit arises.

ix) No under or over absorption of overheads :

In Marginal Costing there is no question of allocation, apportionment or absorption of fixed overheads. Hence, the tedious method of their accounting is eliminated.

x) Facilitates cost control :

By separating the fixed and variable costs, marginal costing provides better means of controlling costs.

xi) Valuable aid to management :

It helps the management with more appropriate information in taking vital business decisions like make or buy, sub-contracting, export order pricing, pricing under recession of continue or discontinue a product/division/ sales territory, selection of suitable product mix etc.

xii) Aid to Profit Planning :

The technique of Marginal Costing helps the management in profit planning. The management can plan the volume of sales for earning a required profit.

5.2 VARIOUS CONCEPTS

Marginal costing is the most important traditional techniques of costing used by the manufacturing industries preferably for profit planning, cost control and managerial decision-making. There is a basic need to understand various concepts used in this most effective technique of cost control, which are discussed as follows :

5.2.1 FIXED COST

Fixed costs are those rigid in nature which remain constant irrespective of the output. It means fixed costs have no effect if there is increase or decrease in output. On the other hand, the fixed cost unit decreases when the output increases and vice-versa. For example, if the fixed cost for producing 5,000 units at 40% capacity is ₹ 10,000 then for producing 10,000 units at 80% capacity also, the fixed cost will remain the same i.e. ₹ 10,000, but the cost per unit will reduce i.e.

- At 40% capacity = $\dfrac{₹ 10,000}{5,000 \text{ Units}}$ = ₹ 2 per unit

- At 80% capacity = $\dfrac{₹ 10,000}{10,000 \text{ Units}}$ = ₹ 1 per unit

Examples of Fixed Costs are Rent of factory premises, Salaries of the managers, Insurance of factory building and Taxes paid to municipality, etc.

These costs are uncontrollable in nature i.e. difficult to control in short-term but in a longer run they can be controlled by using different ways and means.

5.2.2 VARIABLE COST

Variable Costs are which vary directly with the output. It means when the output increases, the variable cost also increases and when the output decreases, the variable cost decreases. But the variable cost per unit remains the same.

For example, if the total production is 10,000 units and the variable cost is ₹ 20,000 at 40% capacity, then if the production is increased to 15,000 units i.e. the variable cost will be ₹ 30,000 i.e. at 60% capacity ₹ 2 per unit. But if the production falls to 5,000 units at 20% capacity, the variable cost will be ₹ 10,000. Thus, the variable cost per unit remains the same irrespective of the output.

- At 40% capacity = $\dfrac{₹\ 20,000}{10,000\ \text{Units}}$ = ₹ 2 per unit

- At 60% capacity = $\dfrac{₹\ 30,000}{15,000\ \text{Units}}$ = ₹ 2 per unit

- At 20% capacity = $\dfrac{₹\ 10,000}{5,000\ \text{Units}}$ = ₹ 2 per unit

Examples of Variable Costs are Direct Material, Direct Labour, Commission to Salesman, Power, etc.

These costs are controllable in nature hence plays an important role in this technique of cost control.

Semi-Variable Cost

These costs are partly fixed and partly variable in nature. The fixed part remaining fixed irrespective of the level of output while the variable portion changes according to the level of production. For example, in case of electricity, we have to pay the rent of the unit which is a fixed cost and we have to pay it whether we use electricity or not, while the other portion in the bill is a variable cost. Examples of semi-variable costs are telephone bills, repairs and maintenance, electricity charges, etc. These costs are also known as "Semi-fixed" costs.

5.2.3 CONTRIBUTION

In marginal costing, contribution has greater significance. The justification for contribution lies in the fact that when two or more products are manufactured by a single unit, the apportionment of fixed costs to different product under marginal costing is simplified. **Contribution** represents the difference between sales and variable cost of sales and is often referred to as "Gross Margin". It can be considered as some sort of fund from and out of which all fixed costs are to be met. Again, the difference between contribution and fixed cost represents either profit or loss as the case may be. The concept of 'contribution' is of immense use in fixing the selling prices, determining the break-even point, selecting the product mix for profit maximisation and also ascertaining the profitability of the product departments etc.

The difference between the marginal cost of the various products manufactured and their respective selling price is the contribution which each product makes towards fixed or period costs and profit.

According to **Watter W. Bigg**. *"Contribution may be defined as the difference between sales value and the marginal cost of sales, and no net profit arises, until the contribution equals the fixed overheads. When this level of output is achieved, the business is said to break-even as neither profit nor loss occurs. Production in excess of that necessary to break-even will result in a profit equivalent to the excess units multiplied by the "contribution" per unit. Conversely, a loss is sustained if output is less than that required to break-even, amounting to the short-fall of units multiplied by the contribution."* Thus, contribution is the difference between product revenue and variable cost of product. It represents the excess of sales over marginal cost (variable cost) that is the amount to meet fixed cost and profit expectation of an organisation. It can be calculated as under.

i) Contribution = Sales – Variable Cost

Contribution per unit = Selling Price – Variable Cost per unit

ii) Contribution = Fixed cost + Profit / Loss

Suppose total sales revenue is ₹ 1,50,000, variable cost is ₹ 60,000 and sales are 1,000 then, contribution will be :

Contribution = ₹ 1,50,000 – ₹ 60,000 = ₹ 90,000

Contribution (per unit)= ₹ 150 – ₹ 60 = ₹ 90

Relationship between Marginal cost and Contribution:

The analysis of marginal cost statement and the contribution above reveals that :

i) Sales (–) Marginal cost = Contribution

ii) Fixed cost (+) Profit = Contribution

By combining the above two equations, we get the fundamental marginal cost equation.

Sales – Marginal Cost = Fixed Cost ± Profit/Loss

The marginal cost equation has practical utility in the sense that if any three factors of the above equation are known, the fourth can be easily found out or computed.

Contribution and Profit:

A product sold at ₹ 50 has a variable cost of ₹ 30 and during the period ended 30th June 2013, 2,000 units were sold. Fixed costs for that period amounted to ₹ 25,000. The contribution and profit would be calculated, as shown in the following table.

	Particulars		Unit Cost ₹	Total Cost ₹	% of Sales
	Selling Price		50	1,00,000	100
Less :	Variable Costs	(–)	30	60,000	60
	∴ Contribution		20	40,000	40
Less :	Fixed Costs	(–)		25,000	
	∴ Profit			15,000	

From the above table, it can be observed that the contribution goes towards the recovery of the fixed overheads and profit. Marginal costing is a technique which can be used as a part of the decision-making process to show the effect of changes possible changes in demand and/or selling prices and/or variable costs. It can for example, be used to identify the most profitable projects; in make or buy decision-making or in deciding whether or not accept a special contract. Variable costs include only those costs which can be identified with and traced to products, for e.g., direct materials, direct expenses and variable overheads. The fixed costs are those which cannot be identified with and traced to the products. They tend to vary more with time than output, and are treated as period costs. This means that the fixed costs are not included in Product costs. They are simply written off, in total, against the total contribution generated from the sale of all the firms's products, for the period in which they were incurred. Refer to Multi-Product Environment Statement shown below. This treatment of fixed costs also means that because they are not included in product costs they are carried forward into the future as part of the valuation of the stocks of work in progress and finished goods.

	Products	'A' ₹	'B' ₹	'C' ₹	'D' ₹	Total ₹
	Contribution	20	34	36	20	110
Less :	Fixed Costs					78
∴	Profit					32

Multi-Product Environment

EXAMPLE

Compute the amount of fixed cost from the information given below :

Sales : ₹ 2,40,000
Variable Cost : ₹ 1,20,000
Profit : ₹ 60,000

ANSWER

As per marginal cost equation.

$$S - V = FC + P$$
$$₹ 2,40,000 - ₹ 1,20,000 = FC + ₹ 60,000$$
$$₹ 1,20,000 = FC + ₹ 60,000$$
$$(-) FC = ₹ 60,000 - ₹ 1,20,000$$
$$(-) FC = (-) ₹ 60,000$$
$$FC = ₹ 60,000$$

5.2.4 PROFIT VOLUME RATIO (P/V RATIO)

The Profit/Volume Ratio also known as 'contribution ratio' or 'marginal ratio' expresses the relationship between contribution and sales. In other words, it is the contribution per rupee of sales. The P/V Ratio may be expressed as under.

$$\text{P/V ratio} = \frac{\text{Contribution}}{\text{Sales}} \times 100 \text{ or } \frac{\text{Contribution per unit}}{\text{Selling price per unit}} \times 100$$

$$\text{Sales} = \frac{\text{Contribution i.e. (FC + Profit)}}{\text{P/V Ratio}} \quad \text{OR}$$

$$\text{Contribution} = \text{Sales} \times \text{P/V Ratio}$$

Since, contribution is equal to sales minus (–) variable cost and also represents the amount of fixed cost and profit expectations, therefore, P/V ratio can also be expressed as

i) $\text{P/V Ratio} = \dfrac{\text{Sales} - \text{Variable Cost}}{\text{Sales}}$

ii) $\text{P/V Ratio} = \dfrac{\text{Fixed Cost} + \text{Profit}}{\text{Sales}}$

As discussed earlier, the fixed cost remains constant in the short-term period, therefore any increase in contribution after the recovery of fixed cost would result straight way in the increase of profit. Thus,

$$\text{P/V Ratio} = \frac{\text{Change in Profit or Change in Contribution}}{\text{Change in Sales}}$$

EXAMPLE

Compute, i) P/V Ratio, ii) Fixed Cost, and iii) Sales Volume to earn a profit of ₹ 1,20,000 from the following information.

Sales : ₹ 1,50,000
Profit : ₹ 15,000
Variable Cost : 80%

ANSWER

Sales = ₹ 1,50,000
Variable Cost = 80%
= $\frac{80}{100}$ × ₹ 1,50,000 = ₹ 1,20,000

i) P/V Ratio = $\frac{S-V}{S} \times 100 = \frac{₹ 1,50,000 - ₹ 1,20,000}{₹ 1,50,000} \times 100 = 20\%$

ii) Contribution = FC + P
₹ 30,000 = FC + ₹ 15,000
(–) FC = ₹ 15,000 – ₹ 30,000
(–) FC = (–) ₹ 15,000
FC = ₹ 15,000

iii) Sales = $\frac{FC + P}{P/V \text{ Ratio}} = \frac{₹ 15,000 + ₹ 15,000}{20} \times 100 = ₹ 1,50,000$

Proof :

Sales = ₹ 1,50,000
Less : V.C. (80%) = ₹ 1,20,000
Contribution = ₹ 30,000
Less : F.C. = 15,000
Profit = **15,000**

EXAMPLE

Assuming that the cost structure and selling prices remains the same in period i) and ii), find out the P/V Ratio.

Periods	Sales ₹	Total Cost ₹
I Quarter	2,80,000	2,50,000
II Quarter	3,20,000	2,80,000

ANSWER

Periods	Sales ₹	Total Cost ₹	Profit ₹
I Quarter	2,80,000	2,50,000	30,000
II Quarter	3,20,000	2,80,000	40,000

P/V Ratio = $\frac{\text{Change in Profit}}{\text{Change in Sales}} \times 100 = \frac{₹ 10,000}{₹ 40,000} \times 100 = 25\%$

5.2.5 BREAK-EVEN POINT

Break-even analysis establishes the relationship between costs and profit with sales volume. It represents a specific method of presenting and studying the inter-relationship between costs, volume and profits. It also helps in the determination of that volume of sales at which costs and revenues are in equilibrium. The equilibrium point is often referred to as the 'break-even point'. The break-even point may be defined as that point of sales volume at which the total revenue is equal to the total cost. Briefly, it is a no-profit, no-loss point. It should be remembered that the break-even point is purely incidental to the Cost Volume-Profit analysis. If all costs are assumed to be variable with sales volume, the break-even point would be at zero sales. On the other hand, if all costs remain fixed, profits would vary disproportionately with sales and the Break-even Point would be at a point, where total sales revenue and fixed cost are in equilibrium.

Break-even analysis is a costing technique that helps executives in profit planning. The narrow interpretation of break-even analysis limits is to the study of break-even point. The break-even point is defined as the volume of activity at which total sales revenue exactly equals total costs of the output produced or sold. Since, at this level of operation sales revenue is adequate to cover all costs to manufacture and sell the product leaving no amount as profit, and therefore, this level is also known as no profit no loss level. Thus, in a situation where total costs of the output consist of only variable costs, the break-even point would be at zero of operation.

Break-even analysis need not be limited merely to seeking the break-even point. In broader sense, break-even analysis refers to the study of relationship between cost, volume, and profit at different levels of sales or production which in technical terminology is known as cost-volume-profit analysis. Cost-Volume-Profit Analysis as a planning tool analyses the inherent relationship between prices, cost structure, volume and profit.

Ahmad Belkooni defines **cost-volume-profit analysis** as *"an examination of cost and revenue behavioural patterns and their relationships with profit. The analysis separates costs into fixed and variable components and determines the levels of activity where costs and revenues are in equilibrium"*.

According to **Schmiedicke and Nagy**, *"cost-volume-profit analysis is an analytical technique which uses the degrees of cost variability for measuring the effect of changes in volume or resulting profits. Such analysis assumes that the plant assets of the firm will remain the same in the short-run, therefore, the established level of fixed cost will also remain unchanged during the period being studied"*.

We define cost-volume-profit analysis as a mature model to study the inter-related relationship between cost, price and profit structure of a company. It is a formal profit planning approach based on established relationship between different factors affecting profit. The usual starting point in such an analysis is the determination of the company's break-even point. Thus, break-even analysis forms just one component of the total system of Cost-Volume-Profit Analysis.

One of the important steps in Cost-Volume-Profit and break-even analysis is that of segregation of costs into fixed and variable costs. If the break-even point is to occur, it becomes essential that the business enterprise has some variable costs and some fixed costs.

Determination of Break-even Point:

The Break-even Point can be determined by the two following methods :
1. Algebric methods. (Mathematical)
    a) Contribution margin technique and
    b) Equation technique.

2. Graphic presentation
   a) Break-even chart and
   b) Profit volume graph.

The break-even point can be computed for a firm manufacturing single product only, in terms of units of product. The BEP is reached when the total proceeds of units sold are equivalent to the total cost incurred-fixed and variable. Each unit of the product sold will cover its variable cost and leave the remainder which is known as the contribution, to cover the fixed costs. The break-even point will occur when adequate units are sold so that total contribution would become equivalent to the total fixed costs. More precisely, contribution per unit while total contribution is equal to unit contribution multiplied by the total units sold. The profit of the unit is obtained by subtracting the fixed cost from the total contribution. The following equation can easily be remembered.

$$\text{Unit Contribution} = \text{Selling price per unit} - \text{Variable Cost per unit}$$
$$\text{Total Contribution} = \text{Unit Contribution} \times \text{Number of units sold}$$
$$\text{Profit} = \text{Total Contribution} - \text{Fixed Costs}$$

5.2.6 MARGIN OF SAFETY

The amount by which the current volume of sales exceeds the break-even sales volume, either in units or rupees represents margin of safety. This is the difference between the total sales figures and the amount of sales at break-even point. It indicates the extend to which sales may decrease before the company suffers a loss. A margin of safety is calculated as follows :

$$M/S = S_A - S_B \quad \text{or} \quad MoS = AS - BS$$

where,

M/S = Margin of safety
S_A = Actual volume of sales
S_B = Break-even volume of sales
MoS = Margin of safety
AS = Actual volume of sales
Bs = Break-even volume of sales

Margin of safety may be expressed as a percentage based either on units or rupee value. For this purpose, the following formulas are used :

$$M/S \text{ (in rupees)} = \frac{\text{Profit}}{\text{P/V Ratio}} \qquad M/S \text{ (in units)} = \frac{\text{Profit}}{\text{Contribution per unit}}$$

The high margin of safety is the sign of prosperity of the business. A low margin would indicate high cost. Such a critical situation calls for :

i) Increase in selling price
ii) Decrease in variable costs
iii) Replacement of existing product line by a more profitable line, and
iv) Increase in volume of production.

MARGINAL COST EQUATIONS

i) **Sales or Selling Price or Market Price or Value of Turnover or Invoice Price or Inflated Price or Loaded Price :**

  = Total Cost + Profit

  = Variable Cost + Fixed Cost + Profit

  = Contribution / P/V Ratio

  = Contribution + Variable Cost

  = Marginal Cost / Marginal Cost Ratio

ii) **Profit or Net Margin or Net Income :**

  = Sales – Total Cost

  = Sales – (Variable Cost + Fixed Cost)

  = Contribution – Fixed Cost

  = Margin of Safety × P/V Ratio

iii) **Loss :**

  = Total Cost – Sales

  = Fixed Cost – Contribution

iv) **Contribution or Gross Margin or Marginal Contribution :**

  = Sales – Variable Cost

  = Fixed Cost + Profit

  = Sales × P/V Ratio

  = Fixed Cost – Loss

  = Fixed Cost / Break-even Units

v) **Fixed Cost, Rigid Cost or Constant Cost :**

  = Total Cost – Variable Cost

  = Contribution – Profit

  = Contribution + Loss

  = Sales – (Variable Cost + Profit)

vi) **Variable Cost or Marginal Cost or Differential Cost :**

  = Total Cost – Fixed Cost

  = Sales – Contribution

  = Sales – (Fixed Cost + Profit)

  = Direct Material + Direct Labour + Direct Expenses + Variable Overheads

vii) **Break-Even Point i.e. BEP (in units) or (in output):**

$$= \frac{\text{Total Fixed Cost}}{\text{Contribution per unit}}$$

$$= \frac{\text{Break-even Sales in } ₹}{\text{Selling Price per unit}}$$

viii) **Break-Even Point i.e. BEP (Sales in Rupees):**

$$= \frac{\text{Total Fixed Cost}}{\text{Contribution per unit}} \times \text{Selling Price per unit}$$

$$= \frac{\text{Total Fixed Cost}}{\text{Total Contribution}} \times \text{Total Sales}$$

$$= \frac{\text{Total Fixed Cost}}{\text{Profit/Volume Ratio}}$$

$$= \frac{\text{Total Fixed Cost}}{1 - \left(\frac{\text{Variable Cost}}{\text{Sales}}\right)}$$

$$= \text{Break-Even Point (Units)} \times \text{Selling Price per unit}$$

ix) **Profit/Volume Ratio or Contribution to Sales Ratio or Contribution Ratio i.e. P/V Ratio:**

$$= \frac{\text{Contribution}}{\text{Sales}} \times 100$$

$$= \frac{\text{Change in Profits}}{\text{Change in Sales}} \times 100$$

$$= \frac{\text{Change in Contribution}}{\text{Change in Sales}} \times 100$$

x) **Margin of Safety:**

$$\text{MS} = \text{Actual Sales} - \text{Break-Even Sales}$$

$$\text{MS} = \frac{\text{Profit}}{\text{P/V Ratio}}$$

$$\text{MS Ratio} = \frac{\text{Profit}}{\text{P/V Ratio}} \times 100$$

$$\text{MS Ratio} = \frac{\text{Margin of Safety}}{\text{Actual Sales}} \times 100$$

xi) **Sales volume to earn required profit (in units) or Sales for desired profit (in units):**

$$= \frac{\text{Total Fixed Cost} + \text{Required Profit}}{\text{Contribution per unit}}$$

xii) **Sales volume to earn required profit (in value) or Sales for desired profit (in ₹):**

$$= \frac{(\text{Total Fixed Cost} + \text{Required Profit}) \times \text{Sales}}{\text{Total Contribution}}$$

$$= \frac{\text{Total Fixed Cost} + \text{Required Profit}}{\text{P/V Ratio}}$$

ILLUSTRATIONS

ILLUSTRATION 1

Rotex India Ltd., Raipur, produces 1,00,000 units and sells them @ ₹ 10 each. The variable cost per unit is ₹ 6 and Total Fixed Cost amounted to ₹ 2,00,000. Calculate Break-even Point in units and sales by following formulae method and graphical presentation method. Also calculate margin of safety, showing angle of incidence.

SOLUTION

A) Formulae Method :

i) Break-even Point (Units) = $\dfrac{\text{Total Fixed Cost}}{\text{Contribution per unit}}$

But,

Contribution per unit = Selling Price per unit – Variable Cost per unit

∴ Break-even Point (Units) = $\dfrac{\text{Total Fixed Cost}}{\text{Selling Price per unit} - \text{Variable Cost}}$

$= \dfrac{₹\,2,00,000}{₹\,10 - ₹\,6}$

$= \dfrac{₹\,2,00,000}{₹\,4}$

= ₹ 50,000 units

ii) Break-even Point (Sales) = Break-even Point (Units) × Selling price per unit

= 50,000 units × ₹ 10

= ₹ 5,00,000

iii) Margin of Safety = Actual Sales – Break-even Sales

= ₹ 1,00,000 – ₹ 5,00,000

= ₹ 5,00,000

B) Graphical Presentation Method :

Break-even Chart is a graphical representation of marginal costing. It indicates the graphical relationship between cost, volume and profits. On the basis of cost data, the Break-even Chart can be drawn as follows :

		₹
i)	Total Actual Sales	10,00,000
	(1,00,000 units × ₹ 10)	
ii)	Total Fixed Cost	2,00,000
iii)	Total Variable Cost	6,00,000
	(1,00,000 units × ₹ 6)	
iv)	Total Profit	2,00,000

Scale,

OX axis ... 1 cm = 10,000 units ... Output in units

OY axis ... 1 cm = ₹ 1,00,000 ... Costs and Sales Revenue

Break-even Chart

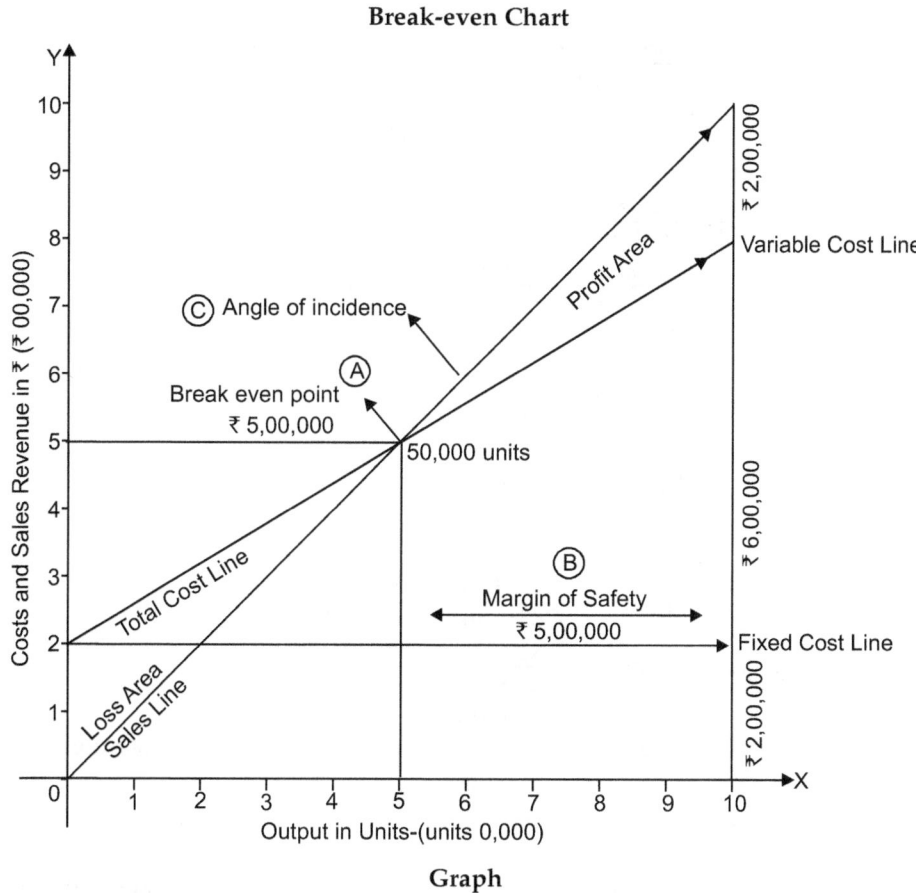

Graph

ILLUSTRATION 2

From the following particulars calculate,

i) Contribution per unit
ii) P/V Ratio
iii) BEP (units and in rupees)
iv) What will be the selling price per unit, if BEP is brought down to 25,000 units?

Fixed expenses ₹ 1,50,000,
Selling price per unit ₹ 15,
Variable Cost per unit ₹ 10.

SOLUTION

i) **Contribution per unit :**

= Selling price per unit – Variable cost per unit
= ₹ 15 – ₹ 10
= ₹ 5

ii) **P/V Ratio :**

$$= \frac{\text{Contribution per unit}}{\text{Selling Price per unit}} \times 100$$

$$= \frac{₹\,5}{₹\,15} \times 100 = \frac{1}{3} \times 100 = 33\,^{1}/_{3}\%$$

iii) **BEP (in rupees) :**

$$= \frac{\text{Fixed Cost}}{\text{P/V Ratio}}$$

$$= \frac{₹\,1{,}50{,}000}{33\,^{1}/_{3}\%} = \frac{₹\,1{,}50{,}000}{^{1}/_{3}} = ₹\,1{,}50{,}000 \times \frac{3}{1}$$

$$= ₹\,4{,}50{,}000$$

BEP (units) :

$$= \frac{\text{Fixed Cost}}{\text{Contribution per unit}}$$

$$= \frac{₹\,1{,}50{,}000}{₹\,5} = 30{,}000 \text{ units}$$

iv) **Selling price per unit :**
where,

$$\text{BEP (units)} = \frac{\text{Fixed Cost}}{\text{Contribution per unit}}$$

$$\therefore \text{Contribution per unit} = \frac{\text{Fixed Cost}}{\text{BEP (Units)}} = \frac{₹\,1{,}50{,}000}{\text{Units 25{,}000}}$$

$$= ₹\,6 \text{ per unit}$$

Selling price per unit = Variable cost per unit + Contribution per unit
$$= ₹\,10 + ₹\,6$$
$$= ₹\,16$$

ILLUSTRATION 3

Find out the selling price per unit if Break-even Point is to be brought down to 9,000 units.

	₹
Marginal cost per unit	75
Fixed Cost	2,70,000
Market price per unit	100

SOLUTION

i) **Calculation of Contribution per unit :**
where,

$$\text{BEP (units)} = \frac{\text{Fixed Cost}}{\text{Contribution per unit}}$$

$$\therefore \text{Contribution per unit} = \frac{\text{Fixed Cost}}{\text{BEP (Units)}}$$

$$= \frac{₹\,2{,}70{,}000}{9{,}000 \text{ units}} = ₹\,30 \text{ per unit}$$

ii) **Calculation of Selling Price per unit :**
Where,

$\therefore$ Contribution per unit = Selling price per unit – Variable cost per unit
$\therefore$ Selling price per unit = Contribution per unit + Variable cost per unit
$$= ₹\,30 + ₹\,75$$
$$= ₹\,105 \text{ per unit}$$

ILLUSTRATION 4

Gasco Ltd., Gurgaon, provides you with the following additional cost data regarding its operations for 2012-13.

- Invoice price ₹ 20 per unit
- Works on Cost – Fixed ₹ 61,000 p.a.
- Production Cost – Marginal ₹ 11 per unit
- Selling Overheads – Rigid ₹ 29,000 p.a.
- Distribution Overheads – Differential ₹ 3 per unit

Calculate –
i) Break-even Point in amount of Sales in rupees.
ii) Number of units to be sold to earn a profit of ₹ 30,000 per year.

SOLUTION

- **Calculation of Contribution per unit :**

		Unit Cost ₹
Invoice Price		20.00
Less : Variable Cost		
i) Production Cost – Marginal	11.00	
ii) Distribution Overheads – Differential	(+) 3.00	
	(–)	14.00
∴ **Contribution**		06.00

- **Calculation of P/V Ratio :**

where,

$$P/V \text{ Ratio} = \frac{\text{Contribution}}{\text{Sales}} \times 100$$

$$= \frac{₹6}{₹20} \times 100$$

$$= 30\%$$

i) Break-even Point in amount of Sales (in rupees) :

$$= \frac{\text{Fixed Cost}}{\text{P/V Ratio}}$$

$$= \frac{\underset{₹61,000}{\text{Works on Cost}} + \underset{₹29,000}{\text{Selling Overheads}}}{30\%}$$

$$= ₹90,000 \times \frac{100}{30}$$

$$= ₹3,00,000$$

ii) Number of units to be sold to earn a profit of ₹ 30,000 per year :

$$= \frac{\text{Fixed Cost + Desired Profit}}{\text{Contribution per unit}}$$

$$= \frac{₹90,000}{₹6}$$

$$= 15,000 \text{ units}$$

ILLUSTRATION 5

From the following cost data, calculate :
i) BEP (units)
ii) BEP (units), if selling price is reduced by 10%.
iii) Selling price per unit if BEP is 8,000 units.

Fixed Cost - ₹ 1,00,000, Variable cost per unit - ₹ 10, Selling price per unit - ₹ 20.

SOLUTION

i) BEP (units) :

$$= \frac{\text{Fixed Cost}}{\text{Contribution per unit}}$$

But,

Contribution per unit = Selling price per unit − Variable cost per unit

∴ BEP (units) $= \dfrac{\text{Fixed Cost}}{\text{Selling price per unit} - \text{Variable cost per unit}}$

$$= \frac{₹\,1,00,000}{₹\,20 - ₹\,10} = \frac{₹\,1,00,000}{₹\,10}$$

= 10,000 units.

ii) BEP (units), if selling price is reduced by 10% :

Original selling price per unit − Reduction by 10% = New selling price per unit.
₹ 20 − ₹ 2 = ₹ 18

BEP (units) :

$$= \frac{\text{Fixed Cost}}{\text{Contribution per unit}}$$

But,

Contribution per unit = Selling price per unit − Variable cost per unit

∴ BEP (units) $= \dfrac{\text{Fixed Cost}}{\text{Selling price per unit} - \text{Variable cost per unit}}$

$$= \frac{₹\,1,00,000}{₹\,18 - ₹\,10} = \frac{₹\,1,00,000}{₹\,8} = 12,500 \text{ units}$$

iii) Selling price per unit if BEP is 8,000 units :

Let X' be the selling price per unit.
where,

BEP (units) $= \dfrac{\text{Fixed Cost}}{\text{Contribution per unit}}$

But,

Contribution per unit = Selling price per unit − Variable cost per unit

∴ BEP (units) $= \dfrac{\text{Fixed Cost}}{\text{Selling price per unit} - \text{Variable cost per unit}}$

∴ 8,000 units $= \dfrac{₹\,1,00,000}{X - ₹\,10}$

∴ 8,000 units × (X − ₹ 10) = ₹ 1,00,000
∴ 8,000 X − ₹ 80,000 = ₹ 1,00,000
∴ 8,000 X = ₹ 1,00,000 + ₹ 80,000
∴ X $= \dfrac{₹\,1,80,000}{8,000 \text{ units}}$ = ₹ 22.50

∴ Selling price per unit = ₹ 22.50

ILLUSTRATION 6

Following cost details are made available by Indian Plastics Ltd., Indapur, for the month October, 2013.

Prime Cost Labour per unit	₹ 3.50
Fixed Overheads	₹ 20,000
Value of Turnover per unit	₹ 20
Productive Wages – Outstanding per unit	Re. 0.50
Basic Material Cost per unit	₹ 6
Variable Overheads – 100% of Direct Labour Cost	10%

You are required to calculate –
i) Break-even Point (Sales Value)
ii) Net Profit, if Sales are 10% and 15% above the Break-even Volume.

SOLUTION

- **Calculation of Contribution per unit :**

where,

	Unit Cost ₹
Selling Price	18.00

$$\left(\begin{array}{cc} \text{Value of Turnover} & \text{Trade Discount @ 10\%} \\ ₹\ 20 & - \quad ₹\ 2 \end{array}\right)$$

Less : Variable Cost

• Basic Material Cost		6.00
• Direct Labour Cost		4.00
• Prime Cost Labour	3.50	
Add : Productive Outstanding Wages	(+) 0.50	
• Variable Overheads		4.00
(100% of Direct Labour Cost i.e. ₹ 4)		__14.00__
∴ **Contribution**		__04.00__

i) Break-even Point Units and Sales :

$$= \frac{\text{Total Fixed Cost}}{\text{Contribution per unit}}$$

$$= \frac{₹\ 20{,}000}{₹\ 4}$$

$$= ₹\ 5{,}000\ \text{Units}$$

	₹
Gross Sales at Break-even	1,00,000
(5,000 Units × ₹ 20)	
Less : Trade Discount	10,000
(10% of ₹ 1,00,000)	(–)
∴ **Net Sales at Break-even**	__90,000__

ii) a) Net Profit, if Sales are 10% above break-even volume :
Revised Sales are 10% above Break-even Volume i.e.

= 5,000 units + (10% of above i.e.) 500 units
= 5,500 units

- Calculation of Net Profit :
   where,
   Contribution = Fixed Cost + Profit
   ∴ Profit = Contribution − Fixed Cost
   = (5,500 units × ₹ 4) − ₹ 20,000
   = ₹ 22,000 − ₹ 20,000
   = ₹ 2,000

b) Net Profit, if Sales are 15% above break-even volume :
Revised Sales are 15% above Break-even Volume i.e.
   = 5,000 units + (15% above i.e.) 750 units
   = 5,750 units

- Calculation of Net Profit :
   where,
   Contribution = Fixed Cost + Profit
   ∴ Profit = Contribution − Fixed Cost
   = (5,750 units × ₹ 4) − ₹ 20,000
   = ₹ 23,000 − ₹ 20,000
   = ₹ 3,000

ILLUSTRATION 7

The following is a Cost Statement of a machine manufactured by Goyal Machineries Ltd., Gondia, for the year ended 31st March, 2013. During the year, the company manufactured 1,000 machines and sold it in the national market.

	Particulars		₹
	Basic Materials		190
Add :	Direct Wages		70
Add :	Productive Expenses	(+)	40
	Prime Cost	**(1)**	300
Add :	Fixed Manufacturing Overheads	(+)	50
	Works Cost	**(2)**	350
Add :	Constant Management Expenses	(+)	20
	Cost of Production	**(3)**	370
Add :	Rigid Selling and Distribution on Cost	(+)	30
	Cost of Sales	**(4)**	400
Add :	Profit	(5) (+)	100
	Selling Price		500

You are required to find out,
i) Break-even Point (units),
ii) The number of machines to be produced and sold to earn the same amount of profit, if the price is to be increased by ₹ 50.

SOLUTION

In the books of Goyal Machineries Ltd., Gondia
Profitability Statement for the year ended 31st March, 2013
(Machines Produced and Sold – 1,000)

	Particulars		₹
	Sales		500
Less :	Variable Cost :		
	• Basic Materials		190
	• Direct Wages		70
	• Productive Expenses	(–)	40
∴	Contribution		200
Less :	Fixed Cost :		
	• Manufacturing Overheads		50
	• Management Expenses		20
	• Selling and Distribution Expenses	(–)	30
∴	**Profit**		**100**

i) Break-even Point (units) :

$$= \frac{\text{Fixed Cost}}{\text{Contribution per unit}}$$

$$= \frac{₹\,1,00,000}{₹\,200}$$

= 500 units.

ii) Number of machines to be produced and sold to earn the same amount of profit, if the price is to be increased by ₹ 50 :

	₹
New Selling Price : (₹ 500 + 50)	550
Less : Variable Cost	(–) 300
∴ Contribution per unit	250

Sales for desired profit in units :

$$= \frac{\text{Total Fixed Cost + Required in Profit}}{\text{Contribution per unit}}$$

$$= \frac{\underset{(₹\,100 \times 1,000\ \text{units})}{₹\,1,00,000} + \underset{(₹\,100 \times 1,000\ \text{units})}{₹\,1,00,000}}{₹\,250} = \frac{₹\,2,00,000}{₹\,250} = 800\ \text{units}$$

ILLUSTRATION 8

Bokaro India Ltd., Badalpur - provides the following cost data relating to one unit of ouptut.

Productive Materials	₹ 50
Variable Works Overheads : 75% of Prime Cost Labour	
Direct Labour	₹ 80
Fixed Establishment Overheads	₹ 2,40,000 p.a.
Market Price	₹ 230

You are required to calculate,
 i) the number of units to be produced and sold in a year to break-even.
 ii) the number of units to be manufactured and sold in a year to make a profit of ₹ 80,000.
 iii) the number of units to be produced and sold to break-even if the selling price is reduced by ₹ 16 each.

SOLUTION

- Calculation of Contribution per unit :
  where,

	Unit Cost ₹
Market Price	230
Less : Variable Cost	
• Productive Materials 50.00	
• Direct Labour (+) 80.00	
• Variable Works Overheads 60.00	
(75% of Prime Cost labour i.e. ₹ 80)	
	(−) 190
∴ **Contribution**	40

i) Number of units to be produced and sold in a year to break-even :
where, Break-even Points (units) =

$= \dfrac{\text{Fixed Cost}}{\text{Contribution per unit}}$

$= \dfrac{₹\,2,40,000}{₹\,40}$

= 6,000 units.

ii) Number of units to be manufactured and sold in a year to make a profit of ₹ 80,000 ?

$= \dfrac{\text{Fixed Cost + Desired Profit}}{\text{Contribution per unit}}$

$= \dfrac{₹\,2,40,000 + ₹\,80,000}{₹\,40}$

$= \dfrac{₹\,3,20,000}{₹\,40}$

= 8,000 units.

iii) Number of units to be produced and sold to break-even, if the selling price is reduced by ₹ 16 each.

- Calculation of Revised Selling Price :

= Old Selling Price − Reduction by
  ₹ 230   ₹ 16

= ₹ 214

- Calculation of Revised Contribution per unit :
  where,

	Unit Cost ₹
Market Price	214.00
Less : Variable Cost	(–) 190.00
∴ Contribution	24.00

Break-even Point (units) :

= $\dfrac{\text{Fixed Cost}}{\text{Contribution per unit}}$

= $\dfrac{₹\,2,40,000}{₹\,24}$

= 10,000 units

ILLUSTRATION 9

The Burma-Shell Ltd., has submitted the following data :

	₹
Selling price per unit	20
Variable cost per unit	16
Total Fixed Cost	20,000

Calculate BEP (units). Also calculate the effect on BEP (units), if

i) Selling price is increased by ₹ 1
ii) Selling price is decreased by ₹ 1
iii) Variable cost is increased by ₹ 1
iv) Variable cost is decreased by ₹ 1
v) Fixed cost is increased by ₹ 5,000
vi) Fixed cost is decreased by ₹ 5,000

SOLUTION

BEP (units) :

= $\dfrac{\text{Fixed Cost}}{\text{Contribution per unit}}$

But,

Contribution per unit = Selling price per unit – Variable cost per unit

∴ BEP (units) = $\dfrac{\text{Fixed Cost}}{\text{Selling price per unit – Variable cost per unit}}$

= $\dfrac{₹\,20,000}{₹\,20 - ₹\,16}$ = $\dfrac{₹\,20,000}{₹\,4}$ = 5,000 units

Calculation of effect on BEP (units) if

i) **Selling Price is increased by Re. 1 :**

Original Selling Price per unit + Increase by ₹ 1 = New Selling Price per unit
    ₹ 20 + ₹ 1 = ₹ 21

BEP (units) = $\dfrac{\text{Fixed Cost}}{\text{Selling Price per unit – Variable Cost per unit}}$

$\dfrac{₹\,20,000}{₹\,21 - ₹\,16}$ = $\dfrac{₹\,20,000}{₹\,5}$ = 4,000 units

ii) **Selling Price is decreased by ₹ 1 :**

Original Selling Price per unit − Decrease by ₹ 1 = New Selling Price per unit

₹ 20 − Re. 1 = ₹ 19

$$\text{BEP (units)} = \frac{\text{Fixed Cost}}{\text{Selling Price per unit} - \text{Variable Cost per unit}}$$

$$\frac{₹\,20{,}000}{₹\,19 - ₹\,16} = \frac{₹\,20{,}000}{₹\,3} = 6{,}667 \text{ units}$$

iii) **Variable Cost is increased by ₹ 1 :**

Original Variable Cost per unit + Increase by ₹ 1 = New Variable Cost per unit

₹ 16 + ₹ 1 = ₹ 17

$$\text{BEP (units)} = \frac{\text{Fixed Cost}}{\text{Selling Price per unit} - \text{Variable Cost per unit}}$$

$$\frac{₹\,20{,}000}{₹\,20 - ₹\,17} = \frac{₹\,20{,}000}{₹\,3} = 6{,}667 \text{ units}$$

iv) **Variable Cost is decreased by ₹ 1 :**

Original Variable Cost per unit − Decrease by ₹ 1 = New Variable Cost per unit

₹ 16 − ₹ 1 = ₹ 15

$$\text{BEP (units)} = \frac{\text{Fixed Cost}}{\text{Selling Price per unit} - \text{Variable Cost per unit}}$$

$$\frac{₹\,20{,}000}{₹\,20 - ₹\,15} = \frac{₹\,20{,}000}{₹\,5} = 4{,}000 \text{ units}$$

v) **Fixed Cost is increased by ₹ 5,000 :**

Original Fixed Cost + Increase by = New Fixed Cost
₹ 20,000 + ₹ 5,000 = ₹ 25,000

$$\text{BEP (units)} = \frac{\text{Fixed Cost}}{\text{Selling Price per unit} - \text{Variable Cost per unit}}$$

$$\frac{₹\,25{,}000}{₹\,20 - ₹\,16} = \frac{₹\,25{,}000}{₹\,4} = 6{,}250 \text{ units}$$

vi) **Fixed Cost is decreased by ₹ 5,000 :**

Original Fixed Cost − Decrease by = New Fixed Cost
₹ 20,000 − ₹ 5,000 = ₹ 15,000

$$\text{BEP (units)} = \frac{\text{Fixed Cost}}{\text{Selling Price per unit} - \text{Variable Cost per unit}}$$

$$= \frac{₹\,15{,}000}{₹\,20 - ₹\,16} = \frac{₹\,15{,}000}{₹\,4} = 3{,}750 \text{ units}$$

ILLUSTRATION 10

A Company has prepared the following budget estimated for the year 2012-2013.

Sales	15,000 units
Fixed Cost	₹ 34,000
Sales Value	₹ 1,50,000
Variable Cost per unit	₹ 6

You are required to calculate,
A) P/V Ratio, BEP (Sales) and Margin of Safety
B) Also calculate the effect of the following.
   i) decrease of 10% in selling price
   ii) increase of 10% in variable cost.

SOLUTION

Selling price per unit $= \dfrac{\text{Sales value}}{\text{Sales units}} = \dfrac{₹1,50,000}{15,000 \text{ units}} = ₹10$

A) i) **P/V Ratio :**

$$= \dfrac{\text{Contribution per unit}}{\text{Selling price per unit}} \times 100$$

But, Contribution per unit = Selling price per unit – Variable Cost per unit

$\therefore$ P/V Ratio $= \dfrac{\text{Selling price per unit} - \text{Variable cost per unit}}{\text{Selling price per unit}} \times 100$

$= \dfrac{₹10 - ₹6}{₹10} \times 100 = \dfrac{₹4}{₹10} \times 100 = 40\%$

ii) **BEP (Sales) :**

$= \dfrac{\text{Fixed Cost}}{\text{P/V Ratio}}$

$= \dfrac{₹34,000}{40\%} = ₹34,000 \times \dfrac{100}{40} = ₹85,000$

iii) **Margin of Safety :**

= Actual Sales – BEP (Sales)

$= \begin{matrix} ₹1,50,000 \\ (15,000 \text{ units} \times ₹10) \end{matrix} - ₹85,000$

= ₹65,000

B) a) **Decrease of 10% in Selling Price :**

Original Selling Price per unit – Decrease of 10% = New Selling Price per unit
₹10 – ₹1 = ₹9

i) **P/V Ratio :**

$= \dfrac{\text{Contribution per unit}}{\text{Selling price per unit}} \times 100$

But, Contribution per unit = Selling Price per unit – Variable Cost per unit

$\therefore$ P/V Ratio $= \dfrac{\text{Selling Price per unit} - \text{Variable Cost per unit}}{\text{Selling Price per unit}} \times 100$

$= \dfrac{₹9 - ₹6}{₹9} \times 100 = \dfrac{₹3}{₹9} \times 100 = 33\dfrac{1}{3}\%$

ii) **BEP (Sales) :**

$= \dfrac{\text{Fixed Cost}}{\text{P/V Ratio}}$

$= \dfrac{₹34,000}{33\dfrac{1}{3}\%} = \dfrac{₹34,000}{1/3} = ₹34,000 \times \dfrac{3}{1}$

= ₹1,02,000

iii) **Margin of Safety :**

$$= \text{Actual Sales} - \text{BEP (Sales)}$$
$$= ₹1,35,000 - ₹1,02,000$$
$$ (15,000 \text{ units} \times ₹9)$$
$$= ₹33,000$$

b) **Increase of 10% in Variable Cost :**

Original Variable Cost per unit + Increase of 10% = New Variable Cost per unit
₹6 + Re. 0.60 = ₹6.60

i) **P/V Ratio :**

$$= \frac{\text{Contribution per unit}}{\text{Selling Price per unit}} \times 100$$

But, Contribution per unit = Selling Price per unit – Variable Cost per unit

$$\therefore \text{P/V Ratio} = \frac{\text{Selling Price per unit} - \text{Variable Cost per unit}}{\text{Selling Price per unit}} \times 100$$

$$= \frac{₹10 - ₹6.60}{₹10} \times 100 = \frac{₹3.40}{₹10} \times 100 = 34\%$$

ii) **BEP (Sales) :**

$$= \frac{\text{Fixed Cost}}{\text{P/V Ratio}}$$

$$= \frac{₹34,000}{34\%} = ₹34,000 \times \frac{100}{34}$$

$$= ₹1,00,000$$

iii) **Margin of Safety :**

$$= \text{Actual Sales} - \text{BEP (Sales)}$$
$$= ₹1,50,000 - ₹1,00,000$$
$$= ₹50,000$$

ILLUSTRATION 11

From the following cost data, you are required to calculate,
i) BEP (units and sales)
ii) Sales required to earn a profit of ₹ 54,000.

Selling Price per unit ₹ 18, Contribution per unit ₹ 6 and Fixed Cost ₹ 84,000.

SOLUTION

i) **BEP (Units) :**

$$= \frac{\text{Fixed Cost}}{\text{Contribution per unit}} = \frac{₹84,000}{₹6} = 14,000 \text{ units}$$

BEP (Sales) :

$$= \frac{\text{Fixed Cost}}{\text{Contribution per unit}} \times \text{Selling Price per unit}$$

$$= \frac{₹84,000}{₹6} \times ₹18 = 14,000 \text{ units} \times ₹18$$

$$= ₹2,52,000$$

Calculation of P/V Ratio :

$$\text{P/V Ratio} = \frac{\text{Contribution per unit}}{\text{Selling Price per unit}} \times 100$$

$$= \frac{₹6}{₹18} \times 100 = \frac{1}{3} \times 100 = 33\,^{1}/_{3}\%$$

ii) Sales required to earn a profit of ₹ 54,000 :

$$P/V \text{ Ratio} = \frac{\text{Contribution}}{\text{Sales}}$$

But,

Contribution = Fixed Cost + Profit

∴ $P/V \text{ Ratio} = \dfrac{\text{Fixed Cost + Profit}}{\text{Sales}}$

∴ $\text{Sales} = \dfrac{\text{Fixed Cost + Profit}}{P/V \text{ Ratio}}$

$= \dfrac{₹84{,}000 + ₹54{,}000}{33\,1/3\%} = \dfrac{₹1{,}38{,}000}{1/3} = ₹1{,}38{,}000 \times \dfrac{3}{1}$

= ₹ 4,14,000

ILLUSTRATION 12

Activa Engineering Co. Ltd., Ahmednagar, provides you with the following cost materials.

Non-variable Cost	₹ 2,000
Variable Cost of Sales	60%
Total Turnover	₹ 10,000
Net Margin	₹ 2,000

Calculate the following :
i) Break-even Sales
ii) Sales Volume to earn a profit of ₹ 6,000 and
iii) Margin of Safety when Sales are ₹ 25,000.

SOLUTION

As Variable Cost of Sales are 60%, the P/V Ratio will be (i.e. 100% – 60%) = 40%.

i) Break-even Sales :

$= \dfrac{\text{Fixed Cost (i.e. Non-variable Cost)}}{P/V \text{ Ratio}}$

$= \dfrac{₹2{,}000}{40\%}$

$= ₹2{,}000 \times \dfrac{100}{40}$

= ₹ 5,000

ii) Sales Volume to earn a profit of ₹ 6,000 :

where,

$P/V \text{ Ratio} = \dfrac{\text{Contribution}}{\text{Sales}}$

But,

$\text{Contribution} = \dfrac{\text{Fixed Cost + Profit}}{\boxed{\text{Sales}}}$

∴ $\text{Sales} = \dfrac{\text{Fixed Cost + Profit}}{P/V \text{ Ratio}}$

$= \dfrac{₹2{,}000 + ₹6{,}000}{40\%}$

$= ₹8{,}000 \times \dfrac{100}{40}$

= ₹ 20,000

Cost Accounting — Marginal Costing

iii) Margin of Safety, when Sales are ₹ 25,000 :

where,

Margin of Safety = Actual Sales – Break-even Sales
= ₹ 25,000 – ₹ 5,000
= ₹ 20,000

ILLUSTRATION 13

Bajaj Auto Ltd., Bilaspur, has submitted the following cost data

	₹
Invoice Price per unit	40
Fixed Production Overheads	1,50,000
Variable Manufacturing Cost per unit	5
Selling on cost – Fixed	20,000
Prime Cost Materials per unit (Variable Cost)	18
Fixed - Distribution Expenses	10,000
Variable Selling overheads per unit	2

Calculate,

i) BEP (Sales)
ii) Number of units to be sold to earn a profit of ₹ 1,20,000.
iii) Number of units to be sold to earn an income of 25% of Sales.

SOLUTION

Calculation of Total Fixed Cost :

	₹
Fixed Production Overheads	1,50,000
Add : Selling on cost – Fixed	20,000
Add : Fixed Distribution Expenses	10,000
∴ Total Fixed Cost	1,80,000

Calculation of Total Variable Cost per unit

	₹
Variable Manufacturing cost per unit	5
Add : Prime Cost materials per unit	18
Add : Variable Selling Overheads per unit	2
∴ Variable Cost per unit	25

Calculation of P/V Ratio :

$$= \frac{\text{Contribution per unit}}{\text{Selling Price per unit}} \times 100$$

But, Contribution per unit = Selling Price per unit – Variable Cost per unit

$$\therefore \text{P/V Ratio} = \frac{\text{Selling Price per unit} - \text{Variable Cost per unit}}{\text{Selling Price per unit}} \times 100$$

$$= \frac{₹40 - ₹25}{₹40} \times 100 = \frac{₹15}{₹40} \times 100 = 37.50\%$$

i) BEP (Sales) :

$$= \frac{\text{Fixed Cost}}{\text{Contribution per unit}} \times \text{Selling Price per unit}$$

Cost Accounting   5.29   Marginal Costing

But,   Contribution per unit = Selling Price per unit − Variable Cost per unit

∴   BEP (Sales) = $\dfrac{\text{Fixed Cost}}{\text{Selling price per unit} - \text{Variable Cost per unit}} \times$ Selling price per unit

$= \dfrac{₹1,80,000}{₹40 - ₹25} \times 40 = \dfrac{₹1,80,000}{₹15} \times ₹40$

$= ₹12,000 \text{ units} \times ₹40$

$= ₹4,80,000$

ii) Number of units to be sold to earn a profit of ₹ 1,20,000 :

where,

P/V Ratio = $\dfrac{\text{Contribution}}{\text{Sales}}$

But, Contribution = Fixed Cost + Profit

∴   P/V Ratio = $\dfrac{\text{Fixed Cost} + \text{Profit}}{\text{Sales}}$

∴   Sales = $\dfrac{\text{Fixed Cost} + \text{Profit}}{37.5\%}$

$= \dfrac{₹1,80,000 + ₹1,20,000}{37.5\%}$

$= ₹3,00,000 \times \dfrac{100}{37.5}$

$= ₹8,00,000$

But,

Number of units to be sold = $\dfrac{\text{Total Sales}}{\text{Selling Price per unit}}$

$= \dfrac{₹8,00,000}{₹40}$

$= 20,000$ units

iii) Number of units to be sold to earn an income of 25% on Sales :

Let x be the number of units to be sold.

∴   x = $\dfrac{\text{Fixed Cost} + \text{Required Profit}}{\text{Contribution per unit}}$

But, Contribution per unit = Selling Price per unit − Variable Cost per unit

∴   x = $\dfrac{\text{Fixed Cost} + \text{Required Profit}}{\text{Selling Price per unit} - \text{Variable Cost per unit}}$

∴   x = $\dfrac{₹1,80,000 + 25\% (x \times 40)}{₹40 - ₹25}$

x = $\dfrac{₹1,80,000 + 10x}{₹15}$

∴   15x = ₹1,80,000 + 10x

∴   15x − 10x = ₹1,80,000

∴   5x = ₹1,80,000

∴   x = $\dfrac{₹1,80,000}{₹5}$

$= 36,000$ units

∴ Number of units to be sold to earn an income of 25% of Sales = 36,000 units.

ILLUSTRATION 14

From the following information, find out :
i)   P/V Ratio   ii) BEP (Sales)   iii) Profit when Sales are ₹ 1,20,000.
iv) Sales required to earn a Profit of ₹ 60,000

	₹
Fixed Cost per unit	40,000
Variable Cost per unit	2
Sales	2,00,000
Selling Price per unit	10

SOLUTION

i) P/V Ratio :

$$= \frac{\text{Contribution per unit}}{\text{Selling Price per unit}} \times 100$$

But,

Contribution per unit = Selling Price per unit − Variable Cost per unit

$$\therefore \text{P/V Ratio} = \frac{\text{Selling Price per unit} - \text{Variable Cost per unit}}{\text{Selling Price per unit}} \times 100$$

$$= \frac{₹10 - ₹2}{₹10} \times 100 = \frac{₹8}{₹10} \times 100 = 80\%$$

ii) BEP (Sales) :

$$= \frac{\text{Fixed Cost}}{\text{P/V Ratio}}$$

$$= \frac{₹40,000}{80\%} = ₹40,000 \times \frac{100}{80} = ₹50,000$$

iii) Profit, when Sales are ₹ 1,20,000 :

where,   P/V Ratio = $\frac{\text{Contribution}}{\text{Sales}}$

But,   Contribution = Fixed Cost + Profit

∴   P/V Ratio = $\frac{\text{Fixed Cost} + \text{Profit}}{\text{Sales}}$

∴   P/V Ratio × Sales = Fixed Cost + Profit

∴   Profit = (P/V Ratio × Sales) − Fixed Cost

∴   = (80% × ₹ 1,20,000) − ₹ 40,000

    = ₹ 96,000 − ₹ 40,000

    = ₹ 56,000

iv) Sales required to earn a profit of ₹ 60,000 :

where,   P/V Ratio = $\frac{\text{Contribution}}{\text{Sales}}$

But,   Contribution = Fixed Cost + Profit

∴   P/V Ratio = $\frac{\text{Fixed Cost} + \text{Profit}}{\text{Sales}}$

∴   Sales = $\frac{\text{Fixed Cost} + \text{Profit}}{\text{P/V Ratio}}$

    = $\frac{₹40,000 + ₹60,000}{80\%}$ = ₹ 1,00,000 × $\frac{100}{80}$

    = ₹ 1,25,000

ILLUSTRATION 15

The following information is obtained from Godrej Ltd., for the year ended 31st March, 2013.

	₹
Sales (1,00,000 Units)	1,00,000
Marginal Cost	60,000
Fixed Cost	30,000

Calculate :
i) P/V Ratio,
ii) BEP (Sales value)
iii) Sales to earn a profit of ₹ 15,000
iv) Profit when sales amounted to ₹ 1,40,000

SOLUTION

i) P/V Ratio :

$$= \frac{\text{Contribution}}{\text{Sales}} \times 100$$

But,

Contribution = Sales − Variable Cost

$$\therefore \text{P/V Ratio} = \frac{\text{Sales} - \text{Variable Cost}}{\text{Sales}} \times 100$$

$$= \frac{₹1,00,000 - ₹60,000}{₹1,00,000} \times 100 = \frac{₹40,000}{₹1,00,000} \times 100$$

$$= 40\%$$

ii) BEP (Sales value) :

$$= \frac{\text{Fixed Cost}}{\text{P/V Ratio}}$$

$$= \frac{₹30,000}{40\%} = ₹30,000 \times \frac{100}{40}$$

$$= ₹75,000$$

iii) Sales to earn a profit of ₹ 15,000 :

where,

$$\text{P/V Ratio} = \frac{\text{Contribution}}{\text{Sales}}$$

But,

Contribution = Fixed Cost + Profit

$$\therefore \text{P/V Ratio} = \frac{\text{Fixed Cost + Profit}}{\text{Sales}}$$

$$\therefore \text{Sales} = \frac{\text{Fixed Cost + Profit}}{\text{P/V Ratio}}$$

$$= \frac{₹30,000 + ₹15,000}{40\%} = ₹45,000 \times \frac{100}{40} = ₹1,12,500$$

iv) Profit when Sales amounted to ₹ 1,40,000 :

where,

$$\text{P/V Ratio} = \frac{\text{Contribution}}{\text{Sales}}$$

But, Contribution = Fixed Cost + Profit

$$\therefore \text{P/V Ratio} = \frac{\text{Fixed Cost + Profit}}{\text{Sales}}$$

∴ P/V Ratio × Sales = Fixed Cost + Profit
∴ Profit = (P/V Ratio × Sales) − Fixed Cost
= (40% × ₹ 1,40,000) − ₹ 30,000
= ₹ 56,000 − ₹ 30,000
= ₹ 26,000

ILLUSTRATION 16

Ashoka Ltd., Aurangabad, furnishes you with the following cost data for the year 2012-2013.

Particulars	Amount
Process Material per unit	₹ 3
Sales	10,000 units
Operating Labour per unit	₹ 3
Fixed Cost	₹ 60,000
Chargeable expenses per unit	₹ 1
Value of Sales per unit	₹ 25
Variable Overheads – 100% of Direct Labour	

You are requested to find out,
i) P/V Ratio, ii) BEP (Sales), iii) Margin of Safety.

SOLUTION

Calculation of Total Variable Cost per unit :

Particulars	₹
Variable Overheads :	
• Process Material	3.00
• Operating Labour	3.00
• Chargeable Expenses	1.00
• Variable Overheads	3.00
(100% of Direct Labour i.e. ₹ 3)	
∴ Variable Cost per unit	10.00

i) **P/V Ratio :**

$$= \frac{\text{Contribution per unit}}{\text{Selling Price per unit}} \times 100$$

But, Contribution per unit = Selling Price per unit − Variable Cost per unit

∴ $$\text{P/V Ratio} = \frac{\text{Selling Price per unit} - \text{Variable Cost per unit}}{\text{Selling Price per unit}} \times 100$$

$$= \frac{₹25 - ₹10}{₹25} \times 100 = \frac{₹15}{₹25} \times 100 = 60\%$$

ii) **BEP (Sales) :**

$$= \frac{\text{Fixed Cost}}{\text{P/V Ratio}}$$

$$= \frac{₹60,000}{60\%} = ₹60,000 \times \frac{100}{60} = ₹1,00,000$$

iii) **Margin of Safety :**

= Actual Sales − BEP (Sales)
= (₹ 25 × 10,000 units) − ₹ 1,00,000
= ₹ 2,50,000 − ₹ 1,00,000 = ₹ 1,50,000

ILLUSTRATION 17

From the following cost data relating to Force India Ltd., Faizpur, you are required to calculate –

i) Sales at Break-even,
ii) Profit at budgeted sales,
iii) Profit, if actual sales be at 80% capacity.

Budgeted Sales for the year 2012-2013 (At 100% Capacity)	₹ 12,00,000
Rigid cost in total	₹ 1,00,000
Chargeable Expenses	02% of Sales
Variable Manufacturing Overheads	10% of Sales
Administrative and Selling on Cost – Variable	08% of Sales
Direct Materials	35% of Sales
Prime Cost Labour	20% of Sales

SOLUTION

In the books of Force India Ltd., Faizpur
Profitability Statement for the year ended 2012-2013
(Normal Capacity – 100%)

	Particulars		₹
	Budgeted Sales		12,00,000
Less :	Variable Cost :		
	• Chargeable Expenses (02% of Sales i.e. ₹ 12,00,000)	24,000	
	• Variable Manufacturing Overheads (10% of Sales i.e. ₹ 12,00,000)	1,20,000	
	• Administrative and Selling on Cost – Variable (08% of Sales i.e. ₹ 12,00,000)	96,000	
	• Direct Materials (35% of Sales i.e. ₹ 12,00,000)	4,20,000	
	• Prime Cost Labour (20% of Sales i.e. ₹ 12,00,000)	2,40,000 (+)	
		(–)	9,00,000
	∴ Contribution		3,00,000
Less :	Fixed Cost		
	i) Rigid Cost	(–)	1,00,000
	∴ Profit at Budgeted Sales		**2,00,000**

Calculation of P/V Ratio :

where,

$$\text{P/V Ratio} = \frac{\text{Contribution}}{\text{Sales}} \times 100$$

$$= \frac{₹\,3,00,000}{₹\,12,00,000} \times 100$$

$$= 25\%$$

i) Sales at Break-even :
where,

$$\text{Break-even Point Sales} = \frac{\text{Fixed Cost}}{\text{P/V Ratio}}$$

$$= \frac{₹1,00,000}{25\%}$$

$$= ₹1,00,000 \times \frac{100}{25}$$

$$= ₹4,00,000$$

ii) Profit at Budgeted Sales :
where,

Contribution = Fixed Cost + Profit

∴ Profit = Contribution − Fixed Cost
= ₹3,00,000 − ₹1,00,000
= ₹2,00,000

iii) Profit, if actual sales be at 80% capacity :

- Calculation of actual sales at 80% capacity

  If 100% Capacity = ₹12,00,000 Actual Sales

  ∴ 80% Capacity = ?

  $$= \frac{80 \times ₹12,00,000}{100}$$

  = ₹9,60,000

- Calculation of profit, if actual sales are ₹9,60,000
  where,

  $$\text{P/V Ratio} = \frac{\text{Contribution}}{\text{Sales}}$$

  But,

  Contribution = Fixed Cost + Profit

  ∴ $$\text{P/V Ratio} = \frac{\text{Fixed Cost} + \boxed{\text{Profit}}}{\text{Sales}}$$

  ∴ P/V Ratio × Sales = Fixed Cost + $\boxed{\text{Profit}}$

  ∴ Profit = (P/V Ratio × Sales) − Fixed Cost

  = (25% × ₹9,60,000) − ₹1,00,000

  = ₹2,40,000 − ₹1,00,000

  = ₹1,40,000

ILLUSTRATION 18

From the following data, calculate,

i) Total Profits   ii) BEP (Sales)   iii) Margin of Safety

Number of units sold	units – 20,000
Fixed Overheads	₹ 50,000
Selling Price per unit	₹ 10
Variable Overheads per unit	₹ 6

SOLUTION

i) Total Profits :

$$\text{Sales} = \text{Total Cost} + \text{Profit}$$

But, Total Cost = Fixed Overheads + Variable Cost

∴ Sales = Fixed Overheads + Variable Cost + Profit

∴ Profits = Sales – (Fixed Overheads + Variable Cost)
= 20,000 units × ₹ 10 – (₹ 50,000 + 20,000 units × ₹ 6)
= ₹ 2,00,000 – (₹ 50,000 + ₹ 1,20,000)
= ₹ 2,00,000 – ₹ 1,70,000
= ₹ 30,000

ii) BEP (Sales) :

$$= \frac{\text{Fixed Cost}}{\text{Contribution per unit}} \times \text{Selling price per unit}$$

But, Contribution per unit = Selling price per unit – Variable cost per unit

∴ $\text{BEP (Sales)} = \frac{\text{Fixed Cost}}{\text{Selling price per unit} - \text{Variable cost per unit}} \times \text{Selling Price per unit}$

$$= \frac{₹\,50{,}000}{₹\,10 - ₹\,6} \times ₹\,10 = \frac{₹\,50{,}000}{₹\,4} \times ₹\,10$$

= ₹ 12,500 × ₹ 10
= ₹ 1,25,000

iii) Margin of Safety :

= Actual Sales – BEP (Sales)
= (20,000 units × ₹ 10) – ₹ 1,25,000
= ₹ 2,00,000 – ₹ 1,25,000
= ₹ 75,000

ILLUSTRATION 19

You are given following cost data :

Total Sales	₹ 4,00,000
Total Variable Cost	₹ 2,00,000
Total Fixed Cost	₹ 1,00,000
Total Units sold	Units 1,00,000

Calculate,
i) Contribution per unit
ii) BEP - units and sales
iii) Margin of Safety
iv) Profit
v) Units to be sold to earn a profit of ₹ 1,40,000

SOLUTION

i) Contribution per unit :

where,

Contribution = Sales – Variable Cost
= ₹ 4,00,000 – ₹ 2,00,000
= ₹ 2,00,000

But,
Contribution per unit :

$$= \frac{\text{Total Contribution}}{\text{Total units sold}}$$

$$= \frac{₹2,00,000}{1,00,000 \text{ units}} = ₹2 \text{ per unit}$$

ii) **BEP (units) :**

$$= \frac{\text{Total Fixed Cost}}{\text{Contribution per unit}}$$

$$= \frac{₹1,00,000}{₹2} = 50,000 \text{ units}$$

Calculation of Selling price per unit :

$$\frac{\text{Total Sales}}{\text{Total units sold}} = \frac{₹4,00,000}{1,00,000 \text{ units}} = ₹4 \text{ per unit}$$

BEP (Sales) :

$$= \frac{\text{Total Fixed Cost}}{\text{Contribution per unit}} \times \text{Selling price per unit}$$

$$= \frac{₹1,00,000}{₹2} \times ₹4$$

$$= 50,000 \text{ units} \times ₹4 = ₹2,00,000.$$

iii) **Margin of Safety :**

$$= \text{Actual Sales} - \text{BEP (Sales)}$$
$$= ₹4,00,000 - ₹2,00,000$$
$$= ₹2,00,000$$

iv) **Profit :**

where,

Contribution = Fixed Cost + Profit

∴ Profit = Contribution − Fixed Cost
= ₹2,00,000 − ₹1,00,000
= ₹1,00,000

v) **Units to be sold to earn a profit of ₹ 1,40,000 :**

Sales volume to earn required profit (units) :

$$= \frac{\text{Total Fixed Cost} + \text{Required Profit}}{\text{Contribution per unit}}$$

$$= \frac{₹1,00,000 + ₹1,40,000}{₹2} = \frac{₹2,40,000}{₹2}$$

$$= 1,20,000 \text{ units}$$

ILLUSTRATION 20

Kiddy Toy's Manufacturing Co., provides the following costing data :

	% of Sales	₹
Marginal Cost	80%	8,00,000
Fixed Cost	10%	1,00,000
Profit	10%	1,00,000
Sales	100%	10,00,000

Cost Accounting — Marginal Costing

You are required to calculate :
i) P/V Ratio, ii) BEP (Sales), iii) Margin of Safety, iv) Margin of Safety Ratio

SOLUTION

i) **P/V Ratio :**

$$= \frac{\text{Contribution}}{\text{Sales}} \times 100$$

But, Contribution = Sales − Variable Cost

$\therefore$ P/V Ratio $= \dfrac{\text{Sales} - \text{Variable Cost}}{\text{Sales}} \times 100$

$= \dfrac{₹10,00,000 - ₹8,00,000}{₹10,00,000} \times 100 = \dfrac{₹2,00,000}{₹10,00,000} \times 100$

$= 20\%$

ii) **BEP (Sales) :**

$= \dfrac{\text{Fixed Cost}}{\text{P/V Ratio}}$

$= \dfrac{₹1,00,000}{20\%} = ₹1,00,000 \times \dfrac{100}{20} = ₹5,00,000$

iii) **Margin of Safety :**

$= \dfrac{\text{Profit}}{\text{P/V Ratio}}$

$= \dfrac{₹1,00,000}{20\%} = ₹1,00,000 \times \dfrac{100}{20}$

$= ₹5,00,000$

iv) **Margin of Safety Ratio :**

$= \dfrac{\text{Actual Sales} - \text{BEP (Sales)}}{\text{Actual Sales}} \times 100$

$= \dfrac{₹10,00,000 - ₹5,00,000}{₹10,00,000} \times 100$

$= \dfrac{₹5,00,000}{₹10,00,000} \times 100$

$= 50\%$

ILLUSTRATION 21

Following is the cost structure of a product Gemini of 2012-2013.

Particulars		Unit Cost ₹
Direct Material		100
Add : Productive Wages	(+)	80
	(+)	20
Add : Variable Overheads		200
Total Variable Cost	(+)	40
Total Cost		240
Add : Profit	(+)	60
Sales		300

Company produced and sold 5,000 units.
You are required to calculate,
i)   P/V Ratio   ii) BEP (Sales)
iii) Margin of Safety   (d) Profit when Sales are ₹ 30,00,000
v)   Sales when Profit are ₹ 1,00,000

SOLUTION

i) P/V Ratio :

$$= \frac{\text{Contribution per unit}}{\text{Selling price per unit}} \times 100$$

But,

Contribution per unit = Selling price per unit – Variable cost per unit

$$\therefore \text{P/V Ratio} = \frac{\text{Selling price per unit} - \text{Variable cost per unit}}{\text{Selling price per unit}} \times 100$$

$$= \frac{₹ 300 - ₹ 200}{₹ 300} \times 100 = \frac{₹ 100}{₹ 300} \times 100$$

$$= 33\,^1/_3\%$$

ii) BEP (Sales) :

$$= \frac{\text{Total Fixed Cost}}{\text{P/V Ratio}}$$

$$= \frac{₹ 40 \times 5,000 \text{ units}}{33\,^1/_3\%} = \frac{₹ 2,00,000}{1/3} = ₹ 2,00,000 \times \frac{3}{1}$$

$$= ₹ 6,00,000$$

iii) Margin of Safety :

= Actual Sales – BEP (Sales)
= (₹ 300 × 5,000 units) – ₹ 6,00,000
= ₹ 15,00,000 – ₹ 6,00,000
= ₹ 9,00,000

iv) Profit when Sales are ₹ 30,00,000 :

where,

$$\text{P/V Ratio} = \frac{\text{Contribution}}{\text{Sales}}$$

But,   Contribution = Fixed Cost + Profit

$$\therefore \text{P/V Ratio} = \frac{\text{Fixed Cost} + \text{Profit}}{\text{Sales}}$$

∴   P/V Ratio × Sales = Fixed Cost + Profit
∴   Profit = (P/V Ratio × Sales) – Fixed Cost
                       = $33\,^1/_3\%$ × ₹ 30,00,000 – (₹ 40 × 5,000 units)
                       = ₹ 10,00,000 – ₹ 2,00,000
                       = ₹ 8,00,000

v) Sales when Profit are ₹ 1,00,000 :

where,

$$\text{P/V Ratio} = \frac{\text{Contribution}}{\text{Sales}}$$

But,

$$\text{Contribution} = \text{Fixed Cost} + \text{Profit}$$

$$\therefore \quad \text{P/V Ratio} = \frac{\text{Fixed Cost} + \text{Profit}}{\text{Sales}}$$

$$\therefore \quad \text{Sales} = \frac{\text{Fixed Cost} + \text{Profit}}{\text{P/V Ratio}}$$

$$= \frac{(₹\,40 \times 5{,}000 \text{ units}) + ₹\,1{,}00{,}000}{33\,^{1}/_{3}\%}$$

$$= \frac{₹\,2{,}00{,}000 + ₹\,1{,}00{,}000}{1/3} = ₹\,3{,}00{,}000 \times \frac{3}{1}$$

$$= ₹\,9{,}00{,}000$$

ILLUSTRATION 22

Bajaj Industries provides the following cost data :

	₹
Sales	1,50,000
Marginal Cost	1,20,000
Gross Profit	60,000
Fixed Overheads	20,000
Net Profit	40,000

You are required to calculate,
i) P/V Ratio
ii) BEP (Sales)
iii) Margin of Safety, when Sales are ₹ 4,00,000
iv) Net Profit, when Sales are ₹ 4,00,000
v) Sales required to earn a profit of ₹ 80,000.

SOLUTION

i) **P/ V Ratio :**

$$= \frac{\text{Contribution}}{\text{Sales}} \times 100$$

But, Contribution = Sales – Variable Cost

$$\therefore \quad \text{P/V Ratio} = \frac{\text{Sales} - \text{Variable Cost}}{\text{Sales}} \times 100$$

$$= \frac{₹\,1{,}50{,}000 - ₹\,1{,}20{,}000}{₹\,1{,}50{,}000} \times 100 = \frac{₹\,30{,}000}{₹\,1{,}50{,}000} \times 100$$

$$= 20\%$$

ii) **BEP (Sales) :**

$$= \frac{\text{Fixed Cost}}{\text{P/V Ratio}}$$

$$= \frac{₹\,20{,}000}{20\%} = ₹\,20{,}000 \times \frac{100}{20} = ₹\,1{,}00{,}000$$

iii) **Margin of Safety, when Sales are ₹ 4,00,000 :**

$$\text{Margin of Safety} = \text{Actual Sales} - \text{BEP (Sales)}$$
$$= ₹ 4,00,000 - ₹ 1,00,000$$
$$= ₹ 3,00,000$$

iv) **Net Profit, when Sales are ₹ 4,00,000 :**

where,
$$\text{P/V Ratio} = \frac{\text{Contribution}}{\text{Sales}}$$

But,
$$\text{Contribution} = \text{Fixed Cost} + \text{Profit}$$
$$\therefore \text{P/V Ratio} = \frac{\text{Fixed Cost} + \text{Profit}}{\text{Sales}}$$
$$\therefore \text{P/V Ratio} \times \text{Sales} = \text{Fixed Cost} + \text{Profit}$$
$$\therefore \text{Profit} = (\text{P/V Ratio} \times \text{Sales}) - \text{Fixed Cost}$$
$$= (20\% \times ₹ 4,00,000) - ₹ 20,000$$
$$= ₹ 80,000 - ₹ 20,000$$
$$= ₹ 60,000$$

v) **Sales required to earn a Profit of ₹ 80,000 :**

where,
$$\text{P/V Ratio} = \frac{\text{Contribution}}{\text{Sales}}$$

But,
$$\text{Contribution} = \text{Fixed Cost} + \text{Profit}$$
$$\therefore \text{P/V Ratio} = \frac{\text{Fixed Cost} + \text{Profit}}{\text{Sales}}$$
$$\therefore \text{Sales} = \frac{\text{Fixed Cost} + \text{Profit}}{\text{P/V Ratio}}$$
$$= \frac{₹ 20,000 + ₹ 80,000}{20\%} = ₹ 1,00,000 \times \frac{100}{20} = ₹ 5,00,000$$

ILLUSTRATION 23

Calculate,

i) P/V Ratio, if a company has fixed expenses of ₹ 90,000 with Sales at ₹ 3,00,000 and a profit of ₹ 60,000.

ii) BEP (Sales), if budgeted output is 80,000 units, fixed cost is ₹ 4,00,000, Selling price per unit is ₹ 20 and Variable cost per unit is ₹ 10.

iii) Sales, if Marginal Cost is ₹ 2,400 and P/V Ratio is 20%.

iv) Margin of Safety, if profit is ₹ 20,000 and P/V Ratio is 40%.

SOLUTION

i) **P/V Ratio :**

$$= \frac{\text{Contribution}}{\text{Sales}} \times 100$$

But, $\text{Contribution} = \text{Fixed Cost} + \text{Profit}$

$$\therefore \text{P/V Ratio} = \frac{\text{Fixed Cost} + \text{Profit}}{\text{Sales}} \times 100$$
$$= \frac{₹ 90,000 + ₹ 60,000}{₹ 3,00,000} \times 100 = \frac{₹ 1,50,000}{₹ 3,00,000} \times 100$$
$$= 50\%$$

Cost Accounting 5.41 Marginal Costing

ii) **BEP (Sales) :**

$$= \frac{\text{Fixed Cost}}{\text{Contribution per unit}} \times \text{Selling price per unit}$$

But,
Contribution per unit = Selling price per unit – Variable cost per unit

$$\therefore \text{BEP (Sales)} = \frac{\text{Fixed Cost}}{\text{Selling price per unit – Variable cost per unit}} \times \text{Selling price per unit}$$

$$= \frac{₹4,00,000}{₹20 - ₹10} \times ₹20 = \frac{₹4,00,000}{₹10} \times ₹20$$

$$= ₹40,000 \text{ units} \times ₹20$$

$$= ₹8,00,000$$

iii) **Sales :**

$$= \frac{\text{Marginal Cost}}{\text{Marginal Cost Ratio}}$$

But,
Marginal Cost Ratio = 100 – (P/V Ratio)

$$\therefore \text{Sales} = \frac{\text{Marginal Cost}}{100 - \text{P/V Ratio}}$$

$$= \frac{₹2,400}{100\% - 20\%} = \frac{₹2,400}{80\%} = ₹2,400 \times \frac{100}{80}$$

$$= ₹3,000$$

iv) **Margin of Safety :**

$$= \frac{\text{Profit}}{\text{P/V Ratio}}$$

$$= \frac{₹20,000}{40\%} = ₹20,000 \times \frac{100}{40}$$

$$= ₹50,000$$

ILLUSTRATION 24

(A) From the following, compute the sales volume in units that will yield a profit of ₹ 25,000.

	₹
Selling price per unit	15
Variable cost per unit	10
Fixed Cost	25,000

(B) From the following information, compute the sales in value to earn a profit of ₹ 2,40,000.

	₹
Sales	12,00,000
Variable Cost	7,50,000
Fixed Cost	3,60,000

SOLUTION

A) Sales volume to earn the required profit in units :

$$= \frac{\text{Fixed Cost + Required Profit}}{\text{Contribution per unit}}$$

But,
Contribution per unit = Selling price per unit – Variable cost per unit

∴ **Sales volume in units :**

$$= \frac{\text{Fixed Cost + Required Profit}}{\text{Selling price per unit – Variable cost per unit}}$$

$$= \frac{₹\,25{,}000 + ₹\,25{,}000}{₹\,15 - ₹\,10} = \frac{₹\,50{,}000}{₹\,5} = 10{,}000 \text{ units}$$

B) Sales volume to earn the required profit in value :

$$= \frac{(\text{Fixed Cost + Required Profit}) \times \text{Sales}}{\text{Contribution}}$$

But, Contribution = Sales – Variable Cost

∴ **Sales volume in value :**

$$= \frac{(\text{Fixed Cost + Required Profit}) \times \text{Sales}}{\text{Sales – Variable Cost}}$$

$$= \frac{(₹\,3{,}60{,}000 + ₹\,2{,}40{,}000) \times ₹\,12{,}00{,}000}{₹\,12{,}00{,}000 - ₹\,7{,}50{,}000}$$

$$= \frac{₹\,6{,}00{,}000 \times ₹\,12{,}00{,}000}{₹\,4{,}50{,}000}$$

$$= ₹\,16{,}00{,}000$$

ILLUSTRATION 25

Mobilink Co., Malad, has fixed overheads of ₹ 90,000 with a turnover of ₹ 3,00,000 and a profit of ₹ 60,000 during the first half year. If in the next half year they suffered a loss of ₹ 30,000, calculate :

a) P/V Ratio, BEP (Sales) and Margin of Safety for the first half year.
b) Expected sales volume for the next half year, assuming that selling price and fixed cost remain unchanged.
c) BEP (sales) and Margin of Safety for the whole year.

SOLUTION

a) i) P/V Ratio :

$$= \frac{\text{Contribution}}{\text{Sales}} \times 100$$

But,

Contribution = Fixed Cost + Profit

∴ P/V Ratio $= \dfrac{\text{Fixed Cost + Profit}}{\text{Sales}} \times 100$

$$= \frac{₹\,90{,}000 + ₹\,60{,}000}{₹\,3{,}00{,}000} \times 100$$

$$= \frac{₹\,1{,}50{,}000}{₹\,3{,}00{,}000} \times 100$$

$$= 50\%$$

ii) BEP (Sales) :

$$= \frac{\text{Fixed Cost}}{\text{P/V Ratio}}$$

$$= \frac{₹\,90{,}000}{50\%} = ₹\,90{,}000 \times \frac{100}{50}$$

$$= ₹\,1{,}80{,}000$$

iii) Margin of Safety :

$$= \text{Actual Sales} - \text{BEP (Sales)}$$
$$= ₹\,3,00,000 - ₹\,1,80,000$$
$$= ₹\,1,20,000$$

b) Expected sales volume for the next half year :

where,

$$\text{P/V Ratio} = \frac{\text{Contribution}}{\text{Sales}}$$

But, Contribution = Fixed Cost − Loss

$$\therefore \text{P/V Ratio} = \frac{\text{Fixed Cost} - \text{Loss}}{\text{Sales}}$$

$$\therefore \text{Sales} = \frac{\text{Fixed Cost} - \text{Loss}}{\text{P/V Ratio}}$$

$$= \frac{₹\,90,000 - ₹\,30,000}{50\%}$$

$$= ₹\,60,000 \times \frac{100}{50}$$

$$= ₹\,1,20,000$$

c) i) BEP (Sales) For The Whole Year :

$$= \frac{\text{Fixed cost for the whole year}}{\text{P/V Ratio}}$$

$$= \frac{₹\,90,000 + ₹\,90,000}{50\%}$$

$$= ₹\,1,80,000 \times \frac{100}{50}$$

$$= ₹\,3,60,000$$

ii) Margin of Safety :

$$= \text{Actual Sales} - \text{BEP (Sales)}$$
$$= (₹\,3,00,000 + ₹\,1,20,000) - ₹\,3,60,000$$
$$= ₹\,4,20,000 - ₹\,3,60,000$$
$$= ₹\,60,000$$

QUESTIONS FOR SELF-STUDY

I. Theory Questions :

i) Define the concept of 'Marginal Cost' and 'Marginal Costing'. State the important characteristics of Marginal Costing.

ii) What is 'Marginal Costing' ? Explain the objectives of Marginal Costing.

iii) State the advantages and limitations of Marginal Costing.

iv) Explain Marginal Costing as a technique of costing.

v) Explain the following concepts :

a) Fixed Cost, b) Variable Cost, c) Marginal Cost, d) Contribution, e) Profit Volume Ratio.

vi) Explain the technique of Marginal Costing and state its importance in decision-making.

vii) How are variable costs and fixed costs treated in Marginal Costing.

viii) Define the term 'Marginal Costing'. Explain the practical uses of Marginal Costing.

ix) State the utility of Marginal Costing in price fixation, during trade depression and for export promotion.

x) In what circumstances would you recommend the management to make use of Marginal Costing ?

xi) What is 'Contribution' ? How it differs from 'Profit' ?

xii) What do you understand by P/V Ratio ? Discuss the importance of P/V Ratio. How P/V Ratio can be improved ?

xiii) What is Break-even Point. Explain the importance of Break-even Point.

xiv) Explain the concept of 'Break-even-Point'. What faculty influences Break-even Point.

xv) What is Margin of Safety ? How can it be increased ?

xvi) Discuss the importance of the following in relation to Marginal Costing

(a) Break-even Point, (b) Margin of Safety, (c) Contribution, (d) Angle of Incidence.

xvii) Explain the concept 'Margin of Safety'. State various ways of improving Margin of Safety.

xviii) Write short notes on :

a) Marginal Cost, b) Fixed Cost, c) Marginal Costing, d) Variable Cost, e) Contribution, f) Margin of Safety, g) Profit Volume Ratio, h) Break-even Point, i) Cost-Volume-Profit Analysis, j) Key Factor, k) Application of Marginal Costing Technique.

xix) Differentiate between :

a) Fixed Cost and Variable Cost, b) Contribution and Profit.

II. Practical Problems :

i) The following are the budgeted cost data of Atlas Co. Ltd., Ahmedabad.

	₹
Total Turnover	6,00,000
Marginal Costs	3,00,000
Fixed Costs	1,50,000

Find out the Break-Even-Point at a) the budgeted data and b) 20% increase in variable cost.

ii) The turnover and profits during the two periods were as follows :

Period	Sales ₹	Profit ₹
One	40,00,000	4,00,000
Two	60,00,000	8,00,000

Assuming that the cost structure and selling price remains the same in the two periods. Calculate – a) Profit-Volume Ratio, b) Break-Even Point (Sales Value), c) The sales required to earn a profit of ₹ 10,00,000, d) Margin of Safety in period two, e) Profit when Sales are ₹ 50,00,000.

iii) From the following cost data calculate – a) Fixed Cost, b) Break-even Point, c) The number of units to be sold to earn a profit of ₹ 40,000.

The selling price is ₹ 100 per unit.

Period	Sales (Units)	Profit/Loss ₹
One	7,000	Loss – 10,000
Two	9,000	Profit - 10,000

iv) From the following find out, a) P/V Ratio, b) Break-even Point, c) Net Profit, if the sales were ₹ 2,50,000, d) Sales to earn a profit of ₹ 70,000.

In the books of A Ltd.

Particulars		₹
Value of Turnover		2,00,000
Less : Variable Cost	(–)	1,20,000
∴ Contribution		80,000
Less : Fixed Cost	(–)	20,000
∴ Profit		60,000

v) Morgan Ltd., Mahim, has prepared the following budget estimates for the year 2012-13.

Sales – 20,000 units

Sales value – ₹ 2,00,000

Variable Cost per unit ₹ 5

Fixed Cost – ₹ 20,000.

You are required to calculate –

i) P/V Ratio, Break-even Point and Margin of Safety in each of the following cases.
- Decrease of 10% in selling price.
- Increase of 10% in variable cost.

vi) Calculate the Break-Even point in the following cases :

Sales (estimated) – ₹ 5,00,000

Fixed costs – ₹ 2,00,000

Variable cost per unit – ₹ 10

Selling price per unit – ₹ 50

vii) Amol Industries supply you with the following information :

    Sales   – ₹ 2,00,000
    Fixed cost   – ₹ 1,00,000
    Variable cost – ₹ 1,30,000

Find out the increase in sales required to break-even.

viii) Chaby Ltd., furnishes you with the following information. Calculate the break-even point and show the same by drawing a graph.

    Sales (value)   – ₹ 1,50,000
    Sales (units)   – 15,000
    Fixed cost   – ₹ 50,000
    Variable costs –
    Direct Material – ₹ 40,000
    Direct Labour   – ₹ 45,000
    Variable overheads – ₹ 35,000

ix) From the following particulars draw a break-even chart and find out the break-even point.

    Variable cost per unit – ₹ 15
    Fixed cost   – ₹ 54,000
    Selling price per unit – ₹ 20

x) From the following particulars, find out the (1) P/V Ratio, (2) BEP (Sales) and (3) Margin of Safety.

	₹	% of Sales
Variable cost	– 10,000	80%
Fixed cost	– 5,000	5%
Profit	– 15,000	15%
	30,000	100%

xi) The sales and profit during the last two years are given below :

	Sales	Profit
2006	– ₹ 20 lakhs	₹ 2 lakhs
2007	– ₹ 30 lakhs	₹ 4 lakhs

Calculate a) P/V Ratio, b) Sales required to earn a profit of ₹ 5 lakhs.

xii) Ashim Ltd., gives you the following information :

    Sales   – ₹ 50,000
    Variable cost – ₹ 25,000
    Fixed cost   – ₹ 10,000

Calculate P/V Ratio, BEP and Margin of Safety. Also calculate the effect of 20% increase in sales price and 20% decrease in sales price.

xiii) The following are the figures obtained from the cost records of Neel Industries :

		₹	₹
Sales	– 5,000 units @ ₹ 4 per unit		20,000
Direct material	–	4,000	
Direct labour	–	5,000	
Variable overheads	–	+ 3,000	
		12,000	
Fixed overheads	–	+ 4,000	16,000
		Net profit	4,000

The company has decided to reduce the selling price by 10%. What extra units should be sold to obtain the same amount of profit ?

xiv) The P/V Ratio and Margin of Safety of Bardhan Industries are 50% and 40% respectively. The Company has a sales volume of ₹ 8,00,000. Calculate the net profit.

xv) The following are the details of Manoj Ltd. for the two products 'A' and 'B' :

	'A' Per unit ₹	'B' Per unit ₹
Sales price –	100	120
Material (₹ 10 per kg) –	20	40
Wages –	30	20
Variable overheads –	8	12
Total fixed costs –	₹ 10,000	

When material is the limiting factor, suggest which product should be produced more.

xvi) The following two proposals are under consideration –
   a) 10% reduction in price to give an increase in sales volume from 5,000 units to 6,500 units.
   b) 10% increase in price with decrease in sales volume from 5,000 units to 4,000 units.
   Following cost data is also being made available :
   Variable Cost per unit – ₹ 50
   Selling Price per unit – ₹ 100
   Fixed Cost – ₹ 1,00,000.

   State which of the two proposals should be recommended to the management, so as to get more profits.

xvii) Godrej Ltd., Goregaon, are currently operating at full capacity, manufactures and sells a product at ₹ 6 each. The existing production is 1,00,000 units per year for which the cost structure is as follows :

	₹
Direct Materials	2,00,000
Prime Cost Labour	50,000
Variable on Cost	2,00,000
Fixed Overheads	50,000
Sales	6,00,000

There is an offer from a reputed buyer for 20,000 units at 5.50 per unit. Acceptance of this order would result in additional fixed cost of ₹ 20,000 per year, for hire of special machinery and payment of overtime premium of 20% for the extra direct labour required. Should the order be accepted ?

xviii) Domino Plastics Co., Dombivili, make plastic trays. An analysis of their cost accounting record reveals the following :

Selling price per tray	₹ 80
Variable cost per tray	₹ 20
Fixed cost for the year	₹ 50,000
Production capacity per year	Trays - 2,000

You are required to find out –
a) Break-even Point (in units)
b) The number of trays to be sold to get a profit of ₹ 30,000.
c) If the company can produce 600 trays more per year with an additional fixed cost of ₹ 2,000, what should be the new selling price of a tray to maintain ₹ 30,000, as at the original data ?

xix) Two competing companies Honda Ltd., and Kinetic Ltd., produce and sell the same type of product in the same market. For the year ended 31st March, 2007, their forecasted Profit and Loss Account are as follows :

	Particulars		Honda Ltd.		Kinetic Ltd.	
	Sales			4,50,000		4,50,000
Less :	Variable Cost		2,70,000		3,60,000	
Less :	Fixed Cost	(+)	1,35,000	(+)	45,000	
				(–) 4,05,000		(–) 4,05,000
	Forecasted Net Profit			45,000		45,000

You are required to calculate,

a) Profit/Volume Ratio, b) Break-even Point (Sales Value), c) State which company is likely to keep greater profit, in conditions of –

i) low demand and ii) high demand.

xx) From the following data, which products would you recommend to produce in a factory, time being the key factor.

Particulars		Product X Unit Cost	Product Y Unit Cost
Prime Cost Materials	₹	24	14
Direct Labour @ Re. 1 per hour	₹	2	3
Variable Overheads @ ₹ 2 per hour	₹	4	6
Selling Price	₹	100	110
Standard time to produce	Hrs.	2	3

✻✻✻

Unit ... 6

STANDARD COSTING

6.1 Meaning and Definitions
6.2 Advantages and Limitations of Standard Costing
6.3 Variance Analysis
    6.3.1 Material Variances
    6.3.2 Labour Variances
* Illustrations
* Questions for Self-Study

Control of cost is one of the most important objectives of cost accounting and cannot be achieved without some standard against which actual can be compared. All managements are interested not only in knowing what costs are, but also how satisfactory they are. The use of standard costs increases cost consciousness among management and employees and can improve business profits by providing a base for performance evaluation. Standard costing, therefore, helps managerial planning and control in a significant manner. This system is now widely used and serves as an effective tool for management control.

Historical cost systems are principally associated with recording of historical, or as they are commonly called actual costs. Basically, there are two types of Costing, viz., Historical Costing and Standard Costing. Historical Costs are the actual costs incurred. The term, Historical Costing may be defined as, "the cost which is accumulated during the process of production by the usual historical costing methods". Historical Costs are incurred during a specified period. In Historical Costing system, the analysis of costs are done only after they are incurred i.e. from the past records. Hence, corrective action to avoid inefficiency and wastages cannot be taken. In order to know before hand, the estimated costs, Standard Costing is used. Standard Costing system is based on the ascertainment and use of pre-determined costs. This system is now widely used and serves as an effective tool for management control.

The recording of historical costs is useful as it determines the cost of resources used towards achieving organisational objectives. **Historical costs**, however, have the following **limitations**.

    i)   Historical costs are allocated after they have been incurred and therefore are ineffective in cost control. The costs have been incurred, they cannot be controlled and no steps can be taken to correct inefficiencies.

    ii)   Historical costs are not helpful in cost reduction since they contain no standards or goals towards which employees can work.

    iii) Historical costs do not serve as a reliable guide to management in the tasks of budgeting, planning, and decision-making. Historical costs reflect a situation in a previous period. But the company, in fact, may be working under conditions different from those prevailing during that previous period. Therefore, historical costs are not useful in budget making, performance evaluation, detecting above or below – standard performance.

6.1 MEANING AND DEFINITIONS

Standard Cost :

The word **'Standard'** means a criterion. Thus, a **Standard Cost** is one which is pre-determined and used as a criterion for measuring the efficiency with which actual cost has been incurred. Standard costs represent 'planned' cost of a product. They are expected to be achieved in a particular production process under normal conditions.

Standard Cost is defined in the C.I.M.A. Official terminology as, *"a predetermined calculation of how much costs should be under specified working conditions. It is built-up from an assessment of the value of cost elements and correlates technical specifications and the qualification of materials, labour and other costs to the prices and/or usage rates expected to apply during the period in which the Standard Cost is intended to be used. Its main purpose is to provide basis for control through variance accounting for the valuation of stock and work-in-progress and in some cases for fixing selling prices".*

A **Standard Cost** is a planned cost for a unit of product or service rendered. **Standard Costs** are highly detailed, scientifically pre-determined costs of material, labour and overhead chargeable to a product or service. Standard Costs represent excellent target costs that should be obtained.

The **Institute of Cost and Management Accountants (U.K.)**, defines **Standard Costs** as *"a pre-determined cost which is calculated from management's standards of efficient operation and the relevant necessary expenditure. It may be used as a basis for price fixing and for cost control through variance analysis".* **Standard cost** expresses what costs should be under attainable good performance. They are projections of what actual cost should be under an assumed set of conditions. The term "standard", has been called by different names in accounting e.g., "a norm", "a model or example or comparison", "a measure of comparison", "a criterion of excellence", "a yardstick", "a benchmark", "an index of waste or potential savings", "a sea level from which to measure cost attitudes", "a guage". A **standard** may be a norm or a measure of comparison in terms of specific items such as pounds or kilograms of materials, labours hours required, hours of plant capacity used.

From the above definition, it is observed that **Standard Cost** is a target cost which must be attained. It is based on technical and engineering studies, production method, material specifications, material and labour price projections.

Standard Costing :

Standard Costing is a technique which uses standards for costs and revenues for the purpose of control through variance analysis. According to C.I.M.A., London, **Standard Costing** is, *"the preparation and use of standard costs, their comparison with actual cost and the analysis of variance to their causes and points of incidence".*

Brown and Harward defines **Standard Costing** as, *"a technique of cost accounting which compares the standard cost of each product or service with the actual costs to determine the efficiency of the operation so that any remedial action may be taken immediately".*

Thus, **Standard Costing** involves the setting of pre-determined cost estimates in order to provide a basis for comparison with actual costs. A **Standard Cost** is a planned cost for a unit of product or service rendered. **Standard Costing** is universally accepted as an effective instrument for cost control in industries. It can be used in conjunction with any method of costing. However, it is specially suitable where the manufacturing method involves production of standardised goods of repetitive nature.

Features of Standard Costing

The following features of Standard Costing can be summarised as follows :
i) In Standard Costing all costs are pre-determined in advance. These pre-determined costs are compared with the actual costs incurred. The difference between the standard cost and the actual cost is known as the Variance. These variances are then analysed and reasons are found out for taking corrective action.
ii) The standards are set, based on the past records and performances.
iii) Comparison between actual performance and standard performance is shown by way of reports which are presented to the top management.
iv) Analysis of variances are made for taking appropriate action according to the nature of expenses, i.e. controllable and uncontrollable.
v) In case of controllable costs, if there is adverse variance, efforts are taken to prevent its recurrence. But in case of uncontrollable costs, the standards are revised.
vi) Standard Costing may be applied to any industry.

Objectives of Standard Costing

The objectives of **Standard Costing** technique can be outlined as follows :
i) To provide a formal basis for assessing performance and efficiency.
ii) To control costs by establishing standards and analysis of variances.
iii) To enable the principle if "Management by Exception" to be practised at the detailed operational level.
iv) To assist in setting of budgets.
v) To assist in assigning responsibility for non-standard performance in order to correct deficiencies or to capitalise on benefits.
vi) To provide a basis for estimating.
vii) To provide guidance on possible ways of improving performance.

Standard Cost and Estimated Cost

Both Estimated Costs and Standard Costs are predetermined costs, determined in advance of production. However, these two types of costs differ in respect of the following aspects.

	Standard Cost		Estimated Cost
i)	It is a specification of what the cost "should be".	i)	It is an estimation of what the cost "will be".
ii)	It is ascertained and applied when Standard costing system is in operation.	ii)	It can be used in any business situation or decision-making, where accurate cost is not required.
iii)	It is "planned" cost and established on a scientific basis.	iii)	It is "predetermined" cost based on past performances.
iv)	It is used for analysis of variances and cost control purposes.	iv)	It is used in decision-making and selection of alternative with maximum profitability.
v)	It is determined for each element of cost in the process of business generally on unit basis i.e. standard hours, standard unit etc.	v)	It is determined generally for the period.
vi)	It is a part of accounting system and thus, finds a place in the accounting records.	vi)	It is used only as a statistical information and hence, are not entered in the account books.

Standard Costing and Budgetary Control

Both techniques of Standard Costing and Budgetary Control are similar in principle, since both are concerned with setting performance and cost levels for control purposes. But they differ in their scope. Standards are unit concept, i.e. they apply to particular products to individual operations or processes. Budgets are concerned with totals they lay down cost limits for function and departments and for the firm as a whole. The important points of distinction between Standard Costing and Budgetary Control are as follows:

	Standard Costing		Budgetary Control
i)	Standard Costs are predetermined scientifically for each element of cost i.e. material, labour and overhead. Standard Costs are fixed for each unit for e.g., hour standard, unit standard, labour mix, material mix etc.	i)	Budgets are based on past performance. It is a written plan covering projected activities of a firm for a definite time period. It is a financial measure of target and achievement.
ii)	It may be expressed both in quantitative and monetary measure.	ii)	It is generally expressed in monetary terms.
iii)	It is concerned with ascertainment and control of costs.	iii)	It is concerned with the overall profitability and financial position of the concern.
iv)	Its emphasis is on what should be the cost.	iv)	Its emphasis is on the level of costs not to be exceeded.
v)	It is determined for each element of cost.	v)	It is determined for a specified period.
vi)	Any variance adverse or favourable is investigated.	vi)	It puts emphasis more on excess over the budget.
vii)	It is related with the control of costs and it is more intensive in scope.	vii)	It is concerned with the operation of business as a whole and it is more extensive.
viii)	It is introduced primarily to ascertain the efficiency and effectiveness of cost performance.	viii)	It is introduced to state in figures as approved plan of action relating to a particular period.
ix)	It is limited to manufacturing activities only.	ix)	It is used for all departments in an organisation.
x)	It is a projection of cost accounts.	x)	It is a projection of financial accounts.
xi)	It is generally used in taxtial decisions like price fixation, computation of product cost, valuation of inventories etc.	xi)	It lays emphasis on policy determination, achievement of goals, co-ordination of different departments and activities etc.
xii)	It is less expensive.	xii)	It is more expensive.
xiii)	It cannot be applied in part.	xiii)	Budgeting may be either partial or comprehensive.

6.2 ADVANTAGES AND LIMITATIONS OF STANDARD COSTING

The important **Advantages of Standard Costing** system are as follows:

i) **Cost Control :**

Standard Costing serves as a measuring rod of operating efficiency and cost control. Under this system, costs are controlled by comparing actual costs with standard costs, analysing the variance and taking corrective action.

ii) **Motivation :**

The standards provide incentive and motivation to work with greater effort. Plans may be formulated to reward those workers who achieve the standards. This increases all-round efficiency and productivity.

iii) **Formulation of price and production policies :**

Standard Costing acts as a valuable guide to management in the formulation of price and production policies. This enables the management in the preparation of price lists for prospective orders and planning production of new products.

iv) **Cost Reporting :**

It provides for prompt reporting of cost for various purposes like fixation of selling price, ascertaining the value of closing stocks and determining the idle capacity. Prompt reporting enhances the value of reports.

v) **Reporting on the principle of exception :**

Attention of the management is drawn to adverse variances which are significant. Analysis of investigating of significant deviations enables the management to take corrective action to prevent their recurrence.

vi) **Basis of inventory valuation :**

It can be used to value stock and provide a basis for setting wage incentive schemes.

vii) **Measurement of efficiency :**

It is a yardstick for evaluating efficiency at all levels. This also facilitates cost control.

viii) **Saving in clerical costs :**

Installation of Standard Costing saves clerical labour and expenses involved in the work of cost accounting. Costing procedure is simplified and the number of forms and records is reduced.

ix) **Budgetary Planning :**

Being pre-determined costs, standard costs are very useful in planning, budgeting and decision-making.

x) **Cost Consciousness :**

Due to emphasis on cost variation, the entire organisation becomes cost-conscious. Employees in production and other departments realise the importance of efficient operations which leads to cost reduction.

xi) **Effective delegation of authority :**

As responsibility is defined clearly, delegation of authority is made more effective.

xii) **All round efficiency :**

Standard Costing facilitates the maximum use of working capital, plant and equipments and other current assets. Wastages of materials is reduced to the minimum and idle time is closely controlled. Consequently, the overall efficiency of the concern is promoted to the maximum extent.

The important Limitations of Standard Costing System are as follows :

i) **Difficulty in setting standards :**

It is quite difficult to establish accurate standards. It requires technical skills. Inaccurate and unreliable standards do more harm than good. Unless standards are accurately set, any performance evaluation will be meaningless.

ii) **More expensive :**

A lot of input data is required which can be expensive. Again revision of standards in the light of changed circumstances becomes expensive. Therefore, it is not suitable for small firms.

iii) **Adverse effect on morale of employees :**

Fixation of inaccurate standards, especially those that are incapable of achievement, adversely affects the morale of employees and acts as a hindrance to increased efficiency.

iv) **Unsuitable where technology changes frequently :**

Standard Costing is not suitable in industries that are subject to frequent technological changes. In case the technique is introduced inspite of such changes, it becomes necessary to constantly revise the standards.

v) **Segregation of Variances :**

For localising deviation and fixing responsibility, it becomes necessary to distinguish between controllable and uncontrollable variances. Such a distinction may not always be possible.

vi) **Price Changes :**

Operation of Standard Costing necessitates the price estimation of the prices of input factors. Such precise estimation may not be possible if prices fluctuate too often.

vii) **Varying levels of output :**

In case of some industries, the capacity utilisation cannot be precisely estimated for absorption of overheads. Accordingly, if the standard level of output set for pre-determining standard costs is not achieved, standard costs do not serve the required purpose.

viii) **Implementation of Standard Costing System :**

Unless, there is much interest on the part of management and complete support and co-operation from employees implementation of Standard Costing system is not possible.

ix) **Difficulty in understanding the technique :**

The research evidence shares that overly elaborate variances are imperfectly understood by line managers and thus, they are likely to be ineffective for control purposes.

x) **Nature of Variance Analysis :**

All forms of variance analysis are post mortem on past events. Obviously, the part cannot be altered so the only value, variances can have is to guide management if identical or similar circumstances occur in the future.

6.3 VARIANCE ANALYSIS

Variance Accounting is a technique whereby the planned activities of an undertaking are expressed in budgets, standard costs, standard selling prices and standard profit margins and the difference between these and the comparable actual results are accounted for. The procedure is to collect, compare, comment and correct.

'Variance' is the difference between planned, budgeted or standard cost and actual costs and similarly in respect of revenues. In short, variance is the difference between standard cost and actual cost.

Variance Analysis is defined by the Terminology as, "that part of Variance Accounting which relates to the analysis into constituent parts of variance between planned and actual performance". Thus, Variance Analysis is the analysis of variance arising in standard costing system into their constituent parts. It is the analysis and comparison of the factors which have caused the differences between pre-determined standards and actual results with a view to eliminating inefficiencies. The purpose of variance analysis is to draw the attention of the management to reasons for the difference between budgeted operated profit and actual operating profit. A break-up of the difference into the various constituent parts will enable management to improve operations, increase efficiency, utilise resources more effectively and reduce costs.

Favourable and Unfavourable Variances :

Cost Variance may either be favourable or unfavourable or adverse. When actual cost is **less than** standard cost, it has a 'favourable' effect on profit and thus it is known as favourable variance. (positive/plus). On the other hand, when actual cost is **more than** standard costs it has an 'adverse' or 'unfavourable' effect on profit and is known as adverse unfavourable or negative (minus) variance.

If only the variances are found, it does not help the management in any way. The analysis of variances and their causes are more important. Variances can again be divided into two categories – a) Controllable and b) Uncontrollable. The controllable variances are those which can be controlled by the management, for e.g., wastage of material, idle time of labour, machine break-down etc. This is because all these costs can be controlled by the incharge of the department who is responsible. On the other hand, some costs are uncontrollable in nature which have to be incurred due to external factors, for e.g., if the minimum wages are increased for the labourers by the Government, the management cannot control this cost. Thus, the management gives more stress on controlling the controllable costs by analysis of the variances.

There are basically three main variances i.e. Direct Material Cost Variance, Direct Labour (Wages) Cost Variance and Overhead Cost Variance

Thus, the addition of all the three factors gives us the **"Total Cost Variance"** which is illustrated as follows.

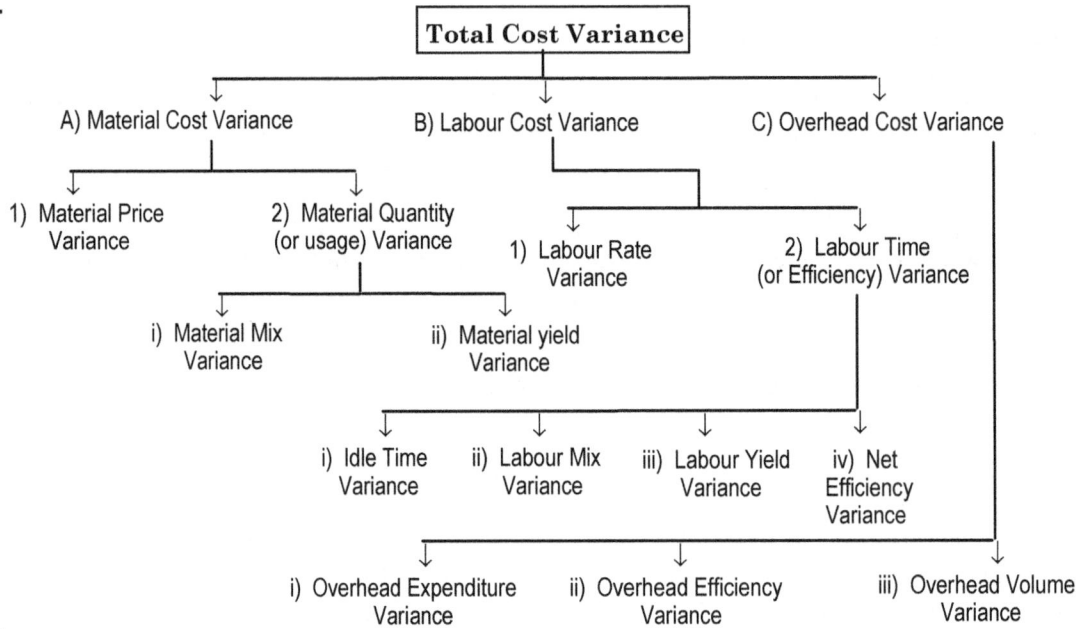

6.3.1 Material Variances

Material Variances includes the following :

A) Material Cost Variance :

Material Cost Variance is also called "Material Total Variance", it is the difference between standard direct material cost of actual production and the actual cost of direct material. It is computed by the following formula :

Material Cost Variance = Standard Cost of Material – Actual Cost of Material.

Thus, in symbol MCV = SC – AC.

OR

Marginal Cost Variance = (Standard Quantity × Standard Price) – (Actual Quantity × Actual Price)

Thus, in symbol MCV = (SQ × SP) – (AQ – AP)

Material Cost Variance is analysed into **two** sub-variances – Material Price Variance and Material Quantity (or usage) Variance.

1) Material Price Variance :

The **Material Price Variance** is the difference between the standard price and the actual purchase price for each unit of material multiplied by the actual quantity of material purchased. It is preferable to base the price variance on the actual quantity of material purchased and not on the actual quantity used in order that price variances can be reported for control purposes as soon as possible i.e. when the materials are purchased. Its formula is :

Material Price Variance = (Standard Price – Actual Price) × Actual Quantity

Thus, in symbol, MPV = (SP – AP) × AQ

Material Price Variance occurs due to the following reasons:
- Change in the purchase price of materials.
- Other materials purchased instead of the standard quality.
- Inability to obtain cash discount.
- Spending more on transportation.
- Emergency purchases to meet urgent orders.
- Hike in taxes and duties levied by the Government.
- Failure to enter into forward contracts.
- Purchases in uneconomical quantities.

Generally, the Purchase Manager is held responsible for the material price variance. But he cannot be held responsible for the uncontrollable expenses, for e.g., rise in prices, Government taxes etc.

2) Material Quantity (or Usage) Variance :

Material Usage Variance is the difference between the standard usage and the actual usage of materials for the output achieved. The Terminology defines Material Usage Variance is, "that portion of the direct materials cost variance which is the difference between the standard quantity specified for the production achieved, whether completed or not, and the actual quantity used, both valued at standard prices". Its formula is :

Material Quantity Variance = (Standard Quantity – Actual Quantity) × Standard Price

Thus, in symbol MQV (or MUV) = (SQ – AQ) × SP

This variance arises mainly due to the following **reasons** :
- Defective materials used in production which results in spoilage of articles.
- Defective tools used, causing breakages, spoilage etc. for which more material is required.
- No proper handling of materials.
- Untrained labourers or trainees spoil more materials.
- Theft/pilferage of materials.
- Changes in the design or specification of the product due to Research and Development or due to change in the customer's choice.
- Using other material mix than the standard mix.
- Inefficient production methods.
- Rigid inspection resulting in more rejections requiring additional materials for rectification.
- Accounting errors.
- Inaccurate standards.
- Increased rate of scrap than anticipated.
- Failure to return excess materials to stores.

Thus, from the above, we derive the formula for Material Cost Variance as –

Material Cost Variance = Material Price Variance + Material Usage Variance

Thus, in symbol MCV = MPV + MUV

Again Material Usage Variance can be classified into –
i) Material Mix Variance
ii) Material Yield Variance

The computation of these variances becomes useful, when products involving a mixture of ingredients are being manufactured.

i) Material Mix Variance :

Material Mix Variance is a part of the Material Usage Variance. Material Mix Variance occurs due to the usage of other mixture of materials rather than the standard mix specified. For example, this variance arises in chemical industries, rubber industries etc. where the standard mixture of chemicals etc. is determined in advance. Any deviation from this standard due to shortage of a particular chemical or due to using substitutes which have different specifications, leads to Material Mix Variance.

Its formula is :

Material Mix Variance = Standard Price × (Standard Quantity Mix − Actual Quantity Mix)

Thus, in symbol MMV = SP × (SQM − AQM)

This formula is used when the actual weight of mix and standard weight of mix do not differ.

Sometimes, there is a need to revise the standards, for e.g., in case of shortage of materials. In this case, the formula for the revised standard is −

MMV = SP × (RSQ − AQ)

where, RSQ = Revised Standard Quantity.

ii) Material Yield Variance :

Material Yield Variance is also a part of the Material Usage Variance. Material Yield Variance arises when the actual yield differs from the standard yield. It is defined as, "the difference between the standard yield specified and the actual yield obtained". This variance is worked out in processing industry, for e.g., chemical industry, where the yield from a material is specified and is expected from a given input of materials. Its formula is −

a) When Standard Mix and Actual Mix are the same :

Material Yield Variance = SC (AY − SY)

where, SC = Standard Cost per unit

SC is calculated as under :

$$SC = \frac{\text{Standard Cost of Standard Mix}}{\text{Net Standard Output (Output − Loss)}}$$

where, AY = Actual Yield

SY = Standard Yield

b) When Actual Mix differs from Standard Mix :

In such a case, the revised standard mix is calculated, so that standard mix is in proportion to actual mix.

Revised Standard Cost per unit is found out as −

$$SC = \frac{\text{Standard Cost of Revised Standard Mix}}{\text{Net Standard Output}}$$

Formula :

MYV = SC (AY − RSY)

where, RSY = Revised Standard Yield

Material Yield Variance is caused due to changes in waste, scrap etc.

6.3.2 Labour Variances

The Labour Variances are more or less the same as material variances. Normally, labour is taken as a variable cost at times it becomes fixed cost as it is not possible to remove or retrench in case of fall or stoppage in production.

Labour Rate Standard :

This is basically dependent on the agreement with the labour unions or rate prevalent in the particular area or industry.

Labour Efficient Standard :

The labour (quantities) efficiency means the number of hours that the appropriate grade of workers will take to perform the necessary work. It is based on the actual performance of the worker or a group of workers posessing average skill and using average effort, while performing manual operations or working or machine under normal conditions. The standard time is fixed considering the past performance or work study. This is on the basis that is acceptable to the workers as well as the management.

B) Labour Cost Variance (Direct Wages Variance):

This is defined as, "the difference between the standard direct labour cost and actual direct labour cost incurred for the production achieved. Its formula is –

Labour Cost Variance = Standard Cost – Actual Cost

Thus, in symbol   LCV = SC – AC

OR

Labour Cost Variance = (Standard Hours × Standard Rate) – (Actual Hours × Actual Rate)

Thus, in symbol LCV = (SH × SR) – (AH × AR)

When the actual hours for production differ from the standard hours, we can use the formula as –

(Standard hours for actual production × SR) – (AH × AR)

The Labour Cost Variance is sub-divided into a) Labour Rate Variance and b) Labour Efficiency Ratio.

1) Labour Rate Variance:

According to the terminology, Labour Rate Variance is "the difference between the standard and actual direct labour hour rate per hour for the total hours worked". Thus, this is "that part of the Labour Cost Variance which is due to the difference between the standard rate specified and the actual rate paid. It is calculated by the following formula:

Labour Rate Variance = (Standard Rate – Actual Rate) × Actual Hours

Thus, in symbol LRV = (SR – AR) × AH

The following are the **reasons** for Labour Rate Variance.

- Changes in basic wage rates.
- Employment of different categories of workers which are different from the standard categories (grades).
- Using different methods for payment of wages.
- Working more hours than specified.
- Trainees are recruited who are not given full wages. This results in favourable variance.
- Payment of day rates although the standards specify piece-rates.
- Night Shift work.
- Promotion of employees without proper authorisation by personal favouritism of supervisors and paying them rates fixed for higher job classifications.

2) Labour Efficiency Variance:

This is also known as Labour Time Variance. Labour Efficiency Variance is the difference between the standard hours allowed and the actual hours worked for the volume of output achieved. The difference is valued at the standard rate. The Terminology defines Labour Efficiency Variance as, "the difference between the standard hours for the actual production achieved and the hours actually worked, valued at standard labour rate". It is calculated as follows:

Labour Efficiency Variance = (Standard Hours – Actual Hours) × Standard Rate

Thus, in symbol LEV = (SH – AH) × SR

Thus, Labour Cost Variance is the sum total of Labour Rate Variance and Labour Efficiency Variance as shown below :

$$LCV = LRV + LEV$$

Labour Efficiency Variance may arise because of the following **reasons** :
- Use of incorrect grade of labour.
- Insufficient training.
- Bad supervision.
- Incorrect instructions.
- Bad working conditions.
- Worker's dissatisfaction.
- Inefficient organisation awaiting for materials, tools and instructions, delay in routing etc.
- Defective machinery and equipment.
- High Labour Turnover
- Fixation of incorrect standards.
- Wrong booking of Job time.
- Power failure, machine breakdown etc.

The Labour Efficiency Variance can be segregated into the following :

i) Idle Time Variance :

It is that part of the Labour Efficiency Variance which is due to the wastage of time over and above the normal idle time. Thus, the idle time variance represents the difference between hours paid and hours worked i.e. idle hours multiplied by the standard wage rate per hour. The causes for such idle time are :
- Breakdown of machines.
- Power failure
- Illness of workers
- Strike by workers.
- Accident or fire in the factory etc.

Formula for Idle Time Variance :

$$\text{Idle Time Variance} = \text{Idle Hours} \times \text{Standard Rate}$$

ii) Labour Mix Variance :

Labour Mix Variance arises when more than one grade of workers (i.e. different mixture of workers) are engaged and the composition of actual grade of workers differs from the standard grade. Its formula is :

$$\text{Labour Mix Variance} = (\text{Revised Standard Time} - \text{Actual Time}) \times \text{Standard Rate}$$

Thus, in symbol $LMV = (RST - AT) \times SR$

where, $RST \text{ means} = \dfrac{\text{Total Actual Time}}{\text{Total Standard Time}} \times \text{Standard Time}$

iii) Labour Yield Variance :

The Labour Yield Variance arises due to the difference in the standard output specified and the actual output obtained –

$$\text{Labour Yield Variance} = \text{Standard Cost per unit} \left(\text{Standard output for actual time} - \text{Actual output} \right)$$

iv) Net Efficiency Variance :

This variance is calculated after deducting idle hours from actual hours. The Efficiency Variance *less* Idle Time Variance is called **Net Efficiency Variance**. Its formula is :

$$\text{Net Efficiency Variance} = \text{Standard Rate} \times \left(\text{Standard Time} - \text{Actual Hours paid} - \text{Idle hours} \right)$$

ILLUSTRATIONS

MATERIAL VARIANCES

ILLUSTRATION 1

From the following cost data, calculate,
i) Material Cost Variance   ii) Material Price Variance   iii) Material Usage Variance

Standard		Actual	
Material required for of finished product	70 kgs	Output	2,10,000 kgs
	100 kgs	Materials used	2,80,000 kgs
Price of materials	₹ 1 per kg	Cost of Materials	₹ 2,52,000

Also verify your results.

SOLUTION

Working Notes :

a) **Calculation of Standard Quantity of material required for Actual Output :**

$\quad$ If 70 kgs output = 100 kgs input

$\therefore \quad$ 2,10,000 kgs output = ?

$\qquad = \dfrac{2,10,000 \text{ kgs} \times 100 \text{ kgs}}{70 \text{ kgs}}$

$\qquad = 3,00,000$ kgs

b) **Calculation of Actual Price per kg :**

$\quad$ If 2,80,000 kgs = ₹ 2,52,000

$\therefore \quad$ 1 kg = ?

$\qquad = \dfrac{1 \text{ kg} \times ₹ 2,52,000}{2,80,000 \text{ kgs}}$

$\qquad = ₹ 0.90$ per kg

Calculation of Material Variances :

i) **Material Cost Variance :** (SQ × SP) – (AQ × AP)
   = (Standard Quantity × Standard Price) – (Actual Quantity × Actual Price)
   = (3,00,000 kgs × ₹ 1) – (2,80,000 kgs × ₹ 0.90)
   = ₹ 3,00,000 – ₹ 2,52,000
   = ₹ 48,000 (Favourable)

ii) **Material Price Variance :** (SP – AP) × AQ
   = (Standard Price – Actual Price) × Actual Quantity
   = (₹ 1.00 – ₹ 0.90) × 2,80,000 kgs
   = ₹ 28,000 (Favourable)

iii) **Material Usage Variance :** (SQ – AQ) × SP
   = (Standard Quantity – Actual Quantity) × Standard Price
   = (3,00,000 kgs – 2,80,000 kgs) × ₹ 1
   = 20,000 kgs × ₹ 1
   = ₹ 20,000 (Favourable)

Verification,

$\qquad$ MCV = MPV + MUV

Material Cost Variance = Material Price Variance + Material Usage Variance

$\qquad$ ₹ 48,000 (F) = ₹ 28,000 (F) + ₹ 20,000 (F)

$\qquad$ **Total ₹ 48,000 (F)** = ₹ 48,000 (F)

ILLUSTRATION 2

Ajanta Chemicals, Aurangabad, are using Standard Costing technique to control their cost. A standard estimate for basic materials of 1,000 units of a commodity is 400 kgs. @ ₹ 2.50 per kgs. During March, 2013, when 2,000 units of a commodity are manufactured it is ascertained that 850 kgs. of materials are actually consumed @ ₹ 2.20 per kg.

Calculate the Material Variances.

SOLUTION

Working Notes :

a) Calculation of Standard Quantity of Material required for actual output :

If 1,000 units = 400 kgs.

∴ 2,000 units = ?

$$= \frac{2{,}000 \text{ units} \times 400 \text{ kgs.}}{1{,}000 \text{ units}}$$

= 800 kgs.

Calculation of Material Variances :

i) Material Cost Variance : (SQ × SP) − (AQ × AP)

= (Standard Quantity × Standard Price) − (Actual Quantity × Actual Price)
= (800 kgs. × ₹ 2.50) − (850 kgs. × ₹ 2.20)
= ₹ 2,000 − ₹ 1,870
= ₹ 130 (Favourable)

ii) Material Price Variance : (SP − AP) × AQ

= (Standard Price − Actual Price) × Actual Quantity
= (₹ 2.50 − ₹ 2.20) × 850 kgs.
= ₹ 0.30 × 850 kgs.
= ₹ 255 (Favourable)

iii) Material Usage Variance : (SQ − AQ) × SP

= (Standard Quantity − Actual Quantity) × Standard Price
= (800 kgs. − 850 kgs.) × ₹ 2.50
= 50 kgs. × ₹ 2.50
= ₹ 125 (Adverse)

Verification,

MCV = MPV + MUV

Material Cost Variance = Material Price Variance + Material Usage Variance

₹ 130 (F) = ₹ 255 (F) + ₹ 125 (A)

∴ Total : ₹ 130 (F) = ₹ 130 (F)

Cost Accounting   6.15   Standard Costing

ILLUSTRATION 3

In Sudarshan Chemicals Ltd., Someshwarnagar, for producing 10 kgs. of a product 'SANNY', the standard requirement is as follows :

Materials	Quantity kgs.	Rate per kg. ₹
C_2	8	6.00
D_1	4	4.00

During January, 2007, 1,000 kgs. of product 'SANNY' were produced. The actual consumption of material is as under :

Materials	Quantity kgs.	Rate per kg. ₹
C_2	750	7.00
D_1	500	5.00

You are required to calculate,

i) Material Cost Variance, ii) Material Price Variance, and iii) Material Usage Variance.

Also, verify the results.

SOLUTION

Working Notes :

a) Calculation of Standard Quantity of Material required for Actual Output of 1,000 kgs :

Material C_2 :

$$\text{If 10 kgs. output} = 8 \text{ kgs. input}$$

∴   1,000 kgs. output = ?

$$= \frac{1,000 \text{ kgs.} \times 8 \text{ kgs.}}{10 \text{ kgs.}}$$

= 800 kgs.

Material D_1 :

If 10 kgs. output = 4 kgs. input

∴   1,000 kgs. output = ?

$$= \frac{1,000 \text{ kgs.} \times 4 \text{ kgs.}}{10 \text{ kgs.}}$$

= 400 kgs.

Calculation of Material Variances :

i) **Material Cost Variance : (SQ × SP) – (AQ × AP)**

= (Standard Quantity × Standard Price) – (Actual Quantity × Actual Price)

Material C_2:

= (800 kgs. × ₹ 6) – (750 kgs. × ₹ 7)

= ₹ 4,800 – ₹ 5,250

= ₹ 450 (Adverse)

Material D_1:

= (400 kgs. × ₹ 4) – (500 kgs. × ₹ 5)

= ₹ 1,600 – ₹ 2,500

= ₹ 900 (Adverse)

ii) **Material Price Variance : (SP – AP) × AQ**

= (Standard Price – Actual Price) × Actual Quantity

Material C_2:

= (₹ 6 – ₹ 7) × 750 kgs.

= ₹ 1 × 750 kgs.

= ₹ 750 (Adverse)

Material D_1:

= (₹ 4 – ₹ 5) × 500 kgs.

= ₹ 1 × 500 kgs.

= ₹ 500 (Adverse)

iii) **Material Usage Variance : (SQ – AQ) × SP**

= (Standard Quantity – Actual Quantity) × Standard Price

Material C_2:

= (800 kgs. – 750 kgs.) × ₹ 6

= 50 kgs. × ₹ 6

= ₹ 300 (Favourable)

Material D_1:

= (400 kgs. – 500 kgs.) × ₹ 4

= 100 kgs. × ₹ 4

= ₹ 400 (Adverse)

Verification,

		MCV	=	MPV + MUV
	Material Cost Variance	=	Material Price Variance + Material Usage Variance
C_2 :	₹ 450 (A)	=	₹ 750 (A) + ₹ 300 (F)
D_1 :	₹ 900 (A)	=	₹ 500 (A) + ₹ 400 (A)
	₹ 1,350 (A)	=	₹ 1,250 (A) + ₹ 100 (A)
∴	Total : ₹ 1,350 (A)	=	₹ 1,350 (A)

ILLUSTRATION 4

The following particulars derived from the cost records are made available from which you are required to find out,

i) Material Cost Variance, ii) Material Price Variance and iii) Material Usage Variance

Opening Stock of Material	...	Nil
Closing Stock of Material	...	1,000 units
Standard quantity of material required per tonne of output	...	50 units
Standard price of material per unit	...	₹ 1.50
Quantity of materials purchased	...	5,000 units
Cost of materials purchased	...	₹ 10,000
Quantity produced	...	100 tonnes

Also verify your results.

SOLUTION

Working Notes :

a) **Calculation of Standard Quantity of materials required :**

$$\text{If 1 tonne} = 50 \text{ units}$$

$$\therefore \quad 100 \text{ tonnes} = ?$$

$$= \frac{100 \text{ tonnes} \times 50 \text{ units}}{1 \text{ tonne}}$$

$$= 5,000 \text{ units}$$

b) **Calculation of Actual Quantity of materials consumed in units :**

= Opening Stock + Purchases − Closing Stock

= Nil + 5,000 units − 1,000 units

= 4,000 units.

c) **Calculation of Actual Price of material per unit :**

$$\text{If 5,000 units} = ₹ 10,000$$

$$\therefore \quad 1 \text{ unit} = ?$$

$$= \frac{1 \text{ unit} \times ₹ 10,000}{5,000 \text{ units}}$$

$$= ₹ 2 \text{ per unit}$$

Calculation of Material Variance :

i) **Material Cost Variance :** $(SQ \times SP) - (AQ \times AP)$

    = (Standard Quantity × Standard Price) − (Actual Quantity × Actual Price)

    = (5,000 units × ₹ 1.50) − (4,000 units × ₹ 2)

    = ₹ 7,500 − ₹ 8,000

    = ₹ 500 (Adverse)

ii) **Material Price Variance :** $(SP - AP) \times AQ$

    = (Standard Price − Actual Price) × Actual Quantity

    = (₹ 1.50 − ₹ 2) × 4,000 units

    = ₹ 0.50 × 4,000 units

    = ₹ 2,000 (Adverse)

iii) **Material Usage Variance :** $(SQ - AQ) \times SP$

    = (Standard Quantity − Actual Quantity) × Standard Price

    = (5,000 units − 4,000 units) × ₹ 1.50

    = 1,000 units × ₹ 1.50

    = ₹ 1,500 (Favourable)

Verification,

    MCV = MPV + MUV

    Material Cost Variance = Material Price Variance + Material Usage Variance

    ₹ 500 (A) = ₹ 2,000 (A) + ₹ 1,500 (F)

∴   Total : ₹ 500 (A) = ₹ 500 (A)

ILLUSTRATION 5

From the following information calculate,

i) Material Cost Variance, ii) Material Price Variance iii) Material Usage Variance and iv) Material Mix Variance

Material	Standard Mix	Actual Mix
'X'	70 kgs @ ₹ 2 per kg	60 kgs @ ₹ 2 per kg
'Y'	30 kgs @ ₹ 4 per kg	50 kgs @ ₹ 5 per kg

SOLUTION

Working Notes :

a) Calculation of Standard Mixing Proportion between Material 'X' and Material 'Y' in kgs.

    Material 'X' : Material 'Y'

    70 kgs : 30 kgs

    7 : 3

b) Calculation of total quantity of Actual Material Consumed :

= Material 'X' + Material 'Y'
= 60 kgs + 50 kgs
= 110 kgs

c) Calculation of Revised Standard Mix in kgs :

= Actual quantity of material consumed × Standard mixing proportion

Material 'X' = 110 kgs × 7/10 = 77 kgs
Material 'Y' = 110 kgs × 3/10 = 33 kgs

Calculation of Material Variances :

i) Material Cost Variance : (SQ × SP) − (AQ × AP)

= (Standard Quantity × Standard Price) − (Actual Quantity × Actual Price)

Material 'X' = (70 kgs × ₹ 2) − (60 kgs × ₹ 2)
= ₹ 140 − ₹ 120
= ₹ 20 (Favourable)

Material 'Y' = (30 kgs × ₹ 4) − (50 kgs × ₹ 5)
= ₹ 120 − ₹ 250
= ₹ 130 (Adverse)

ii) Material Price Variance : (SP − AP) × AQ

= (Standard Price − Actual Price) × Actual Quantity

Material 'X' = (₹ 2 − ₹ 2) × 60 kgs
= NIL × 60 kgs
= NIL

Material 'Y' = (₹ 4 − ₹ 5) × 50 kgs
= ₹ 1 × 50 kgs
= ₹ 50 (Adverse)

iii) Material Usage Variance : (SQ − AQ) × SP

= (Standard Quantity − Actual Quantity) × Standard Price

Material 'X' = (70 kgs − 60 kgs) × ₹ 2
= 10 kgs × ₹ 2
= ₹ 20 (Favourable)

Material 'Y' = (30 kgs − 50 kgs) × ₹ 4
= 20 kgs × ₹ 4
= ₹ 80 (Adverse)

iv) **Material Mix Variance :** (SRM – AM) × SP

= (Standard Revised Mix – Actual Mix) × Standard Price

Material 'X' = (77 kgs – 60 kgs) × ₹ 2
= 17 kgs × ₹ 2
= ₹ 34 (Favourable)

Material 'Y' = (33 kgs – 50 kgs) × ₹ 4
= 17 kgs × ₹ 4
= ₹ 68 (Adverse)

Verification,

MCV = MPV + MUV

Material Cost Variance = Material Price Variance + Material Usage Variance

Material 'X' : ₹ 20 (F) = NIL + ₹ 20 (F)

Material 'Y' : ₹ 130 (A) = ₹ 50 (A) + ₹ 80 (A)

∴ ₹ 110 (A) = ₹ 50 (A) + ₹ 60 (A)

∴ Total : ₹ 110 (A) = ₹ 110 (A)

ILLUSTRATION 6

In Toshniwal Chemicals, Tulapur, for the output of 'Tosha' chemical of 10 kgs., the actual mix differs from the standard mix with a change in output. The cost details for a period of March, 2013, are given below :

Materials	Standard Mix			Actual Mix		
	Quantity kgs.	Price ₹	Cost ₹	Quantity kgs.	Price ₹	Cost ₹
'Bk'	60	20	1,200	75	22	1,650
'Pk'	40	10	400	30	08	240
Total	100		1,600	105		1,890

Calculate the following material variances, i) Material Cost Variance, ii) Material Price Variance, iii) Material Usage Variance and iv) Material Mix Variance.

SOLUTION

Working Notes :

a) **Calculation of Standard Mixing Proportion between Material - 'Bk' and Material - 'Pk'.**

Material - 'Bk' : Material - 'Pk'

60 kgs. : 40 kgs.

3 : 2

b) **Calculation of Total Quantity of actual material consumed :**

= Material - 'Bk' + Material - 'Pk'

= 75 kgs. + 30 kgs.

= 105 kgs.

c) **Calculation of Revised Standard Mix in kgs. :**

$$\text{Material - 'Bk'} = 105 \text{ kgs.} \times \frac{3}{5}$$

$$= 63 \text{ kgs.}$$

$$\text{Material - 'Pk'} = 105 \text{ kgs.} \times \frac{2}{5}$$

$$= 42 \text{ kgs.}$$

Calculation of Material Variances :

i) **Material Cost Variance : (SQ × SP) – (AQ × AP)**

= (Standard Quantity × Standard Price) – (Actual Quantity × Actual Price)

Material - 'Bk' :

= (60 kgs. × ₹ 20) – (75 kgs. × ₹ 22)

= ₹ 1,200 – ₹ 1,650

= ₹ 450 (Adverse)

Material - 'Pk' :

= (40 kgs. × ₹ 10) – (30 kgs. × ₹ 8)

= ₹ 400 – ₹ 240

= ₹ 160 (Favourable)

ii) **Material Price Variance : (SP – AP) × AQ**

= (Standard Price – Actual Price) × Actual Quantity

Material - 'Bk' :

= (₹ 20 – ₹ 22) × 75 kgs.

= ₹ 2 × 75 kgs.

= ₹ 150 (Adverse)

Material - 'Pk' :

= (₹ 10 – ₹ 8) × 30 kgs.

= ₹ 2 × 30 kgs.

= ₹ 60 (Favourable)

iii) **Material Usage Variance : (SQ – AQ) × SP**

= (Standard Quantity – Actual Quantity) × Standard Price

Material - 'Bk' :

- = (60 kgs. − 75 kgs.) × ₹ 20
- = 15 kgs. × ₹ 20
- = ₹ 300 (Adverse)

Material - 'Pk' :

- = (40 kgs. − 30 kgs.) × ₹ 10
- = 10 kgs. × ₹ 10
- = ₹ 100 (Favourable)

iv) **Material Mix Variance : (SRM − AM) × SP**

= (Standard Revised Mix − Actual Mix) × Standard Price

Material - 'Bk' :

- = (63 kgs. − 75 kgs.) × ₹ 20
- = 12 kgs. × ₹ 20
- = ₹ 240 (Adverse)

Material - 'Pk' :

- = (42 kgs. − 30 kgs.) × ₹ 10
- = 12 kgs. × ₹ 10
- = ₹ 120 (Favourable)

Verification,

	MCV	=	MPV + MUV
'Bk' :	₹ 450 (A)	=	₹ 150 (A) + ₹ 300 (A)
'Pk' :	₹ 160 (F)	=	₹ 60 (F) + ₹ 100 (F)
	₹ 290 (A)	=	₹ 90 (A) + ₹ 200 (A)
∴	Total : ₹ 290 (A)	=	₹ 290 (A)

ILLUSTRATION 7

Godrej Co., Gurgaon, manufacturers a product 'Bosin' by mixing three raw materials viz. 'A_1', 'B_2' and 'C_3'. It is ascertained that 125 kgs. of raw materials input are used for every 100 kgs. of output. In January, 2013, there was an output of 5,600 kgs. of product 'Bosin'. The additional cost data relating to the period is as follows :

Raw Material	Standard		Actual	
	Mixing Proportion %	Price per kg. ₹	Mixing Proportion %	Price per kg. ₹
'A_1'	50	40	60	45
'B_2'	30	25	20	20
'C_3'	20	10	20	15

Cost Accounting 6.23 Standard Costing

During the period, the actual quantity of material consumed was 7,000 kgs.

You are required to compute the following material variances and verify the results. i) Material Cost Variance, ii) Material Price Variance, iii) Material Usage Variance and iv) Material Mix Variance.

SOLUTION

Working Notes :

a) **Calculation of Standard Quantity of Material required for Actual Output :**

If 100 kgs. Output = 125 kgs. Input

∴ 5,600 kgs. Ouptut = ?

$= \dfrac{5{,}600 \text{ kgs.} \times 125 \text{ kgs}}{100 \text{ kgs.}}$

= ₹ 7,000 kgs.

Apportionment of Total Standard Quantity (i.e. 7,000 kgs. among Raw Materials 'A_1', 'B_2' and 'C_3' in standard mixing proportion (i.e. 5 : 3 : 2).

'A_1' = 7,000 kgs. × $\dfrac{5}{10}$ = 3,500 kgs.

'B_2' = 7,000 kgs. × $\dfrac{3}{10}$ = 2,100 kgs.

'C_3' = 7,000 kgs. × $\dfrac{2}{10}$ = 1,400 kgs.

b) **Apportionment of Total Actual Quantity (i.e. 7,000 kgs.) among Raw Materials 'A_1', 'B_2' and 'C_3' in actual mixing proportion (i.e. 6 : 2 : 2).**

'A_1' = 7,000 kgs. × $\dfrac{6}{10}$ = 4,200 kgs.

'B_2' = 7,000 kgs. × $\dfrac{2}{10}$ = 1,400 kgs.

'C_3' = 7,000 kgs. × $\dfrac{2}{10}$ = 1,400 kgs.

c) **Calculation of Revised Standard Mix in kgs.**

= Actual Quantity of Material consumed × Standard Mixing Proportion

Material 'A_1' = 7,000 kgs. × $\dfrac{5}{10}$ = 3,500 kgs.

Material 'B_2' = 7,000 kgs. × $\dfrac{3}{10}$ = 2,100 kgs.

Material 'C_3' = 7,000 kgs. × $\dfrac{2}{10}$ = 1,400 kgs.

Calculation of Material Variances :

i) **Material Cost Variance : (SQ × SP) – (AQ × AP)**

= (Standard Quantity × Standard Price) – (Actual Quantity × Actual Price)

Material 'A$_1$':

= (3,500 kgs. × ₹ 40) – (4,200 kgs. × ₹ 45)

= ₹ 1,40,000 – ₹ 1,89,000

= ₹ 49,000 (Adverse)

Material 'B$_2$':

= (2,100 kgs. × ₹ 25) – (1,400 kgs. × ₹ 20)

= ₹ 52,500 – ₹ 28,000

= ₹ 24,500 (Favourable)

Material 'C$_3$':

= (1,400 kgs. × ₹ 10) – (1,400 kgs. × ₹ 15)

= ₹ 14,000 – ₹ 21,000

= ₹ 7,000 (Adverse)

ii) **Material Price Variance : (SP – AP) × AQ**

= (Standard Price – Actual Price) × Actual Quantity

Material 'A$_1$':

= (₹ 40 – ₹ 45) × 4,200 kgs.

= ₹ 5 × 4,200 kgs.

= ₹ 21,000 (Adverse)

Material 'B$_2$':

= (₹ 25 – ₹ 20) × 1,400 kgs.

= ₹ 5 × 1,400 kgs.

= ₹ 7,000 (Favourable)

Material 'C$_3$':

= (₹ 10 – ₹ 15) × 1,400 kgs.

= ₹ 5 × 1,400 kgs.

= ₹ 7,000 (Adverse)

iii) **Material Usage Variance : (SQ – AQ) × SP**

= (Standard Quantity – Actual Quantity) × Standard Price

Material 'A$_1$':

= (3,500 kgs. – 4,200 kgs.) × ₹ 40

= 700 kgs. × ₹ 40

= ₹ 28,000 (Adverse)

Material 'B$_2$':

= (2,100 kgs. – 1,400 kgs.) × ₹ 25

= 700 kgs. × ₹ 25

= ₹ 17,500 (Favourable)

Material 'C$_3$' :

- = (1,400 kgs. – 1,400 kgs.) × ₹ 10
- = NIL × ₹ 10
- = NIL

iv) Material Mix Variance : (RSQ – AQ) × SP

- = (Revised Standard Quantity – Actual Quantity) × Standard Price

Material 'A$_1$' :

- = (3,500 kgs. – 4,200 kgs.) × ₹ 40
- = 700 kgs. × ₹ 40
- = ₹ 28,000 (Adverse)

Material 'B$_2$' :

- = (2,100 kgs. – 1,400 kgs.) × ₹ 25
- = 700 kgs. × ₹ 25
- = ₹ 17,500 (Favourable)

Material 'C$_3$' :

- = (1,400 kgs. – 1,400 kgs.) × ₹ 10
- = NIL × ₹ 10
- = NIL

Verification,

$$\text{MCV} = \text{MPV} + \text{MUV}$$

Material Cost Variance = Material Price Variance + Material Usage Variance

'A$_1$' :	₹ 49,000 (A)	=	₹ 21,000 (A) + ₹ 28,000 (A)
'B$_2$' :	₹ 24,500 (F)	=	₹ 7,000 (F) + ₹ 17,500 (F)
'C$_3$' :	₹ 7,000 (A)	=	₹ 7,000 (A) + NIL
	₹ 31,500 (A)	=	₹ 21,000 (A) + ₹ 10,500 (A)
∴	Total ₹ 31,500 (A)	=	₹ 31,500 (A)

ILLUSTRATION 8

The standard materials cost to produce one tonne of chemical 'Sulpha' is –

- Material 'A$_3$' : 300 kgs. @ ₹ 10 per kg.
- Material 'B$_2$' : 400 kgs. @ ₹ 5 per kg.
- Material 'C$_1$' : 500 kgs. @ ₹ 6 per kg.

During January, 2013, in Alembic Chemicals Ltd., Ahmednagar, 100 tonnes of chemical Sulpha was produced from the usage of,

- Material 'A_3' : 35 Tonnes @ ₹ 9,000 per tonne.
- Material 'B_2' : 42 Tonnes @ ₹ 6,000 per tonne.
- Material 'C_1' : 53 Tonnes @ ₹ 7,000 per tonne.

You are required to calculate, i) Material Cost Variance, ii) Material Price Variance, iii) Material Usage Variance and iv) Material Mix Variance.

Also verify the results.

SOLUTION

Working Notes :

a) Calculation of Standard Quantity of material required for Actual Output of 100 tonnes :

Material 'A_3' :

$$\text{If 1 Tonne} = 300 \text{ kgs.}$$
$$\therefore \quad 100 \text{ Tonnes} = ?$$
$$= \frac{100 \text{ Tonnes} \times 300 \text{kgs.}}{1 \text{ Tonne}}$$
$$= 30,000 \text{ kgs.}$$

Material 'B_2' :

$$\text{If 1 Tonne} = 400 \text{ kgs.}$$
$$\therefore \quad 100 \text{ Tonnes} = ?$$
$$= \frac{100 \text{ Tonnes} \times 400 \text{kgs.}}{1 \text{ Tonne}}$$
$$= 40,000 \text{ kgs.}$$

Material 'C_1' :

$$\text{If 1 Tonne} = 500 \text{ kgs.}$$
$$\therefore \quad 100 \text{ Tonnes} = ?$$
$$= \frac{100 \text{ Tonnes} \times 500 \text{ kgs}}{1 \text{ Tonne}}$$
$$= 50,000 \text{ kgs.}$$

b) Calculation of Actual Quantity of materials used for Actual Output of 100 tonnes in kgs.

(Base = 1 Tonne = 1,000 kgs.)

Material 'A_3' :

$$\text{If 1 Tonne} = 1,000 \text{ kgs.}$$
$$\therefore \quad 35 \text{ Tonnes} = ?$$
$$= \frac{35 \text{ Tonnes} \times 1,000 \text{ kgs}}{1 \text{ Tonne}}$$
$$= 35,000 \text{ kgs.}$$

Material 'B_2':

If 1 Tonne = 1,000 kgs.

∴ 42 Tonnes = ?

= $\dfrac{42 \text{ Tonnes} \times 1{,}000 \text{ kgs.}}{1 \text{ Tonne}}$

= 42,000 kgs.

Material 'C_1':

If 1 Tonne = 1,000 kgs.

∴ 53 Tonnes = ?

= $\dfrac{53 \text{ Tonnes} \times 1{,}000 \text{ kgs.}}{1 \text{ Tonne}}$

= 53,000 kgs.

c) **Calculation of Actual Rate of material per kg.:**

Material 'A_3':

If 1,000 kgs. = ₹ 9,000

∴ 1 kg. = ?

= $\dfrac{1 \text{ kg.} \times ₹ 9{,}000}{1{,}000 \text{ kgs.}}$

= ₹ 9 per kg.

Material 'B_2':

If 1,000 kgs. = ₹ 6,000

∴ 1 kg. = ?

= $\dfrac{1 \text{ kg.} \times ₹ 6{,}000}{1{,}000 \text{ kgs.}}$

= ₹ 6 per kg.

Material 'C_1':

If 1,000 kgs. = ₹ 7,000

∴ 1 kg. = ?

= $\dfrac{1 \text{ kg.} \times ₹ 7{,}000}{1{,}000 \text{ kgs.}}$

= ₹ 7 per kg.

d) **Calculation of Standard Mixing proportion between materials 'A_3', 'B_2' and 'C_1' in kgs.:**

'A_3'	:	'B_2'	:	'C_1'
30,000 kgs.	:	40,000 kgs.	:	50,000 kgs.

∴ 3 : 4 : 5

e) **Calculation of Total Quantity of Actual Material Consumed in kgs.:**

             Material – 'A_3' –   35,000 kgs.

Add: Material – 'B_2' –   42,000 kgs.

Add: Material – 'C_1' –   (+) <u>53,000 kgs.</u>

             ∴ Total   <u>1,30,000 kgs.</u>

f) **Calculation of Standard Revised Mix in kgs.:**

= Actual Total Quantity of Materials consumed × Standard Mixing Proportion

$$\text{Material 'A}_3\text{'} = 1,30,000 \text{ kgs.} \times \frac{3}{12} = 32,500 \text{ kgs.}$$

$$\text{Material 'B}_2\text{'} = 1,30,000 \text{ kgs.} \times \frac{4}{12} = 43,333 \text{ kgs.}$$

$$\text{Material 'C}_1\text{'} = 1,30,000 \text{ kgs.} \times \frac{5}{12} = 54,167 \text{ kgs.}$$

Calculation of Material Variances:

i) **Material Cost Variance : (SQ × SP) – (AQ × AP)**

= (Standard Quantity × Standard Price) – (Actual Quantity × Actual Price)

Material 'A_3':

= (30,000 kgs. × ₹ 10) – (35,000 kgs. × ₹ 9)

= ₹ 3,00,000 – ₹ 3,15,000

= ₹ 15,000 (Adverse)

Material 'B_2':

= (40,000 kgs. × ₹ 5) – (42,000 kgs. × ₹ 6)

= ₹ 2,00,000 – ₹ 2,52,000

= ₹ 52,000 (Adverse)

Material 'C_1':

= (50,000 kgs. × ₹ 6) – (53,000 kgs. × ₹ 7)

= ₹ 3,00,000 – ₹ 3,71,000

= ₹ 71,000 (Adverse)

ii) **Material Price Variance : (SP – AP) × AQ**

= (Standard Price – Actual Price) × Actual Quantity

Material 'A_3':

= (₹ 10 – ₹ 9) × 35,000 kgs.

= ₹ 1 × 35,000 kgs.

= ₹ 35,000 (Favourable)

Material 'B$_2$' :

= (₹ 5 – ₹ 6) × 42,000 kgs.

= ₹ 1 × 42,000 kgs.

= ₹ 42,000 (Adverse)

Material 'C$_1$' :

= (₹ 6 – ₹ 7) × 53,000 kgs.

= ₹ 1 × 53,000 kgs.

= ₹ 53,000 (Adverse)

iii) **Material Usage Variance : (SQ – AQ) × SP**

= (Standard Quantity – Actual Quantity) × Standard Price

Material 'A$_3$' :

= (30,000 kgs. – 35,000 kgs.) × ₹ 10

= 5,000 kgs. × ₹ 10

= ₹ 50,000 (Adverse)

Material 'B$_2$' :

= (40,000 kgs. – 42,000 kgs.) × ₹ 5

= 2,000 kgs. × ₹ 5

= ₹ 10,000 (Adverse)

Material 'C$_1$' :

= (50,000 kgs. – 53,000 kgs.) × ₹ 6

= 3,000 kgs. × ₹ 6

= ₹ 18,000 (Adverse)

iv) **Material Mix Variance : (RSM – AM) × SP**

= (Revised Standard Mix – Actual Mix) × Standard Price

Material 'A$_3$' :

= (32,500 kgs. – 35,000 kgs.) × ₹ 10

= 2,500 kgs. × ₹ 10

= ₹ 25,000 (Adverse)

Material 'B$_2$' :

= (43,333 kgs. – 42,000 kgs.) × ₹ 5

= 1,333 kgs. × ₹ 5

= ₹ 6,665 (Favourable)

Material 'C₁':

= (54,167 kgs. – 53,000 kgs.) × ₹ 6

= 1,167 kgs. × ₹ 6

= ₹ 7,002 (Favourable)

Verification,

$$MCV = MPV + MUV$$

Material Cost Variance = Material Price Variance + Material Usage Variance

'A₃':	₹ 15,000 (A)	=	₹ 35,000 (F) + ₹ 50,000 (A)
'B₂':	₹ 52,000 (A)	=	₹ 42,000 (A) + ₹ 10,000 (A)
'C₁':	₹ 71,000 (A)	=	₹ 53,000 (A) + ₹ 18,000 (A)
	₹ 1,38,000 (A)	=	₹ 60,000 (A) + ₹ 78,000 (A)
∴	Total ₹ 1,38,000 (A)	=	₹ 60,000 (A) + ₹ 78,000 (A)
∴	Total ₹ 1,38,000 (A)	=	₹ 1,38,000 (A)

ILLUSTRATION 9

Calculate Material Cost Variance from the following cost data made available by Modular Electronics Ltd., Mumarabad, for October, 2013.

Basic Materials	Standard		Actual	
	Quantity Units	Price ₹	Quantity Units	Price ₹
'AC'	60	15	50	12
'BC'	50	13	40	15
'CC'	40	12	45	14

Since basic material 'AC' was in short supply, it was decided to decrease its consumption by twelve units and increase the consumption of basic material 'BC' and 'CC' by seven and five units respectively. Also calculate Material Mix Variance and verify your results.

SOLUTION

Working Notes:

a) **Calculation of Standard Revised Mix in kgs.:**

Material – 'AC' = 60 units – 12 units = 48 units

Material – 'BC' = 50 units + 07 units = 57 units

Material- 'CC' = 40 units + 05 units = 45 units

Calculation of Material Variances:

i) **Material Cost Variance: (SQ × SP) – (AQ × AP)**

= (Standard Quantity × Standard Price) – (Actual Quantity × Actual Price)

Material 'AC' :

    = (60 units × ₹ 15) – (50 units × ₹ 12)

    = ₹ 900 – ₹ 600

    = ₹ 300 (Favourable)

Material 'BC' :

    = (50 units × ₹ 13) – (40 units × ₹ 15)

    = ₹ 650 – ₹ 600

    = ₹ 50 (Favourable)

Material 'CC' :

    = (40 units × ₹ 12) – (45 units × ₹ 14)

    = ₹ 480 – ₹ 630

    = ₹ 150 (Adverse)

ii) Material Price Variance : (SP – AP) × AQ

    = (Standard Price – Actual Price) × Actual Quantity

Material 'AC' :

    = (₹ 15 – ₹ 12) × 50 units

    = ₹ 3 × 50 units

    = ₹ 150 (Favourable)

Material 'BC' :

    = (₹ 13 – ₹ 15) × 40 units

    = ₹ 2 × 40 units

    = ₹ 80 (Adverse)

Material 'CC' :

    = (₹ 12 – ₹ 14) × 45 units

    = ₹ 2 × 45 units

    = ₹ 90 (Adverse)

iii) Material Usage Variance : (SQ – AQ) × SP :

    = (Standard Quantity – Actual Quantity) × Standard Price

Material 'AC' :

    = (60 units – 50 units) × ₹ 15

    = 10 units × ₹ 15

    = ₹ 150 (Favourable)

Material 'BC':

= (50 units − 40 units) × ₹ 13

= 10 units × ₹ 13

= ₹ 130 (Favourable)

Material 'CC':

= (40 units − 45 units) × ₹ 12

= 5 units × ₹ 12

= ₹ 60 (Adverse)

iv) **Material Mix Variance : (SRM − AM) × SP**

= (Standard Revised Mix − Actual Mix) × Standard Price

Material 'AC':

= (48 units − 50 units) × ₹ 15

= 2 units × ₹ 15

= ₹ 30 (Adverse)

Material 'BC':

= (57 units − 40 units) × ₹ 13

= 17 units × ₹ 13

= ₹ 221 (Favourable)

Material 'CC':

= (45 units − 45 units) × ₹ 12

= NIL × ₹ 12

= NIL

Verification,

	MCV	=	MPV + MUV
	Material Cost Variance	=	Material Price Variance + Material Usage Variance
	Material 'AC' : ₹ 300 (F)	=	₹ 150 (F) + ₹ 150 (F)
	Material 'BC' : ₹ 50 (F)	=	₹ 80 (A) + ₹ 130 (F)
	Material 'CC' : ₹ 150 (A)	=	₹ 90 (A) + ₹ 60 (A)
	₹ 200 (F)	=	₹ 20 (A) + ₹ 220 (F)
∴	Total : ₹ 200 (F)	=	₹ 200 (F)

ILLUSTRATION 10

Barua Chemicals Ltd., Badalapur, produces certain chemicals, the standard material cost of the same is as follows :

Material 'Alfa' : 40% @ ₹ 20 per tonne

Material 'Bita' : 60% @ ₹ 30 per tonne

A standard production loss of 10% is normally expected in the manufacturing processes. During February, 2013, the results of chemical productions are as follows :

	Units Tonnes
Material 'Alfa' : @ ₹ 18 per tonne	90
Material 'Bita' : @ ₹ 34 per tonne	(+) 110
∴ Input	200
Less : Production Loss	(−) 29
∴ Output	171

You are required to calculate Material Price Variance and Material Yield Variance.

SOLUTION

a) Calculation of Standard Quantity of material required for actual output :

	Units Tonnes
Material 'Alfa'	90
Material 'Bita'	(+) 110
∴ Standard Input	200
Less : Standard Loss i.e. 10% of 200 tons	(−) 20
∴ Standard Output	180

If 180 Tonnes - Output = 200 Tonnes - Input

∴ 171 Tonnes - Output = ?

= $\dfrac{171 \text{ Tonnes} \times 200 \text{ Tonnes}}{180 \text{ Tonnes}}$

= 190 Tonnes

Apportionment of Standard Quantity (i.e. 190 Tonnes) in standard mixing proportion (i.e. 4 : 6)

Material 'Alfa' :

$$190 \text{ Tonnes} \times \frac{4}{10} = 76 \text{ tonnes}$$

Material 'Bita' :

$$190 \text{ Tonnes} \times \frac{6}{10} = 114 \text{ Tonnes}$$

b) Calculation of Standard Cost per unit of output :

	₹
Material 'Alfa' : 76 Tonnes × ₹ 20	1,520
Material 'Bita' : 114 Tonnes × ₹ 30	(+) 3,420
∴ Total Standard Cost	4,940

= $\dfrac{\text{Total Standard Cost of Material}}{\text{Actual Output}}$

= $\dfrac{₹\,4{,}940}{\text{Tonnes }171}$

= ₹ 28.89

Calculation of Material Variances :

i) **Material Price Variance : (SP − AP) × AQ**

   Material 'Alfa' : (₹ 20 − ₹ 18) × 90 Tonnes

   = ₹ 180 (Favourable)

   Material 'Bita' : (₹ 30 − ₹ 34) × 110 Tonnes

   = ₹ 440 (Adverse)

   Total Material Price Variance :

   Material 'Alfa' : ₹ 180 (Favourable)

   Material 'Bita' : ₹ **440 (Adverse)**

   ∴ Total : ₹ **260 (Adverse)**

ii) **Material Yield Variance : (SY − AY) × SC**

   = (Standard Output − Actual Output) × Standard Cost per unit of output

   = (171 Tonnes − 180 Tonnes) × ₹ 28.89

   = 9 Tonnes × ₹ 28.89

   = ₹ 260 (Adverse)

ILLUSTRATION 11

Sudarshan Ltd., Surat, manufacturers a single product, the standard mix of which is as follows :

Material 'Aey' : 60% @ ₹ 10 per kg.

Material 'Bee' : 40% @ ₹ 6 per kg.

Normal loss in production is 20% of input. Due to acute shortage of Material Aey, the standard mix revised accordingly. The cost data relating to the actual results for January, 2013, are as follows :

		Units kgs.
	Material 'Aey' @ ₹ 10 per kg.	200
	Material 'Bee' @ ₹ 5 per kg.	(+) 100
∴	Input	300
Less :	Loss	(−) 60
∴	Output	240

Cost Accounting   6.35   Standard Costing

You are required to calculate, i) Material Cost Variance, ii) Material Price Variance, iii) Material Usage Variance, iv) Material Mix Variance, and v) Material Yield Variance.

Also verify your results.

SOLUTION

Working Notes :

a) **Calculation of Standard Quantity of material required for Actual Output :**

Normal loss in production is 20% of input

$$\underset{100}{\text{Input}} - \underset{20}{\text{Normal loss}} = \underset{80}{\text{Output}}$$

The standard mixing proportion of material 'Aey' and 'Bee' is 60% : 40% i.e. 3 : 2.

Material 'Aey' :

If 80 kg. Output = 60 kgs.

∴   240 kgs. Output = ?

= $\dfrac{240 \text{ kgs.} \times 60 \text{ kgs.}}{80 \text{ kgs.}}$

= 180 kgs.

Material 'Bee' :

If 80 kgs. Output = 40 kgs.

∴   240 kgs. Output = ?

= $\dfrac{240 \text{ kgs.} \times 40 \text{ kgs.}}{80 \text{ kgs.}}$

= 120 kgs.

b) **Calculation of Standard Mixing Proportion between Material Aey and Material Bee**

'Aey' : 'Bee'

60% : 40%

3/5 : 2/5

c) **Calculation of Total Quantity of Actual Material Consumed in kgs. :**

Material 'Aey'		200 kgs.
Add : Material 'Bee'		(+) <u>100 kgs</u>
∴	Total	<u>300 kgs</u>

d) **Calculation of Revised Standard Mix in kgs. :**

= Actual Total Quantity of Materials consumed × Standard Mixing Proportion

Material 'Aye' = 300 kgs. × $\frac{3}{5}$ = 180 kgs.

Material 'Bee' = 300 kgs. × $\frac{2}{5}$ = 120 kgs.

e) **Calculation of Standard Output :**

Total Standard Output	300 kgs.
Less : Normal Loss i.e. 20%	(–) 60 kgs.
∴ Total	240 kgs.

f) **Calculation of Standard Cost per unit of Output :**

Material 'Aey' : 60 kgs. × ₹ 10	₹ 600
Material 'Bee' : 40 kgs. × ₹ 6	(+) 240
∴ Total Cost	₹ 840

$\frac{\text{Input}}{100} - \frac{\text{Normal Loss}}{20} = \frac{\text{Output}}{80}$

= $\frac{\text{Total Standard Cost}}{\text{Net Output}}$

= $\frac{₹ 840}{80 \text{ kgs.}}$

= ₹ 10.50 per kg.

Calculation of Material Variances :

i) **Material Cost Variances : (SQ × SP) – (AQ × AP)**

= (Standard Quantity × Standard Price) – (Actual Quantity × Actual Price)

Material 'Aey' :

= (180 kgs. × ₹ 10) – (200 kgs. × ₹ 10)

= ₹ 1,800 – ₹ 2,000

= ₹ 200 (Adverse)

Material 'Bee' :

= (120 kgs. × ₹ 6) – (100 kgs. × ₹ 5)

= ₹ 720 – ₹ 500

= ₹ 220 (Favourable)

ii) **Material Price Variance : (SP – AP) × AQ**

= (Standard Price – Actual Price) × Actual Quantity

Material 'Aey' :

= (₹ 10 – ₹ 10) × 200 kgs.

= NIL × 200 kgs.

= NIL

Material 'Bee' :

= (₹ 6 – ₹ 5) × 100 kgs.
= ₹ 1 × 100 kgs.
= ₹ 100 (Favourable)

iii) **Material Usage Variance : (SQ – AQ) × SP**

= (Standard Quantity – Actual Quantity) × Standard Price

Material 'Aey' :

= (180 kgs. – 200 kgs.) × ₹ 10
= 20 kgs. × ₹ 10
= ₹ 200 (Adverse)

Material 'Bee' :

= (120 kgs. – 100 kgs.) × ₹ 6
= 20 kgs. × ₹ 6
= ₹ 120 (Favourable)

iv) **Material Mix Variances : (RQS – AQ) × SP**

= (Revised Quantity Standard – Actual Quantity) × Standard Price

Material 'Aey' :

= (180 kgs. – 200 kgs.) × ₹ 10
= 20 kgs. × ₹ 10
= ₹ 200 (Adverse)

Material 'Bee' :

= (120 kgs. – 100 kgs.) × ₹ 6
= 20 kgs. × ₹ 6
= ₹ 120 (Favourable)

v) **Material Yield Variance : (SY – AY) × SC**

= (Standard Yield – Actual Yield) × Standard Cost per unit of output
= (240 kgs. – 240 kgs.) × ₹ 10.50
= NIL × ₹ 10.50
= NIL

Verification,

MCV = MPV + MUV

Material Cost Variance = Material Price Variance + Material Usage Variance

'Aey' : ₹ 200 (A) = NIL + ₹ 200 (A)
'Bee' : ₹ 220 (F) = ₹ 100 (F) + ₹ 120 (F)

₹ 20 (F) = ₹ 100 (F) + ₹ 80 (A)

∴ Total ₹ 20 (F) = ₹ 20 (F)

MUV = MMV + MYV

Material Usage Variance = Material Mix Variance + Material Yield Variance

₹ 80 (A) = ₹ 80 (A) + NIL

∴ Total ₹ 80 (A) = ₹ 80 (A)

ILLUSTRATION 12

Zuari Co. Ltd., Nashik Road, manufacturers certain products. The cost data relating to a standard product for November, 2013, are given below.

Raw Materials		Standard Cost Data		
		Quantity kgs.	Price ₹	Total ₹
'Aspi-1'		500	6.00	3,000
'Bispi-2'		400	3.75	1,500
'Cospi-3'	(+)	300	3.00	900
		1,200		
Less : 10% Normal Loss	(−)	120		
		1,080		5,400

Raw Materials		Actual Cost Data		
		Quantity kgs.	Price ₹	Total ₹
'Aspi-1'		400	6.00	2,400
'Bispi-2'		500	3.60	1,800
'Cospi-3'	(+)	400	2.80	1,120
		1,300		
Less : Actual Loss	(−)	220		
		1,080		5,320

From the above mentioned cost data you are required to calculate,

i) Material Cost Variance, ii) Material Price Variance, iii) Material Usage Variance, iv) Material Mix Variance and v)) Material Yield Variance. Also verify your results.

SOLUTION

Calculation of Material Variances :

i) **Material Cost Variance : (SQ × SP) – (AQ × AP)**

    = (Standard Quantity × Standard Price) – (Actual Quantity × Actual Price)

    = Standard Material Cost for Actual Output – Actual Material Cost for actual output

    = ₹ 5,400 – ₹ 5,320

    = ₹ 80 (Favourable)

    ∴ **Total Material Cost Variance = ₹ 80 (F)**

ii) **Material Price Variance : (SP – AP) × AQ**

    = (Standard Price – Actual Price) × Actual Quantity

Material : 'Aspi-1' :

    = (₹ 6 – ₹ 6) × 400 kgs.

    = NIL × 400 kgs.

    = NIL

Material : 'Bispi-2' :

    = (₹ 3.75 – ₹ 3.60) × 500 kgs.

    = ₹ 0.15 × 500 kgs.

    = ₹ 75 (Favourable)

Material : 'Cospi-3' :

    = (₹ 3 – ₹ 2.80) × 400 kgs.

    = ₹ 0.20 × 400 kgs.

    = ₹ 80 (Favourable)

    ∴ **Total Material Price Variance = NIL + ₹ 75 (F) + ₹ 80 (F) = ₹ 155 (F)**

iii) **Material Usage Variance : (SQ – AQ) × SP**

    = (Standard Quantity – Actual Quantity) × Standard Price

Material : 'Aspi-1' :

    = (500 kgs. – 400 kgs.) × ₹ 6

    = 100 kgs. × ₹ 6

    = ₹ 600 (Favourable)

Material : 'Bispi-2' :

    = (400 kgs. – 500 kgs.) × ₹ 3.75

    = 100 kgs. × ₹ 3.75

    = ₹ 375 (Adverse)

Material : 'Cospi-3' :
- = (300 kgs. − 400 kgs.) × ₹ 3
- = 100 kgs. × ₹ 3
- = ₹ 300 (Adverse)

∴ **Total Material Usage Variance = ₹ 600 (F) + ₹ 375 (A) + ₹ 300 (A) = ₹ 75 (A)**

iv) **Material Mix Variance : (RQS − ARQ) × SP**
   = (Standard Revised Quantity − Actual Quantity) × Standard Price

Material : 'Aspi-1' :
- = (541.67 kgs. − 400 kgs.) × ₹ 6
- = 141.67 kgs. × ₹ 6
- = ₹ 850 (Favourable)

Material : 'Bispi-2' :
- = (433.33 kgs. − 500 kgs.) × ₹ 3.75
- = 66.67 kgs. × ₹ 3.75
- = ₹ 250 (Adverse)

Material : 'Cospi-3' :
- = (325 kgs. − 400 kgs.) × ₹ 3
- = 75 kgs. × ₹ 3
- = ₹ 225 (Adverse)

∴ **Total Material Variance = ₹ 850 (F) + ₹ 250 (A) + ₹ 225 (A) = ₹ 375 (F)**

v) **Material Yield Variance : (SY − AY) × SC**
   = (Standard Yield − Actual Yield) × Standard Cost per unit of output
- = (990 kgs. − 1,080 kgs.) × ₹ 5
- = 90 kgs. × ₹ 5
- = ₹ 450 (A)

∴ **Total Material Yield Variance = ₹ 450 (A).**

Verification,

$$\text{MCV} = \text{MPV} + \text{MUV}$$

Material Cost Variance = Material Price Variance + Material Usage Variance

₹ 80 (F) = ₹ 155 (F) + ₹ 75 (A)

∴ Total ₹ 80 (F) = ₹ 80 (F)

$$\text{MUV} = \text{MMV} + \text{MYV}$$

Material Usage Variance = Material Mix Variance + Material Yield Variance

₹ 75 (A) = ₹ 375 (F) + ₹ 450 (A)

∴ Total : ₹ 75 (A) = ₹ 75 (A)

Working Notes:

a) Calculation of Standard Mixing Proportion between Material Aspi-1, Bispi-2 and Cospi-3.

'Aspi-1'	:	'Bispi-2'	:	'Cospi-3'
500 kgs.	:	400 kgs.	:	300 kgs.
5/12	:	4/12	:	3/12

b) Calculation of Total Quantity of Actual Material Consumed in kgs.

'Aspi-1' + 'Bispi-2' + 'Cospi-3' = Total
400 kgs. + 500 kgs. + 400 kgs. = 1,300 kgs.

c) Calculation of Revised Mix Standard in kgs.

= Actual Total Quantity of Material consumed × Standard Mixing Proportion

Aspi-1 = 1,300 kgs. × $\frac{5}{12}$ = 541.67 kgs.

Bispi-2 = 1,300 kgs. × $\frac{4}{12}$ = 433.33 kgs.

Cospi-3 = 1,300 kgs. × $\frac{3}{12}$ = 325 kgs.

d) Calculation of Standard Output i.e. expected output from actual total quantity of material:

	Kgs.
Expected output from actual quantity	1,300
Less: Standard Normal Loss i.e. 10%	(–) 130
∴ Standard Output	1,170

e) Calculation of Actual Output:

	Kgs.
Output from actual quantity	1,300
Less: Actual Loss	(–) 220
∴ Actual Output	1,080

f) Calculation of Standard Cost per unit of output:

= $\frac{\text{Total Standard Cost}}{\text{Net Output}}$

= $\frac{₹ 5,400}{\text{Kgs. } 1,080}$

= ₹ 5 per kg.

LABOUR VARIANCES

ILLUSTRATION 1

A product requires 10 hours per unit to produce at a standard rate of ₹ 2 per hour. 1,000 units were produced during March, 2013. Actual time taken to produce was 9,000 hours. The actual rate was ₹ 2.50 per hour.

Calculate :

i) Labour Cost Variance, ii) Labour Rate Variance and iii) Labour Efficiency Variance and verify your results.

SOLUTION

Working Notes :

a) Calculation of Standard Labour Hours for Actual Production :

$$\text{If 1 unit} = 10 \text{ hours}$$
$$\therefore 1,000 \text{ units} = ?$$
$$= \frac{1,000 \text{ units} \times 10 \text{ hours}}{1 \text{ unit}}$$
$$= 10,000 \text{ hours}$$

Calculation of Labour Variances :

i) **Labour Cost Variance : (SH × SR) – (AH × AR)**
   = (Standard Hours × Standard Rate) – (Actual Hours × Actual Rate)
   = (10,000 hours × ₹ 2) – (9,000 hours × ₹ 2.50)
   = ₹ 20,000 – ₹ 22,500
   = ₹ 2,500 (Adverse)

ii) **Labour Rate Variance : (SR – AR) × AH**
   = (Standard Rate – Actual Rate) × Actual Hours
   = (₹ 2.00 – ₹ 2.50) × 9,000 Hours
   = ₹ 0.50 × 9,000 Hours
   = ₹ 4,500 (Adverse)

iii) **Labour Efficiency Variance : (SH – AH) × SR**
   = (Standard Hours – Actual Hours) × Standard Rate
   = (10,000 Hours – 9,000 Hours) × ₹ 2
   = 1,000 Hours × ₹ 2
   = ₹ 2,000 (Favourable)

Verification,

$$\text{LCV} = \text{LRV} + \text{LEV}$$

Labour Cost Variance = Labour Rate Variance + Labour Efficiency Variance

₹ 2,500 (A) = ₹ 4,500 (A) + ₹ 2,000 (F)

∴ Total ₹ 2,500 (A) = ₹ 2,500 (A)

Cost Accounting 6.43 Standard Costing

ILLUSTRATION 2

Dynalog India Ltd., Durgapur, provides the following cost details from which you are required to calculate.

i) Labour Cost Variance, ii) Labour Rate Variance and iii) Labour Efficiency Variance.

Standard Hours per unit of output	20 Hours
Standard Rate per hour	₹ 2
Actual Production during October, 2006	2,000 Units
Actual Hours	35,000 Hours
Actual Rate per hour	₹ 5

Also verify your results.

SOLUTION

Working Notes :

a) **Calculation of Standard Labour Hours for Actual Production :**

If 1 unit = 20 Hours

∴ 2,000 units = ?

= $\frac{2{,}000 \text{ units} \times 20 \text{ Hours}}{1 \text{ unit}}$

= 40,000 Hours.

Calculation of Labour Variances :

i) **Labour Cost Variance : (SH × SR) − (AH × AR)**

= (Standard Hours × Standard Rate) − (Actual Hours × Actual Rate)
= (40,000 Hours × ₹ 5) − (35,000 Hours × ₹ 4)
= ₹ 2,00,000 − ₹ 1,40,000
= ₹ 60,000 (Favourable)

ii) **Labour Rate Variance : (SR − AR) × AH**

= (Standard Rate − Actual Rate) × Actual Hours
= (₹ 5 − ₹ 4) × 35,000 Hours
= ₹ 1 × 35,000 Hours
= ₹ 35,000 (Favourable)

iii) **Labour Efficiency Variance : (SH − AH) × SR**

= (Standard Hours − Actual Hours) × Standard Rate
= (40,000 Hours − 35,000 Hours) × ₹ 5
= 5,000 Hours × ₹ 5
= ₹ 25,000 (Favourable)

Verification,

$$LCV = LRV + LEV$$

Labour Cost Variance = Labour Rate Variance + Labour Efficiency Variance

₹ 60,000 (F) = ₹ 35,000 (F) + ₹ 25,000 (F)

∴ Total : ₹ 60,000 (F) = ₹ 60,000 (F)

ILLUSTRATION 3

Elite Co., Erankulam, produces a product, the standard cost card of the same discloses the following information :

- Standard Rate per hour   ₹ 26
- Standard Time for a unit of output   Hours 5

The actual cost data for a particular period are as follows :

- Total number of units produced   Units 200
- Actual hours worked   Hours 900
- Total Labour Cost   ₹ 27,000

You are required to calculate i) Labour Cost Variance, ii) Labour Rate Variance and iii) Labour Efficiency Variance.

Also verify your results.

SOLUTION

Working Notes :

a) **Calculation of Standard Labour Hours for Actual Production :**

If 1 unit = 5 Hours

∴ 200 units = ?

$$= \frac{200 \text{ Units} \times 5 \text{ Hours}}{1 \text{ Unit}}$$

= 1,000 Hours.

b) **Calculation of Actual Rate per hour :**

If 900 Hours = ₹ 27,000

∴ 1 Hour = ?

$$= \frac{1 \text{ Hour} \times ₹ 27,000}{900 \text{ Hours}}$$

= ₹ 30 per hour

Calculation of Labour Variances :

i) **Labour Cost Variance : (SH × SR) – (AH × AR)**
   = (Standard Hours × Standard Rate) – (Actual Hours × Actual Rate)
   = (1,000 Hours × ₹ 26) – (900 Hours × ₹ 30)
   = ₹ 26,000 – ₹ 27,000
   = ₹ 1,000 (Adverse)

ii) **Labour Rate Variance : (SR – AR) × AH**
   = (Standard Rate – Actual Rate) × Actual Hours
   = (₹ 26 – ₹ 30) × 900 Hours
   = ₹ 4 × 900 Hours
   = ₹ 3,600 (Adverse)

iii) **Labour Efficiency Variance : (SH – AH) × SR**
   = (Standard Hours – Actual Hours) × Standard Rate
   = (1,000 Hours – 900 Hours) × ₹ 26
   = 100 Hours × ₹ 26
   = ₹ 2,600 (Favourable)

   Verification,
   LCV = LRV + LEV
   Labour Cost Variance = Labour Rate Variance + Labour Efficiency Variance
   ₹ 1,000 (A) = ₹ 3,600 (A) + ₹ 2,600 (F)
   ∴ Total : ₹ 1,000 (A) = ₹ 1,000 (A)

ILLUSTRATION 4

The standard and actual labour cost information of Champion India Ltd., Churchgate, are summarised as follows :

Standard Time for a job	Hours 1,000
Standard Rate per hour	₹ 5.00
Actual Time taken on the job	Hours 950
Total Wages paid	₹ 4,560

Calculate the Labour Variance and verify your results.

SOLUTION

Working Notes :

a) **Calculation of Actual Rate per hour :**
   If 950 Hours = ₹ 4560
   ∴ 1 Hour = ?

$$= \frac{1 \text{ Hour} \times ₹ 4{,}650}{950 \text{ Hours}}$$

= ₹ 4.90 per hour

Calculation of Labour Variances :

i) **Labour Cost Variance : (SH × SR) – (AH × AR)**

= (Standard Hours × Standard Rate) – (Actual Hours × Actual Rate)

= (1,000 Hours × ₹ 5) – (950 Hours × ₹ 4.80)

= ₹ 5,000 – ₹ 4,560

= ₹ 440 (Favourable)

ii) **Labour Rate Variances : (SR – AR) × AH**

= (Standard Rate – Actual Rate) × Actual Hours

= (5.00 – 4.80) × 950 Hours

= ₹ 0.20 × 950 Hours

= ₹ 190 (Favourable)

iii) **Labour Efficiency Variance : (SH – AH) × SR**

= (Standard Hours – Actual Hours) × Standard Rate

= (1,000 Hours – 950 Hours) × ₹ 5

= 50 Hours × ₹ 5

= ₹ 250 (Favourable)

Verification,

$$\text{LCV} = \text{LRV} + \text{LEV}$$

Labour Cost Variance = Labour Rate Variance + Labour Efficiency Variance

₹ 440 (F) = ₹ 190 (F) + ₹ 250 (F)

∴ Total : ₹ 440 (F) = ₹ 440 (F)

ILLUSTRATION 5

In Chetna Manufacturing Co., Chembur, production of a single product requires three operations viz. Assembly, Electrical and Mechanical. The standard and the actual cost data relating to direct labour are as follows :

Operations	Standard		Actual	
	Hours	Rate ₹	Hours	Rate ₹
Assembly	100	3.00	120	2.00
Electrical	150	4.00	140	5.00
Mechanical	200	5.00	180	6.00
Total	450		440	

Calculate the Labour Variance viz. i) Labour Cost Variance, ii) Labour Rate Variance and iii) Labour Efficiency Variance.

SOLUTION

Calculation of Labour Variances :

i) **Labour Cost Variance : (SH × SR) − (AH × AR)**

= (Standard Hours × Standard Rate) − (Actual Hours × Actual Rate)

Assembly :

= (100 Hrs. × ₹ 3) − (120 Hrs. × ₹ 2)

= ₹ 300 − ₹ 240

= ₹ 60 (Favourable)

Electrical :

= (150 Hrs. × ₹ 4) − (140 Hrs. × ₹ 5)

= ₹ 600 − ₹ 700

= ₹ 100 (Adverse)

Mechanical :

= (200 Hrs. × ₹ 5) − (180 Hrs. × ₹ 6)

= ₹ 1,000 − ₹ 1,080

= ₹ 80 (Adverse)

ii) **Labour Rate Variance : (SR − AR) × AH**

= (Standard Rate − Actual Rate) × Actual Hours

Assembly :

= (₹ 3 − ₹ 2) × 120 Hrs.

= ₹ 1 × 120 Hrs.

= ₹ 120 (Favourable)

Electrical :

= (₹ 4 − ₹ 5) × 140 Hrs.

= ₹ 1 × 140 Hrs.

= ₹ 140 (Adverse)

Mechanical :

= (₹ 5 − ₹ 6) × 180 Hrs.

= ₹ 1 × 180 Hrs.

= ₹ 180 (Adverse)

iii) **Labour Efficiency Variance : (SH − AH) × SR**

= (Standard Hours − Actual Hours) × Standard Rate

Assembly :

- = (100 Hrs. − 120 Hrs.) × ₹ 3
- = 20 Hrs. × ₹ 3
- = ₹ 60 (Adverse)

Electrical :

- = (150 Hrs. − 140 Hrs.) × ₹ 4
- = 10 Hrs. × ₹ 4
- = ₹ 40 (Favourable)

Mechanical :

- = (200 Hrs. − 180 Hrs.) × ₹ 5
- = 20 Hrs. × ₹ 5
- = ₹ 100 (Favourable)

Verification,

$$LCV = LRV + LEV$$

Labour Cost Variance = Labour Rate Variance + Labour Efficiency Variance

Assembly :	₹ 60 (F)	= ₹ 120 (F) + ₹ 60 (A)
Electrical :	₹ 100 (A)	= ₹ 140 (A) + ₹ 40 (F)
Mechanical :	₹ 80 (A)	= ₹ 180 (A) + ₹ 100 (F)
	₹ 120 (A)	= ₹ 200 (A) + ₹ 80 (F)
∴ Total :	₹ 120 (A)	= ₹ 120 (A)

ILLUSTRATION 6

In Mangalam Industries, Malad, the budgeted labour force employed in a welding process is as follows :

- Un-skilled Labour Force :

  200 workers @ ₹ 5 per hour for 40 hours.

- Semi-skilled Labour Force :

  300 workers @ ₹ 6 per hour for 50 hours. The actual labour force during a particular period was as follows :

- Un-skilled Labour Force :

  210 workers @ ₹ 4 per hour for 45 hours.

- Semi-skilled Labour Force :

  290 workers @ ₹ 7 per hour for 45 hours.

Compute the following labour variances, i) Labour Cost Variance, ii) Labour Rate Variance, and iii) Labour Efficiency Variance.

SOLUTION

Calculation of Labour Variances :

i) **Labour Cost Variance : (SH × SR) − (AH × AR)**

    = (Standard Hours × Standard Rate) − (Actual Hours × Actual Rate)

Un-skilled Workers :

    = [(200 workers × 40 Hours) × ₹ 5] − [(210 workers × 45 Hours) × ₹ 4]

    = (8,000 Hrs. × ₹ 5) − (9,450 Hours × ₹ 4)

    = ₹ 40,000 − ₹ 37,800

    = ₹ 2,200 (Favourable)

Semi-skilled Workers :

    = [(300 workers × 50 Hours) × ₹ 6] − [(290 workers × 45 Hours) × ₹ 7]

    = (15,000 Hours × ₹ 6) − (13,050 Hours × ₹ 7)

    = ₹ 90,000 − ₹ 91,350

    = ₹ 1,350 (Adverse)

ii) **Labour Rate Variance : (SR − AR) × AH**

    = (Standard Rate − Actual Rate) × Actual Hours

Unskilled Workers :

    = (₹ 5 − ₹ 4) × 210 workers × 45 Hours

    = ₹ 1 × 9,450 Hours.

    = ₹ 9,450 (Favourable)

Semi-skilled Workers :

    = (₹ 6 − ₹ 7) × 290 Workers × 45 Hours

    = ₹ 1 × 13,050 Hours

    = ₹ 13,050 (Adverse)

iii) **Labour Efficiency Variance : (SH − AH) × SR**

    = (Standard Hours − Actual Hours) × Standard Rate

Un-skilled Workers :

    = (200 workers × 40 Hours) − (210 workers × 45 Hours) × ₹ 5

    = (8,000 Hours − 9,450 Hours) × ₹ 5

    = 1,450 Hours × ₹ 5

    = ₹ 7,250 (Adverse)

Semi-skilled Workers :

    = (300 workers × 50 Hours) − (290 workers × 45 Hours) × ₹ 6

    = (15,000 Hours − 13,050 Hours) × ₹ 6

= 1,950 Hours × ₹ 6
= ₹ 11,700 (Favourable)

Verification,

LCV = LRV + LEV

Labour Cost Variance = Labour Rate Variance + Labour Efficiency Varaince

Semi-skilled Workers : ₹ 2,200 (F) = ₹ 9,450 (F) + ₹ 7,250 (A)

Un-skilled Workers : ₹ 1,350 (A) = ₹ 13,050 (A) + ₹ 11,700 (F)

₹ 850 (F) = ₹ 3,600 (A) + ₹ 4,450 (F)

∴ Total ₹ 850 (F) = ₹ 850 (F)

ILLUSTRATION 7

From the following information, calculate for each of the department,

i) Labour Cost Variance, ii) Labour Rate Variance and iii) Labour Efficiency Variance

		Dept. 'X'	Dept. 'Y'
Gross Direct Wages	₹	26,240	18,900
Standard Hours Produced	Hrs.	8,600	6,000
Standard Rate per hour	₹	3.00	3.40
Actual Hours Worked	Hrs.	8,200	6,300

SOLUTION

Working Notes :

a) Calculation of Actual Rate per hour :

Dept 'X' :

If 8,200 Hours = ₹ 26,240

∴ 1 Hour = ?

$$= \frac{1 \text{ Hour} \times ₹ 26,240}{8,200 \text{ Hours}}$$

= ₹ 3.20

Dept 'Y' :

If 6,300 Hours = ₹ 18,900

∴ 1 Hour = ?

$$= \frac{1 \text{ Hour} \times ₹ 18,900}{6,300 \text{ Hours}}$$

= ₹ 3.00

Calculation of Labour Variances :

i) **Labour Cost Variance :** (SH × SR) – (AH × AR)

= (Standard Hours × Standard Rate) – (Actual Hours × Actual Rate)

Dept. 'X' = (8,600 Hours × ₹ 3.00) – (8,200 Hours × ₹ 3.20)
= ₹ 25,800 – ₹ 26,240
= ₹ 440 (Adverse)

Dept. 'Y' = (6,000 Hours × ₹ 3.40) – (6,300 Hours × ₹ 3.00)
= ₹ 20,400 – ₹ 18,900
= ₹ 1,500 (Favourable)

ii) **Labour Rate Variance :** (SR – AR) × AH

= (Standard Rate – Actual Rate) × Actual Hours

Dept. 'X' : = (₹ 3.00 – ₹ 3.20) × 8,200 Hours
= ₹ 0.20 × 8,200 Hours
= ₹ 1,640 (Adverse)

Dept. 'Y' : = (₹ 3.40 – ₹ 3.00) × 6,300 Hours
= ₹ 0.40 × 6,300 Hours
= ₹ 2,520 (Favourable)

iii) **Labour Efficiency Variance :** (SH – AH) × SR

= (Standard Hours – Actual Hours) × Standard Rate

Dept. 'X' = (8,600 Hours – 8,200 Hours) × ₹ 3.00
= 400 Hours × ₹ 3.00
= ₹ 1,200 (Favourable)

Dept. 'Y' : = (6,000 Hours – 6,300 Hours) × ₹ 3.40
= 300 Hours × ₹ 3.40
= ₹ 1,020 (Adverse)

Verification,

LCV = LRV + LEV

Labour Cost Variance = Labour Rate Variance + Labour Efficiency Variance

Dept. 'X' : ₹ 440 (A) = ₹ 1,640 (A) + ₹ 1,200 (F)
Dept. 'Y' : ₹ 1,500 (F) = ₹ 2,520 (F) + ₹ 1,020 (A)
₹ 1,060 (F) = ₹ 880 (F) + ₹ 180 (F)
Total ₹ 1,060 (F) = ₹ 1,060 (F)

ILLUSTRATION 8

Using the following cost data, calculate,

i) Labour Cost Variance, ii) Labour Rate Variance, iii) Labour Efficiency Variance and iv) Idle Time Variance and verify your results.

Gross Direct Wages	₹ 3,000
Standard Hours produced	Hrs. 1,600
Standard Rate per hour	₹ 1.50
Actual Hours paid	Hrs. 1,500

(out of which hours not worked due to abnormality are 50 hours).

SOLUTION

Working Notes:

a) Calculation of Actual Rate per hour:

$$\text{If } 1,500 \text{ Hours} = ₹ 3,000$$
$$\therefore 1 \text{ Hour} = ?$$
$$= \frac{1 \text{ Hour} \times ₹ 3,000}{1,5000 \text{ Hours}}$$
$$= ₹ 2 \text{ per hour}$$

Calculation of Labour Variances:

i) Labour Cost Variance : (SH × SR) − (AH × AR)
= (Standard Hours × Standard Rate) − (Actual Hours × Actual Rate)
= (1,600 Hours × ₹ 1.50) − (1,500 Hours × ₹ 2.00)
= ₹ 2,400 − ₹ 3,000
= ₹ 600 (Adverse)

ii) Labour Rate Variance : (SR − AR) × AH
= (Standard Rate − Actual Rate) × Actual Hours
= (₹ 1.50 − ₹ 2.00) × 1,500 Hours
= (₹ 0.50 × 1,500 Hours)
= ₹ 750 (Adverse)

iii) Labour Efficiency Variance : (SH − AH) × SR
= (Standard Hours − Actual Hours) × Standard Rate
= (1,600 Hours − 1,450 Hours) × ₹ 1.50
= 150 Hours × ₹ 1.50
= ₹ 225 (Favourable)

iv) Idle Time Variance : IT × SR
= Idle Time × Standard Rate
= 50 Hours × ₹ 1.50
= 75 (Adverse)

Verification,

LCV = LRV + LEV + ITV
Labour Cost Variance = Labour Rate Variance + Labour Efficiency Variance + Idle Time Variance
₹ 600 (A) = ₹ 750 (A) + ₹ 225 (F) + ₹ 75 (A)
∴ **Total ₹ 600 (A) = ₹ 600 (A)**

Cost Accounting   6.53   Standard Costing

ILLUSTRATION 9

Harison Electrical Ltd., Haridwar, provides you the cost details regarding manufacture of certain products for June, 2013.

Standard Time per unit of output	10 Hours
Standard Rate per labour hour	₹ 8
Actual monthly production	1,100 units
Effective hours worked	11,500 Hours
Idle Time	500 Hours
Actual Total Hours paid	12,000 Hours
Total Wage payment for the month	₹ 1,20,000

You are required to find out the labour variances.

SOLUTION

Working Notes :

a) **Calculation of Standard Labour Hours for Actual Production :**

            If 1 unit = 10 Hours

∴   1,100 units = ?

= $\dfrac{1,100 \text{ units} \times 10 \text{ Hours}}{1 \text{ Unit}}$

= 11,000 Hours.

b) **Calculation of Actual Rate per hour :**

         If 12,000 Hours = ₹ 1,20,000 Total Wages

∴   1 Hour = ?

= $\dfrac{1 \text{ Hour} \times ₹ 1,20,000}{12,000 \text{ Hours}}$

= ₹ 10 per labour hour

Calculation of Labour Variances :

i) **Labour Cost Variance : (SH × SR) – (AH × AR)**

  = (Standard Hours × Standard Rate) – (Actual Hours × Actual Rate)

  = (11,000 Hours × ₹ 8) – (12,000 Hours × ₹ 10)

  = ₹ 88,000 – ₹ 1,20,000

  = ₹ 32,000 (Adverse)

ii) **Labour Rate Variance : (SR – AR) × AH**

  = (Standard Rate – Actual Rate) × Actual Hours

  = (₹ 8 – ₹ 10) × 12,000 Hours

  = ₹ 2 × 12,000 Hours

  = ₹ 24,000 (Adverse)

iii) **Labour Efficiency Variance : (SH − AH) × SR**

= (Standard Hours − Actual Hours) × Standard Rate

= (11,000 Hours − 11,500 Hours) × ₹ 8

= 500 Hours × ₹ 8

= ₹ 4,000 (Adverse)

iv) **Idle Time Variance : IT × SR**

= Idle Time × Standard Rate

= 500 Hours × ₹ 8

= ₹ 4,000 (Adverse)

Verification,

LCV = LRV + LEV + ITV

Labour Cost Variance = Labour Rate Variance + Labour Efficiency Variance + Idle Time Variance

₹ 32,000 (A) = ₹ 24,000 (A) + ₹ 4,000 (A) + ₹ 4,000 (A)

∴ Total : ₹ 32,000 (A) = ₹ 32,000 (A)

ILLUSTRATION 10

From the following details, calculate,

i) Labour Cost Variance, ii) Labour Rate Variance, iii) Labour Efficiency Variance and iv) Labour Mix Variance.

Workers	Standard			Actual		
	Hours	Rate ₹	Amount ₹	Hours	Rate ₹	Amount ₹
Skilled	30	5.00	150	32	5.00	160
Un-skilled	40	4.00	160	32	4.25	136
Total	70		310	64		296

SOLUTION

Working Notes :

a) **Calculation of Standard Mixing Proportion between Skilled and Unskilled workers in hours :**

Skilled Workers : Unskilled Workers

30 Hours : 40 Hours

3 : 4

b) **Calculation of total Actual Hours worked for :**

= Skilled workers + Unskilled workers

= 32 Hours + 32 Hours = 64 Hours.

c) **Calculation of Revised Standard Mix in hours :**

= Actual hours worked for × Standard mixing proportion

Skilled workers = 64 Hours × 3/7 = 27.42 i.e. 27 Hours

Unskilled workers = 64 Hours × 4/7 = 36.57 i.e. 37 Hours

Calculation of Labour Variances :

i) **Labour Cost Variance : (SH × SR) – (AH × AR)**
   = (Standard Hours × Standard Rate) – (Actual Hours × Actual Rate)

   Skilled workers = (30 Hours × ₹ 5.00) – (32 Hours × ₹ 5.00)
   = ₹ 150 – ₹ 160
   = ₹ 10 (Adverse)

   Unskilled workers = (40 Hours × ₹ 4.00) – (32 Hours × ₹ 4.25)
   = ₹ 160 – ₹ 136
   = ₹ 24 (Favourable)

ii) **Labour Rate Variance : (SR – AR) × AH**
   = (Standard Rate – Actual Rate) × Actual Hours

   Skilled workers = (₹ 5.00 – ₹ 5.00) × 32 Hours
   = NIL × 32 Hours
   = NIL

   Unskilled workers = (₹ 4.00 – ₹ 4.25) × 32 Hours
   = ₹ 0.25 × 32 Hours
   = ₹ 8 (Adverse)

iii) **Labour Efficiency Variance : (SH – AH) × SR**
   = (Standard Hours – Actual Hours) × Standard Rate

   Skilled workers = (30 Hours – 32 Hours) × ₹ 5
   = 2 Hours × ₹ 5
   = ₹ 10 (Adverse)

   Unskilled workers = (40 Hours – 32 Hours) × ₹ 4
   = 8 Hours × ₹ 4
   = ₹ 32 (Favourable)

iv) **Labour Mix Variance : (RSM – AM) × SR**
   = (Revised Standard Mix – Actual Mix) × Standard Rate

   Skilled workers = (27 Hours – 32 Hours) × ₹ 5.00
   = 5 Hours × ₹ 5.00
   = ₹ 25 (Adverse)

   Unskilled workers = (37 Hours – 32 Hours) × ₹ 4.00
   = 5 Hours × ₹ 4.00
   = ₹ 20 (Favourable)

Verification,

LCV = LRV + LEV

Labour Cost Variance = Labour Rate Variance + Labour Efficiency Variance

Skilled workers : ₹ 10 (A) = NIL + ₹ 10 (A)

Unskilled workers : ₹ 24 (F) = ₹ 8 (A) + ₹ 32 (F)

₹ 14 (F) = ₹ 8 (A) + ₹ 22 (F)

∴ Total **₹ 14 (F)** = **₹ 14 (F)**

ILLUSTRATION 11

From the following cost data made available by Glostar Ltd. Gulbarga, calculate –
i) Labour Cost Variance, ii) Labour Rate Variance, iii) Labour Efficiency Variance, iv) Labour Mix Variance.

The standard labour force for manufacture of a Product 'Marshall' is as follows :
- 20 untrained workers @ ₹ 75 per hour for 50 hours.
- 10 trained workers @ ₹ 1.25 per hour for 50 hours.

Whereas the actual labour force employed for manufacture of a product 'Marshall' is as follows :
- 22 un-trained workers @ ₹ 80 per hour for 50 hours.
- 08 trained workers @ ₹ 1.20 per hour for 50 hours.

Also verify your results.

SOLUTION

Working Notes :

a) Calculation of Standard Labour Cost and Actual Labour Cost :

Category of Workers	Standard			Actual		
	Weeks (Number of Workers × Number of Hours)	Rate (Per Worker per hour) ₹	Amount ₹	Weeks (Number of Workers × Number of Hours)	Rate (Per Worker per hour) ₹	Amount ₹
Un-trained	20 × 50 = 1,000	0.75	750	22 × 50 = 1,100	0.80	880
Trained	10 × 50 = 500	1.25	625	8 × 50 = 400	1.20	480
∴ Total	1,500		1,375	1,500		1,360

b) Calculation of Standard Mixing Proportion of number of untrained and trained workers in hours :

Untrained workers : Trained-workers
1,000 Hours : 500 Hours
$\frac{2}{3}$: $\frac{1}{3}$

c) Calculation of Total Actual Hours worked :

= Untrained workers + Trained workers
   1,100 Hours   400 Hours
= 1,500 Hours

d) Calculation of Revised Standard Mix in hours :

= Actual Hours worked × Standard Mixing Proportion

- **Untrained Workers :**

  = 1,500 Hours × $\frac{2}{3}$

  = 1,000 Hours

- **Trained Workers :**

  = 1,500 Hours × $\frac{1}{3}$

  = 500 Hours

Calculation of Labour Variances :

i) **Labour Cost Variance : (SH × SR) – (AH × AR)**
  = (Standard Hours × Standard Rate) – (Actual Hours × Actual Rate)

Untrained Workers :
  = (1,000 Hours × ₹ 0.75) – (1,100 Hours × ₹ 0.80)
  = ₹ 750 – ₹ 880
  = ₹ 130 (Adverse)

Trained Workers :
  = (500 Hours × ₹ 1.25) – (400 Hours × ₹ 1.20)
  = ₹ 625 – ₹ 480
  = ₹ 145 (Favourable)

ii) **Labour Rate Variance : (SR – AR) × AH**
  = (Standard Rate – Actual Rate) × Actual Hours

Untrained Workers :
  = (₹ 0.75 – ₹ 0.80) × 1,100 Hours
  = ₹ 0.05 × 1,100 Hours
  = ₹ 55 (Adverse)

Trained Workers :
  = (₹ 1.25 – ₹ 1.20) × 400 Hours
  = ₹ 0.05 × 400 Hrs.
  = ₹ 20 (Favourable)

iii) **Labour Efficiency Variance : (SH – AH) × SR**
  = (Standard Hours – Actual Hours) × Standard Rate

Untrained Workers :
  = (1,000 Hours – 1,100 Hours) × ₹ 0.75
  = 100 Hours × ₹ 0.75
  = ₹ 75 (Adverse)

Trained Workers :
  = (500 Hours – 400 Hours) × ₹ 1.25
  = 100 Hours × ₹ 1.25
  = ₹ 125 (Favourable)

iv) **Labour Mix Variance : (RSM – AM) × SR**
  = (Revised Standard Mix – Actual mix) × Standard Rate

Untrained Workers :
  = (1,000 Hours – 1,100 Hours) × ₹ 0.75
  = 100 Hours × ₹ 0.75
  = ₹ 75 (Adverse)

Trained Workers :
  = (500 Hours – 400 Hours) × ₹ 1.25
  = 100 Hours × ₹ 1.25
  = ₹ 125 (Favourable)

Verification,
$$LCV = LRV + LEV$$

Labour Cost Variance = Labour Rate Variance + Labour Efficiency Variance

Untrained Workers :
₹ 130 (A) = ₹ 55 (A) + ₹ 75 (A)

Trained Workers :
₹ 145 (F) = ₹ 20 (F) + ₹ 125 (F)
₹ 15 (F) = ₹ 35 (A) + ₹ 50 (F)

∴ Total : ₹ 15 (F) = ₹ 15 (F)

ILLUSTRATION 12

In Mafatlal Mills Ltd., Mumbai, standard labour cost of producing 500 metre of cloth has been specified as follows :
- Men Workers : 20 Hours @ ₹ 15 per hour.
- Women Workers : 30 Hours @ ₹ 10 per hour.

The actual cost data for producing 500 metre of cloth is as follows :
- Men Workers : 30 Hours @ ₹ 17 per hour.
- Women Workers : 30 Hours @ ₹ 10 per hour

You are required to calculate i) Labour Cost Variance, ii) Labour Rate Variance, iii) Labour Efficiency Variance, iv) Labour Mix Variance, v) Labour Yield Variance.

Also verify your results.

SOLUTION

Calculation of Labour Variances :

i) **Labour Cost Variance : (SH × SR) – (AH × AR)**

= (Standard Hours × Standard Rate) – (Actual Hours × Actual Rate)

- **Men Workers :**
  = (20 Hours × ₹ 15) – (30 Hours × ₹ 17)
  = ₹ 300 – ₹ 510
  = ₹ 210 (Adverse)

- **Women Workers :**
  = (30 Hours × ₹ 10) – (30 Hours × ₹ 10)
  = ₹ 300 – ₹ 300
  = NIL

ii) **Labour Rate Variance : (SR – AR) × AH**

= (Standard Rate – Actual Rate) × Actual Hours

- **Men Workers :**
  = (₹ 15 – ₹ 17) × 30 Hours
  = ₹ 2 × 30 Hours
  = ₹ 60 (Adverse)

- **Women Workers :**
  = (₹ 10 – ₹ 10) × 30 Hours
  = NIL × 30 Hours
  = NIL

iii) **Labour Efficiency Variance : (SH – AH) × SR**
  = (Standard Hours – Actual Hours) × Standard Rate

- **Men Workers :**
  = (20 Hours – 30 Hours) × ₹ 15
  = 10 Hours × ₹ 15
  = ₹ 150 (Adverse)

- **Women Workers :**
  = (30 Hours – 30 Hours) × ₹ 10
  = NIL × ₹ 10
  = NIL

iv) **Labour Mix Variance : (RSM – AM) × SR**
  = (Revised Standard Mix – Actual Mix) × Standard Rate

- **Men Workers :**
  = (24 Hours – 30 Hours) × ₹ 15
  = 6 Hours × ₹ 15
  = ₹ 90 (Adverse)

- **Women Workers :**
  = (36 Hours – 30 Hours) × ₹ 10
  = 6 Hours × ₹ 10
  = ₹ 60 (Favourable)

v) **Labour Yield Variance : (SO – AO) × SC**
  = (Standard Output from actual hours worked – Actual Output) × Standard Cost per metre
  = (600 metre – 500 metre) × ₹ 1.20
  = ₹ 120 (Adverse)

Verification,

LCV = LRV + LEV

Labour Cost Variance = Labour Rate Variance + Labour Efficiency Variance

Men Workers :   ₹ 210 (A) = ₹ 60 (A) + ₹ 150(A)
Women Workers :   NIL = NIL + NIL
       ₹ 210 (A) = ₹ 60 (A) + ₹ 150 (A)
∴ Total : ₹ 210 (A) = ₹ 210 (A)

LEV = LMV – LYV

Labour Efficiency Variance = Labour Mix Variance – Labour Yield Variance
   ₹ 150 (A) = ₹ 30 (A) – ₹ 120 (A)
∴ Total : ₹ 150 (A) = ₹ 150 (A)

Working Notes :

a) **Calculation of Standard Mixing Proportion of men and women workers in hours :**

$$\text{Men Workers} : \text{Women Workers}$$
$$20 \text{ Hours} : 30 \text{ Hours}$$
$$\frac{2}{5} : \frac{3}{5}$$

b) **Calculation of Total Actual Hours Worked :**

= $\frac{\text{Men Workers}}{30 \text{ Hours}} + \frac{\text{Women Workers}}{30 \text{ Hours}}$

= 60 Hours.

c) **Calculation of Revised Standard Mix in hours :**

= Actual Hours worked for × Standard Mixing Proportion

- **Men Workers :**

   = 60 Hours × $\frac{2}{5}$

   = 24 Hours.

- **Women Workers :**

   = 60 Hours × $\frac{3}{5}$

   = 36 Hours

d) **Calculation of Standard Output i.e. expected output from Actual Hours Worked :**

If 50 Standard Hours = 500 Metre Output

∴ 60 Actual Hours = ?

= $\frac{60 \text{ Hours} \times 500 \text{ Metre}}{50 \text{ Hours}}$

= 600 Metre

e) **Calculation of Standard Labour Cost per metre :**

- Total Standard Labour Cost ₹

   Men Workers : (20 Hours × ₹ 15) 300

   Add : Women Workers : (30 Hours × ₹ 10) (+) 300

   ∴ Total 600

   If 500 Metre = ₹ 600 Labour Cost

   ∴ 1 Metre = ?

   = $\frac{1 \text{ Metre} \times ₹ 600}{500 \text{ Metre}}$

   = ₹ 1.20 per metre

COMBINED VARIANCES

ILLUSTRATION 1

For a particular unit of product, the standard data is given below.

	₹
• Material : 5 kgs @ ₹ 40 per kg	200
• Labour : 40 Hours @ ₹ 1 per hour	(+) 40
	240

For actual production of 100 units, the actual data is as follows :

	₹
• Material : 490 kgs @ ₹ 42 per kg	20,580
• Labour : 3,960 Hours @ ₹ 1.10 per hour	(+) 4,356
	24,936

Calculate the following and verify your results.
i) Material Cost Variance, ii) Material Price Variance, iii) Material Usage Variance, iv) Labour Cost Variance, v) Labour Rate Variance and vi) Labour Efficiency Variance.

SOLUTION

Working Notes :

a) Calculation of standard quantity of Material for Actual Production :

If 1 unit = 5 kgs
∴ 100 units = ?

$$= \frac{100 \text{ units} \times 5 \text{ kgs}}{1 \text{ unit}}$$

= 500 kgs

Calculation of Material Variances :

i) **Material Cost Variance : (SQ × SP) – (AQ × AP)**
 = (Standard Quantity × Standard Price) – (Actual Quantity × Actual Price)
 = (500 kgs × ₹ 40) – (490 kgs × ₹ 42)
 = ₹ 20,000 – ₹ 20,580
 = ₹ 580 (Adverse)

ii) **Material Price Variance : (SP – AP) × AQ**
 = Standard Price – Actual Price) × Actual Quantity
 = (₹ 40 – ₹ 42) × 490 kgs
 = ₹ 2 × 490 kgs
 = ₹ 980 (Adverse)

iii) **Material Usage Variance : (SQ – AQ) × SP**
 = (Standard Quantity – Actual Quantity) × Standard Price
 = (500 kgs – 490 kgs) × ₹ 40
 = 10 kgs × ₹ 40
 = ₹ 400 (Favourable)

Verification,

MCV = MPV + MUV
Material Cost Variance = Material Price Variance + Material Usage Variance
₹ 580 (A) = ₹ 980 (A) + ₹ 400 (F)
∴ Total : ₹ 580 (A) = ₹ 580 (A)

Working Notes :
b) Calculation of Standard Labour Hours for Actual Production :

If 1 unit = 40 Hours
∴ 100 units = ?
= $\dfrac{100 \text{ units} \times 40 \text{ Hours}}{1 \text{ unit}}$
= 4,000 Hours

Calculation of Labour Variances :
iv) **Labour Cost Variance : (SH × SR) – (AH × AR)**
 = (Standard Hours × Standard Rate) – (Actual Hours × Actual Rate)
 = (4,000 Hours × ₹ 1.00) – (3,960 Hours × ₹ 1.10)
 = ₹ 4,000 – ₹ 4,356
 = ₹ 356 (Adverse)

v) **Labour Rate Variance : (SR – AR) × AH**
 = (Standard Rate – Actual Rate) × Actual Hours
 = (₹ 1.00 – ₹ 1.10) × 3,960 Hours
 = ₹ 0.10 × 3,960 Hours
 = ₹ 396 (Adverse)

vi) **Labour Efficiency Variance : (SH – AH) × SR**
 = (Standard Hours – Actual Hours) × Standard Rate
 = (4,000 Hours – 3,960 Hours) × ₹ 1.00
 = 40 Hours × ₹ 1.00
 = ₹ 40 (Favourable)

Verification,
 LCV = LRV + LEV
 Labour Cost Variance = Labour Rate Variance + Labour Efficiency Variance
 ₹ 356 (A) = ₹ 396 (A) + ₹ 40 (F)
 ₹ 356 (A) = ₹ 356 (A)

ILLUSTRATION 2

Canon Co. Ltd., Chalisgaon, has submitted the following cost data in relation to a product manufactured in their workshop during October, 2013.

Particulars	Standard Cost	Actual Cost
Raw Materials	1,000 units @ ₹ 6 per unit	1,100 units @ ₹ 7 per unit
Productive Labour	1,600 Hours @ ₹ 5 per hour	1,500 Hours @ ₹ 4 per hour

You are required to calculate i) Material Cost Variance, ii) Material Price Variance, iii) Material Usage Variance, iv) Labour Cost Variance, v) Labour Rate Variance and vi) Labour Efficiency Variance.

SOLUTION

Calculation of Material Variances :
i) **Material Cost Variance : (SQ × SP) – (AQ × AP)**
 = (Standard Quantity × Standard Price) – (Actual Quantity × Actual Price)
 = (1,000 units × ₹ 6) – (1,100 units × ₹ 7)
 = ₹ 6,000 – ₹ 7,700
 = ₹ 1,700 (Adverse)

ii) **Material Price Variance : (SP – AP) × AQ**
 = (Standard Price – Actual Price) × Actual Quantity

= (₹ 6 – ₹ 7) × 1,100 units
   = ₹ 1 × 1,100 units
   = ₹ 1,100 (Adverse)
iii) **Material Usage Variance : (SQ – AQ) × SP**
   = (Standard Quantity – Actual Quantity) × Standard Price
   = (1,000 units – 1,100 units) × ₹ 6
   = 100 units × ₹ 6
   = ₹ 600 (Adverse)
   Verification,
                    MCV = MPV + MUV
   Material Cost Variance = Material Price Variance + Material Usage Variance
                    ₹ 1,700 (A) = ₹ 1,100 (A) + ₹ 600 (A)
   ∴   Total : ₹ 1,700 (A) = ₹ 1,700 (A)

Calculation of Labour Variances :
iv) **Labour Cost Variance : (SH × SR) – (AH × AR)**
   = (Standard Hours × Standard Rate) – (Actual Hours × Actual Rate)
   = (1,600 Hrs. × ₹ 5) – (1,500 Hrs. × ₹ 4)
   = ₹ 8,000 – ₹ 6,000
   = ₹ 2,000 (Favourable)
v) **Labour Rate Variance : (SR – AR) × AH**
   = (Standard Rate – Actual Rate) × Actual Hours
   = (₹ 5 – ₹ 4) × 1,500 Hrs.
   = ₹ 1 × 1,500 Hrs.
   = ₹ 1,500 (Favourable)
vi) **Labour Efficiency Variance : (SH – AH) × SR**
   = (Standard Hours – Actual Hours) × Standard Rate
   = (1,600 Hrs. – 1,500 Hrs.) × ₹ 5
   = 100 Hrs. × ₹ 5
   = ₹ 500 (Favourable)
   Verification,
                    LCV = LRV + LEV
   Labour Cost Variance = Labour Rate Variance + Labour Efficiency Variance
                    ₹ 2,000 (F) = ₹ 1,500 (F) + ₹ 500 (F)
   ∴   Total : ₹ 2,000 (F) = ₹ 2,000 (F)

QUESTIONS FOR SELF-STUDY

I. **Theory Questions :**
   i) Define 'Standard Cost' and 'Standard Costing'. Distinguish between Standard Costing and Budgetary Control.
   ii) Define 'Standard Cost'. What is meant by variance analysis ?
   iii) Enumerate the preliminary tasks required for introducing a Standard Costing system in a factory.
   iv) What is Standard Costing ? What are its advantages and disadvantages.
   v) Explain the advantages and limitations of Standard Costing.
   vi) What is 'Standard Costing' ? State its objectives.
   vii) Distinguish between 'Standard Cost' and 'Estimated Cost'.
   viii) "Variance analysis is an integral part of Standard Costing system". Discuss.

Cost Accounting 6.64 Standard Costing

ix) How do you analyse the variances of material and labour costs.
x) What is meant by 'Variance' and 'Variance Analysis' ? What are the main divisions of Total Cost Variance ?
xi) What is Variance Analysis ? Point out its significance from the point of view of management ?
xii) Define and explain the following terms :
   a) Material Price Variance b) Material Usage Variance
   c) Labour Rate Variance d) Labour Efficiency Variance.
xiii) What are the causes for :
   a) Material Usage Variances b) Labour Efficiency Variances
xiv) Write short notes on :
   a) Material Mix Variance b) Material Yield Variance c) Labour Mix Variance
   d) Labour Yield Variance e) Idle-Time Variance
xv) What is Variance Analysis ? Explain in brief the different types of variances.
xvi) Briefly describe the technique of Standard Costing.
xvii) What do you mean by 'Standard Costing' ? State its features.
xviii) "Standard Costing is a valuable aid to management". Discuss.

II. Practical Problems :

i) A company produces product "A". The following are the details of standard and actual production.

Standard quantity of material per unit	10 kgs.
Standard price	₹ 8 per kg.
Actual number of units produced	500 units
Actual quantity of material used	2,500 kg.
Price of material	₹ 5 per kg.

You are required to calculate,
a) Material Price Variance, b) Material Usage Variance, c) Material Cost Variance.

ii) Ankit Chemical Co., Ajmer, produces a certain chemical, the standard material costs are :
   30% material 'A' @ ₹ 50 per kg.
   70% material 'B' @ ₹ 100 per kg.
   Standard loss expected 10% in production.
   During 2013 – 300 kgs of material 'A' and 'B' were mixed as below :
   185 kgs. of material 'A' @ ₹ 40 per kg.
   115 kgs. of material 'B' @ ₹ 120 per kg.
   The actual production was 200 kgs of chemical.
   Calculate the following variances :
   a)   Material Price, b) Material Mix, c) Material Yield.

iii) Tip Top Industries, Tarapur, furnish the following information.

Material	Standard			Actual		
	Quantity Units	Rate ₹	Amount ₹	Quantity Units	Rate ₹	Amount ₹
Material 'X'	4	2.00	8.00	3	4.00	12.00
Material 'Y'	3	3.00	9.00	2	3.00	6.00
Material 'Z'	2	4.00	8.00	2	5.00	10.00
Total	9		25.00	7		28.00

Compute Material Price, Material Usage and Material Mix Variances.

iv) Calculate : a) Material Cost Variance, b) Material Price Variance, c) Material Usage Variance from the following particulars.

Material	Standard Quantity kgs.	Standard Price ₹	Actual Quantity kgs.	Actual Price ₹
'X'	15	5	18	4
'Y'	20	4	24	3

v) The standard mix of a product is as follows :

Material	Units	Price per unit ps.
'A'	30	20
'B'	20	15
'C'	50	30

Standard loss in production is 10%
There is actual production of 8,000 units from 90 mixes during July, 2013.
The actual purchases and consumption of materials during July, 2013, were.

Material	Units	Price per unit ps.
'A'	2,500	25
'B'	1,600	10
'C'	4,500	40

Compute the various material variances.

vi) Compute a) Labour Cost Variance, b) Labour Rate Variance and c) Labour Efficiency Variance

Standard hours per unit	25 hour
Standard rate	₹ 5 per hour
Actual production	3,000 units
Actual hours	20,000 hour
Actual rate	₹ 4 per hour

vii) From the following particulars, calculate the various labour variances :

Standard time per unit	10 hours per unit
Standard rate	₹ 5 per hour
Actual production	1,500 units
Actual time taken (hours)	18,000
Less : Idle time (hours)	1,000
Total	17,000 hours

The actual wages paid were ₹ 1,14,000 @ ₹ 6 per hour.

viii) A medium scale unit worked for 50 hours a week. It has 100 workers. The following are the other details.

Standard rate per hour	₹ 2
Standard output per gang hour during a week	400 units
10 workers were paid	₹ 1.00 per hour
15 workers were paid	₹ 1.50 per hour
75 workers were paid	₹ 2.00 per hour
The actual production was	20,500 units

Calculate the labour variances

ix) From the data given below, calculate labour variances for the two departments.

Particulars		Department 'A'	Department 'B'
Actual gross wages (direct)	₹	2,000	1,800
Standard hours produced	Hrs.	8,000	6,000
Standard rate per hour	Ps.	30	35
Actual hours worked	Hrs.	8,200	5,800

x) In a factory, 100 workers are engaged and the average rate of wages is 50 ps. per hour. Standard working hours per week are 40 and the standard performance is 10 units per gang hour.

During a week in March, 2007, wages paid for 50 workers were @ 50 paise per hour, 10 workers @ 70 paise per hour and 40 workers at 40 paise per hour. Actual output was 380 units.

The factory did not work for five hours, due to break-down of machinery. Calculate appropriate labour variances.

xi) From the following cost data, you are required to calculate : a) Material Cost Variance, b) Material Price Variance, c) Material Usage Variance and d) Material Mix Variance.

Raw Material	Standard		Actual	
	Quantity Units	Price ₹	Quantity Units	Price ₹
'A_2'	100	4.00	130	3.00
'B_1'	150	5.00	130	6.00
Total	250		260	

Also verify your results.

xii) In Swojus Industries, Surat, during October, 2006, actual mix differs from standard mix but there is a change in output. Output is chemical 'Sopra' : 10 kgs. The cost details for the period are as follows :

Material	Standard Mix		Amount ₹	Actual Mix	Amount ₹
'C'	70 kgs. @ ₹ 30		2,100	75 kgs. @ ₹ 32	2,400
'D'	30 kgs. @ ₹ 20	(+)	600	25 kgs. @ ₹ 18 (+)	450
Total			2,700		2,850

Calculate the following variances a) Material Cost Variance, b) Material Price Variance, c) Material Usage Variance, d) Material Mix Variance and verify your results.

xiii) In Cadbury India Ltd., Chalisgaon, Works Department employed 200 workers @ ₹ 5.50 per hour to manufacture a standard product. During December, 2013, the factory is scheduled to run for 168 hours in a four weekly period. The standard performance is fixed at 60 units per hour. During the month, 18 workers were paid @ ₹ 5 per hour, 12 workers @ ₹ 6 per hour and 8 workers @ ₹ 4 per hour. The factory remain idle for two hours, due to electricity failure. The actual production for the month was 10,100 units.

You are required to calculate a) Labour Cost Variance, b) Labour Rate Variance, c) Labour Efficiency Variance, d) Labour Yield Variance. Verify your results.

xiv) The following labour cost details are made available by Dabur India Ltd., Dombivili.

Gross Direct Wages	₹ 3,000
Standard Hours produced	Hrs. 1,600
Standard Rate per hour	₹ 1.50
Actual Hours paid for	Hrs. 1,500

(of which abnormal idle time is 100 Hours)

Calculate a) Labour Cost Variance, b) Labour Rate Variance, c) Labour Efficiency Variance, d) Idle Time Variance.

xv) It is estimated that a specific job can be completed by employing 10 trained workers for 8 hours and 12 untrained workers for 10 hours each to be paid at a standard rate of ₹ 20 per hour and ₹ 15 per hour respectively.

Actually, 8 trained workers for 12 hours each and 10 untrained workers 8 hours each worked to complete the job @ ₹ 18 and ₹ 20 per labour hour respectively.

You are reqeuired to calculate a) Labour Cost Variance, b) Labour Rate Variance, c) Labour Efficiency Variance, d) Labour Mix Variance and e) Labour Yield Variance. Also verify your results.

***

GLOSSARY
(BASIC COST ACCOUNTING TERMS WITH SIMPLIFIED EXPLANATIONS)

- **Abnormal Costs :** A cost which is normally incurred at a given level of output in the conditions in which that level of output is normally attained.
- **Abnormal Gain :** It is a result of the excess of actual output over normal output due to excellent climatic conditions for production, exceptionally good material, new equipments, etc.
- **Abnormal Loss :** It is the loss caused by abnormal conditions which is excess of actual loss over normal loss which may arise due to poor quality of raw materials, defects in machines, carelessness on the part of workers, etc.
- **Administration Costs :** The sum of these costs of general and management, and of secretarial, accounting and administrative services which cannot be directly related to production, marketing, research and development function of the enterprise.
- **Angle of Incidence :** It is the angle formed through intersection of cost line and sales line.
- **Basic Standard :** It is a standard established for use over a long period from which a current standard be developed.
- **Batch Costing :** It is that form of specific order costing, which applies where similar articles are manufactured in batches either for sale or use, within the undertaking.
- **Break-Even Analysis :** The analysis used to determine the probable profit or loss at any level of production.
- **Break-Even Chart :** A chart indicating graphical relationship between costs, volume and profits.
- **Break-even Point :** It is that level of output and sales, at which there is neither any profit nor any loss.
- **Budget :** It is an estimate of future needs arranged according to an orderly basis, converting some or all activities of an enterprise for a definite period of time.
- **Budget Centre :** It is the section of the organisation of an undertaking defined for the purposes of budgetary control.
- **Budget Manual :** It is a document which sets out, interalia, the responsibilities of the persons engaged in the routine of, and the forms and records required for budgetary control.
- **Budget Period :** It is a period for which a budget is prepared and employed.
- **Budgetary Control :** It is a tool of management used to plan, carry out and control the operations of business. It establishes pre-determined objectives and provides the basis for measuring performance against these objectives.
- **Budgeting :** It is the process of designing, implementing and operating budgets.

- **Capital Costs :** A cost which is intended to benefit in future period.
- **Cash Budget :** It is a forecast of cash position for a particular period.
- **Composite Cost Unit :** It is a unit which measures two characteristics simultaneously. For e.g., per tone-mile, per passenger-kilometre, kilowatt-hour etc.
- **Contract Costing:** It is that form of specific order costing, which applies where work is undertaken regarding customers special requirements and each order is of long duration.
- **Contribution :** It is the difference between sales value and the marginal cost of sales.
- **Controllable Costs :** A cost chargeable to a cost centre, which can be influenced by the actions of the person in whom control of the centre is vested.
- **Cost :** It is the amount of expenditure (actual or notional) incurred on or attributable to a specified thing or activity.
- **Cost Accountancy :** It is the application of costing and cost accounting principles, methods and techniques to the science, art and practice of cost control and the ascertainment of profitability.
- **Cost Accounting :** It is that branch of accounting dealing with the classification, recording, allocation, summarisation and reporting of current and prospective costs.
- **Cost Centre :** It is a location, person or item of equipment for which costs may be ascertained and used for the purpose of control.
- **Cost Classification :** It is a grouping of cost according to their common characteristics.
- **Cost Plus Contracts :** It is that type of account, where a contractor is paid with actual cost of direct materials, direct labour, direct factory expenses and a stipulated amount or percentage of cost to cover overheads and profits.
- **Cost Sheet :** It is a statement which shows the details regarding total cost of the job or a product.
- **Cost Unit :** It is a unit of a quantity of product, service or time in relation to which costs may be ascertained or expressed.
- **Costing :** It is the technique and process of ascertaining costs.
- **Current Standard :** It is a standard established for use over a short period of time, related to current conditions.
- **De-escalation Clause :** It is the clause which provides for a decrease in the contract price due to a decrease in the price of inputs, so that the benefit of price decrease is passed on to the contractee.
- **Development Costs :** The cost of process which begins with the implementation of the decision to produce or new or improved methods and ends with the commencement of formal production of that product or by that method.
- **Direct Expenses :** Costs other than materials or wages which are incurred for a specific product or a saleable service.
- **Direct Labour Costs :** The cost of remuneration for employee's efforts and skills applied directly to a product or saleable service.

- **Direct Material Costs :** The cost of materials entering into and becoming constituent element of a product or saleable service.
- **Distribution Costs :** These are the costs incurred for despatching the products which are ready after packing.
- **Escalation Clause :** It is the clause which aims at safeguarding the interests of the contractor against unforeseen rise in cost.
- **Expenses :** The cost of services provided to an undertaking.
- **Factory Costs :** These are certain indirect expenses incurred by a concern right from the receipt of an order to the final delivery of goods to the customer, or for storing the finished goods in the godowns.
- **Favourable Variance :** It is a positive difference, when actual cost is less than standard cost and it has a favourable effect on profit.
- **Financial Accounting :** It is concerned with recording, classifying, analysing and summarising financial transactions and preparing financial statements with a view to showing profitability and financial state of the affairs of the business.
- **Fixed Budget :** It is a budget which is designed to remain unchanged, irrespective of the level of the activity actually attained.
- **Fixed Cost :** A cost which accrues in relation to the passage of time and which, within certain output and turnover limits, tends to remain unaffected by the fluctuations in the level of activity (of the output or turnover) for e.g., rent, rates, insurance etc.
- **Fixed Costs :** A cost which accrues in relation to the passage of time and which within certain output or turnover limits, tends to be unaffected by the fluctuations in volume of output or turnover.
- **Flexible Budget :** It is a budget which by recognising the difference between fixed, semi-variable cost is designed to change as volume of output changes.
- **Forecasting :** It is a process of predicting the future state of the world in connection with those aspects of the world which are relevant to and likely to affect future activities.
- **Historical Costs :** The costs which are ascertained after these have been incurred.
- **Impersonal Cost Centre :** It is a cost centre which consists of a location or item of equipment.
- **Indirect Expenses :** The expenses other than direct expenses.
- **Indirect Labour Costs :** The Labour Cost other than Direct Labour Cost.
- **Indirect Material Costs :** The Material Cost other than Direct Material Cost.
- **Job Cost Sheet :** It is a cost statement prepared to analyse and ascertain the actual cost incurred with respect to the individual jobs.
- **Job Costing :** It is that form of specific order costing, which applies where work is undertaken regarding customer's special requirements.
- **Job Ticket :** It is a ticket issued by Production Control Department for keeping a track of progress of each job under each operation.

- **Key Factor :** A constraint imposed upon a business which at a point of time or period of time, will limit the volume of output or the activity in the business.
- **Labour Costs :** The sum total of all payments made by the employer to the work-force for performing production activity and the cost to the employer of all benefits granted to the work-force for the same.
- **Margin of Safety :** It is the excess of actual sale over break-even sales.
- **Marginal Cost :** It is the addition to the total costs due to the production of one more unit of output.
- **Marginal Costing :** It is a technique of costing in which only variable manufacturing costs are considered and used, while valuing inventories and determining cost of goods sold.
- **Master Budget :** It is the summary budget incorporating its component – functional budget and which is finally approved, adopted and employed.
- **Material Costs :** The cost of commodities, other than Fixed Assets, introduced in products or consumed in the operation of an organisation.
- **Non-cost Items :** These are certain items of financial nature, which are excluded from the ascertainment of cost.
- **Normal Costs :** A cost which is normally incurred to a given level of output in the condition in which that level of output is normally attained.
- **Normal Loss :** It is the loss of materials under normal conditions, which is unavoidable, as a result normally expected quantity of output is less than the input.
- **Operating Cost :** It is the cost incurred in providing a service.
- **Operating Cost Centre :** It is a cost centre which consists of those machines and persons which carry out the same operations.
- **Operating Cost Sheet :** It is a separate cost sheet maintained for each operation of service generally used for cost ascertainment and cost control.
- **Operating Costing :** It is that form of operation costing, which applies where standardised services are provided either by an undertaking or by a service cost centre within an undertaking.
- **Operation Costing :** The category of basic costing methods applicable where standardised goods or services result from a sequence of repetitive and more or less continuous operations or process to which costs are charged, before being averaged over the units produced during the period.
- **Output Costing :** It is that form of operation costing where large number of identical units are produced.
- **Performance Budgeting :** It is the budgeting which involves determination of responsibility for various levels of management in terms of specific expectations for them in both physical and financial terms.
- **Period Costs :** These are the costs which are associated with a particular accounting period.

- **Personal Cost Centre :** It is a cost centre which consists of a person or group of persons.
- **Pre-determined Costs :** The costs which are ascertained in advance of production on the basis of a specification of all the factors affecting cost.
- **Process Cost Centre :** It is a cost centre which consists of a continuous sequence of operations.
- **Process Costing :** It is that form of operation costing, which applies where the standardised goods are produced.
- **Process Loss :** It is the difference between the input quantity of raw materials and the output quantity.
- **Product Costs :** These are the costs which are directly associated with the product.
- **Production Budget :** It is a budget which provides a well planned forecast of total volume of production with break-up for each product and with detailed schedule of operations together with a forecast of closing inventories.
- **Production Cost Budget :** It is a budget which shows the details of the estimated costs which are required to be incurred as per the quantities shown in the production budget.
- **Production Cost Centre :** It is a cost centre where actual production takes place for e.g., welding, mechanical, electrical, assembly etc.
- **Profit-Volume Ratio :** It is that ratio which expresses the relationship of contribution to sales value.
- **Programme Budgeting :** It is a projection of the Government activities and expenditure thereon for the budget period, classifying budgeted expenses by functions and activities.
- **Purchase Budget :** It is a budget which shows the quantity and value of goods to be purchased during the budget period to meet the day-to-day needs of the business.
- **Research Costs :** The cost of seeking new or improved products, applications of material or methods.
- **Retention Money :** It is the money which serves as a security with the contractee and also acts as a deterrent against leaving the work incomplete by the contractor.
- **Revenue Costs :** A cost which is incurred to benefit the current period.
- **Sales Budget :** It is a budget which gives correct forecast of sales quantities and values for different products and product lines.
- **Scrap :** These are the discarded material having some recovery value, which is usually disposed off without further treatment or re-introduced into the production process in place of raw materials.
- **Selling Cost or Selling Overheads :** These are the costs incurred for attracting the potential customers and retaining the existing customers.
- **Semi-variable Cost :** A cost which has an element of fixity and also of variability for e.g., telephone charges, electricity charges etc.

- **Semi-variable Costs :** A cost containing both fixed and variable elements, which is, therefore, partly affected by fluctuations in the volume of output or turnover.
- **Service Cost Centre :** It is a cost centre which renders services to production department for e.g., power generation plant, repair shop, personnel department etc.
- **Simple Cost Unit :** It is a unit which measure one characteristics such as length or volume or area or weight for e.g., per metre, per kilogram etc.
- **Specific Order Costing :** The category of basic costing methods applicable where the work consists of separate contracts, jobs or batches each of which is authorised by a special order or contract.
- **Standard Cost :** It is a predetermined cost, which is calculated from management standards of efficient operation and the relevant necessary expenditure.
- **Standard Costing :** It is the preparation of use of standard costs, their comparison with actual cost and the analysis of variance to their causes and points of incidence.
- **Sub-Contract Cost :** These are the cost incurred for a sub-contract, where the contractor has entrusted some special work to some expertise sub-contractor for e.g., electrification, sanitary work, welding, digging, installation of lifts, painting work, etc.
- **Uncontrollable Costs :** A cost chargeable to a cost centre which cannot be influenced by the actions of the person in whom control of the centre is vested.
- **Unfavourable Variance :** It is a negative difference, when actual cost is more than standard cost and it has an adverse effect on profit.
- **Variable Cost :** A cost which in aggregate, tends to vary in the direct proportion with the changes in the volume of production or turnover for e.g., direct material cost, direct labour cost, direct expenses etc.
- **Variable Costs :** A cost which in aggregate tends to vary in direct proportions to changes in the volume of output or turnover.
- **Variance Analysis :** It is that part of variance accounting, which relates to the analysis into constituent parts of variance between planned and actual performance.
- **Waste :** These are the discarded substances having no value.
- **Work Certified :** It is the cost of that part of work-in-progress, which is being completed successfully by the contractor and has been approved by the certifier.
- **Work Uncertified :** It is the cost of that part of work-in-progress which is being completed by the contractor, but not approved by the certifier because of the faulty work or the work not according to the specifications.
- **Zero-Base Budgeting :** It is a method of budgeting, whereby all activities are re-evaluated each time a budget is set. Discrete levels of each activity are valued and a combination chosen to match funds available.

***

FORMULAE

1. INTRODUCTION

a) Cost = Usage × Price
b) Price = Cost + Profit
c) Price = Cost − Loss

***

2. ELEMENTS OF COST

a) **Cost of Materials Consumed :**
   = Opening Cost of Raw Materials + Purchases of Raw Materials + Expenses for Purchase of Raw Materials − Closing Stock of Raw Materials − Sale of Scrap of Raw Materials − Defective Materials returned to Suppliers.

b) **Prime Cost :**
   = Direct Materials + Direct Labour + Direct Expenses

c) **Works Cost :**
   = Prime Cost + Factory Overheads

d) **Cost of Production :**
   = Works Cost + Office Overheads

e) **Total Cost :**
   = Cost of Production + Selling and Distribution Overheads

f) **Overheads :**
   = Indirect Materials + Indirect Labour + Indirect Expenses

g) **Conversion Cost :**
   = Direct Labour + Direct Expenses + Overheads

h) **Value of Sales :**
   = Cost of Sales ± Profit/Loss

***

3. METHODS OF COSTING

a) Work Certified = Cash Received + Retention Money
b) Work-in-Progress = Work Certified + Work Uncertified − Cash Received − Reserve
c) Amount of Notional Profit credited to Profit and Loss Account.
   i) If work certified is less than 25% of Contract Value :
      = Nothing is credited to Profit and Loss Account, but everything is transferred to Reserve Account.

ii) If work certified is more than 25%, but less than 50% Of Contract Value :

$$= \frac{1}{3} \times \text{Notional Profit} \times \frac{\text{Cash Received}}{\text{Work Certified}}$$

iii) If work certified is more than 50% of Contract Value :

$$= \frac{2}{3} \times \text{Notional Profit} \times \frac{\text{Cash Received}}{\text{Work Certified}}$$

d) Value of Abnormal Loss/Wastage :

$$= \frac{\text{Normal Cost of Normal Output}}{\text{Normal Output}} \times \text{Units of Abnormal Loss}$$

Value of Abnormal Gain :

$$= \frac{\text{Normal Cost of Normal Output}}{\text{Normal Output}} \times \text{Units of Abnormal Gain}$$

where,

i) Normal Cost = Total Process Cost − Value of Normal Loss.

ii) Normal Output = Input Units entered − Normal Loss in Units.

***

4. BUDGET AND BUDGETARY CONTROL

a) Estimated Production :
= Sales + Closing Stock − Opening Stock

b) Production Cost :
= Direct Material + Direct Labour + Direct Expenses + Factory Overheads

c) Quantity of Materials to be Purchased :
= Material Requirement for Production + Budgeted Closing Stock − Estimated Opening Stock

***

5. MARGINAL COSTING

a) Sales :
 = Total Cost + Profit
 = Variable Cost + Fixed Cost + Profit
 = Contribution/P/V Ratio
 = Contribution + Variable Cost
 = Marginal Cost/Marginal Cost Ratio

b) Profit :
 = Sales − Total Cost
 = Sales − (Variable Cost + Fixed Cost)
 = Contribution − Fixed Cost
 = Margin of Safety × P/V Ratio

c) Loss :
 = Total Cost − Sales
 = Fixed Cost − Contribution

d) **Contribution :**
   - = Sales − Variable Cost
   - = Fixed Cost + Profit
   - = Sales × P/V Ratio
   - = Fixed Cost − Loss
   - = Fixed Cost/Break-even Units

e) **Fixed Cost :**
   - = Total Cost − Variable Cost
   - = Contribution − Profit
   - = Contribution + Loss
   - = Sales − (Variable Cost + Profit)

f) **Variable Cost :**
   - = Total Cost − Fixed Cost
   - = Sales − Contribution
   - = Sales − (Fixed Cost + Profit)
   - = Direct Material + Direct Labour + Direct Expenses + Variable Overheads

g) **Break-Even Point (in units) :**
   - = $\dfrac{\text{Total Fixed Cost}}{\text{Contribution per unit}}$
   - = $\dfrac{\text{Break-even Sales (in Rupees)}}{\text{Selling Price per unit}}$

h) **Break-even Point (in Sales) :**
   - = $\dfrac{\text{Total Fixed Cost}}{\text{Contribution per unit}} \times \text{Selling Price per unit}$
   - = $\dfrac{\text{Total Fixed Cost}}{\text{Total Contribution}} \times \text{Total Sales}$
   - = $\dfrac{\text{Total Fixed Cost}}{\text{P/V Ratio}}$
   - = $\dfrac{\text{Total Fixed Cost}}{1 - \left(\dfrac{\text{Variable Cost}}{\text{Sales}}\right)}$
   - = Break-even Point (Units) × Selling Price per unit

i) **Profit/Volume Ratio :**
   - = $\dfrac{\text{Contribution}}{\text{Sales}} \times 100$
   - = $\dfrac{\text{Change in Profit}}{\text{Change in Sales}} \times 100$
   - = $\dfrac{\text{Change in Contribution}}{\text{Change in Sales}} \times 100$
   - = $\dfrac{\text{Gross Margin}}{\text{Sales Value}}$

j) Margin of Safety :

= Actual Sales − Break-even Sales

= $\dfrac{\text{Profit}}{\text{P/V Ratio}}$

= $\dfrac{\text{Profit} \times \text{Selling Price per unit}}{\text{Selling Price per unit} - \text{Variable Cost per unit}}$

k) Margin of Safety Ratio :

= $\dfrac{\text{Profit}}{\text{P/V Ratio}} \times 100$

= $\dfrac{\text{Margin of Safety}}{\text{Actual Sales}} \times 100$

l) Sales Volume to earn Required Profit (in Units) :

= $\dfrac{\text{Total Fixed Cost} + \text{Required Profit}}{\text{Contribution per unit}}$

m) Sales Volume to earn Required Profit (in Value) :

= $\dfrac{(\text{Total Fixed Cost} + \text{Required Profit}) \times \text{Sales}}{\text{Total Contribution}}$

= $\dfrac{\text{Total Fixed Cost} + \text{Required Profit}}{\text{P/V Ratio}}$

n) Profitability :

= $\dfrac{\text{Contribution}}{\text{Key Factor}}$

***

6. STANDARD COSTING

a) Variance :

= Standard Cost − Actual Cost

b) Direct Material Cost Variance :

= (Standard Quantity × Standard Price) − (Actual Quantity × Actual Price)

c) Direct Material Price Variance :

= (Standard Price − Actual Price) × Actual Quantity

d) Direct Material Usage Variance :

= (Standard Quantity − Actual Quantity) × Standard Price

e) Direct Material Mix Variance :

= Standard Price × (Revised Standard Mix − Actual Mix)

= Standard Price × $\left(\dfrac{\text{Total Actual Quantity}}{\text{Total Standard Quantity}} \times \dfrac{\text{Standard Quantity of Each Material}}{1} - \text{Actual Quantity of Each Material} \right)$

f) Revised Standard Mix :

$$= \frac{\text{Standard Quantity of Each Material}}{\text{Total Standard Quantity}} \times \text{Total Actual Quantity}$$

g) Direct Material Yield Variance :

= (Standard Yield − Actual Yield) × Standard Cost per unit

h) Direct Labour Cost Variance :

= (Standard Hours × Standard Rate) − (Actual Hours × Actual Rate)

i) Direct Labour Rate Variance :

= (Standard Rate − Actual Rate) × Actual Hours

j) Direct Labour Efficiency Variance :

= (Standard Hours − Actual Hours) × Standard Rate

k) Idle Time Variance :

= Idle Hours × Standard Rate

l) Direct Labour Mix Variance :

= (Revised Standard Mix − Actual Mix) × Standard Rate

m) Direct Labour Yield Variance :

= Standard Labour Cost per unit × (Standard Output for Actual Time − Actual Output)

✱✱✱

OBJECTIVE QUESTIONS
(TRUE / FALSE STATEMENTS)

- **State with reasons whether the following statements are True or False :**
    1. Financial Accounting has been developed out of the limitations of Cost Accounting.
    2. Cost is an increase in assets or decrease in liabilities made to secure an economic benefit.
    3. Costing is simply the techniques and process of ascertaining costs.
    4. Cost Accounting can replace Financial Accounting.
    5. Cost Accounting is concerned with cost ascertainment, cost presentation and cost control.
    6. Cost Accountancy is the application of costing and Cost Accounting principles.
    7. A cost unit is a unit of measurement of efficiency.
    8. A cost centre is a location, person or item of equipment, for which costs may be ascertained and used for the purposes of control.
    9. A service cost centre renders services to production departments.
    10. Per passenger-kilometre is an example of composite cost unit in passenger transport company.
    11. A process cost centre is that which consists of a specific process or a continuous sequence of operations.
    12. 'Cost + Profit = Sales' is the equation of costing.
    13. The classification of costs into fixed costs and variable costs helps the management to take vital decisions.
    14. Prime Costs are identifiable.
    15. Depreciation on Fixed Assets is always a Marginal Cost.
    16. Semi-fixed costs are partly controllable and partly uncontrollable.
    17. Fixed Cost decisions, once implemented are irreversible.
    18. Motive power is an example of administration overheads.
    19. Total Fixed Cost always increases in proportion to output.
    20. Period costs are not assigned to products.
    21. Cost-Sheet is a statement which shows only the indirect components of the total cost.
    22. Works Cost is the difference between Gross Cost and Management Cost.
    23. Hire charges of a special machinery is an example of unproductive expenses.
    24. Clay used in bricks manufacturing is an example of indirect material.
    25. Prime Costs are aggregate of indirect materials, indirect labour and indirect expenses.
    26. The difference between cost of sales and value of sales is known as a loss.
    27. Leather used in shoe making business is an example of indirect material.
    28. Underwriting commission is a non-cost item.
    29. Material Cost is the cost of commodities supplied to an undertaking.
    30. All overheads are costs, but all costs may not be overheads.
    31. Cleaning materials used to maintain the machine in factory workshop is an example of Prime Cost Material.
    32. Carriage on Sales is a Prime Cost expense.
    33. Wages paid to watchman is an item of productive labour.
    34. Selling Overheads are the cost of promoting sales and retaining customers.

35. Salary paid to computer operator increases direct labour cost in software industries.
36. All variable costs are direct and indirect costs.
37. Per unit fixed cost is always constant.
38. All costs are variable in the long run.
39. All costs are controllable.
40. All costs are relevant for some decisions or the other.
41. Methods of Costing refers to the process of collecting, arranging, processing and presenting costs.
42. Methods of Costing are introduced for controlling the cost.
43. Job Costing is applicable to cases, where the work is done according to customers' specification.
44. Contract Costing is a method used in civil engineering works, plant installations, etc.
45. A clause providing for reduction in the contract price, in case of falling prices to protect the interest of the contractee is termed as Escalation clause.
46. Retention money is the amount paid to the contractor after the satisfactory completion of the work.
47. Each contract is treated as a separate cost unit.
48. Work certified in a subsequent year is always greater than in the preceding year.
49. Cost-plus-contracts are entered into when the cost of contract can be determined in advance.
50. Process Costing is a method of operation costing.
51. In process manufacturing industries, there is a flow of materials from one operation to the next operation.
52. Each process is treated as a separate cost centre.
53. Normal losses are not charged to the product in Process Costing.
54. Excess of actual loss over normal loss is termed as abnormal loss.
55. The loss inherent in the production process is treated as a normal loss.
56. Process Costing is applicable to those industries, where manufacture of product is of uniform standards.
57. Operating Costing is a part of specific order costing.
58. Operating Costing deals with costing of services.
59. Operating Costing method can suitably be applied in transport undertakings.
60. Operating Costing is used for evaluating alternatives.
61. A standard method of costing cannot be used for all types of industries.
62. Job Costing and Contract Costing are the forms of operation costing.
63. Difference between a job and a contract is that of time involved and cost.
64. Most of the costs in case of contracts are direct costs.
65. Work uncertified does not contain a profit element.
66. Cost of additional work is to be recovered from the contractee.
67. Costing techniques are more useful for cost control purposes.
68. Control processes are more relevant in profit making organisations only.
69. Budgeting should consider developmental opportunities in the industry.
70. Zero Base Budgeting technique delinks current budgets from the past.
71. Budget is an estimate for future needs.
72. Budgeting is the process of designing, implementing and operating budgets.
73. Budgetary control is a tool of management used to plan, carry out and control the operations of business.
74. Long-term budgets are related for a period of 15 to 20 years.
75. Master budget is a summary of all budgets.

76. Scope of budgetary control is wider than that of standard costing.
77. Budgets should adopt participative approach.
78. Marketing Manager is directly responsible for preparation as well as execution of sales budget.
79. The basis for preparing sales budget is production budget.
80. Idle capacity of different machines at different times is brought to light by preparing production budget.
81. Purchase Budgets are to be presented to financial institutions at the time of applying for loans.
82. Cash Budget is prepared by the Finance Manager.
83. Operating Budgets are building blocks for completing a Master Budget.
84. A rigid budget is designed to remain unchanged irrespective of the level of activity actually attained.
85. If the overall business situation is highly dynamic and fast changing use of fixed budgeting is more desirable.
86. Traditional Budgeting is basically retrospective.
87. Conventional Budgeting is accounting-oriented.
88. Zero Base Budgeting requires stricter accountability.
89. Budgets are a communication device also.
90. Cost reduction is the primary objective of budgetary control.
91. Fixed costs are treated as period cost under variable costing.
92. Marginal Costing involves segregation of Fixed and Variable Costs.
93. Marginal Cost is the addition to the total cost due to the production of one more unit of output.
94. Under the system of Marginal Costing, only rigid costs form part of Product Costs.
95. Under the system of Marginal Costing, Constant Costs are treated as Period Costs.
96. Contribution is far better measure of performance than the net profit.
97. Marginal Costing is suitable as a basis for large number of managerial decision-making.
98. Under Marginal Costing, profits fluctuate in harmony with fluctuations in sales.
99. At break-even point, variable cost is always equal to total contribution.
100. Contribution per unit remains constant at all levels of output and sales.
101. Contribution and profits are inversely related.
102. Per Unit Fixed Cost always remains constant.
103. Higher the break-even, lower is the risk.
104. Margin of Safety = Profit ÷ P/V Ratio.
105. Margin of Safety can be increased by reducing Variable Cost.
106. Increase in selling price and a decrease in per unit variable cost leads to an improvement in P/V Ratio.
107. P/V Ratio = Change in Profit ÷ Change in Turnover.
108. Cost-Volume-Profit analysis is an extension of Standard Costing.
109. Variable cost per unit is a better indicator of efficiency than average cost.

Basics of Cost Accounting — Objective Questions

110. Normally prices cannot go below variable cost.
111. Importance of standard costing arises due to limitations of historical costing.
112. Basic standards are for a short period only.
113. Standard costs are always pre-determined.
114. Standard costing is more suitable when production processes are of repetitive character.
115. Ideal standard is one which can be attained under the most favourable conditions possible.
116. The fixation of an effective material usage standard pre-supposes control of material issue and handling.
117. Variance is the difference between standard costs and marginal cost.
118. When actual cost is more than the standard cost, it has a favourable effect on profit.
119. Material price variance arises mainly due to inefficient production methods.
120. Labour efficiency variance may arise because of sufficient training and education.

ANSWERS

True :

3, 5, 6, 8, 9, 10, 11, 12, 13, 14, 16, 17, 20, 22, 26, 28, 29, 30, 34, 35, 36, 38, 40, 41, 43, 44, 46, 47, 48, 50, 51, 52, 54, 55, 56, 58, 59, 60, 61, 63, 64, 65, 66, 67, 69, 70, 71, 72, 73, 75, 76, 77, 83, 84, 86, 87, 88, 89, 90, 91, 92, 93, 95, 96, 97, 98, 100, 104, 106, 107, 109, 110, 111, 113, 114, 115, 116.

False :

1 - Cost Accounting has been developed out of the limitations of Financial Accounting 2 - A decrease in assets or an increase in liabilities, 4 - Both are necessary, 7 - A unit of measurement of cost, 15 - can be a Fixed Cost, 18 - Factory Overheads, 19 - Total Variable Cost, 21 - Shows direct and indirect components of the Total Cost, 23 - Productive expenses, 24 - Direct Material, 25 - are aggregate of direct materials, direct labour and direct expenses, 27 - Direct Material, 31 - Indirect Material, 32 - Distribution overhead, 33 - unproductive labour, 37 - always variable, 39 - are not controllable, 42 - for ascertaining the cost, 45 - De-escalation clause, 49 - Cannot be determined in advance, 53 - are charged to the product, 57 – operation costing, 62 - forms a specific order costing, 68 – in profit making organisations and not for profit organisations also, 74 – for a period of 5 to 10 years, 78 - Sales Manager, 79 - for preparing production budget is sales budget, 80 - by preparing plant utilisation budget, 81 - Cash budgets, 82 - By the Chief Accountant, 85 - Flexible budgeting, 94 - Only Variable Costs, 99 - Fixed Cost, 101 - Adversely related, 102 - Per Unit Variable Cost, 103 - Higher is the risk, 105 - By Reducing Fixed Cost, 108 - Marginal Costing, 112 - long period only, 117 - Standard cost and actual cost, 118 - unfavourable effect, 119 - material usage variance, 120 - insufficient.

FILL IN THE BLANKS

1. Financial Accounting generally discloses profitability of the .... organisation.
2. Both Financial Accounting and Cost Accounting are basically the branches of ....
3. Cost Accounting helps in .... appraisal.
4. Financial Accounts record .... costs, whereas Cost Accounts record .... costs.
5. Emphasis in Financial Accounts is on .... but not on ....
6. Costing is the technique and process of .... costs.
7. Cost Accounting is based on .... system.
8. .... is the application of costing and cost accounting principles, methods and techniques.
9. A small organisation cannot afford an elaborate cost accounting system because it is very ....
10. .... is the amount of expenditure incurred on a given thing.
11. Cost unit is a unit of measurement of ....
12. .... refers to an outflow of resources without any commensurate benefit.
13. Cost unit should be neither too .... nor to ....
14. Repair shop is an example of .... cost centre.
15. Need for Cost Accounting arises due to limitations of .... accounting.
16. .... is a tool for managing planning and control.
17. Cost Accounting focuses on .... not ....
18. Larger the number of alternative techniques of production, greater is the need for ....
19. Cost Accounting is a system of .... and not a postmortem examination.
20. .... cost centre is that which consists of a location or item of equipment.
21. On the basis of .... cost can be classified as fixed, variable and semi-variable.
22. The basic object of Cost Accounting is to ....
23. The main function of Financial Accounting is .... reporting.
24. Direct Cost is .... to cost unit or cost centre, whereas indirect cost is ....
25. .... costs remain constant with changes in volume of output.
26. An estimate is an .... price is a ....and cost is a ....
27. An expenditure which cannot be allocated to a cost centre or a cost unit is termed as .... cost.
28. In cement industries, the cost unit is per ....

29. .... costs benefit the current period only, whereas .... costs benefit more than one particular period.
30. .... is a statement which provides for the assembly of the detailed cost of a cost centre or a cost unit.
31. .... is the physical or mental effort expended in production.
32. Abnormal costs are charged to ....
33. .... costs are based on recorded facts.
34. Pre-determined cost ascertained on scientific basis becomes .... cost.
35. .... costs are the cost directly associated with the product.
36. Primary packing charges is an example of direct .... cost.
37. The Marginal Cost per unit of product remains ....
38. Cost Accounting begins where .... ends.
39. Direct Expenses are also known as .... expenses.
40. .... cost is the cost of seeking new or improved products, applications of material or methods.
41. The sum total of .... cost, production and administration overheads is known as cost of production.
42. Direct cost plus variable overheads is known as .... cost.
43. If profits are 20% of value of turnover and the cost of turnover is Rs. 80,000, the profit will be ....
44. Prime Cost and Overhead Cost makes the .... cost.
45. The aggregate of Direct Wages, Direct Expenses and Manufacturing Overheads is known as .... cost.
46. Costing Methods are used to .... the cost.
47. .... method is applicable to foundries and general engineering workshops.
48. Contract Costing method is used by ....
49. A job is clearly .... throughout the production process.
50. A .... is a cost statement prepared to analyse and ascertain the actual cost incurred with respect to the individual jobs.
51. Job Costing is also known as .... costing because when the work is terminated the job cost sheet has to be completed.
52. In Contract Costing, materials stolen away are to be .... to Contract Account.
53. The main objectives of Job Costing is to ....
54. Under Job Costing .... should be clearly defined.
55. Estimated Cost Sheet can be prepared for submitting ....

56. Job Costing is .... as it involves a lot of clerical work.
57. A .... authorises all concerned departments to commence work on the job.
58. In Contract Costing, the contracts undertaken are generally of large .... involving large.
59. Generally, a job is performed in the .... of the producer, while the contract is executed at customers ....
60. Escalation clause aims at safeguarding the interests of the .... against unforeseen rise in cost.
61. De-escalation clause aims at safeguarding the interests of the ....
62. In Bus Transport undertakings .... is a composite cost unit.
63. Sudarshan Chemicals Ltd., Pune, will employ ....costing as a method of ascertaining costs.
64. In case of textile manufacture, output of weaving process becomes an .... for printing process.
65. Costs at processes are more easily ....
66. Budgets are .... for action.
67. Budgetary control process involves checking and evaluation of .... performance.
68. The document which describes the budgeting organisation, procedures etc. is known as budget ....
69. The budget is an aid to ....
70. The first step in preparing a budget is .... forecast.
71. .... provides maximum flexibility to the top decision-makers in the allocation of resources among different competing demands of activities.
72. .... is a budgetary system, where the input costs are related to the performances.
73. .... budgets are prospective and not retrospective.
74. Flexible budget is also known as .... budget.
75. Cost .... is the primary objective of budgetary control.
76. .... control is a broader term than budgeting.
77. .... are generally made for a longer period than budgets.
78. Budgets are a .... device also.
79. .... costing and budgeting are complementary to each other.
80. Scope of .... control is much wider than that of standard costing.
81. Marginal Costing is not a .... of costing such as job costing.
82. Marginal Cost does not include .... cost.
83. At the break-even point margin of safety is ....

84. Break-even point is ………… by changes in fixed cost.
85. Sales minus Variable Costs = Fixed Cost plus …………
86. Contribution minus ………… Costs = Profit.
87. The margin of safety is the difference between ………… sales and break-even sales.
88. At break-even point ………… is equals to fixed cost.
89. Higher P/V ratio reflects ………… profitability.
90. If nothing is produced, the loss will be equal to …………
91. The break-even point ………… when selling price is increased.
92. The margin of safety can be improved by ………… volume of sales.
93. At break-even point, total cost is equal to …………
94. Marginal costing is a very significant technique widely used for managerial …………
95. ………… is a very important indicator of the profit earning capacity of business.
96. The ………… shows potentiality of the existence of profit.
97. Marginal Costing is a technique of costing, which segregates total cost into ………… and …………
98. ………… factors are to be considered for determination of profitability of a product.
99. Cost-volume-profit analysis is a broader study of …………
100. The break-even chart is an excellent ………… device.
101. Standard costing technique with a process costing system gives best results in ………… industries.
102. When actual cost exceeds the standard cost the difference is termed as ………… variance.
103. Entire technique of standard costing is based on the principle of …………
104. ………… is the relation between the finished product and the raw material input.
105. Time and motion study is used basically to set ………… standard.
106. Employment of skilled person in place of a semi-skilled person results in ………… variance.
107. Compilation of direct material and labour standards entails setting up of ………… and ………… standards.
108. A standard hour is a hypothetical hour, meant for measuring …………
109. ………… costing is necessary for jobbing industry to quote a price and choose a profitable job.
110. The problem of price fluctuations can be overcome to some extent by the use of ………… techniques.
111. Variance analysis involves the calculations and ………… of variances.

Cost Accounting — Fill in the Blanks

112. Importance of standard costing arises, due to limitations of .... costing.

113. The important objective of standard costing is to exercise cost ....

114. Standard costs are always ....

115. .... costing facilitates delegation of authority.

116. Idle time variance shows the impact of time ....

117. .... costs are determined for the costs actually been incurred.

118. .... of standards is a difficult task requiring technical skills and careful investigation into all aspects of costs.

119. A .... standard is a standard established for use over a short period of time, related to current conditions.

120. Material .... variance may arise, due to the changes in the quality of materials purchased.

ANSWERS

1 – entire, 2 – accounting, 3 – performance, 4 – historical – projected, 5 – reporting – control, 6 – ascertaining, 7 – double entry, 8 – Cost Accountancy, 9 – costly, 10 – cost, 11 – cost, 12 – Loss, 13 – big-small, 14 – service, 15 – financial, 16 - Cost Accounting, 17 – costs-revenues, 18 – costing, 19 – foresight, 20 – Impersonal, 21 – behaviour, 22 – control cost, 23 – external, 24 – allocated – apportioned, 25 – fixed, 26 – opinion-policy-fact, 27 – indirect, 28 – tonne, 29 – revenue-capital, 30 – cost sheet, 31 – labour, 32 – Costing Profit and Loss Account, 33 – historical, 34 – standard, 35 – product, 36 – material, 37 – constant, 38 – costing, 39 – chargeable, 40 – Research, 41 – prime, 42 – marginal, 43 – Rs. 20,000, 44 – total, 45 – conversion, 46 – ascertain, 47 – Job Costing, 48 – builders, civil engineering contractors, 49 – identifiable, 50 – Job Cost Sheet, 51 – terminal, 52 – Credited, 53 – ascertain the cost of each job, 54 – cost centres, 55 – tenders, 56 – expensive, 57 – production order, 58 – size-costs, 59 – workshop-site, 60 – contractor, 61 – contractee, 62 – per passenger per km, 63 – process, 64 – input, 65 – controllable, 66 – blue prints, 67 – actual, 68 – manual, 69 – management, 70 – sales, 71 – Zero base budgeting, 72 – performance budgeting, 73 – Programme, 74 – Variable, 75 – control, 76 – Budgetary, 77 – Forecasts, 78 – communication, 79 – Standard, 80 – budgetary, 81 – method, 82 – fixed, 83 – nil, 84 – affected, 85 – profit, 86 – fixed, 87 – actual, 88 – contribution, 89 – greater, 90 – fixed costs, 91 – decreases, 92 – increasing, 93 – revenue, 94 – decision-making, 95 – P/V Ratio, 96 – contribution, 97 – fixed-variable, 98 – key, 99 – break-even analysis, 100 – planning, 101 – process, 102 – adverse, 103 – exception, 104 – yield, 105 – labour time, 106 – substitution, 107 – quantity-price, 108 – output, 109 – Standard, 110 – forecasting, 111 – interpretations, 112 – historical, 113 – control, 114 – pre-determined, 115 – Standard, 116 – lost, 117 – Standard, 118 – Setting, 119 – current, 120 – price.

BIBLIOGRAPHY

1. Advanced Cost Accounting by Saxena and Vasistha.

2. Advanced Cost Accountancy by S. P. Jain and Narong.

3. Cost Accounting by S. N. Maheshwari.

4. Cost Accounting by Ratnam.

5. Practice in Advanced Costing and Management Accounting by Prof. Subhash Jagtap.

6. Cost Accounting - Bhatta HSM, Himalaya Publication.

7. Cost Accounting - Prabhu Dev. Himalaya Publication.

8. Advanced Cost Accounting - Made Gowda, Himalaya Publication.

9. Cost Accounting Principles and Practice by M. N. Arora.
   website: www.icwai.com

***

OCTOBER 2014

B.B.M. (I.B) (Semester - II)

COST ACCOUNTING

Time : 3 Hours   Max. Marks : 80

Instructions to the candidates
1. All questions are compulsory.
2. Figures to the right indicate full marks.

1. (a) **Fill in the blanks (Any Five) :** [5]
    - (i) Wages paid to factory supervision is the example of …… labour.
    - (ii) P/V Ratio is the ratio of …… to sales.
    - (iii) Marginal cost includes direct cost plus …… costs.
    - (iv) Prime costs include only …… costs.
    - (v) …… budget covers all the budgets.
    - (vi) Aggregate of all the direct cost is known as ……

   (b) **Indicate whether the following Statements are true or false (Any Five):** [5]
    - (i) Marginal Costing is a unique method of costing.
    - (ii) When actual cost exceeds the standard cost the difference is termed as negative variance.
    - (iii) Job Cost is suitable for special order.
    - (iv) Flexible Budget is also known as Variable Budget.
    - (v) Variable cost per unit does not remain same.
    - (vi) Semi-fixed costs are partly controllable and partly uncontrollable.

2. Define "Costing" and differentiate between Financial and Cost Accounting : [15]

   OR

   Explain Process costing and state its advantages and disadvantages.

3. Write short notes (Any Three) : [15]
   - (a) Normal Loss and Abnormal Loss
   - (b) Profit Volume Ratio
   - (c) Contract Costing.
   - (d) Features of Job Costing
   - (e) Cost Unit.

4. The following information has been obtained from Samarth Company Ltd. Surat for a quarter ending 31-3-2009. [16]

Stock of raw materials on 1-1-2009	1,00,000
Stock of raw materials on 31-3-2009	74,000
Purchases of raw material	6,00,000
Travelling Expenses	5,000
Carriage Inward	10,000
Carriage Outward	15,000
Depreciation on plant	18,000
Factory rent	12,000
Office rent	10,000
Bad debt	7,000
Productive Wages	20,000
Travellers Salaries and Commission	4,000
Expenses regarding purchases of material	4,000

		Gas, Fuel and Water	8,000
		Manager's Salaries	9,000
		(he devotes 2/3rd of his time to factory)	
		Sales	10,48,000

Prepare a cost sheet showing,

(a) Cost of material consumed, (b) Prime cost, (c) Work cost, (d) Cost of production, (e) Total cost and (f) Profit.

5. (a) Following are the particulars of Bajaj Limited : [12]

Sales : ₹ 1,50,000/-
Marginal Cost : ₹ 1,20,000/-
Gross Profit : ₹ 60,000/-
Fixed Overheads : ₹ 20,000/-
Net Profit : ₹ 40,000/-

You are required to calculate

(i) P/V ratio, (ii) BEP (Sales), (iii) Margin of Safety, (iv) Net Profit when sales are ₹ 4,00,000/-

(b) From the following information related to Rahul traders, Pune prepare flexible budget at 60% and 80% capacity. [12]

Particulars		
(i) **Variable Overheads**		70%
Indirect material		5,000
Indirect labour		15,000
(ii) **Semi variable Overheads**		
Electricity		50,000
Variable 60%		
Fixed 40%		
Repairs and maintenance		5,000
Variable 65%		
Fixed 35%		
(iii) **Fixed Overheads**		
Salaries to staff		10,000
Depreciation on machines		14,000
Insurance on machines		6,000
TOTAL		**1,05,000**

OR

(b) Following is the data given for Sai Enterprises. The standard quantity and standard price of raw material required for 1 unit production is given below.

Material (Kg)	Standard Quantity ₹	Standard Price ₹
Material X	2	3

Actual production for an output of 500 units

Material (Kg)	Standard Quantity ₹	Standard Price ₹
Material X	1100	3.10

April 2015

B.B.M. (I.B) (Semester - II)

COST ACCOUNTING

Time : 3 Hours   Max. Marks : 80

Instructions to the candidates
1. All questions are compulsory.
2. Figures to the right indicate full marks.

1. (a) **Fill in the blanks (Any Five) :** [5]
    (i) Wages paid to factory supervision is the example of …… labour.
    (ii) P/V Ratio is the ratio of …… to sales.
    (iii) Marginal cost includes direct cost plus …… costs.
    (iv) Prime costs include only …… costs.
    (v) …… budget covers all the budgets.
    (vi) Aggregate of all the direct cost is known as ……

   (b) **Indicate whether the following Statements are true or false (Any Five):** [5]
    (i) Marginal Costing is a unique method of costing.
    (ii) When actual cost exceeds the standard cost the difference is termed as negative variance.
    (iii) Job Cost is suitable for special order.
    (iv) Flexible Budget is also known as Variable Budget.
    (v) Variable cost per unit does not remain same.
    (vi) Semi-fixed costs are partly controllable and partly uncontrollable.

2. Explain Process costing and state its advantages and disadvantages. [15]

   OR

   What do you mean by Elements of Cost? Explain the different elements of cost with suitable examples.

3. **Write short notes (Any Three) :** [15]
   (a) Normal Loss and Abnormal Loss
   (b) Contract Costing.
   (c) Cost Unit.
   (d) Labour Variances
   (e) Objectives of Budgetary Control

4. Jindal Manufacturers, Jalgaon furnished the following data relating to the manufacturing of a standard product during the month of March 2009: [16]

Carriage on Purchases of basic materials	200
Raw materials stock as on 31-3-2009	2,850
Sale of scrap raw materials	150
Operating wages payable	600
Stock of raw materials as on 1-3-2009	1,200
Royalty	1,500
Machine hour rate	250
Purchase of raw materials	14,600
Administarion overheads : 10 % of work cost	
Selling and distribution on cost : ₹ 3.60 per unit	
Direct labour charges	4,400
Cost of layout	500

Operation of machine hours
Monthly Production - 1000 units
Units sold - 900 units (@ ₹ 40 per unit)

You are required to prepare a cost sheet showing total cost per unit for the month ended 31-3-2009.

5. (A) From the following information related to castrol Ltd., Cochi prepare flexible budget at 60% and 80% capacity. **[12]**

Particulars

(a)	**Variable Overheads**	70%
	Indirect material	5,000
	Indirect labour	15,000
(b)	**Semi variable Overheads**	
	Electricity	50,000
	Variable 60%	
	Fixed 40%	
	Repairs and maintenance	5,000
	Variable 65%	
	Fixed 35%	
(c)	**Fixed Overheads**	
	Salaries to staff	10,000
	Depreciation on machines	14,000
	Insurance on machines	6,000
	TOTAL	1,05,000

OR

(B) Following is the data given for Sai Enterprises. The standard quantity and standard price of raw material required for 1 unit production is given below. **(12)**

Material (Kg)	Standard Quantity ₹	Standard Price ₹
Material Y	4	2

Actual production for an output of 500 units

Material (Kg)	Actual Quantity ₹	Actual Price ₹
Material Y	1800	2.20

www.ingramcontent.com/pod-product-compliance
Lightning Source LLC
Chambersburg PA
CBHW080726230426
43665CB00020B/2628